Early Childhood Intervention

Working with Families of Young Children with Special Needs

Edited by Hanan Sukkar,
Carl J. Dunst and Jane Kirkby

Routledge
Taylor & Francis Group

LONDON AND NEW YORK

First published 2017
by Routledge

2 Park Square, Milton Park, Abingdon, Oxfordshire OX14 4RN
711 Third Avenue, New York, NY 10017

Routledge is an imprint of the Taylor & Francis Group, an informa business

First issued in paperback 2018

British Library Cataloguing in Publication Data
A catalogue record for this book is available from the British Library

Library of Congress Cataloging in Publication Data
A catalog record for this book has been requested

ISBN: 978-1-138-91851-1 (hbk)
ISBN: 978-1-138-36574-2 (pbk)

Typeset in Galliard
by Apex CoVantage, LLC

Early Childhood Intervention

Early childhood is considered a critical but often vulnerable period in a child's development where early identification and intervention can be crucial for improving children's developmental outcomes. Systems and family-centred perspectives are vital to support families and build their capacities to lead normalised lives with improved family quality of life. This book explores the family-centred practices and systems factors which influence families' experiences raising children with complex needs. It also considers the ways in which professionals can work with families to build and support parent and child competence. Conceptual and practical work from Australia, Canada, Europe and the United States present descriptions of and implications for different family system frameworks and early childhood programs. Contributors in this edited volume bring together contemporary information that bridges the research-to-practice gap in supporting families of young children with disabilities or delays.

Chapters include:

- Early Intervention for Young Children with Developmental Delays: Contributions of the Developmental Systems Approach
- Family Composition and Family Needs in Australia: What Makes a Family?
- Working with Families in Early Childhood Intervention: Family-Centred Practices in an Individualised Funding Landscape
- Family Systems and Family-Centred Intervention Practices in Portugal and Spain: Iberian Reflections on Early Childhood Intervention

This book will attract the attention scholars of Parenting and Families, Child Development and Child Care.

Hanan Sukkar, EdD is Course Leader for the Bachelor of Early Childhood Education at Holmesglen Institute. Over the last 20 years, Hanan has had extensive experience working with families at risk and children with disabilities. Hanan has operated at director level assisting vulnerable families on welfare in the United States and at management level overseeing new migrants in Australia. She has also worked with the Government of Victoria focusing on early intervention, and has held academic positions with Deakin University and Monash University. Hanan has most recently worked as a Senior Associate Research at Semann & Slattery. Hanan's research draws on early childhood intervention and social evaluation.

Carl J. Dunst, PhD is Senior Research Scientist at the Orelena Hawks Puckett Institute, Asheville and Morganton, North Carolina, USA. He has been involved in research and practice with young children and their families for more than 40 years. This work has included the use of family and social systems frameworks for investigating the direct and indirect effects of informal and formal supports on child, parent, and family functioning, and the use of family-centered practices for improving the outcomes associated with early childhood intervention. This research and practice has resulted in a number of frameworks and models for conceptualizing early childhood intervention practices.

Jane Kirkby, EdD is an academic at Monash University, Melbourne, where she lectures in English literacies and curriculum, assessment and pedagogy units in teacher education courses. She is an experienced teacher and school leader, having worked across the early childhood, primary and secondary school levels for 30 years. Jane has implemented major school change initiatives, which involved building relationships and capacity with teachers, administration, parents and community stakeholders. Her research focusses on teachers' professional learning, knowledge exchange and mentoring relationships and with current projects being conducted on boundary crossing in the Early Childhood sector.

Evolving Families
Series Editor: Sivanes Phillipson

This series focuses on issues, challenges and empirical best practices surrounding evolving families that impact upon their survival, development and outcomes. The aim of this series is twofold: (1) to showcase the diversity of evolving families and the multiple factors that make up the function of families and their evolution across time, systems and cultures; and (2) to build on preventative, interventionist, engagement and recovery methods for the promotion of healthy and successful evolving families across generations, social and political contexts and cultures.

1 **Early Childhood Intervention**
  Working with Families of Young Children with Special Needs
  Edited by Hanan Sukkar, Carl J. Dunst and Jane Kirkby

Contents

Figures and tables

Figures

Tables

Foreword

Family-centred practices are a core component of early childhood intervention (ECI); in fact, they are integral to effective services, supports and improved family and child outcomes. I am grateful to Hanan Sukkar, Jane Kirkby and Carl Dunst and the group of likeminded authors they have brought together in this book to provide empirical evidence and explicit practice examples to support this premise. Most notable is how all chapters are grounded in theoretical frameworks that place the family at the centre of ECI supports and services. *Early Childhood Intervention: Working with Families of Young Children with Special Needs* is a book that provides the impetus to reexamine and change our child-focused ECI service models to encompass the family. Over 15 years ago, Carl Dunst and I co-directed a research institute on the role of families in their child's learning. It is no surprise to me that all of these chapters support our preliminary findings and are grounded in the belief system that drove our institute. To say this book is gratifying to me is an understatement!

I, like many others, have long proposed that families should be the target of quality ECI. Granted, families are brought to ECI because of an identified need in their child. However, there are many practical arguments that support the family being at the centre of ECI. Chief among these are the amount of time a family spends with their child, both in the years in ECI and over the child's lifetime. This time is immeasurable, especially in comparison to the amount of time service providers spend with a child and/or family. For example, even if a child spends 40 hours a week in ECI (far more than a typical ECI plan), it is superseded by the amount of time the child spends with their family in the home and the community. Learning theory also suggests that even the most brilliant and gifted ECI practitioner would have to include the family in interventions to insure the generalisation and maintenance of new behaviors across the activities of family living. Lastly, resource limitations and shortages of professionals to deliver ECI have existed for as long as ECI has been available. This situation does not seem as if it will be remedied in the near or not so near future. The utilisation of families as resources across a number of system and program dimensions seems a logical solution to the efficiency of effort needed on many ECI levels, including service delivery.

This book does an admirable job in presenting the accumulating research and practice base that support this focus on family, both across a diversity of family compositions, cultures, and countries, including Australia, Canada, England Portugal, Spain, and the U.S. The information across chapters leaves no doubt that family-centred practices benefit both the family and child, but only when the practices are delivered through an authentic and equitable family professional partnership that builds family capacity and capitalises on strengths. When this occurs, a number of broad and valued outcomes for both children and their families can be achieved.

A content analysis across chapters by the book editors revealed a number of primary and secondary themes that were consistent and fundamental to a new conceptualization of ECI that is relationship driven and strength based, and aimed at building and sustaining family capacity over time. These themes capture the challenges that ECI systems encounter as they shift in focus from the child to the family.

Systems are comprised of personnel, and a paradigm shift to family-centred service delivery will require the involvement of all personnel in the ECI system. While it is easy to identify the changes that have to occur in the theory and practices of personnel who deliver ECI services or provide support to families and children, these changes must be embraced by all personnel involved in the development, funding, governing, administering, training, researching, and measuring of ECI. This will require a fundamental shift in system design and implementation. While implementation science may guide this change, caution is warranted. Fidelity to both the philosophy and implementation of evidence-based and effective family-centred ECI practices must be demonstrated at the family/child level before attempting a scale up to a system level. These concepts and examples are described and illustrated throughout this book.

I close with my opening sentence: Family-centred practices are a core component of early childhood intervention. They are integral to effective services, supports, and improved family and child outcomes. This book leaves no doubt about this and provides evidence to the field to guide the changes that must occur in ECI systems and programs in order to have lasting family and child impacts. I thank the authors for this book to guide the future of ECI.

Mary Beth Bruder
University of Connecticut Health Center,
Farmington, Connecticut, USA

Contributors' biographies

Editors

Hanan Sukkar, EdD is Course Leader for the Bachelor of Early Childhood Education at Holmesglen Institute. Over the last 20 years, Hanan has had extensive experience working with families at risk and children with disabilities. Hanan has operated at director level assisting vulnerable families on welfare in the United States and at management level overseeing new migrants in Australia. She has also worked with the Government of Victoria focusing on early intervention, and has held academic positions with Deakin University and Monash University. Hanan has most recently worked as a Senior Associate Research at Semann & Slattery. Hanan's research draws on early childhood intervention and social evaluation.

Carl J. Dunst, PhD is Senior Research Scientist at the Orelena Hawks Puckett Institute, Asheville and Morganton, North Carolina, USA. He has been involved in research and practice with young children and their families for more than 40 years. This work has included the use of family and social systems frameworks for investigating the direct and indirect effects of informal and formal supports on child, parent, and family functioning, and the use of family-centered practices for improving the outcomes associated with early childhood intervention. This research and practice has resulted in a number of frameworks and models for conceptualizing early childhood intervention practices.

Jane Kirkby, EdD is an academic at Monash University, Melbourne, where she lectures in English literacies and curriculum, assessment and pedagogy units in teacher education courses. She is an experienced teacher and school leader, having worked across the early childhood, primary and secondary school levels for 30 years. Jane has implemented major school change initiatives, which involved building relationships and capacity with teachers, administration, parents and community stakeholders. Her research focusses on teachers' professional learning, knowledge exchange and mentoring relationships and with current projects being conducted on boundary crossing in the Early Childhood sector.

International Authors

Carolyn Blackburn, PhD is Research Fellow in Early Childhood Studies at Birmingham City University, where she is Module Leader for Child Development and Managing Transitions and Co-leader of the Rethinking Childhood Research Cluster. Carolyn teaches across the Faculty of Health, Education and Life Sciences and is an external examiner for the Universities of Bath Spa and Wolverhampton. Carolyn is widely published in the areas of special educational needs and disability and early childhood intervention and has presented her work internationally, most recently in New Zealand and Turkey.

Margarita Cañadas Pérez, PhD is the Director of "the Alqueria" at the Catholic University of Valencia. The Alqueria is a Home- and Community-Based Early Intervention Service that provides home visiting services to approximately 100 families in Valencia. This centre also is an Early Childhood Education Center for children from zero to six. It provides early childhood education in an inclusive environment where children with special needs and disabilities learn and grow side by side with typically developing children. She has a degree in occupational therapy and anthropology, and she is a professor of occupational therapy at the Catholic University of Valencia, Spain.

Climent Giné, PhD is Professor Emeritus at the Ramon Llull University, Barcelona, Spain. His main areas of research focus on the contribution of services to the quality of life of people with intellectual disabilities and their families. He is an AAIDD Fellow.

Michael H. Guralnick, PhD is Director of the Center on Human Development and Disability and Professor of Psychology and Pediatrics at the University of Washington, Seattle, Washington, USA. Dr. Guralnick has directed numerous research, professional training and development projects in the fields of early childhood development and intervention, with a special interest in the design and effectiveness of early intervention programs, peer-related social competence and early childhood inclusion.

Diane Hiebert-Murphy, PhD is a registered psychologist and Professor in the Faculty of Social Work and the Psychological Service Centre at the University of Manitoba. Her research focuses on interventions with families in the contexts of childhood disability and intimate partner violence.

Joana Maria Mas, PhD is Professor in the Faculty of Psychology, Education and, Sports Sciences of Blanquerna, Ramon Llull University, Barcelona, Spain. She is also a member of the coordinating team for the Master's in Early Intervention and Family at Ramon Llull University.

Ana Maria Serrano, PhD is Associate Professor and researcher at the Research Center of Eucation, University of Minho, Portugal. She has been involved in the board of the National Association of Early Intervention (ANIP) in Portugal and is Chair of the European Assocaition of Early Childhood Intervention (EURLYAID).

Barry Trute, PhD is Professor Emeritus of Social Work at two Canadian universities: the University of Calgary, and the University of Manitoba. He was recently ARC Professor of Family Centred Care at the University of Calgary, with split appointments in social work, nursing and paediatrics. Dr. Trute's work includes the advocacy and development of family-centred practice in child health, child disability and child welfare services.

Alexandra Wright, PhD worked as a social work educator with the Faculty of Social Work at the University of Manitoba teaching in the BSW and graduate programmes. She currently holds the position of Executive Director with the Canadian Association for Social Work Education – Association canadienne pour la formation en travail social. Her research interests have focused on human services organisations and effectiveness, culture and climate, policy implementation and evaluation.

Australian Authors

Ian Dempsey, PhD has worked as a special education teacher and a respite care coordinator and is presently an Associate Professor in Special Education at the University of Newcastle, Australia. His research interests include family-centred support approaches, special education law and policy and employment for adults with intellectual disability.

Loraine Fordham, PhD is a lecturer and researcher in the School of Teacher Education at Charles Stuart University, NSW, Australia. Loraine has a PhD in early childhood from Macquarie University and has worked as an academic, researcher and speech pathologist in a range of early childhood, academic, health and community organisations.

John Forster, BA (Hons) is Chief Executive Officer of Noah's Ark Inc, a statewide early intervention and inclusion organisation in Victoria, Australia. Noah's Ark supports over 1,800 families and 2,300 child care and kindergarten programmes. John is a past National President of Early Childhood Intervention Australia, the peak body, and has served on a number of Victorian Government Advisory bodies.

Wendy Goff, MEd is a lecturer at the School of Teacher Education and Early Childhood University of Southern Queensland. Wendy's research interests include adult relationships and how they support the learning and development of children.

Sara Holman, BA (Hons) has been professionally involved with the early years sector over the past 12 years. Her key areas of interest and expertise are diverse, including her involvement in State Government with policy initiatives across the State of Victoria and the Commonwealth in Australia, leadership and management, curriculum, child development, gender and equity, diversity and family-centred practice. She has been a teacher, a project officer in policy, a lecturer at two Victorian Universities and an early intervention key worker. Her biggest inspiration is her 11-year-old daughter, Ella, the creative thinker and the young researcher.

Christine Johnston, PhD is Associate Professor and has a long history of involvement in early childhood intervention. She was the inaugural national President of Early Childhood Intervention Australia and has had a particular focus on family-centred practice and the role of the expert practitioner in her research, writing and supervision of doctoral students. She is currently Director of Engagement and International in the School of Education, Western Sydney University.

Deb Keen, PhD is Professor in Education with the Autism Centre of Excellence in the School of Education and Professional Studies at Griffith University, Brisbane, Australia. She has published extensively from her research into ways to enhance participation and engagement of individuals with autism and their families in home, school and community. She is particularly interested in evidence-based practice, communication, problem behaviour, early intervention and family-centred practice.

Anne Kennedy, EdD works as a consultant, researcher, author and trainer. Anne was a member of the writing team that developed the national Early Years Learning Framework. In her role as chairperson of Community Child Care Association Victoria, she is a strong advocate for equity of access to community-based, not-for-profit education and care services for children and families.

Denise Luscombe, MSc is a paediatric physiotherapist who has worked in the disability field for 30 years. She is currently the National President of Early Childhood Intervention Australia (since 2010) and a Consultant Physiotherapist for the Disability Services Commission (Perth, Western Australia).

June McLoughlin, MEd currently holds positions as the Director of Early Years and Community Engagement at the Colman Foundation, Associate Principal Consultant Early Childhood at the Parenting Research Centre, and the Director of Family and Children's Services at Doveton College. June has extensive experience in both policy and service development and research and practice in the early childhood, family support and children's services fields, which has given her a broad and deep understanding of issues relevant to the needs of parents and their children. June has managed many state and national projects designed to refocus early years services to provide more integrated support for families with young children, with a particular interest in vulnerable children.

Part I

Introduction

The introductory chapter to *Early Childhood Intervention: Working with Families of Young Children with Special Needs* includes descriptions of why family systems and family-centred early childhood intervention hold promise for making a real difference in the lives of infants, toddlers, and preschoolers with special needs and young children with developmental delays due to environmental or biological risk factors and their families. Accordingly, early childhood intervention is conceptualised as a set of different systems-level experiences and opportunities that are expected to offset the development-impeding effects of identified disabilities and risk factors, and family-centred practices are conceptualised as the ways in which early childhood practitioners engage families in competency-enhancing experiences and opportunities in order to have capacity-building and empowering consequences (Espe-Sherwindt, 2008).

The global or universal applicability of ecological systems (Bronfenbrenner, 1994), social systems (Friedman & Allen, 2010), family systems (Cowan, Powell, & Cowan, 1998), and developmental systems (Guralnick, 2001) theories and models as frameworks for conceptualising and operationalising early childhood intervention is based on the fact that children and families throughout the world are themselves social systems embedded in broader-based ecological systems, where the events in these different systems can have either development-impeding or development-enhancing characteristics and consequences. The challenge that early childhood practitioners face when working with family members and engaging families in early childhood intervention is strengthening support systems in ways benefitting young children with special needs and their families. It is also generally recognised that family-centred practices have global and universal applicability, although it has been noted that this approach to early childhood intervention has not yet occurred broadly for a number of reasons (e.g., Bruder, 2000; Dempsey & Keen, 2008; Dunst & Espe-Sherwindt, 2016). Nevertheless, the adoption and use of family-centred practices is now viewed as a type of help-giving approach that can be especially effective in terms of positively influencing families' reactions and adaptations to a child with special needs, their desire and willingness to be involved in early childhood intervention, and for supporting and strengthening family and family member functioning. Accordingly, early childhood practitioners who adhere to family-centred tenets and employ family-centred practices are more likely to be responsive to family and cultural beliefs and values in ways that have broad-based child, parent, and family benefits.

Contributors to *Early Childhood Intervention: Working with Families of Young Children with Special Needs* offer different but compatible perspectives of both family systems and family-centred early childhood intervention. The contents of this volume provide readers with both rich and diverse viewpoints for improving early childhood intervention for young children with special needs and their families.

References

Bronfenbrenner, U. (1994). Ecological models of human development. In T. Husen & N. Postlethwaite (Eds.), *International encyclopedia of education* (2nd ed., Vol. 3, pp. 1643–1647). Oxford, United Kingdom: Elsevier.

Bruder, M. B. (2000). Family-centered early intervention: Clarifying our values for the new millennium. *Topics in Early Childhood Special Education, 20*, 105–116, 122. doi:10.1177/027112140002000206

Cowan, P. A., Powell, D., & Cowan, C. P. (1998). Parenting interventions: A family systems perspective. In W. Damon, I. E. Sigel, & K. A. Renninger (Eds.), *Handbook of child psychology: Vol. 4. Child psychology in practice* (5th ed., pp. 3–72). New York: Wiley.

Dempsey, I., & Keen, D. (2008). A review of processes and outcomes in family-centered services for children with a disability. *Topics in Early Childhood Special Education, 28*, 42–52. doi:10.1177/0271121408316699

Dunst, C. J., & Espe-Sherwindt, M. (2016). Family-centered practices in early childhood intervention. In B. Reichow, B. Boyd, E. Barton, & S. L. Odom (Eds.), *Handbook of early childhood special education* (pp. 37–55). Cham, Switzerland: Springer International.

Espe-Sherwindt, M. (2008). Family-centred practice: Collaboration, competency and evidence. *Support for Learning, 23*, 136–143. doi:10.1111/j.1467-9604.2008.00384.x

Friedman, B. D., & Allen, K. N. (2010). Systems theory. In J. R. Brandell (Ed.), *Theory and practice in clinical social work* (2nd ed., pp. 3–20). Thousand Oaks, CA: Sage.

Guralnick, M. J. (2001). A developmental systems model for early intervention. *Infants & Young Children, 14*(2), 1–18.

1 Family systems and family-centred practices in early childhood intervention

Hanan Sukkar, Carl J. Dunst and Jane Kirkby

The purpose of this volume is to share the thoughts of early childhood researchers and practitioners about different ways family systems theories and family-centred practices have informed how early childhood intervention has been conceptualised and practised. Each chapter in the book includes descriptions of various and unique perspectives for working with young children with special needs and their families. The authors consider approaches to early childhood intervention that can enhance the positive outcomes for children, parents and the family as a whole. The reader will experience a rich array of information that can be used to improve the ways in which early childhood practitioners go about their work with young children and their families.

Children represent our future. Promoting their development and wellbeing is now widely accepted as an essential investment and a moral obligation of society as a whole (Australian Institute of Health and Welfare, 2004). Research focusing on a wide range of wellbeing indicators shows that some countries fare better than others. As a result, no country has it all, and some countries continue to face serious challenges in achieving positive wellbeing outcomes for their children (OECD, 2015). The *How's Life* evaluation, a report that focuses on people's wellbeing in OECD countries, finds that one child in seven still lives in poverty, 10% of children continue to live in a jobless household and one child in 10 reports being bullied in school. Keeping this in mind and taking a closer look at children with a disability or special needs, a review completed by the UCLA Fielding School of Public Health highlights that out of the 190 U.N. countries committed to the Convention on the Rights of the Child (CRC), only 19% ratified the CRC explicitly to protect the right of education for children with disabilities or to prohibit discrimination in education based on a disability (Denly, 2014). Therefore, it is apparent that we, as global citizens of the world, still have a long way to go in meeting the needs of children with a disability and improving their quality of life as well as the life of their families.

The birth of a child sees parents and other givers taking on roles as educators, advocates, information seekers and spokespersons on behalf of their children (Australian Institute of Health and Welfare, 2004; Dunst & Dempsey, 2007).

When that child has disability, the complexities of these roles increase, and often support and resources are required in addition to those that are available within the family (Australian Institute of Health and Welfare, 2004; Barr & Millar, 2003). Families need to understand how their child communicates, interacts and explores their world, which is often different from that of typically developing children (Keilty, 2010). In addition, family members may need supports for learning about the child's life expectancy, patterns of development and any other number of life issues that may not occur whilst raising a typically developing child (Barr & Miller, 2003; Keilty, 2010).

In many cases, parents raising a child with a disability or special needs are asked or encouraged to have a more of hands-on role in caring for their child. However, this cannot be achieved unless parents and professionals work collaboratively and parents feel respected, listened to and treated as equal partners (Barr & Miller, 2003; Keen, 2007). Through the development of strong and healthy relationships, both parents and professionals come to understand, organise and shape the implementation of effective support systems for the child and their family (Guralnick, 2006). In addition, parents can identify the developmental abilities and needs of their child and guide professionals in creating the learning opportunities that are attuned to the child's learning styles (Keilty, 2010).

Families' experiences in raising a child with a disability or special needs

The birth of a child with a disability or a special needs has been found to impose financial, social and physical stress on parents and caregivers, which may include an increase in depression, anger, shock, denial, self-blame and guilt for family members (Heiman, 2002; Lopez, Clifford, Minnes, & Kuntz, 2008). There can be a profound effect on family relationships, including partners' relationships (Brown, Goodman, & Küpper, 2014; Watson, Hayes, & Radford-Paz, 2011). While some relationships may deepen and increase in strength, others may not survive the pressures of rearing a child with a disability. For this reason and more, parents, other carers and partners need to learn how to engage with their extended family members, friends and community to obtain the most suitable supports for the child and family unit. Furthermore, parents must diligently learn how to identify and engage with service providers that are most appropriate for meeting their child's needs (Association for Children with a Disability, 2013).

It has been found, however, that service systems are not always attuned and responsive to family needs (Owen, Gordon, Frederico, & Cooper, 2002). Parents often initiate the process that results in the diagnosis of their child's disability in an effort to better understand their child's atypical behaviour (Watson et al., 2011). From this moment, professionals are duty bound to improve families' abilities to access resources on their own account and identify informal support networks (Owen et al., 2002) and access information and other resources as a means of empowerment and control for parents. Building and strengthening parent and family capacity is considered extremely critical for supporting a child with disability or special needs and in maintaining the family unit intact (Dunst, 2009, 2014; McWilliam, 2010; Moore, 2012). When needed supports and resources are available to families, they are more likely to have positive and rich capacity-building experiences, report fewer concerns and experience better child and family outcomes (Dunst & Trivette, 2009). Further, parents seek help, take steps to decrease stress and build parental resilience (Davis, Day, & Bidmead, 2002; Early Childhood Learning and Knowledge Center, 2007; McWilliam, 2010; Owen et al., 2002). Building constructive and effective parent-professional relationships and partnerships can distinctively improve service provision and provide the child and family with a better quality of life.

Early childhood intervention

There is a significant body of evidence which indicates that intervening early can (1) reduce the effects of a disability and prevent the negative effects associated with poor environmental conditions (Dunst, 2009), (2) provide the foundation and trajectory for children's lifelong learning, development and health outcomes (Blackman, 2002; Fish, 2003; Guralnick, 2005a; Shonkoff & Phillips, 2000), (3) build on and strengthen parents' skills, (4) promote and enhance parents' wellbeing, (5) empower parents to make informed decisions and (6) increase parents' sense of competence and confidence (Dunst & Dempsey, 2007; Dunst & Trivette, 2009).

Early identification and early childhood intervention can be crucial for improving a child's developmental, health and wellbeing outcomes as well as for improving family members' parenting skills (Conlin, 2002; Dunst, 2009; Shonkoff & Garner, 2012). Intervening early can encourage parents to engage their children in early learning opportunities in ways that provide the parents authentic control over the types of supports, resources and services they obtain for their child (Dunst, 2009). Early childhood intervention can also promote respect for racial, cultural and socioeconomic family diversity, and provide services that utilise the natural environment and community-based resources to accommodate the needs of children and families (Rogers, Edgecombe, Kimberley, Barclay, & Humble, 2004).

Early childhood intervention locally, nationally and internationally has been found to be effective in improving child, parent and family outcomes (Guralnick, 1997) and generating benefits to society far beyond program or intervention costs (Centre on the Developing Child at Harvard University, 2007; Shonkoff & Phillips, 2000). The latter benefits can include a decrease in welfare expenditure as well as reduction in the costs of education programs and health services, resulting in long-term savings from government investments (et al., 2000; Shonkoff & Garner 2012; Vimpani, Patton, & Hayes, 2002). One question nevertheless remains. *What are the benefits gained from different approaches to early childhood intervention?* The chapters in this book include descriptions of different social, family and developmental systems approaches to early childhood intervention and the different benefits that are realised from these approaches to intervention.

Family systems and family-centred practices

The ability to both provide children, parents, other primary carers and the family as a whole the supports and resources needed to alleviate or reduce any negative effects associated with the birth and rearing of a child with a disability or delay requires a broader-based perspective of early childhood intervention (Crnic & Stormshak, 1997; Guralnick, Hammond, Neville, & Connor, 2008). The ability to build and strengthen family member capacity as a result of early childhood intervention also necessitates a shift in focus in terms of how family members are involved in early childhood intervention (Korfmacher, Green, Spellman, & Thornburg, 2007). Social and family systems approaches to early childhood intervention have been advanced as ways of broadening the scope of early childhood intervention (Briggs, 1997; Cowan, Powell, & Cowan, 1998; Thurman, 1997), whereas family-centred practices have been advanced as a way of engaging family members in early childhood intervention in a capacity-building manner (Dunst & Espe-Sherwindt, 2016; Epley, Summers, & Turnbull, 2010; Espe-Sherwindt, 2008).

Ecological (Bronfenbrenner, 1992), social (Friedman & Allen, 2010), family (Emery, 2014) and developmental (Guralnick, 2001) systems theories have increasingly been used to broaden the scope and focus of early childhood intervention to include 'interventions' (broadly defined) as the different levels and settings of influence affecting child, parent, other primary carers and family behaviour and functioning. Systems theories and models view the family as a social unit embedded within informal and formal social networks, where events in those units and networks influence the behaviour of a family unit and individual family members to improve child and family outcomes (Dunst & Trivette, 2009). Accordingly, early childhood intervention includes activities in those informal and formal social networks and systems to provide or promote the provision of supports, resources and services needed to improve family member functioning. This includes, but is not limited to, supports, resources and services to improve child, parent, and family wellbeing; family quality of life; parent and other primary carer child rearing confidence and competence; family member self-efficacy beliefs; and child learning, behaviour and development.

Research now indicates that the ways in which families are involved in early childhood intervention matter a great deal if their involvement is to have positive consequences (Dunst, Bruder, & Espe-Sherwindt, 2014; Friend, Summers, & Turnbull, 2009; Korfmacher et al., 2008). Family-centred practices were first introduced as an alternative to professionally-centred practices for changing the ways in which early childhood practitioners interact with and treat families and involve families in early childhood intervention. Family-centred practices constitute a philosophy of care that recognises the constant role of the family in their child's life (Shelton, Jeppson, & Johnson, 1987; Shelton & Stepenak, 1994). This philosophy is based on a set of principles, elements, beliefs and values that describes the scope of how professionals ought to treat and interact with parents, children and other family members to achieve optimal benefits and outcomes

(Dunst & Espe-Sherwindt, 2016). These principles provide professionals a foundation to recognise families' strengths, enhance parent-professional collaborations, promote parent-to-parent support and provide accessible, flexible and responsive early childhood intervention practices (Bruder, 2000; Dunst, 2010; Dunst, Hamby, Johansson, & Trivette, 1991; Dunst & Espe-Sherwindt, 2016; Harbin, McWilliam, & Gallagher, 2003; Keen, 2007; Moore, 2010; Shonkoff & Phillips, 2000). In short, one can summarise that family-centred practices are an approach that seeks to respect family values and preferences, establish a mutually trusting partnership and build on family strengths to improve the quality of life for both the parent and child with additional needs (Dunst, Trivette, & Deal, 1994; Espe-Sherwindt, 2008; Keen, 2007; Moore, 2010; Shonkoff & Phillips, 2000; Turnbull, Turbville, & Turnbull, 2003).

Both social and family systems theories and models and family-centred practices have had significant impacts on how early childhood intervention is now conceptualised and practised. This volume includes advances in the application of these approaches to working with young children with special needs and their families influenced by the contributors' extensive knowledge and experience.

Purpose of the book

Early Childhood Intervention: Working with Families of Young Children with Special Needs is both a scholarly publication and a practical guide that students, practitioners, program directors and policy makers should find informative and helpful in developing a clearer understanding of how to bridge the gaps between theory, research and day-to-day practice. The editors' goal is to present readers with contemporary information which bridges the theory/research to practice gap in working with families of young children with special needs from 'family systems' and 'family-centred' perspectives that can be used to guide their own work with parents and other family members.

The book includes conceptual and practical work from national and international authors in the areas of early childhood education, early childhood intervention, special education, psychology and social work. Experts from Australia, Canada, Great Britain, Portugal, Spain and the United States describe different ways in which family systems and family-centred intervention practices have been used to work with young children with disabilities or delays and their families. The authors' contributions expand upon existing conceptualisations of family systems and family-centred models and practices in ways that should help professionals broaden an understanding for how they can provide the supports, resources and services necessary to address families' individual needs and to improve the early childhood intervention practices with parents and their young children. Equally important, the contributions from Australian authors comprise different perspectives for how to work with families of young children based on the evolving national and state policy and practice changes. Each chapter in this volume draws on research and practice, where authors aim to provide descriptions, implications and lessons learned from using different systems frameworks and different perspectives of family-centred practices for improving early childhood intervention and early childhood education and care based on their own as well as others research and practice. These various perspectives add to the breadth of understanding of family systems and family-centred practices and encourage practitioners to reflect on their own practices in light of the various frames of reference offered by the authors. In summary, this book aims to examine both existing systems and supports available to families raising children in modern and complex societies and the ways in which professions work with families to explore the positive and negative effects of raising a child with special needs.

Overview of the chapters

This book is organised into four main sections. In the first section, *Foundation for working with young children and their families*, both Guralnick and Dunst describe different but compatible models and frameworks for conceptualising and implementing early childhood intervention, both of which have implications for different approaches to family-centred practice, while Dempsey and Keen describe the desired outcomes of family-centred practices and discuss the causal pathways related to family-centred practice and those outcomes.

Guralnick describes the key elements and assumptions of the developmental systems approach to address the needs of young children with disability (Guralnick, 2005a, 2005b). Guralnick's model focuses on how families can provide an optimal developmental environment for their child, and emphasises the importance of incorporating knowledge from the developmental systems approach to support children and families effectively. Guralnick suggests that to do so, it is important to consider child characteristics, family patterns of interaction and the resources that directly influence child and family behaviour and functioning.

Dunst describes different aspects of a family systems approach to early childhood intervention that includes a broad-based definition of intervention, a social systems framework for conceptualising the scope of intervention practices, a capacity-building family-centred paradigm for operationalising early childhood intervention and a model for implementing family systems early childhood intervention practices. The content of each section of the chapter includes research evidence and lessons learned that have been used to facilitate the implementation of early childhood intervention.

Dempsey and Keen outline the development of family-centred practice (FCP) in response to research findings, providing a comprehensive background to current approaches. Their chapter outlines a literature review to examine the causal pathways between family-centred practice and positive life outcomes under three main focal points: explanatory models of the process of FCP, the implementation of FCP and the impact of FCP. Dempsey and Keen conclude their chapter with cautionary words about the need to bridge the difference between a stated belief of practice and the enactment of FCP across a range of services.

In the second section, *Understanding families and family-early childhood practitioner relationships*, Holman explores family composition in Australia and policy implication in the early years, while Kennedy seeks to develop an understanding for the impact of disadvantage and risk factors on families with young children. In addition, Sukkar draws attention to the implications of professional preparation on the provision of family-centred practices.

Holman identifies how our very understanding of the term "family" needs increased scrutiny. She draws on several Australian national and state policy documents to open a discussion on the degree to which the complexity of family structures is recognised and considered by early childhood intervention practitioners as part of their work with families and their children. In particular, Holman suggests that diverse families, already experiencing difficulties in expressing their family identity, may well be little understood and represented in terms of family-centred practice by underprepared service providers.

Kennedy explores how disadvantage and risk factors might affect the capacity and willingness of families and young children to participate in early childhood education and care services. She also includes descriptions of practical strategies to support educators in responding to culturally and ethnically diverse families and their children and highlights the importance of reimagining the partnership between families and professionals.

Sukkar investigates a number of different aspects of family-practitioner relationships, which represent a key foundation for successful early childhood intervention strategies. She explores the impact of developing positive partnerships on the future trajectory of children with disability. Through examining the challenges facing service providers and identifying the implications for professional preparation on service provision, Sukkar presents a framework to support professional preparation into the future.

In the third section, *Working with families and young children in Australia*, Johnston et al. discuss the impact of the National Disability Insurance Scheme (NDIS) and in particular, the effects of an individual funding model on families, professionals and service providers, while Forster describes the impact of the NDIS on professional practice and service provision at a national and local level in Victoria. In the final chapter in this section, Goff and McLoughlin provide the reader a case study of a school-based family-centred approach to supporting the health, development, wellbeing and learning of vulnerable children and their families.

Johnston et al. claim that while the introduction of an individualised funding model is designed to give families of children with disabilities more choice and control over the types of services and supports that best meet their needs, the burden remains with the families to choose well, and the professionals to support the family choice and build family capacity. Furthermore, Johnston et al. argue that early childhood intervention is about the child and the family, and that failure to acknowledge this will lead to poor outcome for the child, family and community.

Forster extends the discussion on the impact of the NDIS in terms of community-based programs. He contends that the introduction of a NDIS in Australia will change the nature of service provision for all persons with disability, including early childhood intervention for young children and their families. Forster also examines some of the factors that led to the different approaches to service provision in both specialist and mainstream early childhood settings.

Goff and McLoughlin describe an example from Doveton College – a Victorian education setting – to identify the steps taken to build a stronger community through early childhood intervention. Doveton College has introduced an innovative educational program which is responsive to its community's needs. The authors provide short case studies to illustrate the varied approaches that are used to implement the Doveton service delivery model. Goff and McLoughlin provide insight into the processes, challenges, opportunities and possibilities embedded in a place-based family-centred community school, established in Australia. Throughout the case study, they also present different approaches and strategies to guide and support professionals in their work with vulnerable children, families and communities.

In the fourth section, *Working with families and young children in other countries*, Serrano and her colleagues from Portugal and Spain, Hiebert-Murphy and her colleagues in Canada and Blackman from England utilise their policy context to describe their individual experiences with family-centred practices and family systems intervention practices.

Serrano et al. present the current status of early childhood intervention in Portugal and Spain, the long path that Portugal has taken in adopting and implementing capacity building family-centred services and how the Portugal model and lessons learned have influenced the adoption of a family-centred early childhood intervention model in Spain. The authors also describe the conceptual differences in early childhood intervention between Spain and Portugal, and how these two countries differ in professional practices and their service delivery approach.

Hiebert-Murphy et al. describe the implication of policy infrastructure on the delivery of child disability services and family-centred practices in Manitoba, Canada. Hiebert-Murphy et al. also examine the role of professional training in transitioning to family-centred services and explore some of the key issues and challenges to implementing family-centred practices.

Blackburn describes parents' experiences with early childhood intervention services for young children with speech, language and communication needs in one local authority in England. She highlights the difficult and subjective nature of early identification of problems with speech, language and communication, and argues that early childhood intervention services are more responsive and accessible to parents whose children have *severe and complex* speech, language and communication needs than they are to those who have *mild to moderate* speech, language and communication needs. Blackburn suggests that this raises questions about how young children with special educational needs and their families are supported and how trajectory can be optimised in line with policy intentions.

The book concludes with a chapter on the future directions of family systems and family-centred early childhood intervention based on different themes that contributors emphasised in their chapters. The themes include a number of considerations involving family systems and family-centred practices and the challenges and opportunities in both approaches to early childhood intervention. The themes also include reflections on and recommendations involving family systems and family-centred practices, and themes involving challenges and opportunities in both approaches to early childhood intervention. The themes afford readers unique opportunities to learn and benefit from the extensive experiences of the contributors.

References

Association for Children with a Disability. (2013). *Helping you and your family.* Retrieved from http://acd.org.au/wp-content/uploads/2014/07/ACD-resource-Helping-You-and-Your-Family-3rd-edition-2013-PDF-1.2MB.pdf

Australian Institute of Health and Welfare-Canberra (2004). *Children with disabilities in Australia.* Retrieved from http://www.aihw.gov.au/WorkArea/Download Asset.aspx?id=6442455787

Barr, O., & Millar, R. (2003). Parents of children with intellectual disabilities: Their expectations and experience of genetic counselling. *Journal of Applied Research in Intellectual Disabilities, 16*(3), 189–204.

Blackman, J.A. (2002). Early intervention: A global perspective. *Infants & Young Children, 15*(2), 11–19.

Briggs, M. H. (1997). A systems model for early intervention teams. In K. G. Butler (Ed.), *Building early intervention teams: Working together for children and families* (pp. 89–122). Gaithersburg, MD: Aspen Publication.

Bronfenbrenner, U. (1992). Ecological systems theory. In R. Vasta (Ed.), *Six theories of child development: Revised formulations and current issues* (pp. 187–248). Philadelphia, PA: Jessica Kingsley.

Brown, C., Goodman, S., & Küpper, L. (2014). *When you learn your child has a disability.* Retrieved from http://www.parentcenterhub.org/repository/journey/

Bruder, M. (2000). Family-centred early intervention: Clarifying our values for the new millennium. *Topics in Early Childhood Special Education, 20*(2), 105–130.

Burke, M. (2012). *Examining family involvement in regular and special education: lessons to be learned for both sides.* Retrieved from https://www.academia.edu/4790232/ Examining_Family_Involvement_in_Regular_and_Special_Education_Lessons_to_ be_Learned_for_Both_Sides_Contents

Centre on the Developing Child at Harvard University. (2007). *A science-based framework for early childhood policy: using evidence to improve outcomes in learning, behavior, and health for vulnerable children.* Retrieved from http://www.developing child.harvard.edu

Conlon, C. (2002). Early intervention. In M.D. Batshaw (Ed.), *Children with disabilities* (pp. 579–588). Australia: MacLennan & Petty Pty Limited.

Cowan, P. A., Powell, D., & Cowan, C. P. (1998). Parenting interventions: A family systems perspective. In W. Damon, I. E. Sigel, & K. A. Renninger (Eds.), *Handbook of child psychology: Vol. 4. Child psychology in practice* (5th ed., pp. 3–72). New York: Wiley.

Crnic, K., & Stormshak, E. (1997). The effectiveness of providing social support for families of children at risk. In M. J. Guralnick (Ed.), *The effectiveness of early intervention* (pp. 209–225). Baltimore, MD: Brookes.

Davis, H., Day, C., & Bidmead, C. (2002). *Working in partnership with parents: the parent advisor model.* London: Harcourt Assessment.

Denly, C. (2014). *A global report card: Are children better off than they were 25 years ago?* Retrieved from http://newsroom.ucla.edu/releases/a-global-report-card-are-children-better-off-than-they-were-25-years-ago

Dunst, C. (2009). Implications of evidence-based practices for personnel preparation development in early childhood intervention. *Infant & Young Children, 22*(1), 44–53.

Dunst, C. (2010). *Advances in the understanding of the characteristics and consequences of family-centered practices.* Retrieved from http://www.puckett.org/presentations/FamCtrdHelpPract_8_2010.pdf

Dunst, C. J. (2014). *Family capacity-building practices: foundations and conceptual model.* Retrieved from http://puckett.org/presentations/FamCapacity_Build_I_2014_Adelaide.pdf

Dunst, C. J., Bruder, M. B., & Espe-Sherwindt, M. (2014). Family capacity-building in early childhood intervention: Do context and setting matter? *School Community Journal, 24*(1), 37–48.

Dunst, C. J., & Dempsey, I. (2007). Family-professional partnerships and parenting competence, confidence, and enjoyment. *International Journal of Disability, Development and Education, 54*(3), 305–318.

Dunst, C. J., & Espe-Sherwindt, M. (2016). Family-centered practices in early childhood intervention. In B. Reichow, B. Boyd, E. Barton, & S. L. Odom (Eds.), *Handbook of early childhood special education* (pp. 37–55). Cham, Switzerland: Springer International.

Dunst, C., Hamby, D., Johanson, C., & Trivette, C. (1991). Family-oriented early intervention policies and practices: Family-centered or not. *Exceptional Children, 58*(2), 115–127.

Dunst, C. J., & Trivette, C. M. (2009). Capacity building family-systems intervention practices. *Journal of Family Social Work, 12*(2), 119–143.

Dunst, C., Trivette, C., & Deal, A. (1994). *Supporting and strengthening families: Methods, strategies and practices.* Cambridge: Brookline Books.

Early Childhood Learning & Knowledge Center. (2007). *Parental resilience: promoting healthy families in your community.* Retrieved from https://www.childwelfare.gov/pubPDFs/packet.pdf

Emery, R. E. (2014). Families as systems: Some thoughts on methods and theory. In S. M. McHale, P. Amato, & A. Booth (Eds.), *Emerging methods in family research* (pp. 109–124). Cham, Switzerland: Springer International Publishing.

Epley, P., Summers, J. A., & Turnbull, A. (2010). Characteristics and trends in family-centered conceptualizations. *Journal of Family Social Work, 13*, 269–285. doi:10.1080/10522150903514017

Espe-Sherwindt, M. (2008). Family-centred practice: Collaboration, competency and evidence. *Support for Learning, 23*, 136–143. doi:10.1111/j.1467-9604.2008.00384.x

Fish, A. (2003). The benefits of early intervention. *Journal of the Economics Institute of Australia, 10*(3), 31–34.

Friedman, B. D., & Allen, K. N. (2010). Systems theory. In J. R. Brandell (Ed.), *Theory and practice in clinical social work* (2nd ed., pp. 3–20). Thousand Oaks, CA: Sage.

Friend, A. C., Summers, J. A., & Turnbull, A. P. (2009). Impacts of family support in early childhood intervention research. *Education and Training in Developmental*

Disabilities, 44(4), 453–470. Retrieved from http://www.beachcenter.org/Research/FullArticles/PDF/Friend_et_al_2009.pdf

Guralnick, M. (1997). Second generation research in the field of early intervention. In M. Guralnick (Ed.), *The effectiveness of early intervention* (pp. 3–20). Baltimore: Paul H.Brookes Publishing Co.

Guralnick, M. J. (2001). A developmental systems model for early intervention. *Infants & Young Children, 14*(2), 1–18.

Guralnick, M. J. (2005a). Early intervention for children with intellectual disabilities: Current knowledge and future prospects. *Journal of Applied Research in Intellectual Disabilities, 18*, 313–324. Retrieved from http://dx.doi.org/10.1111/j.1468-3148.2005.00270.x

Guralnick, M. J. (2005b). *An overview of the developmental systems model for early intervention*. Baltimore, MD: Paul H. Brookes Publishing Co.

Guralnick, M. (2006). The system of early intervention for children with developmental disabilities: Current status and challenges for the future. In J. Jacobson, J. Mulick, & J. Rojahn (Eds.), *Handbook of mental retardation and developmental disabilities* (pp. 465–480). New York: Plenum.

Guralnick, M. J., Hammond, M. A., Neville, B., & Connor, R. T. (2008). The relationship between sources and functions of social support and dimensions of child-and-parent-related stress. *Journal of Intellectual Disability Research, 52*, 1138–1154. doi:10.1111/j.1365-2788.2008.01073.x

Heiman, T. (2002). Parents of children with disabilities: Resilience, coping and future expectations. *Journal of Developmental and Physical Disabilities, 14*(2), 159–171.

Harbin, G., McWilliam, R., & Gallagher, J. (2003). Services for young children with disabilities and their families. In J. Shonkoff & S. Meisels (Eds.), *Handbook of early childhood intervention* (2nd ed., pp. 387–415). Cambridge: Cambridge University.

Karoly, L., Greenwood, P., Everingham, S., Hoube, J., Kilburn, M., Rydell, P., Sanders, M., & Chiesa, J. (2000). *Investing in our children: What we know and don't know about the costs and benefits of early childhood interventions*. Retrieved from https://www.rand.org/content/dam/rand/pubs/monograph_reports/1998/MR898.pdf

Keen, D. (2007). Parents, families, and partnerships: Issues and considerations. *International Journal of Disability, Development and Education, 54*(3), 339–349.

Keilty, B. (2010). *The early intervention guidebook for families and professionals: Parenting for success*. New York: Teacher College, Columbia University.

Korfmacher, J., Green, B., Spellman, M., & Thornburg, K. R. (2007). The helping relationship and program participation in early childhood home visiting. *Infant Mental Health Journal, 28*, 459–480. doi:10.1002/imhj.20148

Korfmacher, J., Green, B., Staerkel, F., Peterson, C., Cook, G., Roggman, L., . . . Schiffman, R. (2008). Parent involvement in early childhood home visiting. *Child and Youth Care Forum, 37*, 171–196. doi:10.1007/s10566-008-9057-3

Lopez, V., Clifford, T., Minnes, P., & Kuntz, H. (2008). *Parental stress and coping in families of children with and without developmental delays*. Retrieved from http://www.oadd.org/publications/journal/issues/vol14no2/download/lopezEtAl.pdf

McWilliam, R. (2010). *Working with families of young children with special needs*. Retrieved from https://books.google.com.au/books/about/Working_with_Families_of_Young_Children.html?id=POu6T4TRm6wC&redir_esc=y

Moore, T. (2010). *Family-centred practice: challenges in working with diverse families*. Retrieved from www.rch.org.au/uploadedFiles/Main/Content/ccch/TM_NMR_ECIS_Professional_Development_Day_10.pdf

Moore, T. (2012). *Rethinking early childhood intervention services: implication for policy and practice.* Retrieved from http://www.rch.org.au/uploadedfiles/main/content/ccch/profdev/ecia_national_conference_2012.pdf

OECD. (2015). *How's life?* Retrieved from http://www.oecd.org/statistics/how-s-life-23089679.htm

Owen, L., Gordon, M., Frederico, M., & Cooper, B. (2002). *Listen to us: supporting families with children with disabilities-identifying service responses that impact on the risk of family breakdown.* Retrieved from http://www.lloydowen.com.au/images/stories/Listen_to_Us_1_Family_Resilience_Project_Title__Executive_Summary_December_02.pdf

Rogers, P., Edgecombe, G., Kimberley, S., Barclay, L., & Humble, R. (2004). *Evaluation of the stronger families and communities strategy 2000-2004: early intervention-particularly in early childhood.* Melbourne: Australian Government: Department of Family and Community Services & RMIT University Circle.

Shelton, T. L., Jeppson, E. S., & Johnson, B. H. (1987). *Family centred care for children with special health care needs.* Washington, DC: Association for the Care of Children's Health.

Shelton, T. L., & Stepanek, J. S. (1994). *Family-centred care for children needing specialised health and developmental services.* Bethesda, MD: Association for the Care of Children's Health.

Shonkoff, J., & Garner, A. (2012). *The lifelong effects of early childhood adversity and toxic stress.* Retrieved from http://pediatrics.aappublications.org/content/pediatrics/early/2011/12/21/peds.2011-2663.full.pdf

Shonkoff, J.P., & Phillips, D.A. (2000). *From neurons to neighborhoods: The science of early childhood development.* Washington D.C: The National Academy of Science.

Turnbull, A., Turbiville, V., & Turnbull, H. (2003). Evolution of family-professional partnerships: Collective empowerment as the model for the early twenty-first century. In J. Shonkoff & S. Meisels (Eds.), *Handbook of early childhood intervention* (pp. 630–650). Cambridge: Cambridge University.

Thurman, S. K. (1997). Systems, ecologies, and the context of early intervention. In S. K. Thurman, J. R. Cornwell, & S. R. Gottwald (Eds.), *Contexts of early intervention: Systems and settings* (pp. 3–17). Baltimore, MD: Brookes.

Vimpani, G., Patton, G., & Hayes, A. (2002). The relevance of child and adolescen development outcomes in education, health and life success. In A. Sanson (Ed.), *Children's health and development: New research directions for Australia* (pp. 14–37). Retrieved from http://www.aifs.gov.au/institute/pubs/resreport8/main.html

Watson, S. L., Hayes, S. A., & Radford-Paz, E. (2011). Research about the journey and initial impact of parents seeking a diagnosis of developmental disability for their child. *International Review of Research in Developmental Disabilities, 40*, 31–71.

Part II

Foundations for working with young children and their families

Both family systems and family-centred early childhood intervention not only broaden the scope of intervention practices, but help elucidate the complex relationships between interrelated and interdependent subsystems where events within and between subsystems affect family, parent, parent-child, and child behaviour and functioning (Bronfenbrenner, 1979, 1986). Different systems theories and models (e.g., Cowan, Powell, & Cowan, 1998; Dent-Read & Zukow-Goldring, 1997; Emery, 2014; Keith, 1995) provide useful frameworks for understanding the factors influencing person-environment interactions and transactions (e.g., Armstrong, Birnie-Lefcovitch, & Ungar, 2005; Munsell, Kilmer, Cook, & Reeve, 2012) and how those interactions and transactions in turn influence child learning and development (Crnic & Greenberg, 1987; Sameroff, 1975).

The chapters in this section of the book provide foundational perspectives for translating basic tenets of systems theories into practice and operationalising early childhood intervention. The authors develop understanding for how family-centred practices – a particular type of practitioner-family interaction and transaction – have direct and indirect effects on the family, parent, and child outcomes that are hypothesised to be the benefits of family systems approaches to early childhood intervention. The chapters, taken together, provide the foundations for the continued rethinking and reimagining of early childhood intervention in order to focus attention on the development-instigating and development-enhancing experiences and opportunities afforded young children and their families.

Both Guralnick (Chapter 2) and Dunst (Chapter 3) describe the key elements and characteristics of different but compatible intervention models informed by systems theories, research, and practice, where each model focuses on the opportunities and experiences that are hypothesised to contribute to better child, parent, and family outcomes. Dempsey and Keen (Chapter 4) describe the particular outcomes that have been found to be associated with family-centred practices and describe a framework (Dempsey & Keen, 2008) for capturing the direct and indirect effects of family-centred practices on child, parent, and family outcomes. The chapters, taken together, provide an expanded perspective for understanding early childhood intervention processes and the benefits associated with family systems and family-centred approaches to intervention.

References

Armstrong, M. I., Birnie-Lefcovitch, S., & Ungar, M. T. (2005). Pathways between social support, family well being, quality of parenting, and child resilience: What we know. *Journal of Child and Family Studies, 14,* 269–281. doi:10.1007/s10826-005-5054-4

Bronfenbrenner, U. (1979). *The ecology of human development: Experiments by nature and design.* Cambridge, MA: Harvard University Press.

Bronfenbrenner, U. (1986). Recent advances in research on the ecology of human development. In R. K. Silbereisen, K. Eyferth, & G. Rudinger (Eds.), *Development as action in context: Problem behavior and normal youth development* (pp. 286–309). New York: Springer-Verlag.

Cowan, P. A., Powell, D., & Cowan, C. P. (1998). Parenting interventions: A family systems perspective. In W. Damon, I. E. Sigel, & K. A. Renninger (Eds.), *Handbook of child psychology: Vol. 4. Child psychology in practice* (5th ed., pp. 3–72). New York: Wiley.

Crnic, K. A., & Greenberg, M. T. (1987). Transactional relationships between perceived family style, risk status, and mother-child interactions in two-year-olds. *Journal of Pediatric Psychology, 12,* 343–362.

Dempsey, I., & Keen, D. (2008). A review of processes and outcomes in family-centered services for children with a disability. *Topics in Early Childhood Special Education, 28,* 42–52. doi:10.1177/0271121408316699

Dent-Read, C., & Zukow-Goldring, P. (Eds.). (1997). *Evolving explanations of development: Ecological approaches to organism-environment systems.* Washington, DC: American Psychological Association.

Emery, R. E. (2014). Families as systems: Some thoughts on methods and theory. In S. M. McHale, P. Amato, & A. Booth (Eds.), *Emerging methods in family research* (pp. 109–124). Cham, Switzerland: Springer International Publishing.

Keith, C. (1995). Family caregiving systems: Models, resources and values. *Journal of Marriage and the Family, 57,* 179–189.

Munsell, E. P., Kilmer, R. P., Cook, J. R., & Reeve, C. L. (2012). The effects of caregiver social connections on caregiver, child, and family well-being. *American Journal of Orthopsychiatry, 82,* 137–145. doi:10.1111/j.1939-0025.2011.01129.x

Sameroff, A. (1975). Transactional models in early social relations. *Human Development, 18,* 65–79.

2 Early intervention for young children with developmental delays

Contributions of the developmental systems approach

Michael J. Guralnick

Those engaged in the field of early intervention today are involved in perhaps its most vibrant historical period. Progress reports summarising innovative projects, journal articles describing new advances, and conference papers alerting us to possible future directions all bring to our attention the extraordinary amount of knowledge being generated with respect to strategies and approaches designed to enhance the development of vulnerable young children. Moreover, dramatic increases are occurring with respect to our understanding as to how development unfolds for vulnerable children and the specific developmental mechanisms, pathways, and influences involved. These advances suggest that a more complete integration of the fields of early child development and early intervention is rapidly approaching. Perhaps most impressive is the diversity of intervention approaches taken to enhance the development of vulnerable children; some addressing a relatively narrow aspect of development, whereas others design and implement more complex and comprehensive sets of intervention strategies. Nevertheless, the vast array of models and intervention strategies that are continually emerging are signs not only of the complexity of the issues that the early intervention field confronts, but also indicate the vigour, commitment, and energy of those seeking to find the most effective means of supporting children's development.

To be effectively applied in early intervention programs, however, this new knowledge must be organised and interpreted in a meaningful context, placing it in a programmatic and developmental framework. Unless this occurs, new knowledge will take the forms of isolated bits of information, creating uncertainty as to how and whether it can be usefully and effectively incorporated into a more comprehensive early intervention program. Accordingly, a systematic approach to early intervention is needed that can provide a framework for incorporating this knowledge and ultimately translating it into a coherent and comprehensive early intervention program at the individual child and family level.

The purpose of this chapter is to outline the elements and assumptions of the developmental systems approach (DSA) to address this issue focusing on young children with developmental delays (Guralnick, 2005a, 2005b). As will be seen, the DSA centres on families as they seek to provide as optimal a developmental environment for their child as possible. At the same time, the DSA recognises the importance of incorporating knowledge from developmental systems as applied to all children. To do so, it is important to consider complex interactions occurring among and within the levels of the child, family patterns of interaction that directly influence the child, and a family's resources. Accordingly, the DSA attempts to integrate the knowledge of the developmental science of normative child development and the knowledge that has been derived from studies of developmental science that focus on circumstances related to risk and disability. Central as well to the DSA is its emphasis on relationships. Through the formation of high-quality relationships with parents, extended family, and others significant in the life of the child, mechanisms of influence are established capable of providing sustained support for the development of young children's social and cognitive competence.

The DSA has been influenced by many existing systems models (e.g., Bronfenbrenner, 2001; Sameroff, 2009) as well as the developmental psychopathology approach designed to apply general developmental systems principles and findings to atypical populations (Cicchetti & Cohen, 2006; Lewis, 2000). A distinguishing feature of the DSA is its application specifically to issues in the early intervention field and its ability to establish a direct connection between developmental science and intervention science. With respect to intervention science and its association with practice, the principles described in Dunst's approach to support family systems in the context of early intervention have been most influential (see Dunst & Trivette, 2009).

The developmental systems approach

Figure 2.1 illustrates the three levels of the DSA and identifies some of the key interrelationships that must be considered within this systems framework. The DSA assumes that the overarching goal of early intervention is to maximise children's social and cognitive competence. It further recognises that in so doing, children will have more adequate internal resources at their disposal to achieve their interpersonal goals as they move through different developmental periods and eventually reach adulthood. Goals therefore range widely over time, such as reducing discomfort to achieving material ends to establishing social connections. The early years provide unique opportunities to establish a positive developmental trajectory in this regard for all children (Shonkoff & Phillips, 2000).

Three interrelated levels of the DSA are identified in Figure 2.1 and are expanded upon in this chapter. The level of child development (first level: social and cognitive competence) identifies components that constitute children's developmental resources and organisational processes which, taken together, are engaged in a systematic and coherent manner when children attempt to achieve their interpersonal goals. To be sure, genetic and epigenetic processes as well as other biological mechanisms have a substantial effect at this level, but all interact over time with experiential factors that are the direct influence of what the DSA refers to as family patterns of interaction (second level). The three major domains

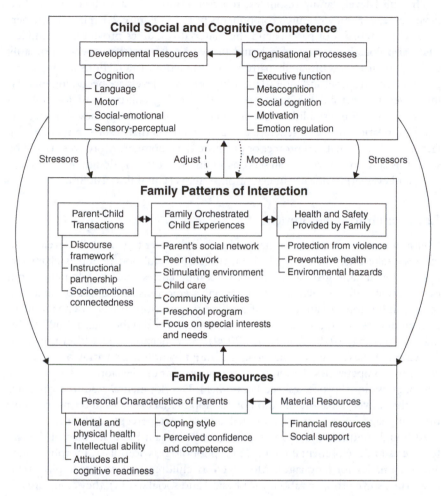

Figure 2.1 The developmental systems approach illustrating the levels, components, and interrelationships of the approach

Source: Adapted from "Why Early Intervention Works: A Systems Perspective," by M. J. Guralnick, 2011, *Infants & Young Children, 24*, pp. 6–28. Copyright 2011 Lippincott Williams & Wilkins.

of family patterns of interaction that influence the level of the child (and therefore children's competencies) are parent-child transactions, family-orchestrated child experiences, and the child's health and safety as provided by the family. Of note, transactions refer to those instances in which true relationships between individuals have been established. Along with their identified components, these three domains constitute the proximal influences on children's developmental resources and organisational processes, and each component within these three domains can serve as a risk or protective factor. Indeed, these proximal influences are the major focus of early intervention.

The third level, family resources, represents more distal influences on child development. Family resource components noted in Figure 2.1 relate to the personal characteristics of parents and the material resources provided by families. They also constitute a set of risk and protective factors that operate primarily through their effects on family patterns of interaction. Interactions among components within a level and interrelationships between levels are becoming increasingly well understood for both typically developing children and for children at risk for, or with, established developmental delays. Indeed, these interactions and interrelationships can generate cumulative effects that result from either risk factors or factors that can protect or promote development. Moreover, as will be seen, this conceptual system can serve as a framework for the design, implementation, and evaluation of early intervention systems (Guralnick, 2005c).

Level of child development

Children's interpersonal goals change dramatically over time as skills develop and interests take different forms. Indeed, the early childhood period is characterised by remarkable growth in children's competencies. Early goals range from more reactive efforts such as regulating one's emotions in the face of uncertain or uncomfortable situations to extraordinary proactive efforts to engage in or gain an understanding of their social and physical world (Chouinard, 2007; Feldman & Masalha, 2010; Woodward, 2009). As conceptualised within the DSA, carrying out these interpersonal goals is realised by utilising an array of social and cognitive competencies that, in turn, are dependent on developmental resources and organisational processes (see Figure 2.1). Developmental resources are similar to the conventional organisation of developmental domains in terms of cognition, language, motor, socio-emotional, and sensory-perceptual abilities.

Although unquestionably interrelated, each domain has a set of well-defined features and developmental course (e.g., phonology, vocabulary, morphosyntax, and pragmatics for language). Moreover, as children seek to accomplish their goals (i.e., solve problems about the physical and social world), they enlist organisational processes as well. These complex and interrelated processes consist of well-conceptualised constructs of executive function, metacognition, social cognition, motivation, and emotion regulation. Although not as easily measured as developmental resources, each nevertheless has a strong empirical basis (Beauchamp & Anderson, 2010; Best & Miller, 2010; Cole, Martin, & Dennis, 2004; Pintrich, 2000). To be sure, unevenness in the relative strength, quality, specific features, and rates of development for both developmental resources and organisational processes are common, yet a coherent pattern of development can be identified that together characterises and constitutes a unique individual as a fully recognisable "self" during the early childhood years.

Developmental constraints for children with delays

There are always variations and perturbations as development unfolds as a consequence of interactions among biological, environmental, and cultural influences.

Despite each child's unique behavioural and developmental pattern, parents and others in the child's sphere of influence are usually able to make adjustments to these characteristics to provide an optimal or near-optimal environment supporting a child's development. Indeed, even in non-optimal environments, most children engage in activities that enable them to extract sufficient information about the physical and social world to support their developing competencies and to carry out their interpersonal goals (Gopnik & Wellman, 2012; Xu & Kushnir, 2013). Resilience is a common characteristic of development.

But the situation changes dramatically when children's development is affected by biological factors that have a substantial adverse effect. Disruption to development of sufficient severity creates constraints on a child's development, potentially producing delays or differences in many areas, including components of both developmental resources and organisational processes. The focus of this chapter is on children where delays are evident during the early childhood period and, at minimum, affect overall aspects of their cognitive development in a significant manner. Formal diagnostic/classification processes, including appropriate assessments of adaptive behaviour, may or may not reveal an aetiology for these delays but the likelihood is that the vast majority of young children identified during this period will experience life-long challenges related to intellectual disability (e.g., Keogh, Bernheimer, & Guthrie, 1997). Although an understanding of what constitutes cognitive development is still evolving, the recent cognitive test battery included as part of the National Institutes of Health Toolbox (Zelazo & Bauer, 2013) identifies the following five areas as critical: (1) executive function and attention; (2) episodic memory (primarily the storage of events, place in time, and their sequence); (3) language (focusing on vocabulary); (4) working memory; and (5) processing speed. These domains are representative of what is referred to as fluid intelligence (related to problem-solving skills and adjustments to the immediate situation and novel events) and to crystallised intelligence (dependent more on experience, such as exposure to new vocabulary words).

Among the many causes of these delays are in-utero exposures to alcohol, drugs, or environmental chemicals, fetal and post-natal infections, exposure to toxins during peri- and post-natal periods, and preterm birth (Diav-Citrin, 2011; Ergaz & Ornoy, 2011; McDermott, Durkin, Schupf, & Stein, 2007; Sansavini, Guarini, & Caselli, 2011). Genetic factors play a major role as well in the form of chromosomal disorders, deletion syndromes, or single-gene disorders (Chelly, Khelfaoui, Francis, Chérif, & Bienvenu, 2006; Mefford, Batshaw, & Hoffman, 2012), or as part of a pattern of polygenic inheritance, usually in combination with significant environmental risks such as chronic poverty (Iarocci & Petrill, 2012). These biological constraints set into motion a developmental pattern that alters specific developmental resources and organisational processes and often requires children to solve their interpersonal goals in different ways using the developmental tools available to them.

For children with genetic disorders in particular, etiologic-specific developmental patterns have been identified that may prompt more innovative intervention approaches, enabling parents to adjust more effectively to their children's developmental and behavioural abilities (Hodapp, Desjardins, & Ricci, 2003).

For example, much is known about the special eye-movement planning problems of children with Williams syndrome, which affects exploration of the visual world, generates general spatial cognitive difficulties, and ultimately adversely influences joint attention episodes so critical for promoting language and other aspects of development (see Brown et al., 2003).

Accordingly, constraints in early aspects of development create a cascade of events that influence developmental patterns over time (Karmiloff-Smith, 2009). As other examples, well-established problems related to emotion regulation, working memory, and social anxiety, among other areas, for children with Fragile X syndrome (Abbeduto, Brady, & Kover, 2007; Cornish, Turk, & Hagerman, 2008; Hagerman, 2011), as well as the executive function, cognitive instabilities, task persistence, and expressive language concerns of children with Down syndrome (Gilmore, Cuskelly, Jobling, & Hayes, 2009; Glenn, Dayus, Cunningham, & Horgan, 2001; Lee et al., 2011; Roberts, Price, & Malkin, 2007; Wishart, 1996) identify issues to be aware of that occur with a higher likelihood for children with these syndromes that affect developmental patterns as they emerge across the early childhood period. At the same time, etiologic-specific information has revealed relative strengths exhibited by children that could be capitalised upon when designing early intervention programs. The relative strength in the use of gestures by children with Down syndrome provides just one example (Lee et al., 2011).

A cornerstone of early intervention has always been its emphasis on individualising supportive approaches. The fact is that despite the usefulness of etiologic-specific information, considerable within-syndrome variability exists. Moreover, etiologic information of developmental value is not available for most children with delays receiving early intervention services. Nevertheless, whenever developmental patterns emerge as a consequence of biological constraints, they increase the likelihood that parents and others playing significant roles in the child's life will have difficulty adjusting to their child's characteristics to establish an optimally supportive developmental environment. It is precisely when these adjustments are not adequate or when it is anticipated that adjustments may not be considered by families that early intervention can have a major influence. More specifically, child-specific characteristics may affect a family's pattern of interactions with their child to the extent that a non-optimal developmental environment is created. These child-specific influences are referred to as stressors within the framework of the DSA (see Figure 2.1) and are discussed shortly.

Family patterns of interaction

Especially for young children, the DSA proposes that, from an experiential perspective, the three types of family patterns of interaction noted above are critical to a child's development. This is the case irrespective of any biological constraints. Without question, biological constraints as reflected in the various developmental resources and organisational processes that underlie children's social and cognitive competence can influence the specific effects a particular level of quality of family patterns of interaction can have on a child's development (see dotted line indicating the moderating effects at the level of child development in Figure 2.1). For example, even linguistic input provided with modest quality by parents is sufficient for children developing typically to extract essential information and develop appropriate language skills. However, children for whom biological constraints exist may well need high-quality linguistic input to achieve the same results (Rowe, Levine, Fisher, & Goldin-Meadow, 2009). Moreover, recent research on genetic factors has revealed how variation in overall sensitivity to environmental inputs also serves as an important moderator of effects (Belsky & Pluess, 2013). Consequently, the message for early intervention is that strategies must be developed to enable parents and others engaging in interactions with the child to adjust to their child's characteristics such that high-quality family patterns of interaction are the result.

Particularly during the first years of a child's life, the quality of relationships in the form of parent-child transactions that are established is the central mechanism that promotes children's social and cognitive competence (see Guralnick, 2011). Emphasis is placed on emerging relationships; constructs characterised by cooperation, synchrony, and positive ambiance (Aksan, Kochanska, & Ortmann, 2006; Feldman, 2007), as well as a shared set of expectations that parents and children are engaged in a collaborative enterprise (Tomasello & Carpenter, 2007). This collaborative enterprise is realised through three interrelated *relationship processes* so that parents (and others) can establish: (1) a discourse framework; (2) an instructional partnership; and (3) socioemotional connectedness. These relationships emerge over time as interactions occur in various contexts and are generated as a result of parents' ability to maintain contingent and predictable patterns of interaction which not only focus on the child in general but also consider the child's specific developmental capabilities, interests, motivational style, and related characteristics. Taken together, this pattern is referred to as "sensitive-responsiveness" (see Ainsworth, Blehar, Waters, & Wall, 1978) and, along with a sufficient level of engagement with the child accompanied by affectively warm interactions, the foundation for building the three relationship processes of parent-child transactions are in place.

The second major feature of family patterns of interaction consists of those experiences orchestrated by families that have the ability to enhance a child's competencies. The components of family-orchestrated child experiences are listed in Figure 2.1. As is the case for parent-child transactions, extensive evidence is available indicating that the quality of each of these experiences contributes to a child's development. Dunst and colleagues in particular (see Dunst, Hamby, Trivette, Raab, & Bruder, 2000) have demonstrated the critical nature of these experiences and the cumulative benefits that result. Moreover, although often constrained by forces well beyond the control of families, it is nevertheless the case that children's health and safety as provided by the family also contribute to children's overall wellbeing and development (e.g., Cole & Winsler, 2010; Strickland et al., 2004).

Accordingly, each of the components of the three family patterns of interaction listed in Figure 2.1 can be said to constitute risk or protective factors. Sufficient evidence is available to suggest that family patterns of interaction influence children's social and cognitive competence through their effects on children's developmental resources and organisational processes. Information with respect to these patterns of influence is available for typically developing children (Guralnick, 2011), for children with established disabilities (Guralnick, 2005a, 2005c, 2016), for children at biological risk due to preterm birth (Guralnick, 2012), and for children at risk due to environmental factors (Guralnick, 2013).

Stressors to family patterns of interaction

The complex child-specific patterns commonly evident for children with developmental delays have the potential to reduce the quality of all of these components of family patterns of interaction, especially those associated with parent-child transactions. Parents can become more directive or even intrusive especially when their child is more passive. They may also find it difficult to engage in joint attention episodes, provide a less enriched linguistic environment for their child, or fail to tailor language exchanges appropriately due to difficulties in reading their child's cues or understanding fully the unevenness of children's developmental resources (e.g., Hauser-Cram, Warfield, Shonkoff, & Krauss, 2001; Murphy & Abbeduto, 2005; Spiker, Boyce, & Boyce, 2002). Family-orchestrated child experiences can also be affected, such as difficulties parents experience in helping to establish and support their child's relationships with peers (Guralnick, 2010).

It is critical to emphasise that despite these challenges, many if not most parents of young children with delays are highly effective, making necessary adjustments to their child's characteristics. That is, they are able to prevent stressors from developing. As one example, forming an instructional partnership with children with delays is often difficult to accomplish, but many parents can indeed make the required adjustments in the level of scaffolding needed to support structured play (Guralnick, Hammond, Neville, & Connor, 2008). Many other examples of highly appropriate and effective parental adjustments to children with delays exist (Bernheimer & Weisner, 2007; Venuti, De Falco, Esposito, & Bornstein, 2009). Consequently, careful assessments of each of the components of family patterns of interaction must be an essential feature of early intervention programs, with substantial intervention activities involving those families who both experience stressors and recognise the value of enhancing all components of family patterns of interaction.

Family resources

Child-specific factors cannot only create stressors at the level of family patterns of interaction, but can also do so with respect to the various components at the level of a family's resources (see Figure 2.1). Components of family resources most vulnerable to stressors are parents' mental health, especially in the context of child behaviour problems, lack of social support, and parents' perceived concerns with respect to their confidence and competence in carrying out the parenting role (Crnic, Pedersen Y Arbona, Baker, & Blacher, 2009; Eisenhower, Baker, & Blacher, 2005; Glidden, 2012). Within the DSA framework and as illustrated in Figure 2.1, family resources directly influence family patterns of interaction. Consequently, stressors to family resources can exacerbate any effects of stressors at the level of family patterns of interaction. Moreover, especially given the association between poverty and the likelihood of having a child with a developmental delay in a family (Emerson & Hatton, 2009), risk factors at the level of family resources are often higher at the outset, even before child-specific stressors add additional risks. A consequence of these interrelated patterns can be a major disruption in the quality of numerous components of a family's pattern of interactions.

Adjustments

It is important to emphasise that most families of children with delays will not require a highly intensive and comprehensive level of early intervention supports and services in order to establish as optimal a developmental environment as possible for their child. Indeed, most families are quite capable of making needed adjustments, often relying on a positive coping style, adequate financial resources, or a supportive social network. Family adaptation, especially over time, is common as appropriate and effective adjustments with respect to specific forms and quality of family patterns of interaction are achieved. There exist, however, subgroups of families who will likely experience difficulties making these adjustments thereby experiencing stressors affecting the level of family patterns of interaction as well as from stressors or pre-existing risk factors at the level of family resources. Together, these challenges cumulate and can create perturbations throughout the entire system. From the child's perspective, this ultimately results in a circumstance in which non-optimal quality of family patterns of interaction are provided. It is through early intervention programs centring on families that these stressors can be addressed, capitalising on protective factors evident in the family structure.

Organisational features of the DSA

One important feature of the DSA is its ability to provide an organisational structure for the many complex components and processes associated with an early intervention program. It also has the potential for organising new knowledge generated by the field, as noted in the introductory section of this chapter. Most evident is that early intervention programs should be designed specifically to enhance the quality of family patterns of interaction. The components selected for inclusion in the DSA at that level are those that have clear and direct relevance to enhancing a child's development. The ultimate success of any early intervention program is its ability to expand a family's capacity to support children's social and cognitive development.

This general approach is outlined in Figure 2.2. With respect to assessment at each level of the DSA, in practice, before a formal early intervention program is designed and implemented, information about a child's overall developmental status is typically available, usually with respect to their developmental resources. Similarly, basic demographic information about the family is usually available, providing some sense for the level of risk and protective factors at the level of family resources. Indeed, larger numbers of paediatricians are gathering information about a family's psychosocial risks through surveillance and use of screening tools that can be utilised by an early intervention team (Garg & Dworkin, 2011).

The key to assessment within the DSA, however, is a careful evaluation of all of the components at the level of family patterns of interaction. This approach then provides an unambiguous structure for gathering critical information about the quality of each component. For example, for parent-child transactions, screening tools related to sensitive-responsiveness, affective warmth, and engagement are available (e.g., Bradley, 2012; Landry, Smith, & Swank, 2006; Tamis-Lemonda, Uzgiris, & Bornstein, 2002). Concerns emerging from the screening process would then lead to a more in-depth assessment of the quality of relationships, focusing on one or more of these three aspects of parent-child transactions. Although relevant instruments capable of capturing the essential features of relationships at various developmental periods consistent with the DSA are now being developed (Aksan et al., 2006), much more needs to be accomplished. As information on these and other forms of assessment relevant to the DSA become available, they can be incorporated into the process. Other, minimally intrusive processes involving parental interviews, questionnaires, or gathering information from service personnel can generate a realistic portrait of the child's experiences

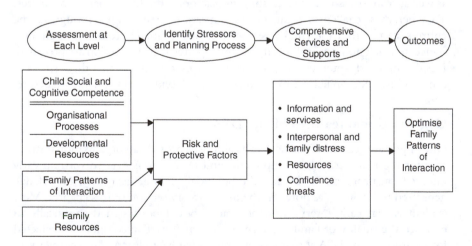

Figure 2.2 Sequence of activities associated with the developmental systems approach designed to optimise family patterns of interaction

Source: Created by the author

as provided by the family, particularly involvement in community activities. Collaborations with health and social service professionals can provide additional information with respect to the child's health and safety provided by the family.

Assessments at each of the three levels of the DSA create the basis for a planning process, organised around the risk and protective factors that are identified. A comprehensive plan of services and supports is then designed, guided by the profile established within the framework of the components at the level of family patterns of interaction and family resources. At the same time, issues identified at the level of child development are considered. At the family resource level, what follows will typically include an array of information and services, including community resources to help address any interpersonal or family concerns, as well as addressing any threats to a parent's confidence in carrying out the parenting role. Once again, as noted in Figure 2.2, the central goal is to optimise family patterns of interaction, and structuring assessments in the form of a partnership with parents helps to organise and make sense of the often unusual complexities associated with supporting children with developmental delays. Working with families to increase their awareness of the power of relationships and identifying the three types of relationship processes can generate a framework for both understanding developmental mechanisms and guiding parent actions. It also provides a common language and a shared set of goals between the parent and the early intervention team.

It is beyond the scope of this chapter to provide details about the intervention options associated with each component of family patterns of interaction or ways to enhance a family's resources, but numerous relevant curricula, strategies, and resources are available. A number of curricula and strategies consistent with the DSA have been summarised (see Spiker, Hebbeler, & Mallik, 2005). Many learning opportunities that are available as part of community activities as articulated by Dunst and colleagues (Dunst et al., 2000), and approaches to enhancing social supports (Dunst, Trivette, & Jodry, 1997) are also well established. Moreover, the DSA can serve as a useful guide to organise new findings relevant to intervention in the field, ones that are sufficiently evidence-based. These strategies can then be considered as possible intervention options for specific components of family patterns of interaction or family resources. As a consequence, existing and new intervention approaches are considered in a context; one that supports an integrated and conceptually coherent approach to supporting and strengthening families.

Problem-solving process

As valuable as an organisational structure may be for any early intervention system, the fact remains that early intervention is a clinical enterprise relying on the ability of all involved to engage in a problem-solving process. Difficulties enhancing the quality of the components of a family's pattern of interaction are inevitable, often arising as children enter different developmental periods. This problem-solving process may require obtaining much more in-depth information at the level of child development, especially with respect to organisational pro-cesses. As a consequence, special adaptations addressing emotion regulation or task motivation may be needed when difficulties emerge forming, for example, a high-quality instructional partnership. Similarly, further probing of the compo-nents of family resources, both the personal characteristics of parents and material resources, may reveal influences at that level that must be urgently addressed or suggest the need for alternative forms of intervention. Family resource issues are sensitive matters, as family systems constitute a complex network of relationships, beliefs, and attitudes. Early intervention activities at this level must be carried out with extreme care, with the recognition that some of the components cannot be easily addressed or will require a long-term investment before an impact is real-ised. Political, social, and community resource constraints must be recognised but not accepted. Creative problem-solving that yields even small gains can have long-term benefits. Early intervention is an ongoing process, the dynamic nature of which continually requires adjustments from all involved.

As Dunst and Trivette (2009) appropriately point out, to be successful, such a process must consider the needs and aspirations of families, their style of relat-ing, and the supports and resources they have available on a regular basis. Rec-ognition of these factors facilitates both the assessment and intervention phases of early intervention as well as the modifications required over time as a result of informal and formal evaluations. Clearly, the success of this process depends importantly on the relationship between early interventionists and family mem-bers. Dunst and Trivette's (2009) twelve principles of effective help-giving pro-vide essential guidelines.

Systems integration and principles

Figure 2.3 provides a flowchart that translates the DSA into a process that can be implemented as part of a system of early intervention practices in community settings (Guralnick, 2001). The sequence of activities ranging from screening through transition planning is designed to integrate the multi-level developmen-tal constructs of the DSA described in this chapter. In addition to these structural features and its developmental orientation, any early intervention system must also be guided by a set of principles and values (Guralnick, 2008). The help-giving principles noted above constitute one key example. Moreover, emphasis in the DSA on relationships within the principle of utilising a developmental framework extends beyond the formation of high-quality parent-child transac-tions to include relationships between early intervention professionals and fami-lies, as well as relationships between children and other adults, especially child care professionals and preschool teachers. Each relationship has somewhat dif-ferent qualities, but yet is essential for the system to operate effectively in order to support a child's development. Other principles and values include ensuring that integration and coordination among all the elements of the system are max-imised, that every effort will be made to include the child in natural settings and, that despite commonalities expected among etiologic subgroups or families with

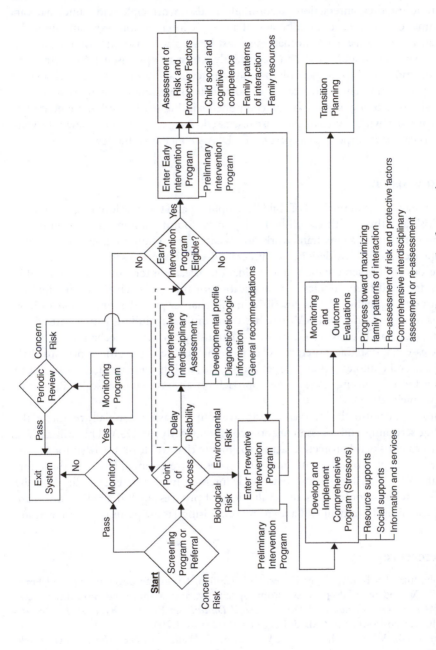

Figure 2.3 The developmental systems approach for early intervention in a proactive framework

Source: Modified from "A Developmental Systems Model for Early Intervention," by M. J. Guralnick, 2001, *Infants & Young Children, 14,* pp. 1–18. Copyright 2001 by Lippincott Williams & Wilkins.

similar demographic characteristics, attention must be given to individualise all components of the system to the unique characteristics of children and families. Ensuring that professionals recognise and understand cultural differences and can adjust their interactions accordingly is also a principle and value that can dramatically influence the outcome of any early intervention program. Similarly, evaluation and feedback mechanisms must be in place given the dynamic nature of development and the need to constantly adjust to optimise family patterns of interaction as much as possible. Finally, curricula and all intervention strategies must not only have evidence to support their effectiveness but must fit within the DSA into one or more of the components in Figure 2.1 and implemented in accordance with the principles just discussed. As a consequence, new interventions can be incorporated as part of the DSA's conceptual framework.

Conclusions

Major advances in the field of child development and the development of children at risk and those with established delays have found common ground in developmental and systems frameworks in recent years. The developmental systems approach is explicitly designed to integrate these perspectives focusing directly on the design, implementation, and evaluation of early intervention for vulnerable children and their families. The application of this approach to young children with developmental delays described in this chapter provides an example of how this might occur. The DSA's emphasis on families, including family patterns of interaction and family resources, with relationships as a core mechanism, provides the essential systemic structure. All of us in the field recognise the enormous challenges and complexities ahead, yet there is increasing evidence that progress can be achieved utilising this systems approach on an international scale (Bruder & Guralnick, 2012).

Implementation by interventionists on a routine basis will initially require gathering screening and assessment tools consistent with the DSA. This will allow a pattern of risk and protective factors to emerge that will form the basis for a comprehensive plan of intervention. Team processes are essential to utilise this information and transform it into day-to-day intervention activities at all levels of the DSA. Regular conferences and evaluations of progress including all involved are critical in order to maintain a focus on optimising family patterns of interaction.

References

Abbeduto, L., Brady, N., & Kover, S. T. (2007). Language development and Fragile X syndrome: Profiles, syndrome-specificity, and within-syndrome differences. *Mental Retardation and Developmental Disabilities Research Reviews, 13*, 36–46. Retrieved from http://dx.doi.org/10.1002/mrdd.20142

Ainsworth, M. S., Blehar, M. C., Waters, E., & Wall, S. (1978). *Patterns of attachment: A psychological study of the strange situation.* Oxford: Erlbaum.

Aksan, N., Kochanska, G., & Ortmann, M. R. (2006). Mutually responsive orientation between parents and their young children: Toward methodological advances in the science of relationships. *Developmental Psychology, 42,* 833–848. Retrieved from http://dx.doi.org/10.1037/0012-1649.42.5.833

Beauchamp, M. H., & Anderson, V. (2010). SOCIAL: An integrative framework for the development of social skills. *Psychological Bulletin, 136,* 39–64. Retrieved from http://dx.doi.org/10.1037/a0017768

Belsky, J., & Pluess, M. (2013). Beyond risk, resilience, and dysregulation: Phenotypic plasticity and human development. *Development and Psychopathology, 25,* 1243–1261. Retrieved from http://dx.doi.org/10.1017/S095457941300059X

Bernheimer, L. P., & Weisner, T. S. (2007). "Let me just tell you what I do all day . . .". *Infants & Young Children, 20,* 192–201. Retrieved from http://dx.doi.org/10.1097.01.IYC.000027775.62819.9b

Best, J. R., & Miller, P. H. (2010). A developmental perspective on executive function. *Child Development, 81,* 1641–1660. Retrieved from http://dx.doi.org/10.1111/j.1467-8624.2010.01499.x

Bradley, R. H. (2012). HOME inventory. In L. M. M. Lewis (Ed.), *The Cambridge handbook of environment in human development* (pp. 568–589). Cambridge: Cambridge University Press.

Bronfenbrenner, U. (2001). Bioecological theory of human development. In N. J. Smelser & B. P. Baltes (Eds.), *International encyclopedia of the social and behavioral sciences* (Vol. 10, pp. 6963–6970). New York: Elsevier.

Brown, J., Johnson, M. H., Paterson, S. J., Gilmore, R., Longhi, E., & Karmiloff-Smith, A. (2003). Spatial representation and attention in toddlers with Williams syndrome and Down syndrome. *Neuropsychologia, 41,* 1037–1046.

Bruder, M. B., & Guralnick, M. J. (2012). From the editor. *Infants & Young Children, 25,* 267–269. Retrieved from http://dx.doi.org/10.1097/IYC.0b013e31826d8242

Chelly, J., Khelfaoui, M., Francis, F., Chérif, B., & Bienvenu, T. (2006). Genetics and pathophysiology of mental retardation. *European Journal of Human Genetics, 14,* 701–713. Retrieved from http://dx.doi.org/10.1038/sj.ejhg.5201595

Chouinard, M. M. (2007). Children's questions: A mechanism for cognitive development. *Monographs of the Society for Research in Child Development, 72,* 1–112. Retrieved from http://dx.doi.org/10.1111/j.1540-5834.2007.00412.x

Cicchetti, D., & Cohen, D. (2006). Development and psychopathology. In D. Cicchetti & D. Cohen (Eds.), *Developmental psychopathology: Vol. 1. Theory and methods* (2nd ed., pp. 1–23). Hoboken, NJ: John Wiley & Sons.

Cole, C., & Winsler, A. (2010). Protecting children from exposure to lead: Old problem, new data, and new policy needs. *Social Policy Report, 24,* 1–29.

Cole, P. M., Martin, S. E., & Dennis, T. A. (2004). Emotion regulation as a scientific construct: Methodological challenges and directions for child development research. *Child Development, 75,* 317–333.

Cornish, K., Turk, J., & Hagerman, R. (2008). The Fragile X continuum: New advances and perspectives. *Journal of Intellectual Disability Research, 52,* 469–482. Retrieved from http://dx.doi.org/10.1111/j.1365-2788.2008.01056.x

Crnic, K. A., Pedersen Y Arbona, A., Baker, B., & Blacher, J. (2009). Mothers and fathers together: Contrasts in parenting across preschool to early school age in children with developmental delays. In L. M. Glidden & M. M. Seltzer (Eds.), *International review of research in mental retardation* (Vol. 37, pp. 1–30). St. Mary's City, MD: Elsevier.

Diav-Citrin, O. (2011). Prenatal exposures associated with neurodevelopmental delay and disabilities. *Developmental Disabilities Research Reviews, 17,* 71–84. Retrieved from http://dx.doi.org/10.1002/ddrr.1102

Dunst, C. J., Hamby, D., Trivette, C. M., Raab, M., & Bruder, M. B. (2000). Every-day family and community life and children's naturally occurring learning opportunities. *Journal of Early Intervention, 23*, 151–164. Retrieved from http://dx.doi.org/10.1177/10538151000230030501

Dunst, C. J., & Trivette, C. M. (2009). Capacity-building family-systems intervention practices. *Journal of Family Social Work, 12*, 119–143. Retrieved from http://dx.doi.org/10.1080/10522150802713322

Dunst, C. J., Trivette, C. M., & Jodry, W. (1997). Influence of social support on children with disabilities and their families. In M. J. Guralnick (Ed.), *The effectiveness of early intervention* (pp. 499–522). Baltimore, MD: Paul H. Brookes Publishing Co.

Eisenhower, A. S., Baker, B. L., & Blacher, J. (2005). Preschool children with intellectual disability: Syndrome specificity, behaviour problems, and maternal well-being. *Journal of Intellectual Disability Research, 49*, 657–671. Retrieved from http://dx.doi.org/10.1111/j.1365-2788.2005.00699.x

Emerson, E., & Hatton, C. (2009). Socioeconomic position, poverty, and family research. In L. M. Glidden & M. M. Seltzer (Eds.), *International review of research in mental retardation* (Vol. 37, pp. 95–130). St. Mary's City, MD: Elsevier.

Ergaz, Z., & Ornoy, A. (2011). Perinatal and early postnatal factors underlying developmental delay and disabilities. *Developmental Disabilities Research Reviews, 17*, 59–70. Retrieved from http://dx.doi.org/10.1002/ddrr.1101

Feldman, R. (2007). Parent-infant synchrony and the construction of shared timing; physiological precursors, developmental outcomes, and risk conditions. *Journal of Child Psychology and Psychiatry, 48*, 329–354. Retrieved from http://dx.doi.org/10.1111/j.1469-7610.2006.01701.x

Feldman, R., & Masalha, S. (2010). Parent-child and triadic antecedents of children's social competence: Cultural specificity, shared process. *Developmental Psychology, 46*, 455–467.

Garg, A., & Dworkin, P. H. (2011). Applying surveillance and screening to family psychosocial issues: Implications for the medical home. *Journal of Developmental & Behavioral Pediatrics, 32*, 418–426. Retrieved from http://dx.doi.org/10.1097/DBP.0b013e3182196726

Gilmore, L., Cuskelly, M., Jobling, A., & Hayes, A. (2009). Maternal support for autonomy: Relationships with persistence for children with Down syndrome and typically developing children. *Research in Developmental Disabilities, 30*, 1023–1033.

Glenn, S., Dayus, B., Cunningham, C., & Horgan, M. (2001). Mastery motivation in children with Down syndrome. *Down Syndrome, Research and Practice, 7*, 52–59.

Glidden, L. M. (2012). Family well-being and children with intellectual disability. In J. A. Burack, R. Hodapp, G. Iarocci, & E. Zigler (Eds.), *The Oxford handbook of intellectual disability and development* (pp. 303–317). Oxford: Oxford University Press.

Gopnik, A., & Wellman, H. M. (2012). Reconstructing constructivism: Causal models, Bayesian learning mechanisms, and the theory theory. *Psychological Bulletin, 138*, 1085–1108. Retrieved from http://dx.doi.org/10.1037/a0028044

Guralnick, M. J. (2001). A developmental systems model for early intervention. *Infants & Young Children, 14*, 1–18.

Guralnick, M. J. (2005a). Early intervention for children with intellectual disabilities: Current knowledge and future prospects. *Journal of Applied Research in Intellectual Disabilities, 18*, 313–324. Retrieved from http://dx.doi.org/10.1111/j.1468-3148.2005.00270.x

Guralnick, M. J. (2005b). An overview of the developmental systems model for early intervention. In M. J. Guralnick (Ed.), *The developmental systems approach to early intervention* (pp. 3–28). Baltimore/MD: Paul H. Brookes Publishing Co.

Guralnick, M. J. (2008). International perspectives on early intervention: A search for common ground. *Journal of Early Intervention, 30*, 90–101. Retrieved from http://dx.doi.org/10.1177/1053815107313483

Guralnick, M. J. (2010). Early intervention approaches to enhance the peer-related social competence of young children with developmental delays: A historical perspective. *Infants & Young Children, 23*, 73–83. Retrieved from http://dx.doi.org/10.1097/IYC.0b013e3181d22e14

Guralnick, M. J. (2011). Why early intervention works: A systems perspective. *Infants & Young Children, 24*, 6–28. Retrieved from http://dx.doi.org/10.1097/IYC.0b013e31820 02cfe

Guralnick, M. J. (2012). Preventive interventions for preterm children: Effectiveness and developmental mechanisms. *Journal of Developmental and Behavioral Pediatrics, 33*, 352–364. Retrieved from http://dx.doi.org/10.1097/DBP.0b013e31824eaa3c

Guralnick, M. J. (2013). Developmental science and preventive interventions for children at environmental risk. *Infants & Young Children, 26*, 270–285. Retrieved from http://dx.doi.org/10.1097/IYC.0b013e3182a6832f

Guralnick, M. J. (2016). Early intervention for children with intellectual disabilities: An update. *Journal of Applied Research in Intellectual Disabilities*. Retrieved from http://dx.doi.org/10.1111/jar.12233

Guralnick, M. J. (Ed.). (2005c). *The developmental systems approach to early intervention*. Baltimore, MD: Brookes.

Guralnick, M. J., Hammond, M. A., Neville, B., & Connor, R. T. (2008). The relationship between sources and functions of social support and dimensions of child- and parent-related stress. *Journal of Intellectual Disability Research, 52*, 1138–1154. Retrieved from http://dx.doi.org/10.1111/j.1365-2788.2008.01073.x

Hagerman, R. J. (2011). Fragile X syndrome and Fragile X-associated disorders. In S. Goldstein & C. R. Reynolds (Eds.), *Handbook of neurodevelopmental and genetic disorders in children* (2nd ed., pp. 276–292). New York: The Guilford Press.

Hauser-Cram, P., Warfield, M. E., Shonkoff, J. P., & Krauss, M. W. (2001). Children with disabilities. *Monographs of the Society for Research in Child Development, 66*, 1–114. Retrieved from http://dx.doi.org/10.1111/1540-5834.00154

Hodapp, R. M., Desjardins, J. L., & Ricci, L. A. (2003). Genetic syndromes of mental retardation. *Infants & Young Children, 16*, 152–160.

Iarocci, G., & Petrill, S. A. (2012). Behavioral genetics, genomics, intelligence, and mental retardation. In J. A. Burack, R. M. Hodapp, G. Iarocci, & E. Zigler (Eds.), *The Oxford handbook of intellectual disability and development* (pp. 13–29). New York: Oxford University Press.

Karmiloff-Smith, A. (2009). Nativism versus neuroconstructivism: Rethinking the study of developmental disorders. *Developmental Psychology, 45*, 56–63. Retrieved from http://dx.doi.org/10.1037/a0014506

Keogh, B. K., Bernheimer, L. P., & Guthrie, D. (1997). Stability and change over time in cognitive level of children with delays. *American Journal on Mental Retardation, 101*, 365–373.

Landry, S. H., Smith, K. E., & Swank, P. R. (2006). Responsive parenting: Establishing early foundations for social, communication, and independent problem-solving skills. *Developmental Psychology, 42*, 627–642.

Lee, N. R., Fidler, D. J., Blakeley-Smith, A., Daunhauer, L., Robinson, C., & Hepburn, S. L. (2011). Caregiver report of executive functioning in a population-based sample of young children with Down syndrome. *American Journal on Intellectual and Developmental Disabilities, 116*, 290–304. Retrieved from http://dx.doi.org/10.1352/1944-7558-116.4.290

Lewis, M. (2000). Toward a development of psychopathology: Models, definitions, and prediction. In A. J. Sameroff, M. Lewis, & S. Miller (Eds.), *Handbook of developmental psychopathology* (pp. 3–22). New York: Kluwer Academic/Plenum Publishers.

McDermott, S., Durkin, M. S., Schupf, N., & Stein, Z. (2007). Epidemiology and etiology of mental retardation. In J. Jacobson, J. Mulick, & J. Rojahn (Eds.), *Handbook of intellectual and developmental disabilities* (pp. 3–40). New York: Springer Science and Business Media.

Mefford, H. C., Batshaw, M., & Hoffman, E. P. (2012). Genomics, intellectual disability, and autism. *New England Journal of Medicine, 366*, 733–743. Retrieved from http://dx.doi.org/10.1056/NEJMra1114194

Murphy, M. M., & Abbeduto, L. (2005). Indirect genetic effects and the early language development of children with genetic mental retardation syndromes: The role of joint attention. *Infants & Young Children, 18*, 47–59.

Pintrich, P. R. (2000). The role of goal orientation in self-regulated learning. In M. Boekaerts, P. R. Pintrich, & M. Zeidner (Eds.), *Handbook of self-regulation* (pp. 451–502). San Diego, CA: Academic Press.

Roberts, J. E., Price, J., & Malkin, C. (2007). Language and communication development in Down syndrome. *Mental Retardation and Developmental Disabilities Research Reviews, 13*, 26–35. Retrieved from http://dx.doi.org/10.1002/mrdd.20136

Rowe, M. L., Levine, S. C., Fisher, J. A., & Goldin-Meadow, S. (2009). Does linguistic input play the same role in language learning for children with and without early brain injury? *Developmental Psychology, 45*, 90–102. Retrieved from http://dx.doi.org/10.1037/a0012848

Sameroff, A. J. (2009). The transactional model. In A. J. Sameroff (Ed.), *The transactional model of development* (pp. 3–21). Washington, DC: American Psychological Association

Sansavini, A., Guarini, A., & Caselli, M. C. (2011). Preterm birth: Neuropsychological profiles and atypical developmental pathways. *Developmental Disabilities Research Reviews, 17*, 102–113. Retrieved from http://dx.doi.org/10.1002/ddrr.1105

Shonkoff, J. P., & Phillips, D. A. (2000). *From neurons to neighborhoods: The science of early child development. Committee on Integrating the Science of Early Childhood Development.* Washington, DC: National Academy Press.

Spiker, D., Boyce, G. C., & Boyce, L. K. (2002). Parent-child interactions when young children have disabilities. In L. M. Glidden (Ed.), *International Review of Research in Mental Retardation* (pp. 35–70). San Diego, CA: Academic Press.

Spiker, D., Hebbeler, K., & Mallik, S. (2005). Developing and implementing early intervention programs for children with established disabilities. In M. J. Guralnick (Ed.), *The developmental systems approach to early intervention* (pp. 305–349). Baltimore, MD: Brookes.

Strickland, B., McPherson, M., Weissman, G., Van Dyck, P., Huang, Z. J., & Newacheck, P. (2004). Access to the medical home: Results of the national survey of children with special health care needs. *Pediatrics, 113*, 1485–1492.

Tamis-Lemonda, C. S., Uzgiris, I. C., & Bornstein, M. H. (2002). Play in parent-child interactions. In M. H. Bornstein (Ed.), *Handbook of parenting: Practical parenting* (Vol. 5, pp. 221–241). Hillsdale, NJ: Lawrence Erlbaum Associates Publishing.

Tomasello, M., & Carpenter, M. (2007). Shared intentionality. *Developmental Science, 10*, 121–125. Retrieved from http://dx.doi.org/10.1111/j.1467-7687.2007.00573.x

Venuti, P., De Falco, S., Esposito, G., & Bornstein, M. H. (2009). Mother-child play: Children with Down syndrome and typical development. *American Journal on Intellectual and Developmental Disabilities, 114*, 274–288. Retrieved from http://dx.doi.org/10.1352/1944-7558-114.4:274-288

Wishart, J. G. (1996). Avoidant learning styles and cognitive development in young children. In B. Stratford & P. Gunn (Eds.), *New approaches to Down syndrome* (pp. 173–205). London: Cassell.

Woodward, A. L. (2009). Infants' grasp of others' intentions. *Current Directions in Psychological Science, 18*, 53–57. Retrieved from http://dx.doi.org/10.1111/j.1467-8721.2009.01605.x

Xu, F., & Kushnir, T. (2013). Infants are rational constructivist learners. *Current Directions in Psychological Science, 22*, 28–32. Retrieved from http://dx.doi.org/10.1177/0963721412469396

Zelazo, P. D., & Bauer, P. J. (2013). National Institutes of Health Toolbox Cognition Battery (NIH Toolbox CB): Validation for children between 3 and 15 years. *Monographs of the Society for Research in Child Development, 78*, 1–155.

3 Family systems early childhood intervention

Carl J. Dunst

Systems theorists postulate that children are embedded in family systems (Emery, 2014) and that families are embedded in broader-based social systems (Friedman & Allen, 2010), and that events within and between systems reverberate and have either or both direct and indirect effects on the behaviour and development of children, their parents, and the family as a whole (Bronfenbrenner, 1992). As noted by Bronfenbrenner (1979),

> *Whether parents can perform effectively in their child-rearing roles within the family depends on the role demands, stresses, and supports emanating from other settings . . . Parents' evaluations of their own capacity to function, as well as their view of their children, are related to such external factors as flexibility of job schedules, adequacy of child care arrangements, the presence of friends and neighbours who can help out in large and small emergencies, the quality of health and social services, and neighbourhood safety.*

> (p. 7)

Elsewhere, commenting specifically on the role of early childhood intervention, Bronfenbrenner (1975) noted,

> *Intervention programs that place major emphasis on involving parents directly in activities fostering their children's development are likely to have constructive impact at any age, but the earlier such activities are begun, and the longer they have continued, the greater the benefit to the children. One major problem still remains . . .[Many] families live under such oppressive circumstances that they are neither willing nor able to participate in the activities required by a parent intervention program. Inadequate health care, poor housing, lack of education, low income, and the necessity for full-time work . . . rob parents of time and energy to spend time with their children . . .*

> (pp. 465–466)

to provide their children development-instigating and development-enhancing learning opportunities (Bronfenbrenner, 1992).

In a study specifically conducted to evaluate the validity of Bronfenbrenner's contentions in terms of parents' involvement in their children's early childhood intervention, results showed that family needs in areas unrelated to their children's early childhood intervention took precedence and interfered with a commitment to carrying out professional recommended child-level interventions (Dunst, Leet, & Trivette, 1988). In instances where early childhood intervention practitioners offer or provide supports and services in response to family needs, those resources often are not compatible with the supports and services parents consider desirable (e.g., Mahoney & Filer, 1996).

The purpose of this chapter is to describe a family systems approach to early childhood intervention that uses social system theory and a confluence of related theoretical formulations and empirical evidence for conceptualising and operationalising a particular approach to working with young children and their parents. The development and evolution of the systems approach to early childhood intervention is described elsewhere (Dunst & Trivette, 2009a). The focus of this chapter is to describe the key elements of the family systems intervention model and their implications for early childhood intervention practice. The family systems approach was initially developed for use with families rearing young children with identified disabilities and developmental delays (e.g., Dunst, 1985; Dunst & Trivette, 1987; Dunst, Trivette, Davis, & Cornwell, 1988; Trivette, Deal, & Dunst, 1986), but has been found applicable for intervening with families having quite varied backgrounds and life circumstances (e.g., Dunst & Trivette, 1997; Dunst, Trivette, & Deal, 1988; Dunst, Vance, & Cooper, 1986).

The family systems intervention model includes an operational definition of early childhood intervention; a social systems perspective of factors influencing child, parent, and family behaviour and functioning; a set of five different but compatible models that, taken together, constitute the key features of a capacity-building paradigm; and a procedural framework for facilitating implementation of family systems intervention practices. The family systems model is one of a number of approaches to working with children and parents that broadens the scope of early childhood intervention to take into consideration complex family situations and the multiple influences of systems factors on child, parent, and family functioning (Barber, Turnbull, Behr, & Kerns, 1988; Cowan, Powell, & Cowan, 1998; Darling, 1989; Guralnick, 2001, this volume).

Definition of early childhood intervention

Early childhood intervention is defined as the *provision or mobilisation of supports and resources to families of young children from informal and formal social network members that directly or indirectly influence and improve parent, family, and child behaviour and functioning in ways having capacity-building consequences.* The experiences, opportunities, advice, guidance, and so forth afforded families by social network members are conceptualised broadly as different types of *interventions* contributing to improved child, parent, and family functioning. The *sine qua non* outcome of the supports and resources afforded to or procured by families include any number of capacity-building and empowering consequences (Dunst & Trivette, 2011; Dunst, Trivette, & LaPointe, 1994).

The family systems definition of early childhood intervention differs from most other definitions by its inclusion of informal supports as a focus of intervention and capacity-building as a primary consequence of the provision or mobilisation of supports and resources. The inclusion of informal supports is based on research showing the manner in which support provided by relatives, friends, neighbours, and other nonprofessionals is related to improved child, parent, and family functioning (Dunst & Trivette, 2009a; Dunst, Trivette, & Jodry, 1997). The focus on capacity-building as an outcome of intervention is based on research demonstrating the manner in which different kinds of experiences and opportunities that have empowering characteristics and consequences in turn influence other aspects of child, parent, and family behaviour and functioning (Bandura, 1997; Dempsey & Keen, 2008; Dunst, Trivette, & Hamby, 2006, 2008; E. A. Skinner, 1995).

Research by colleagues and myself (e.g., Dunst & Trivette, 1990; Dunst, Trivette, & Hamby, 2007a; Dunst et al., 1997) as well as research by others (e.g., Coyne & DeLongis, 1986; Galinsky & Schopler, 1994; Lincoln, 2000) indicates that the manner in which support is provided, offered, or procured matters a great deal if the support has either positive or negative consequences. In a study by Affleck et al. (1989), for example, the investigators found that the provision of professional supports in response to an indicated need for assistance was associated with positive consequences on parents' self-efficacy beliefs and sense of competence, whereas the provision of professional supports in the absence of an indicated need for support had negative consequences on these same outcomes. This is the basis, in part, for the identification of family concerns and priorities as an important component of the approach to early childhood family systems intervention.

Systems theory framework

The provision or mobilisation of supports and resources as part of early childhood intervention is accomplished in the context of a social systems framework where a family is viewed as a social unit embedded within both informal and formal social support networks. According to Bronfenbrenner (1979), the behaviours of a developing child, his or her parents, other family members, and the family unit as a whole are influenced by events occurring in settings beyond the family which can either or both directly and indirectly influence child, parent, and family behaviour and functioning. Figure 3.1 shows a nested environment framework based on Bronfenbrenner's (1979) ecological model with some (but certainly not all) of the sources of influence that are relevant to early childhood intervention. Frameworks like those in Figure 3.1 can be especially useful for mapping the range of supports, resources, and services available to families (e.g., Dunst, Herter, Shields, & Bennis, 2001; McKnight & Kretzmann, 1990; Ordoñez-Jasis & Myck-Wayne, 2012) which constitute the focus of early childhood intervention.

The innermost sphere in Figure 3.1 includes the developing child and the everyday activity settings (Dunst, Hamby, Trivette, Raab, & Bruder, 2002; Farver,

Figure 3.1 Framework for mapping the sources of supports and resources influencing the outcomes of early childhood intervention

Source: Created by the author

1999) where the child interacts with his or her social and non-social environment. According to Bronfenbrenner (1992), child learning and development that takes place in everyday activities is influenced by proximal processes involving the people with whom a child comes in contact, the physical and symbolic features of the settings that invite or interfere with engagement in child interactions, and the personal characteristics of the child that also either invite or interfere with engagement in interactions with other people and the nonsocial environment. The people with whom a child is most likely to come into contact on an everyday basis are immediate family members, including a child's parents, siblings, and other household members. In the context of family systems early childhood intervention, increasing child participation in everyday activities and encouraging parents' or other family members' use of development-enhancing interactive behaviour (e.g., responsiveness to child initiations) is one focus of intervention.

Both the child and his or her family are embedded in sources of both kinship and informal social supports. Kinship support network members include grand-parents, in-laws, the mother's and father's parents, and other blood and marriage relatives. Informal social support network members include friends, neighbours, co-workers, church members, children's peers, and others who are sources of different types of resources. A focus of early childhood intervention at these two spheres of influence is the provision or mobilisation of the supports and resources from social network members so that parents and other primary caregivers have the time and physical and psychological energy to carry out parenting roles in ways that promote and enhance child learning and development.

The sources of support available from professionals include those needed for routine care as well as specialised assistance typically provided in response to such life events as the birth or diagnosis of a child with a disability. Sources of routine care include early care providers, preschool teachers, physicians, health centre nurses, hospitals, employers, and so forth. Specialised sources of support include early childhood intervention practitioners, social workers, speech therapists, occupational therapists, physical/physiotherapists, family resource program pro-viders, medical and health care specialists, and so forth. The role of early child-hood intervention at this sphere of influence is both the provision of supports and resources to a child and parents and assistance with a family obtaining other types of professional help and assistance.

All of the different spheres of influence are further embedded in larger social units and the societal beliefs, attitudes, and values that impinge upon parenting and childrearing practices. The social unit influences include federal, state, and local government laws, and program, agency, and organisation rules, regulations, policies, and procedures that either encourage or discourage the provision of sup-ports, resources, and services to young children and their families. The societal belief appraisals that either encourage or discourage the provision of supports, resources, and services to young children and their families include attitudes toward children with disabilities, the roles and responsibilities of governments toward children with disabilities, the cultural beliefs of different groups of com-munity members, and attitudes toward specific types of parenting practices.

Parents and other primary caregivers' abilities to carry out childrearing roles and provide their child development-enhancing child learning opportunities is dependent, as Bronfenbrenner (1979, 1986) often noted, on the supports and resources at each sphere of influence shown in Figure 3.1. Parents may not, for example, have adequate time, knowledge, or skills if parenting supports are not available in ways facilitating the use of development-enhancing parenting prac-tices. Therefore, in the majority of cases, early childhood intervention will likely occur at multiple spheres of influence for any one child and family.

Capacity-building paradigm

A lesson learned as part of the development of the family systems intervention model was that the manner in which early childhood intervention practitioners worked with young children and their parents mattered a great deal if interventions were to have expected benefits (Dunst & Trivette, 1988b, 1994). This led to rethinking how practitioners should engage families in early childhood intervention (Dunst, 1985, 2000), which in turn resulted in the development of a *capacity-building paradigm* as an alternative to a traditional approach to early childhood intervention (Dunst & Trivette, 2009a).

The models "making up" the capacity-building paradigm and those aligned with a more traditional paradigm are shown in Table 3.1. These contrasting *worldviews* each have different implications for how interventions are conceptualised and implemented. The traditional worldview considers children and families as having deficits and weaknesses that need treatment by professionals to correct problems or abate poor functioning. In contrast, the capacity-building world view considers children and families as having varied strengths and abilities, where the focus of intervention is supporting and promoting competence and other positive aspects of family member functioning (see Dempsey & Keen; Hiebert-Murphy et al., this volume).

The different capacity-building paradigm models each include elements that place primary emphasis on the supports and resources, and experiences and opportunities, afforded or provided children, parents, and families for strengthening existing and promoting the acquisition of new competencies (e.g., Dunst,

Table 3.1 Defining features of contrasting approaches for conceptualising and implementing family systems early childhood intervention

Capacity-Building Paradigm	*Traditional Paradigm*
Promotion Models	*Treatment Models*
Focus on enhancement and optimisation of competence and positive functioning	Focus on remediation of a disorder, problem, or disease, or its consequences
Empowerment Models	*Expertise Models*
Create opportunities for people to exercise existing capabilities as well as develop new competencies	Depend on professional expertise to solve problems for people
Strength-Based Models	*Deficit-Based Models*
Recognise the assets and talents of people, and help people use these competencies to strengthen functioning	Focus on correcting peoples' weaknesses or problems
Resource-Based Models	*Service-Based Models*
Define practices in terms of a broad range of community opportunities and experiences	Define practices primarily in terms of professional services
Family-Centred Models	*Professionally-Centred Models*
View professionals as agents of families who are responsive to family desires and concerns	View professionals as experts who determine the needs of people from their own as opposed to other peoples perspectives

Trivette, & Deal, 1994b; Swanson, Raab, & Dunst, 2011). Promotion models emphasise the enhancement of competence rather than the prevention or treatment of problems (Cowen, 1994; Dunst & Trivette, 2005a; Dunst, Trivette, & Thompson, 1990). Empowerment models emphasise the kinds of experiences and opportunities that are contexts for competence expression (Dunst & Trivette, 1996; Zimmerman, 1990). Strengths-based models emphasise people's competence and how the use of different abilities and interests strengthen family member functioning (Dunst, 2008). Resource-based models emphasise the use of a broad range of supports and resources (rather than only professional services) as the experiences and opportunities for strengthening child, parent, and family functioning (Dunst, Trivette, & Deal, 1994a; Raab, Davis, & Trepanier, 1993). Family-centred models emphasise the pivotal and central roles family members play in decisions about supports and resources best suited for improving parent, family, and child functioning (Dunst, 2002; Dunst & Espe-Sherwindt, 2016). Taken together, the five models provide a particular way of structuring the development and implementation of child and family intervention practices.

The capacity-building paradigm is based on the contention that the outcomes associated with experiences and interventions having capacity-building characteristics should be better than those focusing on treatment of problems or deficits or the prevention of poor outcomes (Bond, 1982; Garbarino, 1992). Findings from a number of studies provide support for the premise that the presence of development-enhancing person and environment factors are associated with value-added positive outcomes (e.g., Kia-Keating, Dowdy, Morgan, & Noam, 2011; Stoddard et al., 2013).

Dunst et al. (2014), in a study of infants and toddlers and their mothers guided by the systems and capacity-building paradigm described in this chapter, investigated the extent to which the presence of intrafamily and extrafamily factors aligned with capacity-building models was associated with child and parent benefits beyond the absence of development-impeding risk factors. Both the mothers' psychological well-being and children's cognitive development were optimised in the presence of multiple enhancement and promotive factors beyond those associated with the absence of development-impeding risk factors (Garbarino, 1992). The pattern of findings not only indicates that the characteristics and consequences of a capacity-building and traditional paradigm differ empirically, but is also consistent with the World Health Organisation (Grad, 2002) definition of health as a state of positive well being and not merely the absence of disease or poor functioning.

Family systems intervention model

The family systems early childhood intervention model is purposively broad in order to accommodate most, if not all, child and family circumstances that early intervention practitioners are likely to encounter in their work with young children and their families. The operational components of the model are shown in Figure 3.2. The model is implemented by using capacity-building help-giving practices to have parents or other primary caregivers identify family concerns and priorities, the supports and resources that can be used to address concerns and

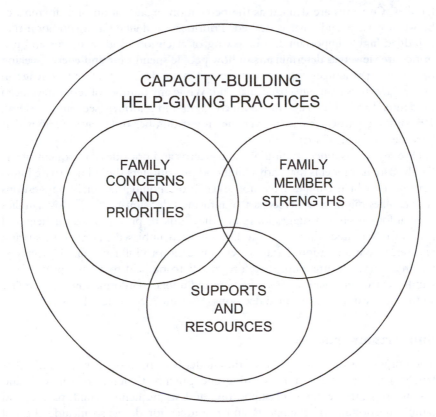

Figure 3.2 Four components of the family systems early childhood intervention model
Source: Created by the author

priorities, and the family member strengths, abilities, and interests used as the skills to obtain supports and resources.

The use of the model to guide interventions is best thought of as a dynamic, fluid process where practices in any one component influence the practices used in the other components (e.g., a family's indicated need for information about a newly diagnosed child condition influencing the person or persons who are best suited for answering questions and explaining the implications for future development). Although each component is described separately for explanatory purposes, the practices in each component are best thought of as a system of interlocking gears where activity in any one component influences activity in each of the other components.

Family concerns and priorities

The purpose of this component of the model is to have parents and other family members identify and base interventions on the concerns and priorities of the families. Concerns are defined as the perception or indication of a discrepancy between what is and what is desired. Priorities are defined as a condition that is judged highly important and deserving of attention. Both concerns and priorities are viewed as determinants of how people spend time and energy seeking or obtaining resources and supports to achieve a desired goal or to engage in desired activities to attain a particular end. While any number of terms have been used interchangeably to describe both concerns and priorities (see Dunst & Deal, 1994), these particular terms cover the largest number of family situations that become the focus of intervention.

One major misunderstanding of the concerns and priorities component of the family systems model is that early childhood practitioners should not share information for which families have not asked, nor should they make suggestions that families might consider as part of informed decision-making. Most families want information and suggestions, and they look to professionals for help and assistance. Granted, there is a fine line between unbiased information sharing and selective information sharing or even coercion to influence family decision-making. Constant attention, therefore, needs to be paid to a basic principle of family-centred practice: Sharing complete and unbiased information with families so that they can make informed decisions (Shelton & Stepanek, 1994).

Supports and resources

The purpose of this component of the model is to promote parents' and other family members' use of both existing and untapped sources of supports and resources as interventions for supporting and strengthening child, parent, and family functioning. The supports and resources for doing so include the full range of information, emotional support, instrumental assistance, experiences, opportunities, and so forth that are available from social network members for addressing and responding to family concerns and priorities. The sources of support and resources include both informal and formal social network members, with the caveat that family members are highly likely to seek out particular social network members depending upon which concerns and priorities are the focus of attention.

As noted earlier, the sources of supports and resources available to families are conceptualised as informal and formal early childhood interventions that are intended to influence child, parent, and family functioning positively. Defining early childhood intervention broadly to include informal supports and resources in addition to professional services "opens up" all kinds of opportunities that otherwise would not be considered legitimate intervention practices. The reconceptualisation of early childhood intervention that includes all types of experiences and opportunities is called resource-based intervention (Raab et al., 1993; Trivette, Dunst, & Deal, 1997). Findings from a research synthesis of resource-based intervention practices studies showed that the use of these practices are associated with positive child, parent, and family outcomes (Mott & Swanson, 2006).

One additional consideration needs to be noted. The supports and resources deemed most appropriate are ones that actively involve family members in obtaining and procuring assistance rather than the noncontingent provision of help (see especially Dunst & Trivette, 1988b). It may seem expedient to provide or give families supports and resources, but doing so deprives them of opportunities to use existing skills or develop new competencies which can perpetuate a need for help (B. F. Skinner, 1978). To the extent that social network members "supply a needed resource but lead a person to see the production of that resource as contingent on what [others] do rather than his or her own behaviour" (Brickman et al., 1983, p. 34), the support may have negative or harmful consequences (see, e.g., Affleck et al., 1989; Dunst, Leet et al., 1988; Mahoney & Filer, 1996).

Family strengths

The purpose of this component of the model is to promote and encourage family members' use of their existing strengths for obtaining desired supports and resources and to engage in desired activities. Whereas family strengths are generally described in terms of different traits (e.g., Curran, 1983; DeFrain & Asay, 2007), it has been found more useful to operationalise strengths as different kinds of family member abilities and interests. Abilities include the behaviour, skills, competencies, and so forth that are used by individual family members and the family as a unit to obtain or procure supports and resources and to engage in activities strengthening child, parent, and family functioning. Interests include the preferences, likes, favourites, and so forth that motivate family members to engage in desired activities.

Strengths-based early childhood intervention is predicated on the premise that building on strengths is more productive than interventions that focus mostly or entirely on family member deficits or poor functioning. As noted by Stoneman (1985), "Every family has strengths and, if the emphasis [of intervention] is on supporting strengths rather than rectifying weaknesses, chances of making a difference in the lives of children are vastly increased" (p. 462). Paraphrasing Rappaport (1981), all families have existing strengths as well as the capacity to become more competent. Strengths-based approaches to intervention are often criticised as ignoring people's problems. This is not the case. Building on and supporting strengths in one or more areas of functioning is viewed as a way to decrease problems or poor functioning in other areas (Schlesinger, 2007; Trute, Benzies, Worthington, Reddon, & Moore, 2010).

Findings from studies that used family member strengths as the building blocks for obtaining supports and resources (e.g., Dunst, 2008; Dunst, Trivette, Gordon, & Pletcher, 1989) or engaging in desired activities (e.g., Dunst & Raab, 2012; Raab, Dunst, & Hamby, 2013) indicate that there are considerably more changes and improvements in child and parent functioning compared to those of more traditional approaches to intervention. Results from two studies are briefly described to illustrate the value-added benefits: a child-level intervention and a parent-level intervention.

One of the most important skills young children with significant developmental delays learn is the ability to use instrumental behaviour to produce environmental consequences. Traditional early childhood intervention typically approaches this by administering some type of developmental scale to identify "missing skills" and by using some type of intervention practice to promote a child's acquisition of the skills. An alternate approach to early childhood intervention is to start with behaviour a child produces but does not use intentionally and to provide the child experiences where the use of the behaviour elicits interesting or reinforcing consequences. In a randomised design study of the two approaches to intervention (termed needs-based and ability-based, respectively) with 20-month-old children functioning at three to five months developmentally (Raab, Dunst, & Hamby, 2016), findings showed that the children in the ability-based group outperformed the children in the needs-based group after only eight weeks of intervention on all six dependent measures constituting the focus of the investigation. Results confirmed the superiority of strengths-based practices for promoting child learning among children who often show considerable difficulty acquiring instrumental behaviour (Hutto, 2007).

Young children in general, and infants and toddlers in particular, are routinely involved in the day-to-day activities of their parents and other family members (e.g., Rogoff, Mosier, Mistry, & Göncü, 1993; Spagnola & Fiese, 2007). In a yet-to-be-published study of young children's learning in the context of participation in everyday activities that their parents identified as either personal abilities or personal interests, results showed that the experiences had both positive parent and child benefits. As hypothesised, parents who indicated that their children benefited from involvement in the parents' strengths-based activities demonstrated more positive parenting confidence, competence, and enjoyment. As also hypothesised, the children manifested more positive and less negative child behaviour as a matter of everyday functioning. In addition, the effects of child participation in strengths-based parent activities on child behaviour were indirectly mediated by parents' sense of their own capabilities. Parents involved in this strengths-based intervention almost unanimously reported positive parent and child benefits from participation in the project.

Capacity-building help-giving practices

The purpose of this component of the model is for practitioners to use capacity-building help-giving practices to facilitate (1) parents' and other family members' identification of concerns and priorities, (2) the sources of supports and resources for addressing concerns and priorities, and (3) family member use of existing strengths and the development of new strengths for obtaining needed supports and resources. As noted by Carkhuff and Anthony (1979), effective help-giving is the act of promoting and supporting family functioning in a way that enhances the acquisition of competencies that permit a greater degree of family control over subsequent activities. The help-giving component of the model includes capacity-building help-giving practices and the particular types of practices that are most likely to have empowering characteristics and consequences.

Studies of the characteristics of effective help-giving practices have identified two clusters of help-giving that have capacity-building influences: *relational help-giving* and *participatory help-giving* (Trivette & Dunst, 2007). Relational help-giving includes practices typically associated with good clinical practice (e.g., active listening, compassion, empathy, respect) and help-giver positive beliefs about family member strengths and capabilities. These types of help-giving practices are often described as relationship-based practices (Trevithick, 2003).

Listening to a family's concerns and asking for clarification or elaboration about what was said is an example of a relational help-giving practice. Participatory help-giving includes practices that are individualised, flexible, and responsive to family concerns and priorities, and which involve informed family choices and involvement in achieving desired goals and outcomes. These types of help-giving practices are often described as capacity-building practices (Dunst & Espe-Sherwindt, 2016; Trivette & Dunst, 2007). Engaging a family member in a process of using information to make an informed decision about care for her child is an example of a participatory help-giving practice.

Research syntheses of the relationships between both types of help-giving practices and parents' personal control appraisals and parent, family, and child behaviour and functioning indicate that both types of helping practices are related to most outcomes, where the relationship between relational and participatory help-giving and parent, family, and child behaviour and functioning is mediated by personal control appraisals (Dunst, Trivette, & Hamby, 2007b; Dunst et al., 2008). In a number of meta-analytic structural equation modelling studies of the effects of relational and participatory help-giving practices on parent and child outcomes, results show that the effects of capacity-building help-giving can be traced to parent well-being mediated by self-efficacy beliefs, parent-child interactions mediated by both parent self-efficacy beliefs and well-being, and child and parent functioning also mediated by parent self-efficacy beliefs and well-being (Dunst & Trivette, 2009b; Dunst, Trivette, & Raab, 2013; Trivette, Dunst, & Hamby, 2010).

Adoption and use of capacity-building help-giving practices necessitate that early childhood intervention practitioners rethink how they interact and work with families of young children with disabilities. Capacity-building help-giving practices, and especially participatory practices, necessitate that practitioners not see themselves as primarily responsible for improving child and family life, but rather for strengthening family members' abilities to improve their own lives. As noted by Skinner (1978), "We may not really help others by doing for them . . . by giving [too] much help we postpone the acquisition of effective behaviour and perpetuate the need for help" (pp. 250–251). Maple (1977) noted that when help-givers see themselves as responsible for doing for families rather than helping families learn to do for themselves, "the [help giver] becomes a star. It is the author's view that your goal as helper is not to learn how to become a star, but rather to help [family members] become 'stars' in some aspects of their lives" (p. 7).

Implications for practice

The family system early childhood intervention model and practices were developed and used by early childhood intervention practitioners working with young children from birth to eight years of age and their families in one early intervention program over the course of 20 years where the model was continually revised and updated based on research, practices, and lessons learned in each component of the model. The bulk of this work is described in a series of publications paralleling the evolution of the model (Dunst, 1985, 2000; Dunst & Trivette, 2009a; Dunst, Trivette, & Deal, 1988; Dunst, Trivette et al., 1994b). The model and practices were also taught to practitioners in other early childhood intervention programs throughout the United States (Dunst, Trivette, & Deal, 2011). The model as well as the components of the model have been adopted by programs and practitioners in a number of other countries for working with children and their families in early childhood intervention, family support, health care, and human services programs (see Dunst & Trivette, 2009a; Serrano et al., this volume).

The model and associated practices have been used with families of young children with identified disabilities, developmental delays, and those at risk for poor outcomes for medical (e.g., low birth weight) or environmental (e.g., multiple family stressors and hassles) factors; pregnant teenagers, teenage parents, same-sex parents, never married parents, and single parent families; blended families, adoptive and foster families, grandparent-headed families, as well as families with other compositions (see Holman, this volume). The model and practices have proven to be flexible enough to accommodate varied and unique family life circumstances while at the same time being structured enough to facilitate active family involvement in ways that build and strengthen child, parent, and family functioning.

A lesson learned from using the family systems early childhood intervention model and practices is that the more straightforward the interventions, the higher the probability that the interventions are implemented as planned and have expected benefits. This is likely the case because "there is evidence that it is easier to achieve high fidelity of simple [rather] than complex interventions . . . because there are fewer 'response barriers' when a model is simple" (Carroll, Patterson, Wood, Booth, Rick, & Balain, 2007). This is the primary reason why there are only four components to the family systems intervention model.

In addition to developing and evaluating the family systems early childhood intervention model and practices, the theoretical, paradigmatic, and research evidence described in this chapter has been used to reconfigure the model and associated practices for specific intervention purposes. Two examples are briefly described next. The first example uses the framework in Figure 3.1 to illustrate how different practices in different spheres of influence can be used to promote parents' use of responsive interactional practices to enhance child learning. The second example uses the framework in Figure 3.2 to illustrate how the family systems intervention model can be used to facilitate parent-mediated everyday child learning opportunities.

Responsive parenting model

It is now generally recognised that child learning and development occurs, to a large degree, in the context of parent-child relationships (Richter, 2004) and parents' use of responsive interactional styles that encourage and support child engagement with his or her parents and the nonsocial environment (Landry, Smith, & Swank, 2006). The extent to which parents are likely to use responsive interactional styles is dependent, in part, on their psychological health where stress is likely to interfere with responsiveness (Guralnick, Hammond, Neville, & Connor, 2008), and positive well-being is likely to encourage responsiveness (Dunst & Trivette, 1988a). Furthermore, enhanced positive well-being is likely to be influenced by the availability of different types of social supports (Levitt, Weber, & Clark, 1986). Positive parent-child relationships and interactions are more likely to be a focus of early childhood intervention when using strengths-based practices (Wilson, 2005) where family-centred practices are used by early childhood practitioners to support parents' use of responsive parenting practices (Mahoney & Wheeden, 1997).

Figure 3.3 shows these different relationships as a series of embedded practices where practices in the different spheres of influence contribute either directly or indirectly to adoption and use of responsive parenting practices for promoting and enhancing child learning and development. Models like the one in Figure 3.3 have been used to conceptualise and implement interventions that included different types of experiences and opportunities to provide or promote social support to parents and to encourage parents' use of responsive parenting practices (e.g., Dunst, Trivette, & Raab, 2014; Dunst, Vance, & Cooper, 1986 Dunst et al. (1986) evaluated the effects of the provision of different types of informal and formal supports on teenage mothers' well-being as well as a particular type of support to encourage the parents' use of responsive parenting practices. Results showed discernible changes and improvements in parent-child interactions over the course of 20 weeks of twice-a-week practitioner-parent support exchanges. Similar results were reported by Dunst et al. (2014) as part of an intervention focusing on parents' use of responsive teaching (a particular type of responsive parenting practice) in the context of everyday family and community activities. A particularly notable finding was parents' judgments of their own parenting confidence and competence in response to the effects of their use of responsive teaching. The model shown in Figure 3.3 could easily be adapted to show the factors in each sphere of influence for any type of early childhood intervention.

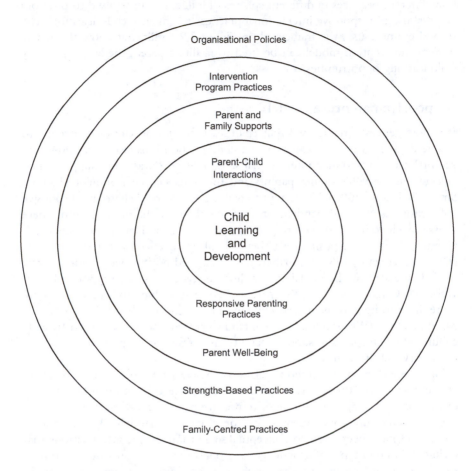

Figure 3.3 Framework for showing the sources of influence on responsive parenting practices and the effects of the practices on child and parent learning and development

Source: Created by the author

Integrated framework model

The bulk of research and practice described in this chapter was used to develop an extension of the family systems model (Figure 3.2) that specifically focused on the use of different types of supports (experiences and opportunities) for promoting parent and child learning and development (Dunst, 2004, 2005). The model is shown in Figure 3.4. The model includes three overlapping components (child learning opportunities, parenting supports, family and community supports) where capacity-building, family-centred practices (Trivette & Dunst, 2007) are used by early childhood practitioners with parents to promote the use of different

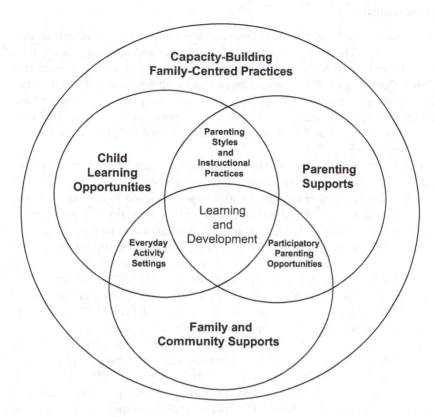

Figure 3.4 Major components and practices of an integrated systems approach to early childhood intervention

Source: Created by the author

development-enhancing experiences and opportunities in the overlapping components. The intersecting sections of the overlapping components include the specific types of practices that are the focus of intervention. The desired outcomes of the practices constituting the focus of intervention are any number of measures of child, parent, and family competence and confidence.

The focus of research and practice on the integrated framework has primarily been the influences of overlapping practices and their intersecting practices (e.g., Dunst, 2008; Dunst, Bruder et al., 2001; Dunst, Hamby, & Brookfield, 2007). The interested reader is referred to Dunst (2005) for descriptions of performance checklists for facilitating the provision of supports and for promoting parents' abilities to provide their children development-enhancing learning opportunities in the context of family, community, parent-child, and other participatory activity settings in ways having capacity-building outcomes (also see Roper & Dunst, 2006). The integrated framework has proven useful for conceptualising, developing, and implementing different kinds of practices in each component of the model.

Conclusion

Families are complex systems that function within the context of equally complex social systems. The nature of this complexity shapes and influences family member roles and responsibilities, including parenting and childrearing (Cowan et al., 1998). Parenting a child in general and a child with special needs in particular is both challenging and rewarding. The extent to which parenting is more rewarding than challenging is dependent upon the supports (broadly defined) available within the family as well as from informal and formal social network members (Bronfenbrenner, 1979).

The family systems early childhood intervention model, and the variants of the model described in this chapter, were developed in response to research, practice, family member comments, and lessons learned indicating that traditional approaches to early childhood intervention were not responsive to the needs of many young children and especially the children's parents. Prior to the development of the family systems model in one early childhood intervention program where the author later became program director, staff were employing a child-focused, deficit-based approach to early childhood intervention (see Dunst & Trivette, 2009a). This included multidisciplinary evaluations that focused almost entirely on identification of children's deficits and "missing skills" where parents were taught to implement professionally prescribed interventions to correct deficits or teach missing skills. Among families who had been involved in the early childhood program more than one year, the subsequent "show rate" for their children's multidisciplinary evaluations was about 30%. (One mother later told me that she became depressed hearing year after year that her child still could not do a [litany of skills].) The "show rate" for home visits was not much better (about 35 to 40%). As part of subsequent open forum parent meetings, large numbers of parents said that the ways in which staff involved them in the children's early childhood intervention made them feel like "bad parents" if they did not follow the staff's prescribed practices. Parents also said that staff did not understand or take into consideration other role demands within and outside the family as part of their intervention practices (see especially Dunst, Leet, & Trivette, 1988).

The shift from deficit-based to strengths-based early childhood early intervention guided by the family systems model took about two to three years. At the time the family systems early childhood intervention model was widely being used, the "show rates" for child evaluations and home visits were 90% or better, and parents almost unanimously reported better staff-family interactions and especially in terms of being treated in a family-centred manner (see Dunst & Trivette, 2005b). This is most likely the case because approaches to early childhood intervention like the one described in this chapter are more effective because family systems intervention practices are responsive to both the broad-based needs of families and changing family life circumstances in ways that support and strengthen child, parent, and family functioning.

References

Affleck, G., Tennen, H., Rowe, J., Roscher, B., & Walker, L. (1989). Effects of formal support on mothers' adaptation to the hospital-to-home transition of high-risk infants: The benefits and costs of helping. *Child Development, 60,* 488–501.

Bandura, A. (1997). *Self-efficacy: The exercise of control.* New York: Freeman.

Barber, P. A., Turnbull, A. P., Behr, S. K., & Kerns, G. M. (1988). A family systems perspective on early childhood special education. In S. L. Odom & M. B. Karnes (Eds.), *Early intervention for infants and children with handicaps: An empirical base* (pp. 179–198). Baltimore, MD: Brooks.

Bond, L. A. (1982). From prevention to promotion: Optimizing infant development. In L. A. Bond & J. M. Joffe (Eds.), *Facilitating infant and early childhood development* (pp. 5–39). Hanover, NH: University Press of New England.

Brickman, P., Kidder, L. H., Coates, D., Rabinowitz, V., Cohn, E., & Karuza, J. (1983). The dilemmas of helping: Making aid fair and effective. In J. D. Fisher, A. Nadler, & B. M. DePaulo (Eds.), *New directions in helping: Vol. 1. Recipient reactions to aid* (pp. 17–49). New York: Academic Press.

Bronfenbrenner, U. (1975). Is early intervention effective? In B. Z. Friedlander, G. M. Sterritt, & G. E. Kirk (Eds.), *Exceptional infant: Vol. 3. Assessment and intervention* (pp. 449–475). New York: Brunner/Mazel.

Bronfenbrenner, U. (1979). *The ecology of human development: Experiments by nature and design.* Cambridge, MA: Harvard University Press.

Bronfenbrenner, U. (1986). Ecology of the family as a context for human development: Research perspectives. *Developmental Psychology, 22,* 723–742.

Bronfenbrenner, U. (1992). Ecological systems theory. In R. Vasta (Ed.), *Six theories of child development: Revised formulations and current issues* (pp. 187–248). Philadelphia, PA: Jessica Kingsley.

Carkhuff, R. R., & Anthony, W. A. (1979). *The skills of helping.* Amherst, MA: Human Resource Development Press.

Carroll, C., Patterson, M., Wood, S., Booth, A., Rick, J., & Balain, S. (2007). A conceptual framework for implementation fidelity. *Implementation Science, 2,* 40. doi:10.1186/1748-5908-2-40

Cowan, P. A., Powell, D., & Cowan, C. P. (1998). Parenting interventions: A family systems perspective. In W. Damon, I. E. Sigel, & K. A. Renninger (Eds.), *Handbook of child psychology: Vol. 4. Child psychology in practice* (5th ed., pp. 3–72). New York: Wiley.

Cowen, E. L. (1994). The enhancement of psychological wellness: Challenges and opportunities. *American Journal of Community Psychology, 22,* 149–179. doi:10.1007/BF02506861

Coyne, J. C., & DeLongis, A. (1986). Going beyond social support: The role of social relationships in adaptation. *Journal of Consulting and Clinical Psychology, 54,* 454–460.

Curran, D. (1983). *Traits of a healthy family: Fifteen traits commonly found in healthy families by those who work with them.* Minneapolis, MN: Winston Press.

Darling, R. B. (1989). Using the social system perspective in early intervention: The value of a sociological approach. *Journal of Early Intervention, 13,* 24–35.

DeFrain, J., & Asay, S. (2007). *Strong families around the world: Strengths-based research and perspectives.* New York: Routledge.

Dempsey, I., & Keen, D. (2008). A review of processes and outcomes in family-centered services for children with a disability. *Topics in Early Childhood Special Education, 28,* 42–52. doi:10.1177/0271121408316699

Dunst, C. J. (1985). Rethinking early intervention. *Analysis and Intervention in Developmental Disabilities, 5,* 165–201. doi:10.1016/S0270-4684(85)80012-4

Dunst, C. J. (2000). Revisiting "rethinking early intervention." *Topics in Early Childhood Special Education, 20,* 95–104. doi:10.1177/027112140002000205

Dunst, C. J. (2002). Family-centered practices: Birth through high school. *Journal of Special Education, 36,* 139–147. doi:10.1177/00224669020360030401

Dunst, C. J. (2004). An integrated framework for practicing early childhood intervention and family support. *Perspectives in Education, 22*(2), 1–16.

Dunst, C. J. (2005). Framework for practicing evidence-based early childhood intervention and family support. *CASEinPoint, 1*(1), 1–11.

Dunst, C. J. (2008). *Parent and community assets as sources of young children's learning opportunities* (Revised and expanded ed.). Asheville, NC: Winterberry Press.

Dunst, C. J., Bruder, M. B., Trivette, C. M., Hamby, D., Raab, M., & McLean, M. (2001). Characteristics and consequences of everyday natural learning opportunities. *Topics in Early Childhood Special Education, 21,* 68–92. doi:10.1177/027112140102100202

Dunst, C. J., & Deal, A. G. (1994). Needs-based family-centered intervention practices. In C. J. Dunst, C. M. Trivette, & A. G. Deal (Eds.), *Supporting and strengthening families: Methods, strategies and practices* (pp. 90–104). Cambridge, MA: Brookline Books.

Dunst, C. J., & Espe-Sherwindt, M. (2016). Family-centered practices in early childhood intervention. In B. Reichow, B. Boyd, E. Barton, & S. L. Odom (Eds.), *Handbook of early childhood special education* (pp. 37–55). Cham, Switzerland: Springer International.

Dunst, C. J., Hamby, D., Trivette, C. M., Raab, M., & Bruder, M. B. (2002). Young children's participation in everyday family and community activity. *Psychological Reports, 91,* 875–897. doi:10.2466/PR0.91.7.875-897

Dunst, C. J., Hamby, D. W., & Brookfield, J. (2007). Modeling the effects of early childhood intervention variables on parent and family well-being. *Journal of Applied Quantitative Methods, 2,* 268–288.

Dunst, C. J., Herter, S., Shields, H., & Bennis, L. (2001). Mapping community-based natural learning opportunities. *Young Exceptional Children, 4*(4), 16–24. doi:10.1177/109625060100400403

Dunst, C. J., Leet, H. E., & Trivette, C. M. (1988). Family resources, personal well-being, and early intervention. *Journal of Special Education, 22,* 108–116. doi:10.1177/002246698802200112

Dunst, C. J., & Raab, M. (2012). Interest-based child participation in everyday learning activities. In N. M. Seel (Ed.), *Encyclopedia of the sciences of learning* (pp. 1621–1623). New York: Springer.

Dunst, C. J., & Trivette, C. M. (1987). Enabling and empowering families: Conceptual and intervention issues. *School Psychology Review, 16,* 443–456.

Dunst, C. J., & Trivette, C. M. (1988a). Determinants of parent and child interactive behavior. In K. Marfo (Ed.), *Parent-child interaction and developmental disabilities: Theory, research, and intervention* (pp. 3–31). New York: Praeger.

Dunst, C. J., & Trivette, C. M. (1988b). Helping, helplessness, and harm. In J. C. Witt, S. N. Elliott, & F. M. Gresham (Eds.), *Handbook of behavior therapy in education* (pp. 343–376). New York: Plenum Press.

Dunst, C. J., & Trivette, C. M. (1990). Assessment of social support in early intervention programs. In S. Meisels & J. Shonkoff (Eds.), *Handbook of early intervention* (pp. 326–349). New York: Cambridge University Press.

Dunst, C. J., & Trivette, C. M. (1994). What is effective helping? In C. J. Dunst, C. M. Trivette, & A. G. Deal (Eds.), *Supporting and strengthening families: Methods, strategies and practices* (pp. 162–170). Cambridge, MA: Brookline Books.

Dunst, C. J., & Trivette, C. M. (1996). Empowerment, effective helpgiving practices and family-centered care. *Pediatric Nursing, 22,* 334–337, 343.

Dunst, C. J., & Trivette, C. M. (1997). Early intervention with young at-risk children and their families. In R. Ammerman & M. Hersen (Eds.), *Handbook of prevention and treatment with children and adolescents: Intervention in the real world* (pp. 157–180). New York: Wiley.

Dunst, C. J., & Trivette, C. M. (2005a). Family resource programs, promotion models, and enhancement outcomes. *Practical Evaluation Reports, 1*(1), 1–5. Retrieved from http://www.practicalevaluation.org/reports/cpereport_vol1_no1.pdf

Dunst, C. J., & Trivette, C. M. (2005b). *Measuring and evaluating family support program quality.* Asheville, NC: Winterberry Press.

Dunst, C. J., & Trivette, C. M. (2009a). Capacity-building family systems intervention practices. *Journal of Family Social Work, 12*(2), 119–143. doi:10.1080/10522150802713322

Dunst, C. J., & Trivette, C. M. (2009b). Meta-analytic structural equation modeling of the influences of family-centered care on parent and child psychological health. *International Journal of Pediatrics, 2009,* 1–9. doi:10.1155/2009/596840

Dunst, C. J., & Trivette, C. M. (2011, May). *Characteristics and consequences of family capacity-building practices.* Paper presented at the 3rd Conference of the International Society on Early Intervention, New York.

Dunst, C. J., Trivette, C. M., Davis, M., & Cornwell, J. (1988). Enabling and empowering families of children with health impairments. *Children's Health Care, 17,* 71–81. doi:10.1207/s15326888chc1702_2

Dunst, C. J., Trivette, C. M., & Deal, A. G. (1988). *Enabling and empowering families: Principles and guidelines for practice.* Cambridge, MA: Brookline Books.

Dunst, C. J., Trivette, C. M., & Deal, A. G. (1994a). Resource-based family-centered intervention practices. In C. J. Dunst, C. M. Trivette, & A. G. Deal (Eds.), *Supporting and strengthening families: Methods, strategies and practices* (pp. 140–151). Cambridge, MA: Brookline Books.

Dunst, C. J., Trivette, C. M., & Deal, A. G. (2011). Effects of in-service training on early intervention practitioners' use of family systems intervention practices in the USA. *Professional Development in Education, 37,* 181–196. doi:10.1080/194152 57.2010.527779

Dunst, C. J., Trivette, C. M., & Deal, A. G. (Eds.). (1994b). *Supporting and strengthening families: Methods, strategies and practices.* Cambridge, MA: Brookline Books.

Dunst, C. J., Trivette, C. M., Gordon, N. J., & Pletcher, L. L. (1989). Building and mobilizing informal family support networks. In G. H. Singer & L. Irvin (Eds.), *Support for caregiving families: Enabling positive adaptation to disability* (pp. 121–141). Baltimore, MD: Brookes.

Dunst, C. J., Trivette, C. M., & Hamby, D. W. (2006). *Family support program quality and parent, family and child benefits.* Asheville, NC: Winterberry Press.

Dunst, C. J., Trivette, C. M., & Hamby, D. W. (2007a). *A matter of family-centered helpgiving practices: The ways family support program staff interact with and treat parents contributes to program participant benefits.* Asheville, NC: Winterberry Press.

Dunst, C. J., Trivette, C. M., & Hamby, D. W. (2007b). Meta-analysis of family-centered helpgiving practices research. *Mental Retardation and Developmental Disabilities Research Reviews, 13,* 370–378. doi:10.1002/mrdd.20176

Dunst, C. J., Trivette, C. M., & Hamby, D. W. (2008). *Research synthesis and meta-analysis of studies of family-centered practices.* Asheville, NC: Winterberry Press.

Dunst, C. J., Trivette, C. M., & Hamby, D. W. (2014). Relationships between family risk and opportunity factors and parent and child functioning. *Journal of Educational and Developmental Psychology, 4*(2), 10–23. doi:10.5539/jedp.v4n2p10

Dunst, C. J., Trivette, C. M., & Jodry, W. (1997). Influences of social support on children with disabilities and their families. In M. Guralnick (Ed.), *The effectiveness of early intervention* (pp. 499–522). Baltimore, MD: Brookes.

Dunst, C. J., Trivette, C. M., & LaPointe, N. (1994). Meaning and key characteristics of empowerment. In C. J. Dunst, C. M. Trivette, & A. G. Deal (Eds.), *Supporting and strengthening families: Methods, strategies and practices* (pp. 12–28). Cambridge, MA: Brookline Books.

Dunst, C. J., Trivette, C. M., & Raab, M. (2013, October). *Pathways of influence of early intervention on family, parent and child outcomes.* Paper presented at the Division for Early Childhood 29th Annual International Conference on Young Children with Special Needs and Their Families, San Francisco. Available at www.puckett.org/presentations.

Dunst, C. J., Trivette, C. M., & Raab, M. (2014). Everyday child language learning early intervention practices. *Infants & Young Children, 27*(3), 207–219. doi:10.1097/IYC.0000000000000015

Dunst, C. J., Trivette, C. M., & Thompson, R. B. (1990). Supporting and strengthening family functioning: Toward a congruence between principles and practice. *Prevention in Human Services, 9*(1), 19–43. doi:10.1300/J293v09n01_02

Dunst, C. J., Vance, S. D., & Cooper, C. S. (1986). A social systems perspective of adolescent pregnancy: Determinants of parent and parent-child behavior. *Infant Mental Health Journal, 7,* 34–48.

Emery, R. E. (2014). Families as systems: Some thoughts on methods and theory. In S. M. McHale, P. Amato, & A. Booth (Eds.), *Emerging methods in family research* (pp. 109–124). Cham, Switzerland: Springer International Publishing.

Farver, J. A. M. (1999). Activity setting analysis: A model for examining the role of culture in development. In A. Göncü (Ed.), *Children's engagement in the world: Sociocultural perspectives* (pp. 99–127). Cambridge: Cambridge University Press.

Friedman, B. D., & Allen, K. N. (2010). Systems theory. In J. R. Brandell (Ed.), *Theory and practice in clinical social work* (2nd ed., pp. 3–20). Thousand Oaks, CA: Sage.

Galinsky, M. J., & Schopler, J. H. (1994). Negative experiences in support groups. *Social Work in Health Care, 20*(1), 77–95.

Garbarino, J. (1992). *Children and families in the social environment* (2nd ed.). New York: de Gruyter.

Grad, F. P. (2002). The preamble of the constitution of the World Health Organization. *Bulletin of the World Health Organization, 80*(12), 981–982. doi:10.1590/S0042-96862002001200014

Guralnick, M. J. (2001). A developmental systems model for early intervention. *Infants & Young Children, 14*(2), 1–18.

Guralnick, M. J., Hammond, M. A., Neville, B., & Connor, R. T. (2008). The relationship between sources and functions of social support and dimensions of child-and-parent-related stress. *Journal of Intellectual Disability Research, 52,* 1138–1154. doi:10.1111/j.1365-2788.2008.01073.x

Hutto, M. D. (2007). *Latency to learn in contingency studies of young children with disabilities or developmental delays.* Asheville, NC: Winterberry Press.

Kia-Keating, M., Dowdy, E., Morgan, M. L., & Noam, G. G. (2011). Protecting and promoting: An integrative conceptual model for healthy development of adolescents. *Journal of Adolescent Health, 48*(3), 220–228. doi:10.1016/j.jadohealth.2010.08.006

Landry, S. H., Smith, K. E., & Swank, P. R. (2006). Responsive parenting: Establishing early foundations for social, communication, and independent problem-solving skills. *Developmental Psychology, 42,* 627–642.

Levitt, M. J., Weber, R. A., & Clark, M. C. (1986). Social network relationships as sources of maternal support and well-being. *Developmental Psychology, 22,* 310–316.

Lincoln, K. D. (2000). Social support, negative social interactions, and psychological well-being. *Social Service Review, 74,* 231–252.

Mahoney, G., & Filer, J. (1996). How responsive is early intervention to the priorities and needs of families? *Topics in Early Childhood Special Education, 16,* 437–457.

Mahoney, G., & Wheeden, C. A. (1997). Parent-child interaction – The foundation for family-centered early intervention practice. *Topics in Early Childhood Special Education, 17*(2), 165–184. doi:10.1177/027112149701700204

Maple, F. F. (1977). *Shared decision making.* Beverly Hills, CA: Sage.

McKnight, J. L., & Kretzmann, J. (1990). *Mapping community capacity.* Evanston, IL: Center for Urban Affairs and Policy Research, Northwestern University.

Mott, D. W., & Swanson, J. (2006). A research synthesis of resource-based intervention practice studies. *CASEinPoint, 2*(10), 1–13.

Ordoñez-Jasis, R., & Myck-Wayne, J. (2012). Community mapping in action: Uncovering resources and assets for young children and their families. *Young Exceptional Children, 15*(3), 31–45. doi:10.1177/1096250612451756

Raab, M., Davis, M. S., & Trepanier, A. M. (1993). Resources vs. services: Changing the focus of intervention with infants and toddlers with special needs. *Infants & Young Children, 5*(3), 1–11.

Raab, M., Dunst, C. J., & Hamby, D. W. (2013). Relationship between young children's interests and early language learning. *Everyday Child Language Learning Reports, 5,* 1–14.

Raab, M., Dunst, C. J., & Hamby, D. W. (2016). Effectiveness of contrasting approaches to response-contingent learning among children with signficant developmental delays and disabilities. *Research and Practice for Persons with Severe Disabilities, 41*(1), 36–51.

Rappaport, J. (1981). In praise of paradox: A social policy of empowerment over prevention. *American Journal of Community Psychology, 9,* 1–25. doi:10.1007/BF00896357

Richter, L. (2004). *The importance of caregiver-child interactions for the survival and healthy development of young children: A review.* Geneva, Switzerland: World Health Organization, Department of Child and Adolescent Health and Development.

Rogoff, B., Mosier, C., Mistry, J., & Göncü, A. (1993). Toddlers' guided participation with their caregivers in cultural activity. In E. A. Forman, N. Minick, & C. A. Stone (Eds.), *Contexts for learning: Sociocultural dynamics in children's development* (pp. 230–253). New York: Oxford University Press.

Roper, N., & Dunst, C. J. (2006). Early childhood intervention competency checklists. *CASEtools, 2*(7), 1–14.

Schlesinger, B. (2007). *Strengths in families: Accentuating the positive.* Ottawa, Ontario: Vanier Institute of the Family.

Shelton, T. L., & Stepanek, J. S. (1994). *Family-centered care for children needing specialized health and developmental services* (3rd ed.). Bethesda, MD: Association for the Care of Children's Health.

Skinner, B. F. (1978). The ethics of helping people. In L. Wispé (Ed.), *Altruism, sympathy, and helping: Psychological and sociological principles* (pp. 249–262). New York: Academic Press.

Skinner, E. A. (1995). *Perceived control, motivation, and coping.* Thousand Oaks, CA: Sage.

Spagnola, M., & Fiese, B. H. (2007). Family routines and rituals: A context for development in the lives of young children. *Infants & Young Children, 20*(4), 284–299. doi:10.1097/01.IYC.0000290352.32170.5a

Stoddard, S. A., Whiteside, L., Zimmerman, M. A., Cunningham, R. M., Chermack, S. T., & Walton, M. A. (2013). The relationship between cumulative risk and promotive factors and vilolent behavior among urban adolescents. *American Journal of Community Psychology, 51*(1–2), 57–65. doi:10.1007/s10464-012-9541-7

Stoneman, Z. (1985). Family involvement in early childhood special education programs. In N. Fallen & W. Umansky (Eds.), *Young children with special needs* (2nd ed., pp. 442–469). Columbus, OH: Charles Merrill.

Swanson, J., Raab, M., & Dunst, C. J. (2011). Strengthening family capacity to provide young children everyday natural learning opportunities. *Journal of Early Childhood Research, 9,* 66–80. doi:10.1177/1476718X10368588

Trevithick, P. (2003). Effective relationship-based practice: A theoretical exploration. *Journal of Social Work Practice, 17*(2), 163–176. doi:10.1080/026505302000145699

Trivette, C. M., Deal, A., & Dunst, C. J. (1986). Family needs, sources of support, and professional roles: Critical elements of family systems assessment and intervention. *Diagnostique, 11,* 246–267.

Trivette, C. M., & Dunst, C. J. (2007). *Capacity-building family-centered helpgiving practices.* Asheville, NC: Winterberry Press.

Trivette, C. M., Dunst, C. J., & Deal, A. G. (1997). Resource-based approach to early intervention. In S. K. Thurman, J. R. Cornwell, & S. R. Gottwald (Eds.), *Contexts of early intervention: Systems and settings* (pp. 73–92). Baltimore, MD: Brookes.

Trivette, C. M., Dunst, C. J., & Hamby, D. W. (2010). Influences of family-systems intervention practices on parent-child interactions and child development. *Topics in Early Childhood Special Education, 30,* 3–19. doi:10.1177/0271121410364250

Trute, B., Benzies, K. M., Worthington, C., Reddon, J. R., & Moore, M. (2010). Accentuate the positive to mitigate the negative: Mother psychological coping resources and family adjustment in childhood disability. *Journal of Intellectual and Developmental Disability, 35,* 36–43. doi:10.3109/13668250903496328

Wilson, L. L. (2005). Characteristics and consequences of capacity-building parenting supports. *CASEmakers, 1*(4), 1–3.

Zimmerman, M. A. (1990). Toward a theory of learned hopefulness: A structural model analysis of participation and empowerment. *Journal of Research in Personality, 24,* 71–86. doi:10.1016/0092-6566(90)90007-S

4 Desirable outcomes associated with family-centred practices for young children with a disability

Ian Dempsey and Deb Keen

Attention to desirable outcomes for families with a member with a disability is warranted for at least two reasons. First, it is well known that a wide variety of physical, psychological, and financial indicators for such families are relatively poor in comparison to families without a member with a disability (Bailey, Golden, Roberts, & Ford, 2007; Peer & Hillman, 2014). Second, across all developed countries, family support programs are increasingly required to demonstrate accountability to their stakeholders (e.g., Australian Department of Families, Housing, Community Services and Indigenous Affairs, 2012). In light of these two factors, practitioners who provide family support, including family-centred services to families with a young child with a disability, need to understand the mechanisms by which their support leads to desirable outcomes and demonstrate the improved outcomes for the families with whom they work. In some countries, accountability data are limited to measures of the processes that the service engages in when interacting with their client group(s) (Bailey, Raspa, & Fox, 2012). In this respect, such data are problematic because, on their own, evidence of the provision of service is no guarantee that meaningful and valued outcomes for others eventuate. This chapter attempts to addresses this deficiency by clarifying the causal pathways between family-centred practices and desirable outcomes for families, and by highlighting potentially desirable outcomes that family-centred practices should be using as indicators of a successful program of support.

Family-centred practices

A family-centred approach to support has dominated the field of early intervention over the last two decades. This approach is built on the foundational work of ecological theory (Bronfenbrenner, 1992), help-giving theory (Trivette, Dunst, & Hamby, 1996), empowerment theory (Rappaport, 1981), and social support theory (Cohen & Wills, 1985). In brief, family-centred practice fosters family engagement, collaboration, and decision-making, sees families as partners, and focuses on family strengths in the process of facilitating child development. As Brewer and colleagues (1989) noted, integral to this approach is the notion that "families be supported in their natural care-giving and decision-making roles by building on their unique strengths as people and families" (p. 1105).

In the 30 years since Dunst (1985) argued that family empowerment should be the primary outcome from family-centred early intervention, the components of that empowerment have been discussed in a variety of forums. Examples of these components include parenting self-efficacy and personal self-efficacy, parenting skills, reduced parental stress, participation in community activities, knowledge of child development, family quality of life, access to support systems, and self-advocacy (Bailey et al, 1998; Dempsey & Foreman, 1997; Dempsey & Keen, 2008; Dunst, Trivette, & Hamby, 2007; Park et al., 2003). Using factor analysis techniques, Raspa et al. (2010) found that family outcomes from early intervention clustered into a family knowledge and ability area, and a family support and community services area.

Allied to this work on parent outcomes is a large body of literature that describes the principles of support assumed to be both directly, indirectly, and causally related to desirable family outcomes. These principles encompass family decision-making and engagement, meaningful communication and collaboration between families and professionals, an emphasis on child and family strengths, abilities, and interests rather than perceived deficiencies, and opportunities for families to strengthen their informal community networks and supports (Bailey et al., 2011; Blue-Banning, Summers, Frankland, Nelson, & Beegle, 2004; Trivette & Dunst, 2000).

In 2008, we reviewed empirical evidence related to processes and outcomes for family-centred services for families with a young child with a disability (Dempsey & Keen, 2008). At that time, we concluded that there was a relatively small research base on which to understand the relationships that exist between service delivery processes and child and parent outcomes. However, we found enough evidence in the research literature to conclude that provision of family-centred help-giving was directly related to parent sense of control, parent self-efficacy, and parent satisfaction with the service support received. Family-centred practice was indirectly related to a number of parent and child outcomes including parent stress, parenting capacity, and child development. Furthermore, parent appraisals of control and parenting self-efficacy mediated the impact of help giving practices on parent and child outcomes. Additional evidence for the efficacy of family-centred principles has more recently emerged from individual research studies, and from a number of literature reviews and meta-analyses. Consequently, the purpose of the present chapter is to check the extent to which more recent research has reified family-centred theory, to chart the evolution of theoretical models of family-centred practice, and to isolate the gaps in our knowledge.

To achieve this aim, we employed searches using the terms *family-centered*, *empowerment, early intervention, child** and *disabil** using EBSCO™, PsychINFO™ and Google Scholar databases, supplemented by general internet search engine enquiries. Studies were selected only if the research data examined the relationship between family-centred practice and parent or child outcomes, and only if there was evidence that the practices described in the study were indeed family-centred. Finally, we focused on studies published between 2007 and 2014.

Review of recent research on the relationship between family-centred practice and parent and child outcomes

In a pilot study with 33 families from Newcastle, Australia, Dempsey, Keen, Pennell, O'Reilly, and Neilands (2009) found statistically significant relationships between several components of family-centred practice, as reported by parents with a young child with a disability, and parent stress. Over 40% of the variance in parent stress was accounted for by how comfortable parents said they felt with support staff and how autonomous parents believed they were in the decision-making associated with the support of their children. Fordham, Gibson, and Bowes (2011) found similar relationships among a sample of 130 families receiving early intervention support. There were significant positive relationships between families' perceived provision of family-centred practices and both family empowerment and several aspects of social support (i.e., support from friends, family, and professionals).

There have been several literature reviews of family-centred practice involving different populations of children. Kuhlthau et al. (2011) conducted a systematic review of family-centred practices focusing specifically on the family-provider partnership for children with chronic physical, developmental, behavioural, or emotional conditions. They found evidence for positive relationships between the use of family-centred care and outcomes such as health status, family functioning, and communication. In addition, McBroom and Enriquez (2009) reviewed nine studies from the US and Sweden involving the families of adolescents with Type 1 Diabetes. There was evidence that following the implementation of a family-centred intervention, family dynamics improved and there was reduced family conflict.

The most comprehensive reviews of the family-centred research are the seven meta-analyses conducted by Carl Dunst and his colleagues. We now examine three of these that have used large sample sizes and/or have made substantial contributions to our understanding of family systems approaches. A full list of all meta-analytic studies appears in Dunst, Trivette, and Hamby (2010, p. 4). In the first of these reviews, Dunst, Trivette, and Hamby (2007) examined 38 research reports with over 11,000 participants from seven countries. The principal findings were that there were statistically significant associations between the use of family-centred practices and six desirable outcomes (parent satisfaction, parent self-efficacy, extent of social support, child behaviour, parental well-being, and parenting behaviour). The effect sizes of these associations ranged from large (for outcomes more proximally related to family-centred practice, such as self-efficacy) to small (for outcomes more distally related, such as parenting behaviour).

This meta-analysis also clarified statistical associations between different types of family-centred practice (relational and participatory practice) and desirable outcomes. Relational practices include active listening, empathy, and respect; participatory practices facilitate family choice and engagement in decision-making. While both types of family-centred practice were significantly associated with desirable outcomes, participatory practices made the largest contribution to these relationships.

The second of these meta-analyses reviewed 15 studies with over 2,900 participants in two US states (Dunst & Trivette, 2009). Structural equation modelling (SEM) was used to test a causal model of family-centred practice. The principal finding was that the higher the level of family-centred practice judged to be provided by professionals, the stronger was parents' self-efficacy (i.e., sense of control over professional and personal life events), and in turn, the higher the parent and child psychological health. Both relational and participatory practices were highly correlated and were strongly related to family-centred practice. The findings from this study have helped to explain the role of parent self-efficacy in positively influencing both parent and child psychological health and well-being.

In the final meta-analysis we report here, Dunst, Trivette, and Hamby (2010) examined eight US studies with 910 participants. The SEM confirmatory model tested in this study included family systems intervention practices (i.e., strategies to meet family needs, access social supports, and to encourage family strengths), as well as relational and participatory practices, as components that both directly or indirectly influence parent self-efficacy, parent well-being, and child development. The model also incorporated parent, family, and child characteristics as relevant independent variables. In addition to supporting the results of the earlier meta-analyses, this study made an important contribution to understanding how family systems practices interact with other processes and outcomes in the family-centred model guiding the conduct of the research synthesis.

Explanatory models of processes associated with the outcomes of family-centred practice

To help incorporate the principal research findings from the 2007–2014 period into the family-centred research base, we now examine how the family-centred model has changed over time in response to these findings. By the late 1980s, there was increasing professional insight into a number of social science theories and the relationship between those theories and family systems. Julian Rappaport (1981) argued that the principal goal for psychology was to empower individuals to better look after themselves, and Uri Bronfenbrenner (1992) had developed ecological systems theory, which explained the interactions between individuals, their communities, and the wider society. Furthermore, there was a greater understanding of the crucial role that both formal and informal social networks play in enhancing quality of life for individuals and families (Cohen & Wills, 1985).

Among the first of those to synthesise these ostensibly disparate theories into an enhanced understanding of family support were Dunst, Trivette, and Deal (1988). Dunst and his colleagues explained that the role of the service provider in assisting families was not only to provide direct support to children with additional needs, but also to facilitate the family's engagement with a range of relevant informal supports within their environment. Integral to this process was assisting families to meet their unique needs and the encouragement of family strengths to assist in building family capacity.

At this early stage of family-centred theory, appropriate social support was hypothesised to impact most directly on family well-being and family functioning, and more indirectly on parent-child interaction and on child development. The first cell of Figure 4.1 shows the relationships between these processes and outcomes as described by Dunst, Trivette, and Deal (1988). At this point in the evolution of family-centred theory, the components and operation of practitioner behaviour to enable and to empower families were yet to be described and tested. However, empirical research over the next two decades was able to more effectively differentiate these help-giving processes and to test some important components of family-centred theory.

By the late 1990s, many studies had shown a strong relationship between family-centred practice and desirable service outcomes, including parent satisfaction with services, parent self-efficacy beliefs, and parents' sense of control. During this time, there was also an appreciation that family-centred practice encompassed not only practices designed to build a trusting relationship with parents, but also a set of practices designed to engage parents in activities that built their parenting confidence and their parenting skills. This period of time also provided insight into a number of important mediating variables that interacted with these processes and outcomes (Dempsey & Keen, 2008). The second cell of Figure 4.1 describes our

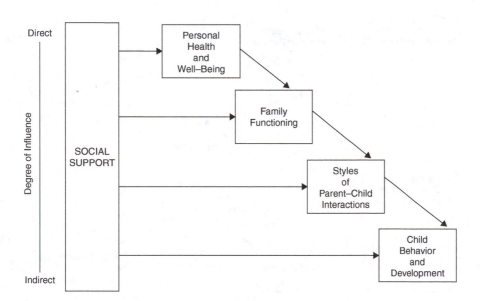

Figure 4.1a Evolution of family-centred theory

Source: Dunst, C. J., Trivette, C. M., & Deal, A. G. (1988). *Enabling and empowering families: Principles and guidelines for practice.* Cambridge, MA: Brookline Books. Reprinted with permission.

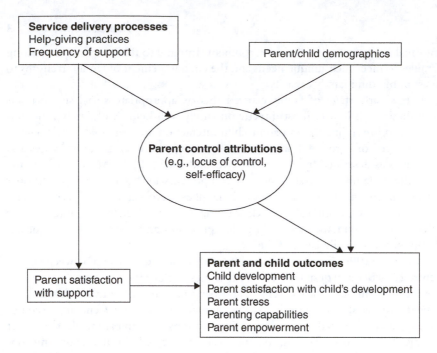

Figure 4.1b Evolution of family-centred theory

Source: Dempsey, I., and Keen, D. (2008). A review of processes and outcomes in family-centred services for children with a disability. *Topics in Early Childhood Special Education*, 28, 42–52. doi:10.1177/0271121408316699

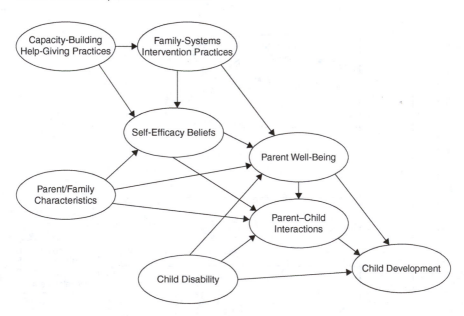

Figure 4.1c Evolution of family-centred theory

Source: Trivette, C. M., Dunst, C. J., and Hamby, D. W. (2010). Influences of family systems intervention practices on parent-child interactions and child development. *Topics in Early Childhood Special Education*, 30, 3–19. doi:10.1177/0271121410364250

understanding of family-centred theory by the mid-2000s. Among other things, this model highlights the importance of parent attributions (e.g., parenting self-efficacy) in the interaction between family-centred practice and a widening range of parent and child outcomes. However, this model was limited in the number of independent and dependent variables examined and that the strength of the relationship between these variables had yet to be fully synthesised.

The meta-analyses in the late 2000s by Dunst and his colleagues were integral to further refinement of family-centred theory. In particular, these analyses quantified the practical importance of the relationships between components of the family-centred model, as well as demonstrating causal pathways between these components. Taken as a whole, the empirical research of the last 25 years has consistently supported the principal features of Dunst, Trivette, and Deal's (1988) original model. Hypothesised direct and indirect relationships between enabling practices and both child and family outcomes have been established in a wide variety of settings and across a wide variety of participants. More importantly, the research shows that beneficial outcomes from family-centred practice depend not just on what support is provided, but also on how that support is provided. Although research has provided evidence that family-centred practice contributes to positive outcomes for children and families, the extent to which such outcomes are achieved is highly dependent on effective implementation of family-centred practice in the community.

Implementation of family-centred practices

There is evidence to suggest that there have been difficulties in implementing family-centred practices in community-based settings. For example, Wright and Hiebert-Murphy (2010) investigated professionals' perceptions of organisational factors that supported or hindered the implementation of family-centred practice. They interviewed 36 staff from two disability service agencies in Canada. The researchers found that organisational culture and climate (e.g., caseload size and activity, supervision, and training), policy limitations, and collateral services (e.g., interdisciplinary and cross-agency collaboration) negatively impacted on the successful implementation of family-centred practice. Other studies have examined the extent to which individual practitioners implement family-centred practices. Fingerhut et al. (2013) interviewed 28 occupational therapists across home, clinic, and school settings. They found a continuum of family-centred practice was demonstrated among practitioners and this varied across settings: the home setting was found to be most family-centred and the school setting the least family-centred.

It could be argued that effective implementation is the next major challenge for family-centred practice. Issues associated with the translation of research into practice are not unique to family-centred practice and there has been increasing attention across the social sciences and education fields over the past few years in translational research. Sometimes referred to as knowledge transfer or implementation science, translational research is the study of "methods to promote the systematic uptake of research findings and other evidence-based practices into routine practice" (Eccles & Mittman, 2006, p. 1). It is clear from previous research that the uptake of particular practices is not automatic and that providing guidelines, policies, information, and training are not sufficient in themselves to ensure the uptake and maintenance of practices over time (Fixsen, Naoom, Blasé, Friedman, & Wallace, 2005).

A range of factors may limit the uptake of family-centred practice in community-based organisations. These factors can be grouped into one of three categories: the nature of the support practices being implemented (e.g., cultural fit, relevance, practicality); users (e.g., knowledge and use of the support practices, skills required, available time); and the institutional context (e.g., resources, organisational culture and structures, training) (Cook & Odom, 2013). There has been very little research undertaken on the nature of support practices and the instructional context. However, in relation to users, Sewell (2012) recently reviewed the literature on teacher preparation in family-centred practices in the field of early childhood and concluded, "teachers find the idea of partnering with families a daunting and unmanageable task due to lack of preparation and training" (p. 262). This review highlighted the need for translational research focused on developing more effective approaches to increasing knowledge and skills of service providers to implement family-centred practices in some contexts. However, enhancing knowledge and skills in family-centred practice does not ensure implementation. Overall, the implementation picture is complex and must take account of not only user variables, but also other factors associated with specific support practices being promoted and institutional context variables.

The extent to which service providers can address challenges associated with the implementation of family-centred practice will determine to what extent this process will become part of everyday practice. Only then may positive outcomes for individuals and their families known to be possible through decades of research be realised. However, the successful implementation of this process demands an understanding of the family-centred model, including an understanding of the outcomes that may develop from family-centred practice. We now turn to such outcomes.

Determining whether family-centred practices are associated with desirable outcomes

Earlier in the chapter, we discussed the limitations of measuring the use of family-centred processes as the only indicator of service quality. Knowing that service staff have implemented family-centred procedures and policy is an important first step in checking on service quality. For example, it is important to know that opportunities for capacity-building and decision-making have been provided to families. However, as shown in Figure 4.1, service delivery processes interact in complex ways with a variety of intermediate and terminal family and child outcomes. Checking on desirable outcomes assumed to develop from the provision of family-centred practice is an important additional step in monitoring service quality, but only if those measured outcomes are meaningful and relevant to families.

One commonly used assessment of service quality has been user satisfaction with the service, but this approach also has an important limitation as a measure of service quality. Asking someone to rate their satisfaction with a service is effectively a rating of another's behaviour and not a rating of whether the service has been helpful to the recipient. Further, satisfaction with service may not always be causally related to other desirable outcomes and satisfaction is influenced by numerous factors, not just service factors (Rodger, Keen, Braithwaite, & Cook, 2008).

In a helpful discussion of outcomes measurement in disability services, Quilliam and Wilson (2011) noted that there are many potentially relevant outcomes measures of disability services that provide helpful advice to practitioners in selecting or developing such measures. Quilliam and Wilson's (2011, p. 13–14) criteria are summarised below, as they specifically relate to measurement in a family-centred context:

- measure outcomes, rather than processes or throughputs,
- use a number of different measures (e.g., both child and family outcomes),
- use measures that are meaningful to those completing them,
- measures should be relatively brief and easy to use,
- measures need to be based on self-report rather than use of a proxy to answer for the individual,
- use measures that require low amounts of administrative and data analysis time, and
- collect information about the things that both enhance and inhibit achievement of desirable outcomes.

One additional criterion to the above list is to use the same instrument over time to determine if change has occurred. For example, have a family's perceptions of their circumstances changed over six or 12 months and has that change (or lack of it) been appreciated by the family? To assist practitioners in identifying and interpreting potentially useful outcome measures, we briefly review three measures: the Family Quality of Life Scale; the Social Network Index; and the Personal Growth Initiative Scale II. This review is neither comprehensive nor an endorsement of the selected measure as the only alternative. Rather, the review may alert practitioners to the options that are available to them. In this regard, practitioners may find the Measurement Instrument Database for the Social Sciences (MIDSS) (2014) helpful in locating instruments.

The Family Quality of Life Scale (Beach Centre on Disabilities, 2014) comprises 25 questions that measure family satisfaction with their quality of family life, potentially a desirable outcome from family-centred practice. Groups of questions measure family interaction, parenting, emotional well-being, physical/ material well-being, and disability-related support. Building and strengthening networks with both formal and informal forms of support is a cornerstone of the family-centred model (Dunst, Trivette, & Deal, 1988). In this regard, the Social Network Index (Cohen et al., 1997) assesses participation in 12 types of social relationships with others such as spouse, parents, children and other close family members, friends, workmates, and members of community organisations. This 12-item scale can either be self-completed or completed by interview.

Finally, we give an example of a capacity-building measure that may be well-suited to determining the extent to which family-centred practice for a family or families may be assisting them to develop competence and confidence. The 16-item Personal Growth Initiative Scale II (Robitschek et al., 2012) assesses a person's active engagement in personal change across the areas of readiness for change, planfulness, using resources, and intentional behaviour. Each of these scales, along with scoring instructions, is freely available from MIDSS.

Conclusion

Our goal in this chapter has been to enhance our understanding of the family-centred model. We reviewed the recent research that identifies the causal pathways between family-centred practice and desirable outcomes for families with a young child with a disability. Finally, we highlighted the importance of checking if desirable outcomes (beyond satisfaction with services or service providers) are associated with family-centred practice. We regard these as important activities because family-centred practitioners cannot reasonably expect to be successful in their endeavours without an understanding of the premise of their support.

Finally, we have argued that one of the principal challenges for family-centred practice into the future is to assist practitioners to implement that practice with fidelity. As Bailey and colleagues have noted, ". . . the principles of family-centered care have little meaning if they are only adopted as a belief system without corresponding application across various practice settings that comprise early intervention" (Bailey, Raspa, Sam, & Humphreys, 2011, p. 679).

The information contained in this chapter holds a number of implications for service providers at both the individual and organisational levels. There is now a large body of evidence, presented in this chapter, to support the use of a range of family-centred practices and practitioners need to be informed of these practices. In many cases, this may occur through formal, discipline-specific qualifications, while in others, in-service professional development may be required and organisations should plan to address these needs on a regular basis.

It is important to recognise, however, that while knowledge of family-centred practice is necessary, it is clearly not sufficient to ensure the effective use of these practices. There are two aspects to effective use that service providers must consider: implementation and evaluation. Implementation of family-centred practices by individual practitioners is more likely to be effective within a whole-of-organisation framework where the organisational culture supports the use of evidence-based practices (Russell et al., 2010). Determining if family-centred practices are being used effectively must be done in a transparent, explicit, and systematic manner. A variety of assessment tools are available to service providers for this purpose and can be combined with informal measures such as interviews with individuals and their families. Ultimately, the most important indicator of effective use of family-centred practices by service providers will be the achievement, for individuals and families, of a range of valued outcomes.

References

Australian Department of Families, Housing, Community Services and Indigenous Affairs (2012). *Family support program: FSP data system protocols.* Retrieved from http://www.dss.gov.au/our-responsibilities/families-and-children/publica tions-articles/fsp-data-system-protocols

Bailey, D. B., Golden, R. N., Roberts, J., & Ford, A. (2007). Maternal depression and developmental disability: research critique. *Mental Retardation and Developmental Disabilities Research Reviews, 13,* 321–329.

Bailey, D. B., McWilliam, R. A., Darkes, L. A., Hebbeler, K., Simeonsson, R. J., Spiker, D., & Wagner, M. (1998). Family outcomes in early intervention: A framework for program evaluation and efficacy research. *Exceptional Children, 64,* 313–328. doi:10.1177/001440299806400302

Bailey, D. B., Raspa, M., & Fox, L. C. (2012). What is the future of family outcomes and family-centered services. *Topics in Early Childhood Special Education, 31,* 216–223. doi:10.1177/0271121411427077

Bailey, D. B., Raspa, M., Sam, A., & Humphreys, B. (2011). Promoting family outcomes in early intervention. In J. Kauffman & D. Hallahan (Eds.), *Handbook of special education* (pp. 668–684). New York: Routledge.

Beach Center on Disabilities. (2014). *Family quality of life scale.* Retrieved from http://www.beachcenter.org/resource_library/beach_resource_detail_page.aspx? intResourceID=2391&JScript=1

Blue-Banning, M., Summers, J. A., Frankland, H. C., Nelson, L. L., & Beegle, G. (2004). Dimensions of family and professional partnerships: constructive guidelines for collaboration. *Exceptional Children, 70,* 167–184. doi:10. 1177/001440290407000203

Brewer, E. J., McPherson, M., Magrab, P. R., & Hutchins, V. L. (1989). Family-centered, community-based, coordinated care for children with special health care needs. *Pediatrics, 83,* 1055–1060. doi:10.1007/s10995-008-0321-9

Bronfenbrenner, U. (1992). Ecological systems theory. In R. Vasta (Ed.), *Six theories of child development: Revised formulations and current issues* (pp. 187–249). London: Jessica Kingsley.

Cohen, S., Doyle, W. J., Skoner, D. P., Rabin, B. S., & Gwaltney, J. M., Jr. (1997). Social ties and susceptibility to the common cold. *Journal of the American Medical Association, 277,* 1940–1944.

Cohen, S., & Wills, T. A. (1985). Stress, social support, and the buffering hypothesis. *Psychological Bulletin, 98,* 310–357. doi:10.1037/0033-2909.98.2.310

Cook, B., & Odom, S. (2013). Evidence-based practices and implementation science in special education. *Exceptional Children, 79,* 135–144. doi:10.1177/ 001440291307900201

Dempsey, I., & Foreman, P. (1997). Towards a clarification of empowerment as an outcome of disability service provision. *International Journal of Disability, Development and Education, 44,* 289–305. doi:10.1080/0156655970440402

Dempsey, I., & Keen, D. (2008). A review of processes and outcomes in family-centered services for children with a disability. *Topics in Early Childhood Special Education, 28*(1), 42–52. doi:10.1177/0271121408316699

Dempsey, I., Keen, D., Pennell, D., O'Reilly, J., & Neilands, J. (2009). Parent stress, parenting competence and family-centered support to young children with an intellectual or developmental disability. *Research in Developmental Disabilities, 30*, 558–566. doi:10.1016/j.ridd.2008.08.005

Dunst, C. J. (1985). Rethinking early intervention. *Analysis and Intervention in Developmental Disabilities, 5*, 165–201. doi:10.1016/S0270-4684(85)80012-4

Dunst, C. J., & Trivette, C. M. (2009). Meta-analytic structural equation modeling of the influences of family-centered care on parent and child psychological health. *International Journal of Pediatrics, 2009*, Article ID 576840, 1–9, doi:10.1155/2009/576840

Dunst, C. J., Trivette, C. M., & Deal, A. G. (1988). *Enabling and empowering families: Principles and guidelines for practice.* Cambridge, MA: Brookline.

Dunst, C. J., Trivette, C. M., & Hamby, D. W. (2010). Influences of family-systems intervention practices on parent–child interactions and child development. *Topics in Early Childhood Special Education, 30*, 3–19. doi:10.1177/0271121410364250

Dunst, C. J., Trivette, C. M., & Hamby, D. W. (2007). Meta-analysis of family-centered helpgiving practices research. *Mental Retardation and Developmental Disabilities Research Reviews, 13*, 370–378. doi:10.1002/mrdd.20176

Eccles, M., & Mittman, B. (2006). Welcome to implementation science. *Implementation Science, 1*, 1–3. doi:10.1186/1748-5908-1-1

Fingerhut, P., Piro, J., Sutton, A., Campbell, R., Lewis, C., Lawji, D., & Martinez, N. (2013). Family-centered principles implemented in home-based, clinic-based, and school-based pediatric settings. *The American Journal of Occupational Therapy, 67*, 228–235. doi:10.5014/ajot.2013.006957

Fixsen, D. L., Naoom, S. F., Blase, K. A., Friedman, R. M., & Wallace, F. (2005). *Implementation research: A synthesis of the literature.* Tampa, FL: University of South Florida, Louis de la Parte Florida Mental Health Institute, The National Implementation Network.

Fordham, L., Gibson, F., & Bowes, J. (2011). Information and professional support: Key factors in the provision of family-centred early childhood intervention services. *Child: Care, Health and Development, 38*(5), 647–653. doi:10.1111/j.1365-2214.2011.01324.x

Kuhlthau, K. A., Bloom, S., Van Cleave, J., Knapp, A. A., Romm, D., Klatka, K., Homer, C. J., Newacheck, P. W., & Perrin, J. M. (2011). Evidence for family-centered care for children with special health care needs: A systematic review. *Academic Pediatrics, 11*, 136–143. doi:10.1016/j.acap.2010.12.014

McBroom, L. A., & Enriquez, M. (2009). Review of family-centered interventions to enhance the health outcomes of children with type 1 diabetes. *The Diabetes Educator, 35*, 428–438. doi:10.1177/0145721709332814

Measurement Instrument Database for the Social Sciences (MIDSS) (2014). *Home Page.* Retrieved from http://www.midss.org/

Park, J., Hoffman, L., Marquis, J., Turnbull, A. P., Poston, D., Mannan, H., Wang, M., & Nelson, L. L. (2003). Toward assessing family outcomes of service delivery: Validation of a family quality of life survey. *Journal of Intellectual Disability Research, 47*, 367–384. doi:10.1046/j.1365-2788.2003.00497.x

Peer, J. W., & Hillman, S. B. (2014). Stress and resilience for parents of children with intellectual and developmental disabilities: A review of key factors and recommendations for practitioners. *Journal of Policy and Practice in Intellectual Disabilities, 11*, 92–98. doi:10.1111/jppi.12072

Quilliam, C., & Wilson, E. (2011). *Literature review outcomes measurement in disability services: a review of policy contexts, measurement approaches and selected measurement tools.* Retrieved from http://www.scopevic.org.au/index.php/cms/frontend/resource/id/1425/name/moss_lit_review.pdf

Rappaport, J. (1981). In praise of paradox: A social policy of empowerment over prevention. *American Journal of Community Psychology, 9,* 1–25. doi:10.1007/BF00896357

Raspa, M., Bailey, D. B., Olmsted, M. G., Nelson, R., Robinson, N., Simpson, M. E., Guillen, C., & Houts, R. (2010). Measuring family outcomes in early intervention: Findings from a large-scale assessment. *Exceptional Children, 76,* 496–510. doi:10.1177/001440291007600407

Robitschek, C., Ashton, M. W., Spering, C. C., Geiger, N., Byers, D., Schotts, G. C., & Thoen, M. (2012). Development and psychometric properties of the personal growth initiative scale – II. *Journal of Counseling Psychology, 59,* 274–287. doi:10.1037/a0027310

Rodger, S., Keen, D., Braithwaite, M., & Cook, S. (2008). Mothers' satisfaction with a home based early intervention programme for children with ASD. *Journal of Applied Research in Intellectual Disabilities, 21,* 174–182. doi:10.1111/j.1468-3148.2007.00393.x

Russell, D., Rivard, L., Walter, S., Rosenbaum, P., Roxborough, L., Cameron, D., Darrah, J., Bartlett, D., Hanna, S., & Avery, L. (2010). Using knowledge brokers to facilitate the uptake of pediatric measurement tools into clinical practice: A before-after intervention study. *Implementation Science, 5*(92). doi:10.1186/1748-5908-5-9

Sewell, T. (2012). Are we adequately preparing teachers to partner with families? *Early Childhood Education Journal, 40,* 259–263. doi:10.1007/s10643-008-0268

Trivette, C. M., & Dunst, C. J. (2000). Recommended practices in family-based practices. In S. Sandall, M. E. McLean, & B. J. Smith (Eds.), *DEC recommended practices in early intervention/early childhood special education* (pp. 39–46). Longmont, CO: Sopris West.

Trivette, C. M., Dunst, C. J., & Hamby, D. (1996). Characteristics and consequences of help-giving practices in contrasting human services programs. *American Journal of Community Psychology, 24,* 273–293. doi:10.1007/BF02510402

Wright, A., & Hiebert-Murphy, D. (2010). Professionals' perspectives on organizational factors that support or hinder the successful implementation of family-centered practice. *Journal of Family Social Work, 13,* 114–130. doi:10.1080/10522150903503036

Part III

Understanding families and family-early childhood practitioner relationships

Both family systems and family-centred approaches to early childhood intervention recognise and take into consideration family and cultural diversity in order to ensure that intervention practices are sensitive to and respectful of family beliefs, desires, and preferences. This is accomplished, to a large degree, by the relationships early childhood practitioners have with families and family members, and especially relationships that support and strengthen family competence and confidence.

Early childhood intervention is now practised throughout most of the world (e.g., European Commission/EACEA/Eurydice, 2015; Guralnick, 2005; New & Cochran, 2007; Odom, Hanson, Blackman, & Kaul, 2003). In many countries, and especially those that differ considerably in the ethnic, linguistic, and religious makeup of their citizens (Fearon, 2003), such diversity demands highly individualised practices in order for early childhood intervention to be culturally sensitive and competent. Within this diversity, however, is one common feature: the family (however defined) as the primary social context for child learning and development, and carer-child interactions as sources of variation in child learning, development, and socialisation. As noted by Richter (2004), caregiver sensitivity and responsiveness to child behaviour shapes and influences social acculturation where these "nurturing caregiver-child relationships have universal features across cultures, regardless of differences in specific child care practices" (p. 3).

The importance of caregiver-child interactions is no doubt the reason so many approaches to early childhood intervention place primary emphasis on influencing caregiving practices, and why supporting and promoting caregiver competence and confidence are viewed as a primary way to have capacity-building and empowering consequences. The chapters in this section of the book include insights and guidance for adopting practices that strengthen carer-child and family-practitioner relationships from family systems and family-centred approaches to early childhood intervention.

References

European Commission/EACEA/Eurydice. (2015). *Early childhood education and care systems in Europe. National information sheets – 2014/15. Eurydice facts and figures.* Luxembourg: Office of the European Union.

Fearon, J. D. (2003). Ethnic and cultural diversity by country. *Journal of Economic Growth, 8*(2), 195–222. doi:10.1023/A:1024419522867

Guralnick, M. J. (Ed.). (2005). *The developmental systems approach to early intervention.* Baltimore, MD: Brookes.

New, R. S., & Cochran, M. M. (2007). *Early childhood education: An international encyclopedia* (Vol. 1). Westport, CT: Praeger Publishers.

Odom, S. L., Hanson, M. J., Blackman, J. A., & Kaul, S. (2003). *Early intervention practices around the world.* Baltimore, MD: Brookes.

Richter, L. (2004). *The importance of caregiver-child interactions for the survival and healthy development of young children: A review.* Geneva, Switzerland: World Health Organisation, Department of Child and Adolescent Health and Development.

5 Family composition and family needs in Australia

What makes a family?

Sara Holman

Family systems across Australia could be classified as complex, as they are diverse in structure and representation due to significant change in fertility options, the life expectancy of time spent in relationships (demographically speaking) and a sense of the shifting social, cultural and economical values of Australia in the present day (De Vaus, 2009). No longer are we portrayed as the "typical," homogenous, traditional, nuclear family presented back in the 1950s era of Australia. Families are diverse and this is highlighted and considered within a myriad of further information or even influence, such as gender, culture, marital status, children; who can be brought into the family system through biological parenting, step-parenting, adoption, or perhaps assisted through in vitro fertilisation (IVF), which enables the eggs of a woman's ovary to be removed and fertilised with sperm through laboratory processes, and then the fertilised egg is returned back into the woman's uterus (IVF Australia, 2015). There are also children who come under the guardianship of family members such as older siblings and grandparents as well as family friends. The reasons for these arrangements are complex and may include parental deaths, the inability of a parent/s to carry out adequate parenting, court rulings or simply decisions by biological parents who are struggling for any number of reasons. When I refer to "complex" family systems, it derives from a place of respect and interest associated with the diverse nature of families across the States and Territories of Australia. Our diverse nation is recorded predominantly through the Australian Bureau of Statistics (ABS) information.

For the purpose of representing the ABS data in an authentic and statistically minded gathering of information, it is fair to highlight that there are people who choose to keep their information exempt from such surveys (such as that which is presented in the ABS data). This chapter will provide readers with a deeper understanding and broader context to represent our family compositions or perhaps systems across Australia.

This chapter also explores how children from diverse families experience the qualities, or perhaps disharmony in expressing their voice about their community, identity and belonging. It investigates whether there is a disjunction between policy imperatives and how diverse families experience such values and practices encouraging their participation and relationships between educators and diverse families. The early childhood policy frameworks promote an ideal practice, but I am eager to discuss if such positive values are being enacted in practices towards our diverse families within early childhood settings. The early childhood frameworks suggest a broad range of appropriate practices and are simply frameworks for guidance. To interpret the frameworks and magnify the essence of their policy intentions would also expose gaps and resistance to knowledge, practice and the desire of families to convey their truth, beliefs and values without prejudice and simply the need for acceptance without explanation.

Current family structures across Australia

Families are no longer defined by the nuclear structure, as was the case in the past. Our children transition and interact amongst a reality that warrants a sincere need to re-connect to the question: what makes a family?

"Families can be described or characterised as big, small, extended, nuclear, multi-generational, with one parent, two parents, same sex parents, and grandparents" (Carpenter, 2002). Discussions in this chapter will focus on an Australian context examining family systems and family dynamics across current early childhood frameworks, Government policy and its implication in practice for educators across the early years. The early childhood sector has responded to the early years frameworks conservatively through both moral obligation and a need to conscientiously utlilise the available frameworks according to direction from the Government, funding and the requirement to present the National Quality Standards (ACECQA, NQS, 2011) across Australia. This uniform approach by the Federal Government is welcomed by many in the early childhood sector, yet early childhood educators must reflect whether their responses are connected to a genuine partnership with families or perhaps they have chosen to opt for a superficial engagement where diverse families partner with early childhood services and educators on the surface yet experience invisibility in family structure, functions and true acceptance (Slattebol & Ferfolja, 2007).

The latest Australian Bureau of Statistics data from 2011 highlights that there are 5,584,000 families across Australia (Australian Institute of Family Studies, n.d). The majority of this number (close to 75% of this total number) represents couples without children (37.8%) and couples with dependent children (aligning closely with couples without children at 36.7%). The remaining 25% of the total number of families across Australia include one-parent families with dependent children (10.6%), couples with non-dependent children (7.9%), one-parent families with non-dependent children (5.3%) and "other" family types (1.7%) (AIFS, n.d).

To understand these data, it is vital to understand five key definitions that relate to family types as defined by the Australian Bureau of Statistics, which include (1) Couple family; (2) Dependent children (3) Non-dependent child; (4) One-parent family and (5) Other family (AIFS, n.d).

A couple family is identified as "[a] family based on two persons who are in a registered or de facto marriage and who are usually resident in the same household. A couple family without children may have other relatives, such as ancestors, present. A couple family with children may have adult children and/or other relatives present" (AIFS, n.d).

Couples with dependent children are "[a]ll family members under 15 years of age; family members aged 15–19 years attending school or aged 15–24 years attending a tertiary educational institution full-time (except those classified as husbands, wives or lone parents)" (AIFS, n.d). Non-dependent child families are classified, "[i]n couple or one-parent families, sons or daughters who are aged over 15 years and who are not full-time students aged 15–24 years (except those classified as husbands, wives or lone parents)" (AIFS, n.d).

One-parent families are "[a] family consisting of a lone parent with at least one dependent or non-dependent child (regardless of age) who is also usually resident in the household. The family may also include any number of other dependent children, non-dependent children and other related individuals" (AIFS, n.d).

Lastly, Other family offers a broad definition, which articulates, "A family of related individuals residing in the same household. These individuals do not form a couple or parent-child relationship with any other person in the household and are not attached to a couple or one-parent family in the household. For example, a "household consisting of a brother and sister only" (AIFS, n.d).

For the sake of statistical data, the definitions of families are represented across numeric representation connected to a glossary that provides broad terminology of these particular families, which are a "best fit" to our cultural and perhaps atypical values and beliefs. The broadest definition of "family" clarifies that a family is made up of, "Two or more persons, one of whom is aged 15 years and over, who are related by blood, marriage (registered or de facto), adoption, step or fostering; and who are usually resident in the same household" (AIFS, n.d).

Furthermore, it is interesting to note that Co-habitation (also known as a de-facto relationship) is strictly "restricted to heterosexual relationships" (AIFS, n.d). The temptation to ponder this definition is far reaching, as I consider same-sex families and wonder where they would fit into the Australian family identity. Davies and Robinson (2013) argue about the constructs of same-sex families and their identity, which is not represented accurately with the Queer dissonance fractured and is often compounded by the contradictory space of the neoliberal framework of current Government within Australia. Furthermore, Davies and Semann (2013) reiterate this view through a detailed conversation with Jonathan Silin, author of, *Sex, Death and the Education of Children: Our Passion for Ignorance in the Age of AIDS* (1995), one of the key figures in the reconceptualist movement of early childhood embracing critical perspectives to early childhood education, challenging constructs of gender and sexuality within the domain of equity and social justice. Twenty years on from this influential book by Silin (1995), the equity debate continues to prevail in same-sex representation, Government policy and social attitude.

Again, it appears that a broad definition of family is constrained to the "statistical norm," and the complexity of this definition exhausts beyond the numeric realms as some families are not presented adequately or precisely based on data which have been available in Australia since 1996, particularly in relation to same-sex families (Qu & Weston, 2013). Qu and Weston's (2013) report also attributes rising figures of same-sex families in the 2011 ABS figures to "an increasing willingness for such couples to disclose their relationship [who] are more prepared to form a couple household, rather than to maintain separate homes" (p. 9). In 1996, same-sex couples were represented by 0.3% of the population as opposed to 0.7% in the 2011 Census data. This shift has been partially attributed to support services for same-sex identified individuals, couples and their families and the overall willingness for society, and particularly those closely associated with a person who identifies as same-sex, to reduce the feelings of isolation and express greater acceptance of their sexual orientation (AIFS, n.d).

The family systems theory framework (Dunst & Trivette, 2009) supports the concept of family capacity-building and family-centred practices. If we are to consider the child in the context of their family, policies and frameworks then the early childhood sector must reflect and address the array of complexities within the family unit. Perhaps even family composition becomes irrelevant when early childhood practitioners simply redirect their focus to capture family need. A capacity-building approach addresses the functionality and future direction of any family regardless of their composition as a strength-based approach and encompasses the ability of the family to move forward and guide their direction through decision-making processes which enable families to take a leadership role positioned with confidence. The family systems theory framework (Dunst & Trivette, 2009) will be discussed in greater detail later on in this chapter.

As in the mainstream educational sector, the same appreciation and relation to diverse families must exist in the early intervention sector. Families confronted with the realities of a child with a disability and/or an additional need would not respond well to practitioners who compound processes with additional or undue stress. It would be expected that early intervention practitioners would in fact exhibit better responsive, acceptable behaviours to diverse families accessing early intervention services (Sukkar, 2011).

Definition of family

To interpret the definition of family is complex, as family represents a variety of meanings to most people (Robinson, 2009; Robinson & Diaz, 2006). It is important to establish and underpin a well-rounded interpretation to present the broad scope of family structures within Australia. Robinson and Diaz (2006) argue that the concept of family is "a powerful and pervasive word in our culture and represents a highly unstable and contradictory space" (p. 82). Furthermore, the definition of family can be accentuated through connection to one's identity and belonging to a particular culture. In turn, this belonging can be confirmed or denied allowing for this space to interplay with "highly contested issues" (p. 82). In addition, the discourse of the nuclear, heteronormative family pervades consistently throughout society and even within early childhood education, which features "the dominant discursive values and practices that operate in the broader society" (p. 83). Robinson (2009) also states, "with increasing variability in family structure and type over time, the idea of achieving a single, workable definition appears elusive for researchers, service providers and policy makers alike" (p. 5).

For a broad definition, I believe that Carpenter's adaptation (2012) of Winton's (1990) definition of family has described families in a comprehensive sense, which includes same-sex parented families articulating that,

> *families are big, small, extended, nuclear, multi-generational, with one parent, two parents, same sex parents, and grandparents. We live under one roof or many. A family can be as temporary as a few weeks, as permanent as forever. We become part of a family by birth, adoption, marriage or from a desire for mutual support. A family is a culture unto itself, with different values and unique ways of realising its dreams. Together, our families become the source of our rich cultural heritage and spiritual diversity. Our families create neighbourhoods, communities, states and nations.*
>
> (Carpenter, 2012)

On the one hand, definitions such as those briefly described above point to understandings of families as legitimately taking diverse forms; on the other hand, there continues to be debate about the value or worth of particular family types in comparison to others (Silverstein & Auerbach, 2006). In early childhood education, it is critical to form associations with families, and yet typically, early childhood professionals enter the workforce with little guidance or knowledge as to how build such relationships with any type of family (Christian, 2006; Ratcliff & Hunt, 2009; Sewell, 2012).

Family structure: Parents with children

Regardless of how two parents come together, I would like to propose an argument to articulate that family is defined as parents with children. The children may have been conceived as part of a previous relationship, born to parents through natural means, IVF, artificial insemination, adoption, foster parenting or perhaps a surrogate mother. Literature to support this claim is diverse and spans a variety of disciplines (Becker, 2012; Carlson & Berger, 2013; Gennetian, 2005; Livermore, 2012a, 2012b; McLanahan & Beck, 2010; Thevenon & Luci, 2012).

Livermore (2012b) states that families should "care for and support one another," which includes the "proper role" of caring, protecting and supporting the development of children within their care (p. 1). Throughout Livermore's discussion on law-related policies involving family, she refers to children as a constant in the link to policy matters covering family issues. For example, her explanation of marriage, divorce and relationship issues presents policies that must always "meet their children's needs" (p. 1). Further comments on this argument refer to family within Australia described as a, "nuclear family consisting of a mother, a father and one or more children who are the direct biological descendants of and are physically born to their parents" (Livermore, 2012a, p. 2). This is followed by a statement that "a large and increasing proportion of families in Australia do not fit this definition" (p. 2). Livermore (2012a) delves further and expands on this discussion, stating that a variety of fertility arrangements, surrogacy, blended families, adopted children, single-parent, step-parent and same-sex families are in fact a "common" representation of families who have children with "powerful social, cultural, psychological and even biological ties to adults other than the people who care for them on a day-to-day basis" (p. 2).

Family system framework

What do we know for sure when considering the rich tapestry of families across Australia? We know families are diverse; we know that children are supported in ways that represent the morals, values and histories of those who raise them in their specified family unit. I would like to extend the perception of Australian families and consider capacity building as a form of strengthening family units through the specific family-centred practices articulated by Dunst and Trivette (2009).

Capacity building evolved from the backlash of the clinical/traditional deficit models popular from the 1960s to the 1980s. These earlier models silenced the voices of families and disregarded their knowledge of their children. A "fix it" concept was enacted which paid little or no attention to viewing the child as primarily connected to their family or environment. This occurred particularly in relation to families and children with a disability (Dunst & Trivette, 2009). To place families in a position where they were consistently reminded of their deficit connects critically to disempowerment, whereas empowerment reinforces capacity-building models and practices, aligns with strength-based approaches, stimulating dispositions of hope and a willingness to strengthen one's knowledge, practice and, essentially, morale. These concepts originated through Bronfenbrenner (1975), who identified the quintessential gap between deficit-based medical models and the benefit of building capacity in parents who would eventually lead in the time, energy and direction needed to support the development of their child. In advancement and planning towards future families, Dunst and his team reviewed theories associated with social systems (Bronfenbrenner, 1979), empowerment (Rappaport, 1981), family strengths (Stinnett & Defrain, 1985), social support (Gottlieb, 1981), and help-giving (Brickman et al., 1982) theories.

The background of these theories formulated part of the systems theory framework and the key considerations noted by Dunst and Trivette (2009) that emphasised the importance of both formal and informal supports, resources and the notion that these supports and resources were embedded within the social system framework. The support and resources are captured across the following activities, "experiences, opportunities, advice, guidance, material assistance, information, and so forth" (Dunst & Trivette, 2009, p. 127–128). The Australian experience of such activities varies from state to state and territory. Much of our "supports" are connected to wider Federal Government funding and State Government funding. The complexities of the non-government organisations aligning with Government organisational support is consistently seen in areas associated with the economy, legislation, new and evolving technologies that may connect or even isolate families and varying societal values (Weston & Qu, 2014). There has been constant debate in the areas of education, health and the provision of social services. Families are faced with a myriad of choices, yet access to these services is complex, confusing and to say the least, lacks consumer interest because the access is difficult to navigate. The debate is a federal versus state-based debate as Governments struggle to find the answers to the best way of delivering funding and services to families across Australia. With the rollout of the National Disability Insurance Scheme, Australia may witness a positive change in the support provided to people with disability (NDIS, 2015).

If early childhood professionals are to consider the child in the context of their family, policies and frameworks then the early childhood sector must reflect and address the array of complexities within the family unit and provide educators with some descriptors or examples of what a "diverse" family may be. In their current form, the early childhood frameworks are too broad and open for a sector that is continually growing and has experienced significant change over the past ten years. Direct explanations of "diversity" and clear expectations for practice would eradicate the status quo, which means that families are treated according to the experience and broad practice of those who have worked closely with a cross section of diverse families.

Australian early years pedagogical frameworks

To consider the child in the context of their family, policies and relevant frameworks within the early childhood sector must reflect and address complexities within the family unit. The federal-governed framework available to all States and Territories within Australia, the Early Years Learning Framework, provides a broad context to understand one of the key tools utilised in the early years sector across Australia. I will also dissect the Victorian Early Years Learning and Development Framework as another significant document, which has been used in the State of Victoria since 2009. Together, these frameworks provide context and evidence of the representation of diverse families across key pedagogical principles, which are communicated through the role of the family, partnerships with educators, the role of the community, child identity, equity and diversity.

The Federal Early Years Learning Framework, "Belonging, Being and Becoming," is a relatively safe, holistic, open-ended framework for the early years.

Examination of this document finds that specific types of families are not mentioned, for example "diverse" families are mentioned but not explained (Australian Government: Department of Education and Training, 2009).

Early Years Learning Framework

The Early Years Learning Framework (EYLF) was developed across 2008 by the Council of Australian Governments to provide an educational foundation where children aged birth to five would access quality programs that are enriched and complemented through the transition to school process (Department of Education Employment and Workplace Relations, 2009). The EYLF is based upon family-centred practices and the principles framed in the United Nations Convention on the Rights of the Child. The Convention provides an overarching philosophy, which includes a child's right to education, and respect for family makeup, culture, identity and languages (United Nations, 1990). The national framework may be utilised as a complementary document to a state framework, or educators can chose to use the EYLF on its own to assist educators in providing a rich learning experience for young children.

Before delving into the concepts of this national framework it is important to consider the title of the EYLF, as it draws upon strong ideals connected to identity. The EYLF is named Belonging, Being, Becoming, and the terms are defined in the foreword of "A Vision for Children's Learning." *Belonging* encapsulates experience, a connection to where one comes from, and extends on connections to community, a child's identity and their individual links to their beginnings in life. *Being* is described as the present, the present experience, and the events that affect a child now, developing, challenging and working through the child's range of relationships. *Becoming* is the notion of identity; ideals associated with capacity building, nurturing strengths, the intense journey of growth during these early years and a child's early contributions to society (Australian Government, Department of Education and Training, 2009). To understand the structure of the EYLF it is important to connect with the five learning outcomes, which are:

1   children have a strong sense of identity,
2   children are connected with and contribute to their world,
3   children have a strong sense of wellbeing,
4   children are confident and involved learners, and
5   children are effective communicators.

(Australian Government: Department of Education and Training, 2009)

This framework is then implemented with the core elements: principles, practices and learning outcomes (see Figure 5.1).

The key elements addressed in this chapter are critical to gain a broad perspective of the national framework as it relates to the way that we should interact with and involve families. As discussed above, each of the following learning outcomes is underpinned by a learning outcome that relates to specific areas. For

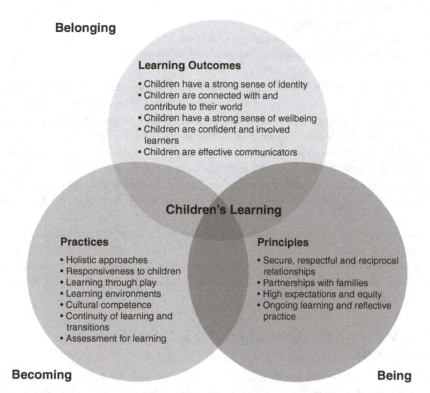

Belonging

Learning Outcomes

- Children have a strong sense of identity
- Children are connected with and contribute to their world
- Children have a strong sense of wellbeing
- Children are confident and involved learners
- Children are effective communicators

Children's Learning

Practices

- Holistic approaches
- Responsiveness to children
- Learning through play
- Learning environments
- Cultural competence
- Continuity of learning and transitions
- Assessment for learning

Principles

- Secure, respectful and reciprocal relationships
- Partnerships with families
- High expectations and equity
- Ongoing learning and reflective practice

Becoming

Being

Figure 5.1 Elements of the Early Years Learning Framework

Source: Adapted from the Early Years Learning Framework (Australian Government: Department of Education and Training, 2009).

the purpose of this chapter, my intention is to concentrate on family, identity, diversity, gender, community and pedagogy.

In the Principles element, the following aspects relate to the dynamics of diverse families:

1   secure, respectful and reciprocal relationships,
2   partnerships with families,
3   high expectations and equity, and
4   respect for diversity.

Under the Practice element, the following aspects also influence the chosen areas family, identity, diversity, gender, community and pedagogy:

1   holistic approaches,
2   responsiveness to children,
3   intentional teaching,

4   learning environments,
5   cultural competence,
6   continuity of learning and transitions, and
7   assessment for learning.

Furthermore, the EYLF emphasises a variety of theoretical underpinnings that may inform an educator's practice, programming, reflection and assessment. Socio-cultural theories promote the central contribution of family, culture and community, while aligning with the social and cultural perspectives of learning (Australian Government, Department of Education and Training, 2009). Critical theory is also identified as a key theory that questions the practice of educators and the way that "their decisions may affect children differently" (Australian Government, Department of Education and Training, 2009, p. 11).

In addition, post-structuralist theories "offer insights into issues of power, equity and social justice in early childhood settings" (p. 11). These theories allow us to examine the links to policy, practice and eventually the influence of these theories, if any, on children and families who identify themselves as diverse families.

The Victorian Early Years Learning and Development Framework

The State of Victoria implemented the Victorian Early Years Learning and Development Framework (VEYLDF) in November of 2009. This framework focuses on children from birth to eight years with a specific understanding that children's learning and development occurs in the context of their family and broader community (Department of Education and Early Childhood Development, 2009). The Victorian framework mirrors the federal Early Years Learning Framework in providing a similar context whereby the information suggested for "best practice" in relation to pedagogical material represents diverse families, yet does not delve deeper to specify what are considered "diverse families". It would be beneficial to include some descriptors in the glossary of what "diverse families" may look like, such as family structures, relationships and the best way to program according to these definitions. This would allow educators to consider a greater scope of diverse families without simply depicting the nuclear family in their environments based on an assumption of their community. Examples of case studies in the document that depict "diverse families" would also be ideal.

Practice Principles throughout the VEYLDF are defined as "the foundations for professional practice for early childhood professionals working with Victorian children from birth to eight years and their families" (DEECD, 2009, p. 9). While this framework offers ideal Practice Principles that are unique and intrinsically linked, it is important to highlight the language and explicit intentions underpinning these principles. My chapter aims to focus on how these recurring principles would relate to single-parent families, same-sex families and their children, grandparents raising children as a family, adoption, foster parenting and other examples of diverse family settings. These Practice Principles include but are not limited to the role of the family, partnerships with educators, and the role of community, child identity, equity and diversity.

The role of family

An overall assessment of the role of families in this policy document can be summed up in one sentence: "families are children's first and most important educators" (DEECD, 2009, p. 7). This view underpins the Minister's message in the foreword, the statements on vision and purpose, practice principles, early years learning and development outcomes, and children's transitions: the conclusion highlights families as a central influence to the growth, development and education of children. This view of families originates from an ecological model of child development designed by Bronfenbrenner (1979). In his model, the child is central to development, with concentric circles that expand outwards to define the level of influence from inwards to outwards and outwards to inwards. First and foremost, the family has the greatest impact on the child, followed by friendship and informal networks, the broader community, formal networks and formal services and lastly, the Government and external environmental influences, such as policy, economics and social impacts (p. 43). These types of influences are represented in Figure 5.2.

The influence of this model is evident throughout the Victorian policy document; the use of inclusive language gives a strong moral imperative that early childhood educators must "ensure that the interests, abilities and culture of every child and their family are understood, valued and respected (DEECD, 2009). In the section named Collaborative Practice, family-centred practice emphasises the view that the family plays a "pivotal role" in children's learning and development as educators "actively engage families and children in planning children's learning and development" (p. 10).

Family partnerships with educators

Leading on from the importance of family in a child's early education, the VEY-LDF clearly stipulates that responsive communication and effective learning develop through strong partnerships between families and educators (DEECD, 2009). Strong partnerships are built upon relationships that are described as dignified, respectful, culturally responsive, caring and nurturing (DEECD, 2009). The achieved outcome of genuine partnerships should "expand children's knowledge and understanding of the world and promote their health, safety and wellbeing" (p. 9).

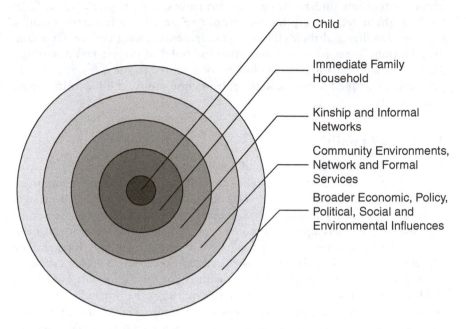

Child

Immediate Family
Household

Kinship and Informal
Networks

Community Environments,
Network and Formal
Services

Broader Economic, Policy,
Political, Social and
Environmental Influences

Figure 5.2 The ecological model of child development

Source: Adapted from the Victorian Early Years Learning and Development Framework (Victorian Government: Department of Education and Training, 2016).

The first practice principle features *family-centred practice*, and it is evident throughout the description of this principle that families are meant to be interwoven in the decisions, planning, feedback and cultural understanding of programming, especially when partnerships are reciprocal, warm and authentic (DEECD, 2009). Practice Principle three, *high expectations for every child*, provides a broader perspective of partnerships, encouraging educators to "work with families to support children's learning and development at home and in the community" (p. 10). Furthermore, Practice Principle five, *respectful relationships and responsive engagement*, infers that interactions are pivotal in creating an understanding of the individual child to ensure that the planning of programs and environments promote the growth of capacity, within a culturally responsive, meaningful educational experience (DEECD, 2009). Lastly, Practice Principle seven, *assessment for learning and development*, acknowledges the key role of families and enlists the assistance of families in developing a holistic view when contributing to assessment to expand on knowledge of the child's experiences, family values, beliefs and related family goals (DEECD, 2009).

The idea of partnerships between families and educators is an integral concept throughout the practice principles. The seriousness with which this is regarded is emphasised across multiple principles, which stipulate that without genuine partnerships, educators, programs and even child development will not meet the expected standards (DEECD, 2009). In such a policy context, it is notable that same-sex families are not specifically addressed in this framework.

Role of community

All families are part of a greater community, and the VEYLDF defines a community as any "social or cultural groups or networks that share a common purpose, heritage, rights and responsibilities and/or other bonds" (DEECD, 2009, p. 51). One of the measures in Practice Principle seven, *assessment for learning and development*, recognises the cultural importance and cultural knowledge connected to children's communities and supports this awareness through the way in which children learn and develop (DEECD, 2009). Outcome one, *children have a strong sense of identity*, underlines that children learn explicitly and develop agency through engaging with and expressing unique elements of their community (DEECD, 2009). The core value underpinning outcome two, *children are connected with and contribute to their world*, states, "children develop a sense of belonging to groups and communities and an understanding of the reciprocal rights and responsibilities necessary for active civic participation" (p. 21). These values are strong indicators of how we should perform in an equitable community and can be interpreted as normative aspirations throughout society.

Child identity and reflection of normative aspirations within society

The VEYLDF refers to child identity frequently within both the practice principles and the outcomes; the VEYLDF includes the claim that child identity is evident when children readily demonstrate growth formed through experience, learning and throughout personal assessment and reflection upon their own learning. The majority of this early learning and influence over identity occurs in the early years during the unique connections with family and community (DEECD, 2009). Outcome one, *children have a strong sense of identity*, even ascertains the power and promotion of child identity. Identity correlates with solid relationships and entitles a "strong sense of self" which in turn mirrors a stable connection to community. Confidence is embodied through challenge, collaboration, reflection, humility, friendship, social awareness, cultural identity and the ability to express home language (DEECD, 2009). Educators are advised that "respect for diversity assists children to begin to appreciate the similarities and differences between individual and groups, including different cultural groups" (p. 18). Child identity highlights the acceptance of diversity and strengthens the need to perform equitable processes in being mindful of the child and their developing identity. In response to these policy principles regarding identity, it is important to highlight the specific questions for this chapter. I believe it is vital to examine if child identity issues are enacted in relation to the children from diverse families and specifically, same-sex families, and whether such children are receiving the same rights-based treatment as those from heterosexual families. All children have a right for their family identity to be respected, and this should not be hindered by the beliefs and assumptions of educators or anyone else in the early learning community.

Equity and diversity

As noted above, equity and diversity are core themes interwoven across the practice principles and outcomes, indicating that these are intended to govern attitude, practice, planning and family relations. The vision and purpose of the VEYLDF states, "families and communities in which children live are diverse" (DEECD, 2009, p. 7). Practice Principle four, *equity* and *diversity*, highlights this principle by stating, "children's personal, family and cultural histories shape their learning and development" (p. 11). This statement develops and promotes child learning when educators celebrate children's culture, their home language and identification of required intervention. In addition, a child's sense of identity, place and their contribution to sustainability all resound to the positive practice of embracing equity and diversity practices (DEECD, 2009).

Diverse families and early intervention

The lack of identity for diverse families does affect the respectful delivery of programmes in mainstream early childhood settings. These are credible implications for the Practice of Educators. Consider mainstream settings and services, and then shift your focus to consider the implications for settings such as presenting diverse families in the programming and funding of early intervention services, and the direct correlation with universal services, such as maternal health services, playgroups, child care and preschool, which are all essentially preventative interventions and/or social supports which are not therapy derived (Moore, McDonald, Robinson, Goldfeld, West, & Oberklaid, 2014). If we struggle to present diverse families in mainstream settings, how would this affect our diverse families interacting with the additional services in the early intervention sector?

Whilst Australia is mandated from a legal perspective to provide inclusive education for children with disabilities, this access and participation do not apply to child care (Sukkar, 2013). It is fair to state that the first National Quality Framework supports the inclusion of children with disabilities both from a "theoretical and philosophical foundation for respecting diversity and acting for equity and inclusion for all children in Early Childhood Education and Care programs" (p. 99). If diverse families are not represented in their significant and unique forms, then "respecting diversity" and children with a disability may indeed contribute another layer of complexity for diverse families accessing support through early intervention and early childhood education services. This is especially in regard to the lack of mandated inclusivity for children with disabilities, coupled with a broad terminology of "diverse" families in the early years frameworks. Some critics may even view the approach to disability and diverse families as tokenistic and problematic as the policy is underpinned within a philosophical stance and the delivery of early childhood intervention services critically lacks consistency in deliverable service and funds (Sukkar, 2013; Kemp & Hayes, 2005).

The provision of funding across Australia relies predominantly on formal diagnosis. When funded, a family's choice of where to utilise this funding is determined by parents/caregivers alongside the organisation coordinating these services. However, options are complex with little support across systems which are varied, intricate and often lacking in consistent communication with one another (Sukkar, 2013). Rolfe (2004) reiterates that the consistency of care is prime for young children with the caregiving styles of families to be valued, incorporated and engrained in professional interactions, education and support services. To provide this optimal support, diverse families must be considered and represented in this approach. A system which relies heavily on the choice and organisation capabilities of unique families may be vulnerable as supports are limited and consistency of support and funding are sporadic at best. If this is the broad picture across our States and Territories, the additional pressure of explaining one's story and the time committed to the embroiled paperwork may even present our diverse families with an overload of information, contemplation and confusion during what could be a period of uncertainty and overwhelming information exchange.

Implications for educators across the early years

Educators in the early years have qualifications; they are deemed as professionals in education and hold significant knowledge to support their practice. As a minimum, a Certificate III is required to work in an early years service. To become a programme leader requires greater responsibility in areas associated with practice, planning, teamwork, family and community engagement and greater knowledge attached to theory, research and overall experience. This type of role requires a Diploma of Children's Services (or a similar Diploma). To become an early childhood teacher, one must obtain a Bachelor of Early Childhood Education, or similar relevant degree as articulated by the Australian Children's Education and Care Quality Authority (Australian Children's Education and Care Quality Authority, n.d). Barriers in services and the connection to diverse families can be challenging. Graduates are armed with skills and some practical experience prior to entering the sector but the reality of working with families is fragmented, as there is not enough experience of working with diverse families. Clearly, diverse families are not specifically articulated within early childhood policy, or within the education of our graduates in their chosen studies within the early years.

For example, sexuality and same-sex families are not presented adequately in early years education or within the experiences provided during educational practice and supports leading up to graduation. Units which not only focus on family-centred practice but also use examples of diverse family units across Australia would provide additional context to students; role-play of possible exchanges with a variety of diverse family examples would allow students to practice their responses in a safe environment that encourages reflective practice. The use of a mentor teacher for graduates in their formative teaching experiences would assist a supported transition to the challenges one may face in their first years of teaching. Weekly meetings with a mentor teacher and connections to teacher networks in the graduate teacher's area would promote healthy discussion and an exploration of how to approach practice based on real examples provided by teachers who have been in the sector for a substantial time, and who have a proven track record of engaging in reflective and reflexive practice. Perhaps from a federal level of Government, as part of the NQS, teachers who mentor or engage in these specific network groups would need to undergo a formal assessment of their practice, philosophy and programming on the job. A clear link to providing supports, specific policy-related documents that highlight diverse families and a requirement to provide experience with diverse families prior to graduation provide a conclusion to this chapter.

Conclusion

In light of the increased complexity of the meaning of family, this chapter has questioned whether the Australian early childhood sector has enabled diverse families to explore partnerships with early childhood services and educators, or indeed, if there is a culture of "invisibility" in relation to diverse families, particularly same-sex identified families who are yet to enjoy the full political and social support of their identity and meaning, even in our early childhood frameworks.

Families are how they define themselves; families define their values and morals; families depict their truth. Government, society, history, religion and media have their voice about what defines a family. Like Martin Luther King Jr., I have a dream that families can live in peace defined only by what they value; by what their truth is; without judgement; indignation; hate; only justice for their personal truth.

In Australia, "the land of the lucky," our families also deserve access to supports and services that are streamlined, non-confrontational, linked in information (to eradicate the duplication of family information) through a central database online and a federally formatted system to connect funding, accessibility and consistent resourcing channels that are fair and equitable to all.

The early years policy context was used as a background to this chapter to consider the experiences of early years educators who work alongside diverse families. The specific focus of this chapter is the sociological analysis of diverse families in early childhood education. My last questions function as an impetus to examine identity and power relations through questioning: what is the identity of diverse families in early childhood education encompassing the early intervention sector? and how do the power relations affect both diverse families and educators in early childhood? The structure of investigating early childhood settings and educators is centred on how early childhood systems and educators enact policy in relation to the inclusion of families and the recognition of difference, or perceived difference. More specifically, I challenge the early childhood sector to explore the perceptions, experience and challenges that face diverse families, particularly same-sex families within the programs implemented in early childhood educational settings by providing programs that represent diverse families; facilitating sincere group discussions with children about diverse family groups; informative and meaningful program planning which is inclusive of all families; the ability to respond to parents who may be confronted by the diverse family representations through the educator articulating their practice, connecting to their centre philosophy and relevant research knowledge.

The way in which diverse families navigate the systems they are in will perpetuate and generate discussion that involves Government systems, early childhood policy, the practice of educators, the educator's "lived" experience, and the complexity of the early childhood environment. Educators can support change through reflective and reflexive practice that generates a coherent supportive program that mirrors the diversity of families in our national identity.

Implications for policy and practice

As articulated across this chapter, there are some broad and specific considerations and suggestions for policy and practice in the realm of the representation and support for diverse families. Greater research is building in relation to the benefits of the social structures of diverse families, but this information must be constantly reflected in our early childhood frameworks with a need to update the material/examples in these frameworks every few years.

Policy frameworks must provide clear definitions of "diverse" families. The interpretation of "diverse" is currently dependent on the educator's own knowledge and experiences to date. To eradicate assumptions of family, educators and children alike would benefit from understanding the variety of "diverse" families across Australia.

Mentor teacher programs would enable graduate teachers to reflect and share experience with a well-rounded professional who has been assessed by the Australian Children's Education and Care Quality Authority (ACEQA) as providing appropriate support to practice and programming. Early learning educator networks would also provide educators with a platform to discuss their relations with families with strength-based educators who contribute positively in professionally performing networks.

Mandatory units at university must also provide key knowledge associated with family-centred practice and the types of families/diverse family units that students will be interacting with on a daily basis. Practical units must also include interviews with mentor teachers about the diverse family experiences and respectful strategies to support diverse families. The Federal framework and any State-aligned framework would be easier to access (in retaining knowledge) if case studies relating to diverse families are presented in these specified documents.

Lastly, the sociological impacts of diverse families are far reaching when our Government of the day does not support diverse family units through marriage equality for same-sex couples. Across 20 countries same-sex marriage has been legalised, including the Netherlands, Belgium, Spain, Canada, South Africa,

Norway, Sweden, Portugal, Iceland, Argentina, Denmark, Brazil, France, Uruguay, New Zealand, the United Kingdom, Luxembourg, Finland, Ireland and the United States (Freedom to Marry, 2015).

Change filters down from good leadership. If the elected Liberal Government in Australia does not support the right for same-sex couples to marry, a distinct message is formulated whereby our nation is given a false message about families that include same-sex couples. Tanya Plibersek from the Labour opposition articulated her concerns over this matter to the public on the 12th of August 2015, that regardless of the liberal and national parties opting for a "no" vote and instead the offer of a plebiscite or referendum to vote for marriage equality the communication was still clear,

> *a lot of people would have heard that refusal to have a vote on this issue as a message to gay and lesbian Australians that they're second-class citizens and that their relationships are second-class relationships and I don't want that sentiment to stand in the Australian community. I want same-sex-attracted teenagers to understand that their government and their nation accepts them as they are, for who they are.*

(Plibersek, 2015)

Tanya Plibersek also mentioned on Wednesday 12th of August to journalists outside Parliament and within Parliament that "children who have two Mums or two Dads are just fine" and that there are many people in Australia that "don't support discrimination of any group in our community" (Plibersek, 2015). For families who have defined themselves as a same-sex family and have a child with a disability and/or additional need, not only are they confronted with the lack of funding in resources and support in the early intervention sector (Sukkar, 2011), in addition, the lack of acknowledgement of their family and ability to enjoy a legalised marriage adds to the stressors of the family unit. In our current political climate, the Prime Minister and his Government are yet to accept diverse families from a legal and political standpoint. Our families and children in the present and future deserve acceptance. One day you or I may read the last section of this chapter and be genuinely surprised at the events discussed here. For now, this is the reality and one which the Australian community will continue to debate. For our children we need to embrace diversity, which is rich across Australia. Whilst there is much work to be done across early childhood and policy, the shifting perception of family will one day evolve to diversity being embraced as the "norm."

References

Australian Children's Education and Care Quality Authority. (n.d). *Educator qualifications*. Retrieved from http://www.acecqa.gov.au/educators-and-providers1/qualifications

Australian Government: Department of Education and Training. (2009). *Belonging, Being and Becoming: The Early Years Learning Framework for Australia*. Retrieved from https://docs.education.gov.au/documents/belonging-being-becoming- early-years-learning-framework-australia

Australian Institute of Family Studies. (n.d). *Family facts and figures: Australian families.* Retrieved from https://www3.aifs.gov.au/institute/info/charts/family structure/index.html#ftype2011

Australian Institute of Family Studies. (n.d). *Family facts and figures glossary.* Retrieved from https://www3.aifs.gov.au/institute/info/charts/glossary.html

Brickman, P., Rabinowitz, V. C., Karuza, J., Jr., Coates, D., Cohn, E., & Kidder, L. (1982). Models of helping and coping. *American Psychologist, 37*, 368–384.

Bronfenbrenner, U. (1975). Is early intervention effective? In B. Z. Friedlander, G. M. Sterritt, & G. E. Kirk (Eds.), *Exceptional infant: Vol. 3. Assessment and intervention* (pp. 449–475). New York: Brunner/Mazel.

Bronfenbrenner, U. (1979). *The ecology of human development: Experiments by nature and design.* Cambridge, MA: Harvard University Press.

Becker, A. (2012). What's marriage (and family) got to do with it? Support for same-sex marriage, legal unions, and gay and lesbian couples raising children. *Social Science Quarterly, 93*(4), 1007–1029. doi:10.1111/j.1540-6237.2012.00844.x

Carlson, M., & Berger, L. (2013). What kids fet from parents: Packages of parental involvement across complex family forms. *Social Service Review, 87*(2), 213–249.

Carpenter, B. (2002). *The family context community and society. Complex needs.* Retrieved from http://www.ssatuk.co.uk/ssat/support/sen/resources-and-documents/complex-needs-booklet-series/

Carpenter, B. (2012). *Talking to families; listening to families.* Retrieved from www.complexneeds.org.uk

Christian, L. G. (2006). Understanding families: Applying family systems theory to early childhood practice. *Young Children, 61*(1), 12–20.

Davies, C., & Robinson, K. H. (2013). Reconceptualising family: Negotiating sexuality in a governmental climate of neoliberalism. *Contemporary Issues in Early Childhood, 14*(1), 39–53. Retrieved from http://dx.doi.org/10.2304/ciec.2013.14.1.39

Davies, C., & Semann, A. (2013). In conversation with Jonathan Silin. *Contemporary Issues in Early Childhood, 14*(1), 1–7.

Department of Education and Early Childhood Development. (2009). *Victorian Early Years Learning and Development Framework.* East Melbourne: Early Childhood Strategy Division Department of Education and Early Childhood Development Victorian Curriculum and Assessment Authority.

Department of Education and Training. (2009). *Victorian Early Years Learning and Development Framework.* East Melbourne: Early Childhood Strategy Division Department of Education and Training and Early Childhood Development Victorian Curriculum and Assessment Authority.

De Vaus, E. (2009). *Diversity and change in Australian families: Statistical profiles.* Retrieved from https://aifs.gov.au/sites/default/files/publication-documents/DiversityAndChange.pdf

Dunst, C. J., & Trivette, C. M. (2009). Capacity-building family-systems intervention practices. *Journal of Family Social Work, 12*, 119–143.

Freedom to Marry. (2015). *The freedom to marry internationally.* Retrieved from http://www.freedomtomarry.org/landscape/entry/c/international

Gennetian, L. (2005). One or two parents? Half or step siblings? The effect of family structure on young children's achievement. *Journal of Population Economics, 18*, 415–436. doi:10.1007/s00148-004-0215-0

Gottlieb, B. H. (1981). *Social networks and social support*. Beverly Hills, CA: Sage.

IVF Australia. (2015). *IVF Treatment: What Is IVF?* Retrieved from http://ivf.com. au/fertility-treatment/ivf-treatment#what-is-ivf-

Kemp, C., & Hayes, A. (2005). Early intervention in Australia: The challenge of systems implementation. In M. Guralnick (Ed.), *The developmental systems approach to early intervention* (pp. 401–423). Baltimore, MD: Paul H. Brookes.

Livermore, M. (2012a). Families: Fundamental concepts. *Hot Topics: Legal Issues in Plain Language, 82*, 2–8.

Livermore, M. (2012b). Families: Government and family. *Legal Issues in Plain Language, 82*, 1.

McLanahan, S., & Beck, A. (2010). Parental relationships in fragile families. *The Future of Children, 20*(2), 17–37.

Moore, T. G., McDonald, M., Robinson, R., Goldfeld, S., West, S., & Oberklaid, F. (2014). *Childcare and early childhood learning: Response to the productivity commission's inquiry into childcare and early childhood learning*. Parkville, Victoria: Centre for Community Child Health, Murdoch Childrens Research Institute, The Royal Children's Hospital.

National Disability Insurance Scheme. (2015). *National disability insurance scheme website*. Retrieved from http://www.ndis.gov.au/about-us

Plibersek, T. (2015). *Marriage equality*. Retrieved from http://www.tanyaplibersek.com/transcripts

Qu, L., & Weston, R. (2013). *Austrian households and families*. Retrieved from https://aifs.gov.au/sites/default/files/publication-documents/aft4.pdf

Rappaport, J. (1981). In praise of paradox: A social policy of empowerment over prevention. *American Journal of Community Psychology, 9*(1), 1–25.

Rutcliff, N., & Hunt, G. (2009). Building teacher-family partnerships the role of teacher preparation programs. *Education, 129*(3), 495–505.

Robinson, E. (2009). Refining our understanding of family relationships. *Family Matters, 82*, 5–7.

Robinson, K. H., & Diaz, C. J. (2006). *Diversity and difference in early childhood education*. Maidenhead: Open University Press.

Rolfe, S. (2004). *Rethinking attachment for early childhood practice*. Crows Nest: Allen & Unwin.

Sewell, T. (2012). Are we adequately preparing teachers to partner with families? *Early Childhood Education Journal, 40*, 259–263. doi:10.1007/s10643-011-0503-8

Jonathan, G. S. (1995). *Sex death and the education of children: Our passion for ignorance in the age of AIDS*. New York: Teachers College Press.

Silverstein, L., & Auerbach, C. (2006). Valuing connection over disconnection: Response to Perlesz. *Journal of Feminist Family Therapy, 18*(4), 89–92.

Skattebol, J., & Ferfolja, T. (2007). Voices from an enclave Lesbian mothers' experiences of child care. *Australian Journal of Early Childhood, 32*(1), 10–18.

Stinnett, N., & DeFrain, J. (1985). *Secrets of strong families*. Boston, MA: Little, Brown.

Sukkar, H. (2011). *The road map to building new dreams: Raising a child with developmental delay or disability*. Doctorate, Melbourne Graduate School of Education, The University of Melbourne.

Sukkar, H. (2013). Early childhood intervention: An Australian perspective. *Infants & Young Children, 26*(2), 94–110.

Thevenon, O., & Luci, A. (2012). Reconciling work, family and child outcomes: What implications for family support policies? *Population Research and Policy Review, 31*(6), 855–882. doi:10.1007/s11113-012-9254-5

United Nations. (1990). Convention on the rights of the child. Retrieved from http://www.unicef.org.au/Upload/UNICEF/Media/Our%20work/childfriendly crc.pdf

Weston, R., & Qu, L. (2014). Trends in family functions, forms and functioning. Essential issues for policy development and legislation, *Family Matters, 95*, 76–84.

Winton P. J. (1990). Promoting a normalizing approach to families: Integrating theory with practice. *Topics in Early Childhood Special Education, 1*(2), 90–103.

6 Reimagining family partnerships

Shifting practice from a focus on disadvantage to engagement and empowerment

Anne Kennedy

This chapter aims to deepen understanding of the impact of significant disadvantage and risk factors on families with young children and how this might affect their capacity and or willingness to participate in universal education and care services. The chapter includes descriptions of practical strategies to support educators responding ethically to families and children living with complex and often intergenerational disadvantage and risk factors. At the heart of this chapter lies a belief that reimagining partnerships with families recognises that they are the most important people in their children's lives. Through engaging with and empowering families and children, educators acknowledge them as active holders of rights.

Contemporary contexts for families and children

Australian society experiences significant and continuous social, economic, and cultural changes. These changes impact on the life experiences and life chances of children and families and on education and care services, including school-age care programs, long day care, family day care, and preschools. Over the past decade there have been identified increases in:

- domestic violence,
- child protection reports,
- homelessness for families with children,
- the cost of housing and rental costs,
- addiction or abuse of alcohol and drugs,
- mental health diagnoses,
- settlement of refugee families, and
- the number of women with young children who are working.

(Australian Council of Social Services, 2014; Australian Bureau of Statistics, 2012; Australian Institute of Health and Wellbeing, 2014; Refugee Council of Australia, 2013)

Snapshot of poverty in Australia

The rise in the number of families living below or close to the poverty line provides a context for significant disadvantage and risk. The Australian Council of Social Services (ACOSS, 2014) defines poverty as being in receipt of 50% of the median income level, which is around $AU640 per week for a single parent with two children. ACOSS statistics highlight additional contexts for poverty in Australia:

- 17.7% (603,000) of children live below the poverty line.
- 13.8% of people in capital cities live below the poverty line with slightly higher rates in rural communities.
- Over 30% of people living below the poverty line are working and are not on social security benefits.

Research and statistical data also show that people from particular demographic categories are at much higher risk for living below the poverty line. Single parents, people with disabilities, refugees, and Aboriginal and Torres Strait Islander people are included in the "at greater risk" for poverty category.

Risk factors for families and children interact with each other in complex ways to increase the challenges people experience in their daily lives. For example, domestic violence increases the risk of homelessness, especially for women and children, and poverty increases a range of health risks. The combination of several significant risk factors such as poverty, homelessness and mental illness impacts on people's capacity to participate in their community, socially, economically or educationally. Evidence suggests that families and children with the most complex risk factors are less likely to participate in universal services such as preschool or child care (Centre for Community Child Health, 2010).

Research also shows that protective factors can reduce the negative impact of risk factors. Protective factors for a child at risk might include extended family support, engagement in a quality education and care setting, and access to services such as a maternal and child health nurse or a family-focused general practitioner (Walker et al., 2011).

The statistical data and research evidence on the contexts that impact on the lives of children and families, and especially the contexts related to risk factors, reveal implications for governments, services, and professionals. The complexity and inter-connectedness of these risk factors requires well-resourced, collaborative, integrated response systems and ways of working. As the data indicate, a "one size fits all" or a siloed approach by professionals will not reduce entrenched or intergenerational disadvantage and vulnerability. A further implication from the statistical evidence is the need for educators to recognise the diversity of families and children who may be at risk. Mental health or domestic violence issues, for example, occur within families from across the economic spectrum.

Research foundations and theoretical contexts

Research evidence and three theoretical frameworks inform the discussion in this chapter:

1   feminist, "ethics of care" theories and frameworks (Tronto, 1993; Nussbaum, 1999),
2   principles of family-centred practice (Allen & Petr, 1998; Dunst, 2002), and
3   social ecology theory (Bronfenbrenner, 1979, 2005).

The common threads of respect for human rights; commitment to equity and redressing disadvantage; the importance of relationships; and responsiveness to the rights, agency, choices and strengths within families, children and communities are evident in the theoretical informants for this chapter. These connecting threads are powerful theories for educators interested in working in ethical ways with families, children and communities (Moss, 2014).

Bronfenbrenner's social ecology model (1979, 2005) supports understanding the interconnectedness and interdependency between individuals, families, communities and the settings or systems in which they live or work and with the wider society. The model identifies how different systems or settings both influence and are influenced by people over time. As Hill and Nichols (2004) explain:

> *Systems operate on a number of levels: there are the immediate settings in which a person is situated, termed 'micro-systems,' such as the family, the neighbourhood and the school; there are larger multi-site institutions such as churches and corporations; and there are even broader and less tangible groupings of knowledge and practices such as cultures and ideologies* (macro-systems).
>
> (p. 164)

The social ecology model acknowledges the interrelationship between different settings in which a child or family participates and the importance of the *quality* of the interrelationships and interconnectedness between different settings in the micro-system. If the interrelationship between a family and settings such as a school or a child care centre is respectful and based on a collaborative partnership approach, the quality of the connection is high and positive outcomes for a family, child and educators are more likely to be achieved (La Placa & Corlyon, 2014; Scott, 2013).

The principles of "family centred practice" advanced by Allen and Petr (1998) and Dunst (2002) provide a further layer of understanding in relation to how and why professionals engage with families and children within the different settings or systems identified by Bronfenbrenner (Espe-Sherwindt, 2008). The four core principles of family centred practice identified by Allen and Petr are:

1   the centrality of the family as the unit of attention,
2   an emphasis on maximising family choice,

3 a strengths rather than a deficits perspective, and
4 cultural sensitivity.

Similar family-centred practice principles and values are evident in the Principles and Practices of the national *Belonging, Being and Becoming: The Early Years Learning Framework for Australia* (Department of Education, Employment and Workplace Relations, 2009; EYLF 2009) and the *My Time Our Place: Framework for School Age Care* (DEEWR, FSAC, 2011). These include the practice of *cultural competence* and the principles of *secure, respectful and reciprocal relationships; partnerships; high expectations and equity and respect for diversity*, which resonate with the principles of family-centred practice.

Feminist theories on the "ethics of care" also focus on the quality of connections between the different systems or settings where children and families participate. Nussbaum's (1999) argument on human rights and our obligations to each other, for example, connects with the principles of family-centred practice and the social ecology model:

> *But the goal should always be to put people in a position of agency and choice, not to push them into functioning in ways deemed desirable. I argue that this is no mere parochial Western ideology but expresses the joy most people have in using their own bodies and minds.*

(p. 11)

In a similar way, Tronto's theorising on the "ethics of care" defines caring as a "habit of mind" combined with practical acts of caring that are attentive, responsible, competent and responsive to the other and the particular contexts of their lives (1993). Caring relationships in this approach are not like a warm blanket that surrounds others or a mere backdrop to the work of educators (Malaguzzi, 1993). Ethical caring demands a willingness to recognise the centrality of building relationships that respect and respond to difference and diversity in non-judgemental and responsive ways.

The principle of respecting people's agency, choices and difference is challenging for professionals working with families and children living with complex risk factors. Finding ways to support families and children, using our professional expertise without diminishing the expertise and authority of families and children, requires deep sensitivity to the ethics of our work (Moss, 2014).

Terminology

This chapter uses the terms "vulnerable," "disadvantaged" and "at risk" to describe the life contexts for certain children and their families. Vulnerability and disadvantage are not the entire story for a child, just as the term "disability" is not the entire story for some children. Every child and family has agency, strengths and interests that are important aspects of their story and lives. In order to recognise a more holistic, positive and accurate image for children and families, this chapter does not refer to "vulnerable children" or "at risk children," but rather, talks about children living with risk factors, disadvantage or with vulnerabilities. In using these terms, it is important to note that how we name people influences how we interact, treat and respond to them in our practice. Using the term "disadvantaged children" may inadvertently limit our expectations for them (Dahlberg, Moss, & Pence, 1999).

Practice strategies from the education and care sector

A range of ethical strategies to support meaningful engagement and partnerships with children and families living with significant and complex risk factors is identified through ongoing conversations with several education and care services. Many of the children in these services are known, or are at risk of being known, to child protection services. Poverty, refugee status, unemployment, addiction, mental health problems and homelessness further complicate these families' lives.

Evidence indicates that participation and engagement in education and care settings are less likely or less regular for children living with significant disadvantage or vulnerabilities (Centre for Community Child Health, 2010). While affordability and availability of places are relevant to this matter, there are other issues to consider. Families living with multiple complexities or risks may find an affordable place for their children, but the setting might not offer the welcome and support necessary for their continued participation and engagement. Unless families feel a sense of belonging and welcome, they are likely to disengage or have irregular attendance (La Placa & Corlyon, 2014).

Process matters of quality focus on relationships, pedagogy, partnerships and collaboration (Huntsman, 2008). These processes link to the quality standards in the Australian National Quality Standards (Australian Children's Education and Care Quality Authority, NQS, 2011) and the learning frameworks. The following theoretically and research-informed engagement strategies include practices in relation to children, families, pedagogy, educators and other professionals.

Primary carer approach

A misunderstood and under-utilised strategy for supporting children and families is to use a primary carer or primary contact approach. This approach recognises that entering a new service can be overwhelming for a child and family, especially when a family is unsure or defensive because of previous negative experiences with other organisations, agencies or institutions. The primary carer approach aims to:

- reduce the number of staff that families develop trusting relationships with during the settling-in phase especially,
- support a partnership with families in educating and caring for their child, and
- ensure that every child and family is acknowledged and supported.

As a primary carer, an educator takes special responsibility for:

- monitoring and supporting the child and family orientation and transition into the setting process,
- meeting with the family regularly to identify shared aspirations or goals and to develop shared strategies to support those goals,
- talking with families on how the strategies are working in the centre and at home, and
- taking main responsibility for daily care practices, such as nappy changing or toileting, especially during the transition period.

Adopting a primary carer approach does not mean that educators are only aware of or support their primary care children and families. Every staff member is expected to be supportive of all the children and families they encounter each day. This expectation is important because educators working different shifts or taking holidays, for example, would not be available for their primary care children. One strategy to support educators knowing about the children and families in the centre is to have focused discussions about a child's learning, development and wellbeing with the primary carer leading the discussion. Other educators contribute their perspectives to support the development of shared understandings and action plans for each child.

Focusing on family strengths

The following is an example of focusing on family strengths implemented in one setting. Margaret, an experienced coordinator of a child care centre in what is described as a 'highly disadvantaged' community, reflects on working with families using a strengths-based approach that nurtures respectful relationships:

> *We try to remain open-minded and to suspend judgements. We don't assume or presume or pre-judge which is difficult when family values, priorities and practices are different from your own. Educators need to be well informed about keeping their judgements in check so that we build trusting relationships with every family. We focus on family strengths including their resilience, adaptability and capacity to recognise genuineness and authenticity in our relationships and interactions with them. Small things are praised and affirmed.*

This example also reinforces the importance of understanding your own values, beliefs and life experiences and how they influence the way you respond to families and children. Margaret reminds us about not making assumptions or being judgemental about a parent's literacy skills, for example:

> *We have to remember to consider a parent's literacy levels. For example, we don't just talk about the sign in book and where it is located. I might go to the book and put my finger on the child's printed name and say this is where you sign your*

child in each day. We watch for clues about a parent's capacity to write their name and the time of departure and sometimes I will say, 'Would you like me to sign in for you?'

Education and care services committed to the ethics of care and family-centred practice hold high expectations for every family and child by valuing and believing in every child and family's strengths and capabilities. High expectations are also about equity and equal opportunity matters. Every child and family has the right to access and participate in education and care services (equal opportunity), and some will require additional support to enable their access and participation (equity).

Parent-professional partnerships

Families have a right as the most important people in their children's lives to be respected, consulted and supported. The Early Years Learning Framework (2009) talks about "genuine partnerships" with families where we value each other's knowledge, roles, experiences, perspectives and contributions. Shifting from viewing parents as 'helpers' or the beneficiaries of our niceness, to a position of sharing power with them as partners in educating and caring for children requires serious thinking and responsive actions. Having conversations with families about difficult issues is easier if educators have established respectful partnerships with them. As one educator explains:

> *The parents we work with rarely get praise from others. We look for positives and give praise. Sometimes we have to talk about issues that arise in their parenting that are not in children's best interests. If a child arrives at the centre in their night nappy several times in a week, we will talk with the parent about this by asking how we can support them to change this practice. Because we build respectful relationships with parents from enrolment, we can have these types of conversations because they trust us, and they know we always acknowledge good aspects of their parenting.*

Communicating with families

Rinaldi (2006) reminds us that genuine and meaningful partnerships require new tools (how we communicate), new content (what we communicate about), and new methods (where and when we meet to communicate). Staff working with families in the Pen Green Centre in the United Kingdom use communication strategies to support families feeling valued, equal and active partners in their children's learning (Whalley, 2006). Staff and families make, watch and discuss video clips of children's play in the centre or at home in order to develop shared learning and development intentions and practices.

Home visits at the family's invitation also support new ways of communicating and building partnerships. For example, an educator working in a child care centre explained how she builds trust and learns more about a family, and they about her, through visiting families in their home. Home visits with one family included cooking dinner with the parent and then sharing the meal with her and the children. On other visits, the educator brought games they could play together or a video to watch with the children and their parent. A positive outcome from these visits is the strengthening of relationships between the children and the parent from the shared enjoyment of home based experiences.

Reducing risks for families and children

Partnerships with families living with complex issues often require services to respond to urgent problems, as Margaret identifies:

> *Sometimes we are responding to urgent needs. We have to be prepared for the urgency involved or that is necessary. Recently three families with two or three children told us that they would be homeless in three weeks' time. We referred the families to housing and welfare agencies in our community and encouraged them to keep bringing the children to the centre as this would support the children through a difficult time of change. I also copied paperwork for them so that they had the necessary information to provide to other agencies.*

Service providers have identified increased risks for children and families when a centre is closed over extended holiday periods. One education and care service has achieved improvements in families' capacity to cope when the service is closed. They use a range of strategies to reduce the risks for families and children including:

- providing families with verbal reminders about the closure for several weeks prior to the holiday period,
- letting families know which local agencies or community services are open over the holiday period, including where food vouchers are available,
- calling local agencies and services and reminding them that families might be needing additional support during the holidays because the centre is closed, and
- letting families know about community services and activities they can access with or for their children such as children's playgrounds in local parks or local vacation care programs.

Intentional pedagogy strategies

> *. . . pedagogy must be understood as 'a relation, a network of obligation,' and the pedagogical relationship is one which requires 'infinite attention to the other.'*
>
> (Brooker, 2009, p. 107)

The national vision for children's lives as being characterised by *"belonging, being and becoming"* (Early Years Learning Framework, 2009, p. 7) underpins pedagogy enacting respect for the uniqueness of and complexities present in children's and families' lives. The framework emphasises that curriculum in education and care settings is enacted from the time of children's arrival to the time of their departure, including daily routines and learning experiences, both planned and spontaneous. A child care centre shows "infinite attention" to children and families through careful attention to child and family transitions into the centre each day, as Kate's reflection reveals:

> *Families and children experience a strong sense of welcome and belonging in the centre. Every day, we convey a purposeful greeting of waiting with pleasure for them and their child to arrive. We are genuine in our welcome, so that families and children get a sense that we really care for them and their child, and that what is being provided is not just a care environment, but also a learning environment. For example, in promoting a sense of belonging for the children we supported them in designing, drawing and sewing of their own cushions which they use every day.*

Kate recognises the importance of knowing the children's interests, strengths and abilities in order to intentionally build on and extend what they know and can do. She makes some interesting observations and practical suggestions.

> *I have found that many of the preschool-aged children we work with have missed out on sensory play experiences as babies and toddlers. They enjoy having regular access to those experiences and they need intentional support to explore sensory materials in basic ways, touching, smelling, or moving things around, for example, before they are ready to progress in how they play and learn with these materials.*
>
> *Language, literacy and concept skills are often delayed, so we are very purposeful in how we plan and support improving children's understandings and skills in these areas of learning. We purposefully focus on experiences that promote learning about everyday living, such as shopping, the days of the week and the sequence of routines such as dressing or meal times and developing shared rules for living and playing together. We believe that every interaction with a child is important. We provide literacy and language enrichment experiences through music, stories, play and conversations. We model clarity in articulation, and we listen carefully and allow unhurried wait times for responses from the children. We model the language of empathy by acknowledging children's feelings – "I know you feel cross when you have to wait" and offering our support – "Would you like me to help you with that?" We also respect a child's right for time away from others or for individual time with one of us.*

Teamwork is necessary when educators are engaged in meaningful conversations with children to extend their thinking and learning, as Kate explains:

> *Teamwork is very important. For example, when one educator is deeply engaged with two children, the other educators respect the importance of this and take*

responsibility for working with the other children. As a team we hope to convey a sense of enjoying learning together with the children and their families.

Focusing on attachment

While all the children have experienced or continue to experience trauma or stress for different reasons, we notice that some of the children are independent in self-help skills and are good observers. We understand those skills might come from the need to be hyper-vigilant to avoid harm or because adults are not always able to meet their physical needs. Being physically and emotionally available to the children for comfort and to support their sense of being safe is important. We sit with them rather than hovering over them as that adds to their anxiousness. When children feel safe, they are ready to explore, play and to enjoy learning with others.

Kate's reflections and practical ideas indicate her understanding of attachment theories and the impact of stress and trauma on children's wellbeing, learning and development. McLean (2014, p. 195) argues for "conceptual clarity and rigour in applying the concept of attachment to the care of vulnerable children." Attachment theories identify different attachment styles and different attachment patterns. Young children filter their life experiences through their sense of safety, the reliability of the adults who care for them and their feelings of self worth (McLean, 2014, p. 197). Attachment with caring others is central to children's sense of safety and their sense of self worth.

The Early Years Learning Framework recognises the importance of attachment in both the Principles and Practices. *Principle 1. Secure, respectful and reciprocal relationships* states, "Babies' first attachments within their families and within other trusting relationships provide them with a secure base for exploration and learning" (Early Years Learning Framework, p. 12). Identifying the type of relationships, environments, routines and pedagogy that supports every child to feel safe, secure and valued is an ethical responsibility for educators.

Supporting educators' wellbeing

Educators working with children and families living with complex risk factors, including trauma or significant disadvantage, often face ongoing challenges in their workplace that require targeted or specific strategies to ensure their wellbeing is not compromised. Research indicates that educators whose wellbeing is compromised or who are depressed themselves are less likely to be emotionally available or attuned to the needs of children and their families. They are also more likely to take stress or sick leave or to leave the service, which impacts on continuity of provision for children and families (Hamre & Pianta, 2004; Morrison, 2007; Shonkoff, 2011).

While vicarious stress or trauma is recognised in the welfare sector in particular, it is not widely understood in the education and care sector. Recognising the nature of vicarious stress or trauma and its impact on staff is an important issue for management and leadership teams working in the education and care sector. Vicarious stress or trauma is a normal response to the impact of working constantly and closely with children and families who are traumatised and stressed by their life experiences. Vicarious stress or trauma impacts on staff mental, physical and emotional wellbeing (Morrison, 2007).

Research and evidence-based practice identify organisational and personal or self-care strategies to support the management of vicarious stress and trauma (Bell, Kulkarni, & Dalton, 2003; Morrison, 2007). Self-care strategies, including regular exercise, maintaining outside interests or hobbies and debriefing with trusted others, can support educators in managing their stress levels at work.

Organisational strategies, including providing staff with regular access to qualified reflective supervisors for debriefing and support, building a culture of peer support in the service and providing ongoing professional learning on related topics to increase the shared and individual professional knowledge base, are important practices. Margaret, a coordinator of a child care centre, comments on how she recognises and responds to stress in staff:

> As the coordinator, I support staff to recognise there are limits to what the centre can do and provide. We do what we can and we also need to have a break, to rest and recover from our complex work during the holiday period.

Regular staff meetings with a focused agenda and respect for every member's contribution support reflection, reviewing and changing practice in response to shared discussion on significant issues.

Collaborative practice strategies

Education and care services engaging with families and children living with significant risk and disadvantage understand the value of collaborating with families, other professionals, agencies and community members. They recognise that some families and children require more comprehensive and coordinated support networks and services. The principles of family-centred practice and inclusion affirm the value of collaborative partnership approaches (Dunst, 2002).

The following examples for supporting families and children show collaborative practice in action.

- books available free to families through a community group that collects books from local schools and then distributes them to local education and care services,
- free fresh fruit and vegetables organised by a local church-based charity and made available for families in a child care centre,
- clothing "swap" stall in the foyer maintained by families with support from the centre coordinator,
- a partnership with a local high school and garden nursery supported the development of a vegetable garden in a preschool. Food is grown, harvested, cooked and shared with families,

- appointments for specialist services organised with families and taking place in a community space within a child and family service,
- offering maternal and child health services in an early childhood education and care service through collaboration between management, educators and maternal child health nurses,
- a range of professionals including educators, infant mental health specialists, family support workers, maternal and child health nurses, and inclusion key workers work collaboratively to support families and children,
- supported playgroups provided in an integrated service in collaboration with a playgroup association and service management, and
- bilingual-bicultural workers accessed through a resource agency to support refugee families, children and educators.

These examples of collaborative practice contribute in powerful ways to ensuring every family and child feels welcome, supported and valued. Adopting community-based or professional collaborative approaches to supporting families and children requires commitment and a willingness to take leadership for initiating change.

Implications for practice

There are important implications for educators from the research evidence, theoretical frameworks and practice examples discussed in this chapter.

Uphold commitments to social justice, equity and inclusion. These principles underpin family-centred practice and the ethics of care. Examining your own values and beliefs in connection with issues such as inclusion or equity is an important step in challenging and changing practices that exclude, disadvantage or marginalise particular families and children.

Build professional knowledge and skills through an ongoing commitment to reflecting on the research literature and undertaking professional learning relevant to engaging with families and children living with complex and interrelated risk factors.

Utilise and grow the evidence base through using research evidence and theories to inform your practice and theorising from your practice evidence through reflection and using inquiry-based approaches. This two-way approach strengthens and grows the evidence base and supports transformation of practice and improved outcomes for children and families.

Focus on relationships with children, families and colleagues that are respectful, responsive and reciprocal in order to build mutual trust and to enact power *with* rather than power *over* others.

Facilitate collaboration with other professionals and the local community in recognition of the complexity and challenges of families' lives. Families and children living with vulnerabilities and risks require support that is connected, integrated and collaborative.

Conclusion

As the title for this chapter indicates, reimagining family partnerships by enacting practices that are focused on engaging and empowering families and children requires shifts or changes in thinking and in practice. Educators like Margaret, Kate and others provide inspiration and practical examples of how education and care services can enact that shift. While engaging and empowering families and children is challenging work, it reflects our professionalism and is an expression of our commitment to a more just and inclusive society.

References

Australian Bureau of Statistics (ABS). (2012). *Personal safety, Australia*. Retrieved from www.abs.gov.au

Australian Children's Education and Care Quality Authority. (2011). *Guide to the national quality standard*. ACT, Canberra: Author.

Australian Council of Social Services (ACOSS). (2014). *Poverty in Australia Report*. Retireved from www.acoss.org.au

Australian Institute of Health and Wellbeing. (2014). *Mental health services in brief*. Cat. No. HSE 154. Canberra: AIHW. Retrieved from www.aihw.gov.au

Allen, R., & Petr, C. (1998). Rethinking family centred practice. *American Journal of Orthopsychiatry, 68*(1), 4–16.

Bell, H., Kulkarni, S., & Dalton, L. (2003). Organisational prevention of vicarious trauma. *Families in Society: The Journal of Contemporary Services, 84*(4), 463–470.

Bronfenbrenner, U. (1979). *The ecology of human development: Experiments by nature and design*. Cambridge, MA: Harvard University Press.

Bronfenbrenner, U. (Ed.). (2005). *Making human beings human: Bioecological perspectives on human development*. (Article 1, pp. 3–15). Thousand Oaks, CA: Sage.

Brooker, L. (2009). 'Just like having a best friend'- how babies and toddlers construct relationships with their key workers in nurseries. In T. Papatheodorou & J. Moyles (Eds.), *Learning together in the early years: Exploring relational pedagogy* (pp. 98–108). Abingdon, Oxon: Routledge.

Centre for Community Child Health. (2010). *Policy brief no 18: Engaging marginalised and vulnerable families*. Retrieved from www.rch.org.au/ccchpolicybriefs.cfm

Dahlberg, G., Moss, P., & Pence, A. (1999). *Beyond quality in education and care: Post modern perspectives*. London: Routledge.

Department of Education, Employment and Workforce Relations. (2009). *Belonging, being and becoming: The early years framework for Australia*. ACT, Canberra: Author.

Department of Education, Employment and Workforce Relations. (2011). *My time, our place: Framework for school age care in Australia*. ACT, Canberra: Author.

Dunst, C. J. (2002). Family centred practices: Birth through high school. *The Journal of Special Education, 36*(3), 139–147.

Espe-Sherwindt, M. (2008). Family-centred practice: Collaboration, competency and evidence. *Support for Learning, 23*(3), 136–143.

Hamre, B., & Pianta, R. (2004). Self reported depression in non-familial caregivers: Prevalence and associations with caregiver behaviour in child-care settings. *Early Childhood Research Quarterly, 19*(2), 297–318.

Hill, S., & Nichols, S. (2004). Multiple pathways between home and school literacies. In A. Anning, J. Cullen, & M. Fleer (Eds.), *Early childhood education: Society and culture* (pp. 169–184). London: Sage Publications.

Hunstman, L. (2008). *Determinants of quality in childcare: A review of the research evidence.* NSW Department of Community Services.

La Placa, V., & Corlyon, J. (2014). Barriers to inclusion and successful engagement of parents in mainstream services: Evidence and research. *Journal of Childhood Services, 9*(3), 220–234.

Malaguzzi, L. (1993). For an education based on relationships. *Young Children, 49*(1), 9–12.

McLean, S. (2014). Attachment theory: From concept to supporting children in out-of-home care. In F. Arney & D. Scott (Eds.), *Working with vulnerable families: A partnership approach* (2nd ed., pp. 194–212). New York: Cambridge University Press.

Morrison, Z. (2007). 'Feeling heavy': Vicarious trauma and other issues facing those who work in the sexual assault field. *Australian Institute of Family Studies, ACSSA Wrap*, September, No 4. Retrieved from www.aifs.gov.au/acssa

Moss, P. (2014). *Transformative change and real utopias in early childhood education: A story of democracy, experimentation and potentiality.* Abingdon, Oxon: Routledge.

Nussbaum, M. (1999). *Sex and social justice.* New York/Oxford: Oxford University Press.

Refugee Council of Australia. (2013). *Housing issues for refugee and asylum seekers in Australia: literature review.* Retrieved from www.refugeecouncil.org.au

Rinaldi, C. (2006). *In dialogue with Reggio Emilia: Listening, researching and learning.* London: Routledge.

Scott, D. (2013). Family-centred practice in early childhood settings. In F. Arney & D. Scott (Eds.), *Working with vulnerable families: A partnership approach* (2nd ed., pp. 42–56). Port Melbourne: Cambridge University Press.

Scott, D., Arney, F., & Vimpani, G. (2013). Think child, think family, think community. In F. Arney & D. Scott (Eds.), *Working with vulnerable families: A partnership approach* (2nd ed., pp. 6–23). Port Melbourne: Cambridge University Press.

Shonkoff, J. (2011). Protecting brains, not simply stimulating minds. *Science, 333*, 982–983.

Tronto, J. (1993). *Moral boundaries: A political argument for the ethics of care.* London: Routledge.

Walker, S. P., Wachs, T. D., Grantham-McGregor, S., Black, M., Nelson, C., Huffman, S. L., Baker-Henningham, H., Chang, S. M., Hamadani, J., Lozoff, B., Meeks Gardner, J. M., Powell, C. A., Rahman, A., & Richter, L. (2011). Inequality in early childhood: Risk and protective factors for early childhood development. *The Lancet, 378*(9799), 1325–1338.

Whalley, M. (2006). *Involving parents in their children's learning.* London: Paul Chapman Publishing.

7 Working with families to develop parent-professional partnerships

Implications for professional preparation

Hanan Sukkar

Developing early childhood intervention programs and practices for families raising children with developmental delays or disabilities is well documented in the literature. Many of the articles reviewed by the author in this chapter highlight the relationship between parents and their children and parents and practitioners, which eventually represents a key foundation for successful early childhood intervention strategies (Blue-Banning, Summers, Frankland, Nelson, & Beegle, 2004; Bruder, 2010; Dunst & Dempsey, 2007; Dodd, Saggers, & Wildy, 2009; Espe-Sherwindt, 2008). The importance of partnerships between families and practitioners have been found in many studies and identify that the provision of early support enables families to better engage with their children in a responsive and interactive style (KPMG, 2014). Hence, in delivering family-centred practices, it is essential for practitioners to recognise and understand the diversity in families' needs, priorities and desires, and focus on working with children in the context of the family unit and not as an isolated case of child support. This chapter will aim to explore family-practitioner relationships with a particular focus on early childhood intervention programs and explore the effect of developing positive partnerships on the future trajectory of children with developmental delays or disabilities.

Parent-professional relationships in early childhood intervention

Positive relationships and partnerships can enhance child and family quality of life and other positive outcomes (Bailey et al., 1998; Summers et al., 2007). Research has proven that parents who experience positive and equitable relationships with early childhood intervention practitioners are much more likely to engage in their child's learning and development experiences. They are also more likely to feel valued for their contribution and develop a stronger self-esteem. Parents in well-balanced partnerships have been found to be associated with higher levels of satisfaction, take more action and show more awareness of available resources in the early years, which can effectively support their child's progression. More significantly, parents in positive professional relationships are able to acquire general problem-solving skills to assist them in developing strategies beyond the early year's experiences (Davis, Days, & Bidmead, 2002; Keen, 2007).

Developing effective relationships

Developing effective communication channels and creating positive interpersonal relationships is central in the work of early childhood professionals (Epps & Jackson, 2000). The importance of effective communication cannot be overstated in early childhood intervention programs. Therefore, it is logical that communication with parents and extended family members is jargon free, clear, respectful and honest. Communication with parents must also be based on sincerity and respect and should enable parents and family members to feel good about themselves (Bruder & Dunst, 2005; Christian, 2006; Davis, Day, & Bidmead, 2002; Epps & Jackson, 2000; Keen, 2007; Porter & McKenzie, 2000). This idea is based on the principle that no matter how different families appear to be from the outside, they all have common needs and characteristics; they are just manifested in different ways (Christian, 2006; Porter & McKenzie, 2000).

In constructing a collaborative relationship with families, professionals need to engage in genuine partnerships. This requires relationships to be guided by families' priorities and supported by the practitioners' specialised knowledge base (Owen, Gordon, Frederico, & Cooper, 2002). In practice, this means that early childhood intervention professionals need to recognise and acknowledge family strengths; use family assets as a foundation for improving functioning; involve families in identifying desired goals and courses of action; enhance families' existing capacities; and nurture the development of new skills in a deliberate, conscious manner. Consequently, professionals using family-centred interventions should aim to help families become their own change agents; that is, to promote empowerment by building capacity, competence and confidence in parenting and navigating systems to access resources that address the child and family needs (Dunst, Boyd, Trivette, & Hamby, 2002; Dunst & Dempsey, 2007; Dunst, 2009; Owen, Gordon, Frederico, & Cooper, 2002).

Parent-professional partnerships have been traditionally marked by the presence of a dominant power structure. This is a clinical model of relationships, where professionals have control over the resources and information shared with parents and family members. Professionals also exert the decision-making control and are deemed to have a higher level of competence. Professionals who employ this model also are known to work as clinicians and define parental problems through "diagnoses" and the provision of "treatments" (Turnbull, Turbiville, & Turnbull, 2003). However, recent literature suggests that the concept of relationship and power distribution between professionals and families has changed. Both parents and professionals have become the focus of intervention and the means through which intervention is delivered (Moore, 2007a). This is because parents and professionals each bring useful and complementary strengths into the relationship. Hence, there is a place for both to equally contribute towards the child's needs (Arthur et al., 2005).

Thus, to develop effective and successful parent-professional partnerships, relationships should be based on the assumption that parents and professionals share a common focus; namely, the parent's child. Looking with a clearer lens, one can recognise that professionals bring to the relationship an in-depth understanding and experience of the service system, expertise with professional literature and research and the knowledge of how a particular discipline can contribute to the child's and family's well-being. On the other hand, parents bring to the relationship a strong commitment to their child and family, the knowledge of how to meet the family and individual needs and the expertise and knowledge about their own child's behaviour and development (Fields-Smith & Neuharth-Pritchett, 2009; Moore, 2007b; Porter & McKenzie, 2000).

In Australia, educational enrolment and transition policies and disability discrimination legislation acknowledge and promote the involvement of parents in educational decision-making and educational transitions (Australian Government, 2005). But the question is, what set of skills do professionals need to use with families facing complex challenges in raising a child with developmental delays or disabilities?

Qualifying set of skills

Moore (2007a) suggests that in order to enhance the relationship between parents and professionals, the following set of skills should be considered:

- attunement and engagement,
- responsiveness,
- open communication,
- capacity to manage communication breakdowns,
- emotional openness,
- reflexivity and the ability to manage one's own feelings and emotions,
- empowerment and strength-building,
- moderating stress and challenges, and
- building coherent narratives that assist people in making sense of their lives and experiences.

These explicit traits have been identified in a number of different international studies (e.g., Davis, Day, & Bidmead, 2002; Dunst, 2010; Epps & Jackson, 2000; Guralnick, 2005a; Porter & McKenzie, 2000; Turnbull, Turbiville, & Turnbull, 2003), which affirm that by using the set of interpersonal skills suggested above, professionals can strengthen their relationships with parents and extended families and support children with developmental delays or disabilities. True commitments can be developed between parents and professionals, and expertise from both ends of the spectrum can be celebrated (Davis, Day, & Bidmead, 2002; Porter & McKenzie, 2000). Professionals can also acknowledge parents' control over family choices, and recognise that effective intervention strategies are influenced by their own actions, strengths and their ability to work with families in a capacity-building fashion (Guralnick, 2006; Rix, Paige-Smith, & Jones, 2008).

Therefore, partnership in this context is envisaged as a decision-making process governed by consensus (Dunst & Dempsey, 2007; Dunst, Trivette, & Hamby, 2002; Espe-Sherwindt, 2008). Professionals understand that parents are the senior partners in the relationship, that is, they have the ultimate decision-making authority around their child's development and learning (Dunst & Dempsey, 2007). However, this leads us to ask, what is the exact role of the early childhood intervention professionals in this context?

Role of early childhood intervention professionals

In portraying the role of early childhood intervention professional, the author suggests focusing on four important pillars: children, families, early childhood practitioners and communities.

Working with children

In working with children, the early childhood intervention professional should demonstrate interpersonal warmth and welcome for all families and children. Specifically, they should aspire to promote positive attachment between children and their parents, identify children's functional and developmental capacities and needs, analyse the child's home environments and identify what adaptations are needed to ensure the child's full participation and engagement, analyse the child's home environments and identify which learning opportunities exist or can be created to maximise the child's practice of key skills, support parents in implementing adaptations and maximising learning opportunities for the child, monitor the impact of these strategies on the child's developmental and functional skills and child's participation/engagement in activities and, most importantly, strengthen the capacity of universal services to meet the needs of all children through fully inclusive programs (Early Childhood Australia and Early Childhood Intervention Australia, 2012; Moore, 2012).

Working with families

In working with families, the role of the early childhood intervention professional should be to help families identify their needs, mobilise resources and access to services, as well as build positive social support networks. Early childhood intervention professionals should work with community-based supports to build family-friendly services. They should also work with other relevant family services to provide integrated supports, assist parents in meeting the needs of their children and promote the capacity of other community-based services to support parents in their caregiving roles (Moore, 2012).

Working with early childhood practitioners

In working with early childhood educators, the role of the early childhood intervention professional should incorporate developing a shared knowledge, a common language and mutually supportive practices in universal programs (Early Childhood Australia and Early Childhood Intervention Australia, 2012). In addition, the role of the early childhood intervention professional should promote positive attachment between early childhood professionals and children, and identify children's functional and developmental capacities and needs. Early childhood intervention professionals should have the capacity to analyse the child's early years' setting and identify the adaptations needed to ensure full participation and engagement in activities. Early childhood intervention professionals should have the skills to analyse and identify what learning opportunities exist or can be created to maximise children's practices of key skills. They should also be able to support early childhood educators in implementing adaptations and maximising learning opportunities for children with developmental delays or disabilities. Early childhood intervention professionals should have the capacity to monitor the impact of these strategies on children' acquisition of developmental and functional skills and the children's participation and engagement in everyday activity (Moore, 2012).

Working with community programs and settings

In working with the community, the role of the early childhood intervention professional should be to promote community understanding and acceptance of children with developmental delays or disabilities and their families, advocate for the rights of children with developmental delays or disabilities and their families to have full access to community programs and settings, promote the quality of life for young children with developmental delays or disabilities and their families, analyse and identify what adaptations are needed to ensure children's full participation and engagement in activities, support community staff in implementing adaptations that will allow the child's full participation, monitor the impact of these strategies on the child's participation and engagement in activities and increase the capacity of universal community services to meet the needs of all children through fully inclusive services (Moore, 2012).

Still, in every relationship, there are challenges. In the context of early childhood intervention, professionals might struggle to include families at the most basic level of intervention, let alone have the capacity to build constructive relationships with parents when the family is going through difficult times accepting their child's delay or disability. Gathering information about where families go and how they engage in everyday life experiences is pivotal to the development of authentic and transparent parent-professional partnerships (Espe-Sherwindt,

2008; Woods & Lindeman, 2008). So what other challenges face early intervention professionals and providers in supporting children and families?

Challenges facing early childhood intervention professionals and service providers

Professionals may find it difficult to effectively work with families (Arthur, Becher, Death, Dockett, & Farmer, 2005; Eakin, n.d.; Fields-Smith & Neutharth-Pritchett, 2009; Oates, 2010), and this can impose considerable demands on the psychosocial qualities of the early childhood professionals (Davis, Day, & Bidmead, 2002). Being warm and caring and using excellent communication does not necessarily mean that a professional is family-centred. Professionals seeking to be family-centred need to focus on developing trusting and supportive relationships. This means abandoning control and judgement, but at the same time utilising their specialised practices and expertise to build family capacity and create opportunities for parents to become agents of change in their children's lives (Espe-Sherwindt, 2008).

Developing positive relationships in family-centred early childhood intervention programs is highly demanding. Professionals need to have the time and resources to establish trusting and supporting relationships with families in typical early intervention programs. They also require higher levels of skills and knowledge, more up-to-date training and support, a considerable amount of supervision and mentoring and awareness of policy and its implication for early intervention services (Caldwell, 1986; Davis, Day, & Bidmead, 2002). For professionals, this means that drawing on relevant research and evidence-based practice is essential for developing effective relationships (Caldwell, 1986; Guralnick, 2005b).

If professionals are to acquire and use the skills necessary to work in partnership with parents, opportunities need to be created for early childhood intervention professionals to engage in learning, along with service providers and families, about innovative intervention practices that aim to strengthen their professional competence and confidence, increase parents' and families' involvement in early intervention and enhance children's developmental and educational outcomes (Dunst, 2015; Grace, Llewellyn, Wedgwood, Fenech, & McConnell, 2008; Swanson, Raab, & Dunst, 2011). The implication for service providers in this instance involves taking into account the adequacy of resources necessary to establish and maintain a workforce capable of delivering credible family-centred early intervention services. In addition, this also involves significant planning with significant input from families so that adequate and efficient systems of care are developed (Epps & Jackson, 2000).

Kemp and Hayes (2005) argue that there is a shortage of research on early intervention provision in Australia, and therefore, the contribution of Australian research for informing early childhood intervention is very limited. They also claim that what is considered to be effective practice is not particularly based on experiential research, but rather reflects current trends or expert opinion on early intervention programs. While there is recognition that family-centred practice in early childhood intervention benefits young children and their families, the totality of its principles has not yet been instilled into existing interventions (Dodd, Saggers, & Wildy, 2009; Epps & Jackson, 2000). Professionals lack the training on how to address complex and sensitive family issues. They also lack the knowledge of resources and services available in the community to assist families and children (Bruder & Dunst, 2005; Davis, Day, & Bidmead, 2002; Dunst, 2008; Dunst, 2009; Epps & Jackson, 2000; Espe-Sherwindt, 2008; Habbin, McWilliam, & Gallagher, 2003; Hefner, 2008; Klein & Gilkerson, 2003; Nieto, 2004; Sarros, 2002). Professionals receive little, if any, professional preparation, guidance or support in how to participate and engage in family-centred practice in their undergraduate courses (Bruder & Dunst, 2005; Bruder, 2010; Malone, Straka, & Logan 2000; Nieto, 2004; Sukkar, 2011). Equally, professional development courses in early intervention programs are rare and mentorship opportunities are very limited (Bruder & Dunst, 2005; Bruder, 2010; Sukkar, 2011). This appears to be a weak, yet critical, element in early intervention systems. Research focused on early intervention personnel affirm that the lack of appropriate tertiary education courses, professional development opportunities and mentorship programs can negatively influence the quality of services provided to children and families in early intervention programs (Bruder, 2010; Dunst, 2009; Dunst, 2015; Sukkar, 2011).

Influence of tertiary education, professional development and mentorship on early childhood intervention

The extent to which early childhood professionals have been adequately trained and prepared to work with children with developmental delays or disabilities and their families has been central to early childhood research and program evaluation (Davies, 2007; Davis, Day, & Bidmead, 2002; Dunst, 2009; Jackson & Fawcett, 2009; Moore, 2005). It is recognised that tertiary education, ongoing professional development and mentorship play a critical role in shaping the relationship between parents and professionals, improving children's lifelong outcomes and strengthening professionals' capacity.

Tertiary education

In Australia, the early childhood intervention practitioner competency document indicates that early intervention practitioners, at a minimum, are required to have a tertiary qualification in early childhood education, social work or therapeutic disciplines (Hollo, 2009). Their training must prepare them to offer a mix of one-on-one intervention and group interventions to children and families as well as allow them to function in centre-based and community-based services with government and non-government agencies. The qualification must also allow professionals to operate efficiently within a system of colleagues (Hollo, 2009).

However, early intervention professionals locally and internationally receive little if any preparation in relation to working with families and family-centred intervention. This has been articulated clearly by researchers in the United States, the United Kingdom and Australia (Centre for Community Child Health, 2002). In fact, many of the universities that are preparing early childhood special education professionals do not include disciplines such as speech pathology, psychology, occupational or physical therapy in their tertiary program (Bruder & Dunst, 2005; Dunst, 2009). Dunst (2009) claims that students receive only limited education, if any, to address the personal skills required to working with complex families and to build positive relationships. This is because tertiary institutions receive limited funds for education and allied health studies to allow for the development of a comprehensive four-year degree that incorporates family-centred and other evidence-based practices (Bruder & Dunst, 2005; Sukkar, 2011). Also, changes in higher education programs, including those for early intervention programs, are not easily sustained. Faculty organisational structures and administration processes have been described as having an adverse impact on the development of supportive and more relevant early intervention courses (Bruder & Dunst, 2005).

It is, therefore, not surprising that professionals and families alike report discrepancies between recommended practices for early intervention, as identified through evidence-based literature and actual service delivery practices (Bruder & Dunst, 2005; Dunst, 2009). Sadly, research indicates that interdisciplinary and transdisciplinary practices have become extremely difficult for professionals and students to embrace (Bruder & Dunst, 2005; Espe-Sherwindt, 2008; Klein & Gillkerson, 2003, p. 483). On a more positive note, the gap in professional knowledge and skills can be addressed, in part, by preparing future professionals to think about early intervention more critically. Undergraduate students and professionals need to know the current thinking about what is considered to be the foundation for evidence-based practice. They also need to know how to differentiate between the different definitions of evidence-based practices. More importantly, future professionals need to have a working knowledge of research and need to learn how to examine research findings and be able to question how research findings can inform current and future practice (Dunst, 2009). Thus, to secure the development of a skilful early intervention workforce, service providers, managers and leaders in early childhood intervention should offer extensive professional development opportunities for its allied health professionals and early childhood educators (Epps & Jackson, 2000; Habbin, McWilliam, & Gallagher, 2003; Hefner, 2008; Klein & Gilkerson, 2003; Sarros, 2002).

Professional development

Studies by researchers such as Bruder and Dunst (2005), Christian (2006), Harbin, McWilliam and Gallagher (2003), Klein and Gilkerson (2003), Turnbull, Turbiville, and Turnbull (2003) and Shonkoff and Phillips (2000) indicate that there is consistency in the literature about the types of attributes early intervention professionals must attain to assist and support families. According to the experts, professionals should show responsiveness and sensitivity to families' needs and wants, and have the ability to distinguish between the two to be effective. Their relationships with families should be strength-based and help families recognise their children's skills. Professionals should also demonstrate flexibility and have the ability to provide families with opportunities to discuss their issues and concerns without any pressure. More importantly, professionals should be trained to acknowledge and respect parents as experts in relation to their child's development and experiences.

What can be done to support early childhood intervention practitioners in Australia and internationally?

Enough evidence has been provided to confirm that early intervention professionals confront numerous challenges in their work with children, parents and extended families. At a local level in Australia, a major challenge comprises not having a coherent framework to advise and guide professional practice. For example, looking at the State of Victoria, Moore (2008) claims that the State does not have a framework that covers pre-service skills, knowledge and values or induction procedures for new staff. Similarly, the Department of Education and Training in Victoria (2010) argues that while guidelines currently exist to support practice, these do not necessarily amount to a comprehensive framework encompassing all aspects of service delivery, professional competencies or child and family livelihood (Department of Education and Early Childhood Development, Murdoch Children's Research Institute, Centre for Community Child Health and The Royal Children's Hospital Melbourne, 2010).

Lack of clear infrastructures, appropriate work conditions, abundance of resources and enhanced remuneration means that it will be difficult to attract and retain capable early intervention professionals. As a result, these inadequacies will also represent a significant flaw in the quality of the early childhood intervention services. Therefore, it can be argued that a framework of guidelines and principles that inform professionals about their practice, and is linked to a clear career structure, is necessary to build a strong profession (Shonkoff & Phillips, 2000). Such a framework would underpin the training and support that professionals need to approach families about difficult issues, access and supervision, and prevents professional burnout (Tomlin & Hadadian, 2007). So where to from here? And how can professionals be supported in the work they do?

A new vision around professional development

Developing professional skills in early intervention extends beyond attending professional development sessions or training courses. Internal and external supervision, coaching and mentoring, creating workplaces that focus on learning and supporting workers to become reflective practitioners are equally critical in developing the identity of the practitioner in early intervention.

Early childhood intervention professionals require professional learning opportunities that not only draw on specialised information about children and family needs, but also focus on strategies to deal with complex family circumstances with confidence and compassion. Professionals in early intervention are often entrenched in their clinical and medical practices and do not necessarily value or understand family-centred practice as a key social model. Thus professional learning opportunities should include unpacking the concept of family-centred practice, that is, how to build capacity in families, develop effective parent-professional relationships and promote effective help giving strategies. At entry-level, early intervention professionals require opportunities not only to understand the theoretical benefits of family-centred practices, but also to use these practices and philosophies with appropriate peer support and mentorship (Dodd, Saggers, & Wildy, 2009; Mandell & Murray, 2009).

Many early childhood intervention professionals have the capacity to manage children's and families' mental health concerns and stressors. Yet, they lack the ability to understand their own needs for similar supports (Tomlin & Hadadian, 2007). Reflective practice assists practitioners in recognising their strengths as well as their own limitations. As a professional in early childhood intervention, being open and reflective is something to which one must aspire and achieve. It is often the key to effective practice in complex situations (Myers, 2010). It is evident that no professional, regardless of their practice is going to improve, if there is not a conscious attempt made to engage them in reflection (Sukkar, 2011). This suggests an important dimension of professional development, which includes the opportunity for early intervention practitioners to identify, develop and reflect upon their service delivery strategies with children and families in early intervention (Özdemir, 2007). According to Tomlin and Hadadian (2007), "nurturing the nurturer" and learning how to shift their own personal and professional values and attitudes is imperative in supporting professionals aspiring to deliver family-centred interventions.

As a result, effective early intervention programs should consider promoting mentorship opportunities, which in turn enhance professionals' self-esteem, increase trust amongst colleagues, create a positive work environment, improve the quality of services and decrease staff turnover (Habbin, McWilliam, & Gallagher, 2003; Hefner, 2008; Sarros, 2002). Effective early intervention programs should also engage early childhood intervention professionals in the process of transformation, showing integrity at all times, and demonstrating commitment and passion for the development of a learning environment that can improve the quality of service provision (Weekes, 2003; Carpenter, 2005).

Moving practitioners from professionally-driven practices to family-centred practices requires a major revamp of professional practice in early childhood intervention services in Australia and elsewhere (Özdemir, 2007). This typically includes an in-depth evaluation of the way professionals work with parents and the way parents respond to professionals and services (Sukkar, 2011). Figure 7.1 represents a suggested model to guide professional practice into the future. This

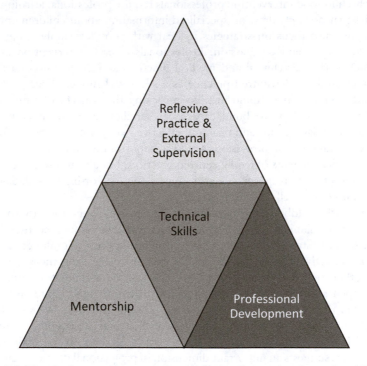

Figure 7.1 The basic requirements for professional practice in early childhood
          intervention

Source: Created by the author

logic model acknowledges the technical skills professionals bring with them
through tertiary education as a basic requirement. It also recognises the importance of professional development in sustaining that knowledge obtained at tertiary level and in further developing professionals' capacity. However, moving
forward, the author suggests that the provision of adequate mentoring and the
development of critical reflective skills to guide professional practice are critical to sustaining the well-being of professionals. Therefore, it is important to
develop a community of practice that nurtures the development and wellbeing of
practitioners over time and sustains the quality of early intervention provided to
children and parents (Sukkar, 2011).

Conclusion

Over the last four decades, family-centred practice has been used as a vehicle
to support children and families, enhance the sense of community, mobilise
resources and support, share responsibility and collaboration, promote family
choice and family control and protect family integrity and family functioning

(Bruder, 2000; Dunst, Hamby, Johanson, & Trivette, 1991). In early childhood intervention particularly, professionals seem to play a critical role in working with families. They are seen as agents of families, and intervene only to maximize family competency and capability in making sound decisions for their children (Dunst, Hamby, Johanson, & Trivette, 1991; Bruder, 2000).

In this chapter, the author touched on the role of professionals in early childhood intervention, the characteristics of parent-professional partnerships, the interpersonal skills that are vital in developing effective partnerships, the challenges that hinder the quality of relationships and the pathways which support the role of professionals over time. With an interest in early intervention professionals, the author suggested a new vision that includes the use of external mentors, training in critical reflections and the establishment of communities of learners to improve practitioners' personal and professional competence and confidence. The author believes that this triangular approach has the power to shape parent-professional relationships and enhance the quality of services provided for children with developmental delays or disabilities.

References

Arthur, L., Becher, B., Death, E., Dockett, S., & Farmer, S. (2005). *Programming and planning in early childhood settings*. South Melbourne, Australia: Thomson.

Australian Government. (2005). *Disability standards for education*. Retrieved from http://docs.education.gov.au/node/16354

Bailey, D., McWilliam, R., Darkes, L., Hebbler, K., Simeonsonn, R., Spiker, D., & Wagner, M. (1998). Family outcomes in early intervention: A framework for program evaluation and efficacy research. *Exceptional Children, 64*(3), 313–328.

Blue-Banning, M., Summers, J., Frankland, H., Nelson, L., & Beegle, G. (2004). Dimensions of family and professional partners: Constructive guidelines for collaboration. *Council for Exceptional Children, 7*(2), 167–184.

Bruder, M. B. (2000). Family-centered early intervention: Clarifying our values for the new millennium. *Topics in Early Childhood Special Education, 20*(2), 105–130.

Bruder, M. (2010). Early childhood intervention: A promise to children and families for their future. *Council for Exceptional Children, 76*(3), 339–355.

Bruder, M., & Dunst, C. (2005). Personnel preparation in recommended early intervention practices: Degree of emphasis across disciplines. *Topics in Early Childhood Special Education, 25*(1), 25–33.

Carpenter, B. (2005). Early childhood intervention: Possibilities and prospects for professionals, families and children. *British Journal of Special Education, 32*(4), 176–183.

Caldwell, B. M. (1986). Future direction for early intervention. *Peabody Journal of Education, 65*(1), 29–41.

Centre for Community Child Health. (2002). *New frontiers in early childhood inclusion*. Retrieved from http://www.noahsarkinc.org.au/wp-content/uploads/2013/03/New-Frontiers-in-Early-Childhood-Inclusion-2.pdf

Christian, L. (2006). *Understanding families: applying family systems theory to early childhood practice*. Retrieved from https://www.naeyc.org/files/yc/file/200601/ChristianBTJ.pdf

Davies, S. (2007). *Team around the child: Working together in early childhood intervention.* Australia: Kurrajong Waratah.

Davis, H., Day, C., & Bidmead, C. (2002). *Working in partnership with parents: The parent advisor model.* London: Harcourt Assessment.

Department of Education and Early Childhood Development, Murdoch Childrens Research Institute, Centre for Community Child Health, & The Royal Children's Hospital Melbourne (2010). *Early childhood intervention reform project executive summary.* Retrieved from http://www.education.vic.gov.au/Documents/childhood/providers/needs/ecislitreviewexecsum.pdf

Dodd, J., Saggers, S., & Wildy, H. (2009). Constructing the ideal family for family-centred practice: Challenges for delivery. *Disability & Society, 24*(2), 173–186.

Dunst, C. J. (2008). *Parent and community assets as sources of young children's learning opportunities.* Retrieved from https://www.wbpress.com/shop/parent-and-community-assets-as-sources-of-young-childrens-learning-opportunities-revised-and-expanded/

Dunst, C. (2009). Implications of evidence-based practices for personnel preparation development in early childhood intervention. *Infant & Young Children, 22*(1), 44–53.

Dunst, C. (2010). *Advances in the understanding of the characteristics and consequences of family-centered practices.* Retrieved from http://www.puckett.org/presentations/FamCtrdHelpPract_8_2010.pdf

Dunst, C. (2015). *Improving the design and implementation of in-service professional development in early childhood intervention.* Retrieved from http://journals.lww.com/iycjournal/Fulltext/2015/07000/Improving_the_Design_and_Implementation_of.2.aspx

Dunst, C., Boyd, K., Trivette, C., & Hamby, D. (2002). Family-oriented program models and professional help giving practices. *Family Relations, 51*(3), 221–229.

Dunst, C. J., Hamby, D., Johanson, C., & Trivette, C. M. (1991). Family-oriented early intervention policies and practices: Family-centered or not. *Exceptional Children, 58*(2), 115–127.

Dunst, C., & Dempsey, I. (2007). Family- professional partnership and parenting competence, confidence and enjoyment. *Journal of Disability, Development and Education, 54*(3), 305–318.

Eakin, L. (n.d.). *Parent/family involvement in early childhood intervention.* Retrieved from http://www.learninglinks.org.au/wp-content/uploads/2012/11/LLIS-53_Parent-Involve.pdf

Early Childhood Australia & Early Childhood Intervention Australia. (2012). *Position on the inclusion of children with a disability in early childhood education and care.* Retrieved from http://www.ecia.org.au/documents/item/31

Epps, S., & Jackson, B. J. (2000). *Empowered families, successful children: Early intervention programs that work.* Washington, DC: American Psychological Association.

Epse-Sherwindt, M. (2008). Family-centred practice: Collaboration, competency and evidence. *Support for Learning, 23*(3), 136–143.

Fields-Smith, C., & Neuharth-Pritchett, S. (2009). Families as decision makers: When researchers and advocates work together. *Childhood Education, 85*(4), 237–242.

Grace, R., Llewellyn, G., Wedgwood, N., Fenech, M., & McConnell, D. (2008). Far from ideal: Every day experiences of mothers and early childhood professionals negotiating an inclusive early childhood experience in the Australian context. *Topics in Early Childhood Special Education, 28*(1), 18–30.

Guralnick, M. (2005a). *Inclusion as a core principle in the early intervention system.* In M. Gurlanick (Ed.), *The developmental system approach to early intervention* (pp. 59–69). Baltimore, MD: Paul H. Brookes Publishing Co.

Guralnick, M. (2005b). An overview of the developmental systems model for early intervention. In M. Gurlanick (Ed.), *The developmental system approach to early intervention* (pp. 3–28). Baltimore, MD: Paul H. Brookes Publishing Co.

Guralnick, M. (2006). The system of early intervention for children with developmental disabilities: Current status and challenges for the future. In J. Jacobson, J. Mulick, & J. Rojahn (Eds.), *Handbook of mental retardation and developmental disabilities* (pp. 465–480). New York: Plenum.

Harbin, G., McWilliam, R., & Gallagher, J. (2003). Services for young children with disabilities and their families. In J. Shonkoff & S. Meisels (Eds.), *Handbook of early childhood intervention* (2nd ed., pp, 387–415). Cambridge: Cambridge University.

Hefener, T. (2008). *Professional development: the cornerstone for trust and empowerment.* Retrieved from http://eclkc.ohs.acf.hhs.gov/hslc/ttasystem/pd/fsd/All%20Staff/prodev_art_00022_060905.html

Hollo, A. (2009). *Early childhood intervention practitioner competencies.* Retrieved from http://www.eciavic.org.au/documents/item/24

Jackson, S., & Fawcett, M. (2009). Early childhood policy and services. In T. Maynard & N. Thomas (Eds.), *An introduction early childhood studies* (pp. 117–133). London: Sage Publications Ltd.

Keen, D. (2007). Parents, families, and partnerships: Issues and considerations. *International Journal of Disability, Development and Education, 54*(3), 339–349.

Kemp, C., & Hayes, A. (2005). Early intervention in Australia: The challenge of systems implementation. In M. Guralnick (Ed.), *The developmental systems approach to early intervention* (pp. 401–423). Baltimore, MD: Paul Brookes Publishing Co.

Klein, N., & Gilkerson, L. (2003). Personnel preparation for early childhood intervention programs. In J. Shonkoff & S. Meisels (Eds.), *Handbook of early childhood intervention* (pp. 454–483). Cambridge: Cambridge University.

KPMG. (2014). *Early childhood intervention – an overview of best practice.* Retrieved from http://www.communityservices.act.gov.au/__data/assets/pdf_file/0007/635695/Early-Intervention-Best-Practice.pdf

Malone, M., Straka, E., & Kent, L. (2000). *Professional development in early intervention: Creating inservice training opportunities.* Retrieved from http://journals.lww.com/iycjournal/Abstract/2000/12040/Professional_Development_in_Early_Intervention_.10.aspx

Malone, M. D., Straka, E., & Logan, K. R. (2000). Professional development in early intervention: Creating effective inservice training opportunities. *Infants & Young Children, 12*(4), 53–62.

Mandell, C., & Murray, M. (2009). Administrators' understanding and use of family-centered practices. *Journal of Early Intervention, 32*(1), 17–37.

Moore, T. (2005). *What do we need to know to work effectively with young children and families? Towards a core curriculum.* Retrieved from http://www.rch.org.au/uploadedFiles/Main/Content/ccch/TM_AIFSConf05_Core_curriculum.pdf

Moore, T. (2007a). *The nature and role of relationships in early childhood intervention services.* Retrieved from http://www.rch.org.au/emplibrary/ccch/TM_ISEI Conf07_Nature_role_rships.pdf

Moore, T. (2007b). *Outcomes-based early childhood intervention for young children with developmental disabilities and their families.* Retrieved from http://www.rch.org.au/emplibrary/ccch/TM_NZ_EC_Conv07_paper.pdf

Moore, T. G. (2008). *Beyond the evidence: building universal early childhood services from the ground up.* Retrieved from http://www.rch.org.au/uploadedFiles/Main/Content/ccch/ECIA-NatConf08-McGregorAddress-paper.pdf

Moore, T. (2012). *Rethinking early childhood intervention services: implications for policy and practice.* Retrieved from http://www.rch.org.au/uploadedFiles/Main/Content/ccch/profdev/ECIA_National_Conference_2012.pdf

Myers, K. (2010). *Reflexive practice: Professional thinking for a turbulent world.* New York: Palgrave MacMillan.

Nieto, S. (2004). *Affirming diversity: The socio-political context of multicultural education.* Boston, MD: Pearson.

Oates, J. (2010). *Early childhood in focus 5: Supporting parents.* Maidenhead: The Open University.

Owen, L., Gordon, M., Frederico, M., & Cooper, B. (2002). *Listen to us: supporting families with children with disabilities: identifying service responses that impact on the risk of family breakdown.* Retrieved from http://www.nda.gov.au/cproot/493/2/ListentoUsFRPFullReport.pdf

Özdemir, S. (2007). *A paradigm shift in early intervention services: from child centerdness to family centerdness.* Retrieved from http://dergiler.ankara.edu.tr/dergiler/26/920/11475.pdf

Porter, L., & McKenzie, S. (2000). *Professional collaboration with parents of children with disabilities.* London: Whurr Publishers.

Rix, J., Paige-Smith, A., & Jones, H. (2008). 'Until the cows came home": Issues for early intervention activities? Parental perspectives on the early years learning of their children with Down syndrome. *Contemporary Issues in Early Childhood, 9*(1), 66–77.

Sarros, J. (2002). The heart and soul of leadership: The personal journey. In C. Baker & R. Coy (Eds.), *The heart and soul of leadership* (pp. 6–22). Queensland, Australia: McGraw Hill.

Shonkoff, J. P., & Phillips, D. A. (2000). *From neurons to neighborhoods: The science of early childhood development.* Washington, DC: The National Academy of Science.

Sukkar, H. (2011). *The road map to building new dreams: Raising a child with developmental delay or disability.* Doctorate, Melbourne Graduate School of Education, The University of Melbourne.

Summers, J. A., Marquis, J., Mannan, H., Turnbull, A. P., Fleming, K., Poston, D., Wang, M., & Kupzyk, K. (2007). Relationship of perceived adequacy of services, family-professional partnerships, and family quality of life in early childhood service programs. *International Journal of Disability, Development and Education, 54*(3), 319–338.

Swanson, J., Raab, M., & Dunst, C. (2011). Strengthening family capacity to provide young children everyday natural learning opportunities. *Journal of Early Childhood Research, 9*(1), 66–80.

Tomlin, A., & Hadadian, A. (2007). Early intervention providers and high-risk families. *Early Child Development and Care, 177*(2), 187–194.

Turnbull, A., Turbiville, V., & Turnbull, H. (2003). *Evolution of family-professional partnerships: Collective empowerment as the model for the early twenty-first century.*

In J. Shonkoff & S. Meisels (Eds.), *Handbook of early childhood intervention* (pp. 630–650). Cambridge: Cambridge University.

Weekes, R. (2003). Courage. In C. Baker & R. Coy (Eds.), *The 7 heavenly virtues of leadership* (pp. 31–56). Sydney: McGraw Hill.

Woods, J. J., & Lindeman, D. P. (2008). Gathering and giving information with families. *Infant & Young Children, 21*(4), 272–284.

Part IV

Working with families and young children in Australia

The chapters in this section of the book place early childhood intervention in Australia in broader-based ecological systems frameworks that include explicit recognition of, and the need to forge, collaborative relationships with other programs, organisations, and agencies also working with young children and their families. Goff and McLoughlin (Chapter 10), for example, describe how Bronfenbrenner's (1992, 1994) ecological systems theory was used to identify and target the provision of supports, resources, and services that are embedded within a school providing early childhood intervention (early learning, schooling, playgroups, maternal and child health care, family supports), those provided by professionals from other agencies at the school (allied health, general practitioners, paediatricians, refugee services, adult education and training), and those provided through referrals to other organisations and professionals (housing, counselling, financial supports). The chapter provides an excellent example of how social systems theory was used to operationalise an ecological approach to early childhood intervention.

All three chapters include descriptions of how family-centred practices are used to provide and promote the provision of supports, resources, and services to young children and their families, and how family-centred practices can be used to overcome obstacles and barriers to involve parents and other primary carers meaningfully in early childhood intervention. The contributors provide readers with examples of how their efforts to promote the use of family-centred practices have informed early childhood intervention.

Forster describes how the Australian National Disability Insurance Scheme (NDIS) is changing "the nature of services for all persons with a disability, including young children" (Forster, Chapter 9), and Johnson et al. (Chapter 8) describe the conditions under which NDIS funding needs to be provided in order for this type of early childhood intervention to have family-centred characteristics and consequences. Notwithstanding the fact that the short-term and long-term impacts of the NDIS on how early childhood intervention is being changed or altered is yet to be determined, the NDIS is an example of how a macrosystem factor (Bronfenbrenner, 1979) can inform discussions about the ways in which early childhood intervention is potentially changed by a macrosystem event.

References

Bronfenbrenner, U. (1979). *The ecology of human development: Experiments by nature and design*. Cambridge, MA: Harvard University Press.

Bronfenbrenner, U. (1992). Ecological systems theory. In R. Vasta (Ed.), *Six theories of child development: Revised formulations and current issues* (pp. 187–248). Philadelphia, PA: Jessica Kingsley.

Bronfenbrenner, U. (1994). Ecological models of human development. In T. Husen & N. Postlethwaite (Eds.), *International encyclopedia of education* (2nd ed., Vol. 3, pp. 1643–1647). Oxford: Elsevier.

8 Working with families as part of early childhood intervention services

Family-centred practice in an individualised funding landscape

Christine Johnston, Denise Luscombe and Loraine Fordham

Australia has long put family-centred practice at the policy centre of early childhood intervention (Brock et al., 1996; Johnston, 2003). However, its implementation has been less assured with researchers such as Summers et al. (2005), and later Fordham, Gibson, and Bowes (2011), stating that whilst most service providers would characterise their practice as family-centred, that is frequently not the experience reported by families. Indeed, Fordham et al. (2011) reported that approximately half of the 130 family participants in their study stated that they were not experiencing family-centred care. Nor is this an isolated finding. For example, Turnbull, Turbiville and Turnbull (2000) and more recently, Arney and Scott (2013), have pointed to a continued focus on developing the child's skills and behaviours, with family involvement most generally confined to the mother. Service providers aspire to and embrace the philosophy but continue to have difficulty working in ways which fully engage the family in the decision-making which is at the heart of family-centred practice.

Although not a focus of the present discussion, it is useful to consider the ten behaviours that Dunst (1997) set down as core practices and which have been summarised by Fordham and Johnston (2014):

1 treat families with respect,
2 work in partnership and collaboration,
3 share information completely and in an unbiased manner,
4 be sensitive and responsive to family diversity,
5 promote family choices and family decision-making,
6 base intervention on family-identified desires and needs,
7 provide individualised support and resources,
8 utilise a broad range of formal and informal supports and resources,
9 employ competency enhancing help-giving styles, and
10 enhance family strengths and capabilities.

Consideration of these practices suggests that they can be divided into those that speak to the ways in which professionals interact with parents and families on a personal level and those which are concerned with the "what," "where" and "how" of intervention strategies and their implementation. This being so, it is not surprising that Dunst (2002) has pointed to what may be the central difficulty in achieving family-centred practice by noting that it demands that professionals have both relational and participatory skills. He contends that although many professionals are able to fulfil the relational component, they are less able to implement the participatory.

This is borne out consistently in research which has studied families' perceptions of the extent to which the services they receive are family-centred. Much of this research has used the Measure of Processes of Care instruments developed by King, Rosenbaum and King (1995) and has habitually found that parents and/or carers rate most highly items on the sub-scale related to respectful and supportive care and lowest on the sub-scale which relates to professionals' providing general information. This is the case for research conducted in Canada (King, King, & Rosenbaum, 1996), the Netherlands (Siebes et al., 2007), Finland (Jeglinsky, Autti-Rämö, & Brogren Carlberg, 2011) and Australia (Dickens, Matthews, & Thompson, 2010; Dyke, Buttigieg, Blackmore, & Ghose, 2006; Fordham et al., 2011; Karlsson, Johnston, & Barker, under review; Raghavendra, Murchland, Bentley, Wake-Dyster, & Lyons, 2007). The similarity in the findings is striking and cannot be seen as simply an artefact of the scale being used: professionals falter when it comes to working in partnerships with families where the skills and knowledge of both are to be equally valued and decisions about intervention jointly made.

It is critical to understand the reason behind these findings in order for the best outcomes to be achieved, especially given that the basic tenets and principles of family-centred practice have been so clearly articulated and over a long period of time (Dunst, 1997; Dunst, Trivette, & Deal, 1988). In an attempt to address the discrepancy between family-centred rhetoric and reality, the Workgroup on Principles and Practices in Natural Environments (2008) set out seven principles which, if followed, would result in best practice in delivering services in natural environments. Each principle is accompanied by a list of key concepts and a series of examples of what the principle looks like and does not look like in practice. Essentially, this is a checklist of the dos and don'ts of good practice, and one which, it might be assumed, would be easy to implement. Yet, despite such support, the implementation of family-centred practice remains elusive.

If professionals are to act in partnership with the families of young children with disabilities, two supporting elements are needed: professionals must have the skills and disposition needed to be family-centred practitioners, and the service system itself must enable family-centred practice to occur. The first can best be addressed through building the capacity of the workforce. This must encompass not only development of their specific discipline skills (in some ways, this is the least important), but also their ability to collaborate with other professionals and families, and to share their skills and knowledge with other professionals and key care providers. At the centre of building staff capacity is effective professional development and the mentoring or coaching of staff by practitioner experts. The second element, that of establishing a service system that not only allows but demands family-centred practice, is now facing a new challenge: that of the impact of individual funding. It is within this new context that family-centred practice must now occur and professionals find new ways of working in partnership with parents and other professionals.

The impact of individual funding

The introduction of the National Disability Insurance Scheme (NDIS) in Australia brings individual funding to all eligible individuals with disabilities from birth to the age of 65 (NDIS, n.d.). Under such a model, a finite amount of money is allocated to the individual (or in the case of children, to their family) on a scale of entitlement related to assessed need. This need is determined by the impact of the disability on functioning and other factors such as disadvantage and vulnerability. Eligible people, or participants (as they are called in the NDIS), register to receive services and support, and work with a Planning Support Coordinator to develop a service plan that meets their and, where relevant, their family's needs. This service plan informs how an individual funding package is developed to enable each participant to purchase the services outlined in their plan. Whilst the full rollout of the full scheme will not commence until July 2019, trial sites have been operating since July 2013. In an environment where families have the ability to purchase services from a range of providers, the specialised, multidisciplinary team which utilises a key worker team model of service delivery (where families are allocated one team member who engages and works with the family as the conduit for the team, and who enlists the support and expertise of other team members in a timely fashion to meet the needs of the family and child, where required) is under threat.

Individual funding for adults with a disability is not new: it has been a growing trend internationally for more than 30 years (Fisher et al., 2010), with significant evidence to support its benefits (Lord & Hutchison, 2003; Lord, Kemp, & Dingwall, 2006; Spalding, 2008). It might be argued that its main advantage is that it increases the choice and control people with disabilities and their families/carers have over services and supports (Buchanan, 2003; Ottmann & Laragy, 2009). In this model, decision-making is theoretically vested in the individual with the disability and their advocate(s), and not in the professional providing services. The approach then, it is argued, is person-centred.

Furthermore, individual funding has also been found to have a positive impact on the families of those with disabilities, with Buchanan (2003) finding that it empowered family members. This has also been supported by Tyson, Brewis and Crosby (2010), who found that families reported having an increased quality of life as measured by their social life, ability to undertake employment and access to supports that allowed them to continue in their caring role. It has been shown that the benefits go beyond those arising from direct therapeutic interventions and enhance well-being: outcomes that are congruent with the aims of early childhood intervention. Although individual funding on a national basis has only more recently been made available to young children with disabilities and their families in Australia, it is becoming apparent that similar benefits accrue to its use with families reporting increased well-being, resilience and independence (Robinson, Gendera, Fisher, Clements, & Eastman, 2011). Therefore, individual funding is not only compatible with family-centred practice, but is also focused on the key element of choice. There are, however, some caveats that need to be applied, as utilising individual funding effectively is not without its difficulties.

Implementing effective family-centred funding

For individual funding to be effective for families who have a young child with a disability, a number of factors need to be considered and addressed. Four can be deemed critical and will be considered in turn:

1   flexibility in the model at a systemic level,
2   parents'/carers' capacity for decision-making,
3   parents'/carers' access to information in forms which are meaningful to them, and
4   the capacity building of professionals.

Flexibility in the model at a systemic level

With the rollout of the NDIS, it is expected that the marketplace and the workforce will adapt and evolve to the demands of people with disabilities (KPMG, 2014). There is the opportunity for new providers to enter the workforce and current providers to modify their work, depending on what is demanded of them. More particularly, it is apparent that private and sole providers are likely to take a larger role in service delivery. This is not an issue in itself and only becomes so if it results in a fragmentation of family-centred practice, with the loss of a collaborative team approach, and a return to a model where professionals work in isolation, placing additional stresses on families as they attempt to negotiate multiple professional agendas.

Families consistently point to their preference for having fewer professionals to work with and point to the benefit of a case-coordinator or key worker who can both advocate and mentor the parents/carers as they come to understand the system and how it may best meet the needs of their child and family (Moseley & Colley, 2011). Relationships continue to emerge as an important part of parents' negotiating the system: having stable, professional relationships with those who work with the child and family is seen by families as essential to good outcomes (Johnston, Tracey, Mahmic, & Papps, 2013). In this connection, it is interesting to note how many times the word "trusted" in reference to professionals appears in the brochures available for download from the NDIS website. Relational practices are a key component of family-centred practice.

The preference for more stable relationships has been recognised by the National Disability Insurance Agency (NDIS website, n.d.) with their acceptance of the need for a team approach to early childhood intervention. A paper entitled *Early childhood intervention – transdisciplinary approach to service provision* located on the NDIS website (6 May, 2014) states that service providers will be asked to estimate the cost of delivering a suite of interventions that include the availability of a range of disciplines required for a child, the allocation of a key worker, the delivery of the services in the child's usual setting (such as their home or early childhood education and care setting) and the provision of educational/ information materials to inform the family on how best to guide the child's development. An important point to realise here is that parent education appears to be confined to the provision of materials; it would seem that it does not allow for alternative modes of family support, such as workshops, to be offered as part of the package. If so, this is a serious omission, as it does not acknowledge family diversity. Parental language, cultural and educational background must be taken into consideration and a variety of learning opportunities offered to meet specific family needs. However, what is stated is a very clear recognition of the need to continue to pursue family-centred practice. As always, the challenge will lie in its implementation.

Parents' and carers' capacity for decision-making

It would be naive to suggest that it is only under individualised funding models that families need to make choices and decide what suite of services best meets their needs and those of their child. This has always been so. The difference with this model is that the allocation of funds places a greater onus on the family to choose wisely and well, lest those limited monies be expended to little effect. Indeed, Johnston et al. (2013) found that this was something that concerned families and that two opposing strategies were evident. In the focus groups they conducted with families already receiving individual funding, some parents reported spending the money as quickly as they could, both because they were concerned that the scheme might end and because they understood how critical it is to intervene early. For other parents the reverse occurred: they were so concerned about not spending the limited funds well that they were not expending them at all or, at best, very slowly. What both approaches appear to share is the lack of a clear service plan.

As Johnston et al. (2013) have stated, this points to the necessity for families to have the capacity to use the funding available in ways which result in the best outcomes both for the child and family. Furthermore, they argue that beginning such capacity building as soon as possible after the disability is identified will have long-term effects on family functioning and child outcomes. The effects of skills learned will be applied as the child moves from early childhood intervention to school and thence to employment or after school options. Determining what types of skills and knowledge are needed is critical if best outcomes are to be achieved. For example, being able to manage the budget allocated is an essential skill as two parents noted again in the Johnston et al. (2013) study.

> *Trying to break the money down into smaller parts. For example working out how much physio sessions cost and then working out how many physio sessions that would mean. So the physio and I sat down and we worked out that we have enough money if we just wanted to use the money for physio we have enough money for private physio once a week until . . . turns seven. So then for example my physio's going away for four weeks, I've made sure that I've organised another four weeks of therapy with somebody else. So I'm making the best use of that money but it would be hard on your own.*
>
> (Parent, WA)

> *I think budgeting and money, people who are good at budgeting would definitely be good at that. People who are not, it's just a lot of budgeting.*
>
> (Parent, WA)

Care must be taken lest this adds to the stresses already being experienced by the family. As the parents note, some are better at budgeting than others. One solution is for one of the professionals or the agency with whom the family is working to do the budgeting for them, a second is for them to work together on it and a third is for parents to be provided with training to enable them to manage the funds themselves. The last seems the most appropriate and militates against a conflict of interest that could arise were a professional receiving some of the funding to assist. Financial literacy is an important skill in this framework. How parents might best be assisted to develop this skill if they do not already have it has yet to be determined. Such training does not fall under the funding possibilities of the NDIS.

A final consideration is the obvious one that not all parents come to the situation with equal levels of education, English facility and previous contact with disability. Not all are at the same stage in their understanding of the implications of disability for their child, themselves and their family. The individual needs of families must therefore be addressed in equal measure as the individual needs of the child. It is critical that families are supported to make effective choices for their young child and family in this new landscape and that service delivery models are developed which enable the capacities of parents/carers to grow.

Parents' and carers' access to information in forms which are meaningful to them

At the centre of parental capacity building is information. Without adequate and appropriate information, decision-making is compromised. However, as already noted, "providing general information" is an area where professionals are perceived as performing poorly by families (e.g., Fordham et al., 2011; Jeglinsky et al., 2011; King et al., 1996; Siebes et al., 2007). In many respects, the reverse might be expected. Providing information to assist parental decision-making seems both an obvious undertaking and one which is relatively straightforward. Why, then, is this not the perception of families? Three possibilities arise: is it that the information is not provided? Or is it not provided consistently? Or is it not provided in a form that is easily interpreted and used by parents?

Much of the information on the NDIS, on disability and on service availability is presented on the internet. Consideration needs to be given to whether providing key information in this way is meeting families' needs. Johnston et al. (2013) surveyed 306 parents and conducted 14 focus groups to explore the information requirements of families with a child with a disability and the sources used to meet these needs. More than half of those responding to the survey had some experience of individual funding. Of interest is the reported source of information used when finding out how to access funding and services. For those who had experience of individual funding, 77.5% reported that early childhood intervention (ECI) staff were their main source of information with the internet rating second (65.9%), early childhood community nurses third (67.7%) with other parents of children with additional needs also being sources of information (58.8%). Clearly, parents are using multiple sources of information in their decision-making. The importance of personal contact was summed up by two parents in a focus group who said:

> *I'd rather sit in like face to face with someone so I can understand what they're saying and explain it to me, what it's about, and then sort of getting on the internet to read it.*

The other parent took this point further and saw the professional as someone who could help them save time by giving information quickly. She said:

> *You have to remember that parents are very time poor so you know I think just simple information, straight forward information is probably a key because again, parents are time poor, you can only spend so long on the computer.*

When asked how confident they felt that they had sufficient information to make decisions about their child, only 19.3% of parents/carers who had experience of individual funding said they were very confident, with 25.7% saying they were somewhat confident (Johnston et al., 2013). Such a finding is of concern as parents and carers are called upon to decide how to spend the funds they are given. Participants in the Johnston et al. (2013) study were also asked to set out their preferences for website design given the role that the internet will take. In order of importance, they thought that the following information was needed on websites: frequently asked questions, hints and tips, finding local information, information from research and information on specific disabilities. They also stated, in order of importance, that the information should be in a number of languages, utilise videos or audio recordings, have pictures, be easy to navigate and be easy to understand. Finally, they wanted the websites to be interactive with the following components, again ranked in order: blogs, to be able to contact the site by email, for there to be a discussion forum, to enable connection to other parents and, finally, connection to therapists and teachers.

What must be considered is that not all parents have equal confidence using the internet. Indeed, some may not have access to it. Hence, it may be useful for services to make a computer station available to families and to coach them in how to access reliable information. Where parents are less likely to come to a service, community libraries might offer a similar service. Families not only need easy access to information but also need to be able to discern the quality of the content and the credibility of the author. This means that the skills necessary to evaluate the efficacy of the interventions and approaches become highly relevant under an individual funding model, where the ability of families to make considered choices for their child and family is paramount.

The capacity building of professionals

Given the move to individual funding, it is evident that early childhood intervention professionals require expanded skill sets to those of the past. Each discipline's technical and clinical skills are no longer enough. For example, with the move to family capacity building, professionals need to enhance their knowledge and expertise in relation to developing therapeutic partnerships with families and building caregiver capacity (Friedman, 2012; Hollo, 2009; Sandall, McLean, & Smith, 2000).

However, ECI is a specialist area for most allied health professionals, with limited training in paediatric disability included in undergraduate discipline-based courses. As a result, new graduates require additional training and development when entering the sector. Generally, supervision and support for professional development activities have fallen to the employer. Similarly, it has been the responsibility of the individual ECI professional to undertake professional development opportunities through professional and peak bodies.

Under the NDIS funding model, the ability of individuals and organisations to fund employee professional development is compromised as attendance at training sessions reduces the income of the service provider. This occurs as the practitioner loses fee-related work whilst increasing expenses through the need to cover the cost of the specific training. At a time when ECI professionals require additional skills, there is less support for them to gain these skills. This has been recognised as a challenge in overseas vendor models of service provision (Bethell, Reuland, Halfon, & Schor, 2004; McWilliam, 2015; Salisbury & Cushing, 2013) and is one that needs to be addressed given the impact of high-quality professional development.

Research shows that high-quality professional development utilising effective adult learning strategies can lead to fidelity of practice (Dunst, Trivette, & Raab, 2015; Snyder, Hemmeter, & McLaughlin, 2011). If the practices being taught are themselves evidence-based, this will lead to high-quality early childhood intervention outcomes (Dunst, 2009; Dunst et al., 2015; Snyder et al., 2011).

Snyder et al. (2011) note that professional training and development have been identified as important drivers in supporting ECI professionals' implementation of evidence-based practice and improving developmental and learning outcomes for young children. It is acknowledged that effective ECI professionals with fundamental skills and competencies are required within programs that provide services to children with disabilities and their families. It is also acknowledged that inclusive mainstream and community settings are essential for a child and family's participation in these contexts. Determining how to ensure that these professionals and practitioners have the knowledge and competencies required to be effective in improving early childhood intervention outcomes for the child and family is vital. Thus, research has targeted professional development implementation and knowledge transfer practices that create effective practitioner behaviour change (Bruder, Dunst, Wilson, & Stayton, 2013; Dunst, Trivette, & Raab, 2013; Fixsen, Naoom, Blase, Friedman, & Wallace, 2005; National Professional Development Centre on Inclusion, 2008). This research should form the basis for professional development strategies.

Further to Snyder et al.'s (2011) research, Bruder et al. (2013) found the more in-services attended by practitioners, the higher they rated themselves as confident and competent in using a number of different ECI practices. Provision of quality professional development with outcomes related to changing practitioner behaviour requires not only time and money, but also a commitment to ongoing personal development. As already noted, the move to individual funding and its possible impact on ongoing professional development means that alternative training and development formats will need to be explored. Formats that take advantage of online technology, such as webinars and e-learning courses, and on-the-job opportunities and support will enable ready access to professional development that does not always require a significant outlay of additional professional time. Training and development in these formats can be incorporated into everyday practice (i.e., occur in real practice) or can be completed during pockets of spare time during the working day or alternatively outside of work hours (e.g., webinars, online learning).

However, components of professional development that have been found to be effective in changing practitioner behaviour include having clear objectives for the training, utilising active learning methods such as on-the-job training, demonstration and modelling of skills, coaching, consultation or mentoring (including coach-guided reflection), self-assessment of mastery of the practice and clinical supervision (Bruder et al., 2013; Dunst & Trivette, 2012; Dunst et al., 2013; 2015; Joyce & Showers, 2002; National Professional Development Centre on Inclusion, 2008; Snyder et al., 2011). In addition, frequent and distributed opportunities to implement the practices directly in the context required after training (i.e., the practice has a high relevancy to current work) are paramount to embed practice change (Dunst & Trivette, 2012; Snyder et al., 2011). Online learning and webinars must therefore occur in conjunction with embedded practice, opportunities for reflection and interaction with peers and expert mentors.

Perhaps not surprisingly, given the intensity of such an approach to training and development, Bruder, Mogro-Wilson, Stayton, Smith and Dietrich (2009) concluded that few ECI practitioners were receiving the systematic implementation support contained within the aforementioned practices to ensure the outcome of fidelity or mastery of practice. This could translate to a significant amount of time and money being wasted on professional development that does not alter the behaviour or practices of the participants, and which therefore does not achieve the outcomes of increasing the competence of the workforce or sector.

Miller and Stayton (2005) focused on this when they concluded that there is a need to extend professional development beyond the individual to the system in which they are working. Indeed, no matter what the skill or intervention being learned, professional development must occur within the context of family-centred practice and demonstrate ways in which it can be implemented in a natural environment and in partnership with the family.

To deliver change of practice requires a long-term approach that focuses on practitioner self-reflection and self-identification of gaps in knowledge as well as strategies to address these needs. Similarly, change of practice can be enabled or sustained through peer support and facilitated collaboration such as communities of practice or study groups (National Professional Development Centre on Inclusion, 2008). Emphasis must be given to the capacity building of professionals at both the system and service levels.

Implications for practice

What, then, are the implications for practice and for the ways in which individual funding is implemented? The following arise from the issues raised and can be grouped according to whether they relate to the system, the service provider or more specifically to the individual professional.

Implications for the system:

- There is a need for skilled planning coordinators who have a sound understanding of early childhood intervention and what constitutes best practice,
- Entry to service provision should be seamless and welcoming,
- Processes and procedures must enable collaborative teamwork, the role of a key worker and the provision of services in natural environments,
- Information on the funding, intervention and support must be available in multiple formats and languages,
- Information and support should be tailored to the stage of diagnosis or familiarity with the system,
- Training and education sessions should be available to parents and carers,
- Professional development should be available to professionals in ways which promote fidelity of practice, and
- Services should be encouraged to evaluate the efficacy of their practice.

Implications for services:

- Services should have easily navigable websites that allow direct contact as needed and set out key information about:
  - what services are offered,
  - the cost,
  - staff, their qualifications and experience, and
  - evidence for the service approaches.

- Commitment to ongoing professional development of staff related to specific discipline areas and delivered with a view to its implementation in a family-centred context,
- Provision of information sessions and training as needed for parents around system requirements, budgeting, goal setting and working with professionals and their child, and
- Ongoing evaluation of the efficacy of the approaches to intervention and working with families used in the service.

Implications for individual professionals:

- Development of positive, professional relationships with families,
- Commitment to working in true partnerships with parents and carers,
- Willingness to work in a collaborative team and share knowledge and expertise with other professionals,
- Willingness to take on the role of key worker with a family, with its intrinsic responsibilities,
- Involvement in ongoing professional development that has at its aim fidelity of practice, and
- Ongoing evaluation of own practice that is rooted in action research and based on reflection of the extent to which agreed family goals are being met.

Conclusion

The introduction of an individualised funding model is designed to give parents/carers of children with disabilities more choice and control over the types of services and supports that best meet their needs. But if the burden is on families to choose well, the burden is equally on professionals to support and build their capacity to do that. Perhaps now more than ever, service providers will be expected to furnish families with information, supports and other resources that enable families to make better informed and financially prudent decisions. Fundamental to this aspiration remains the understanding that early childhood intervention is not child focused: It is about the child *and* their family. Failure to act upon this knowledge will not lead to the best outcomes for the child, the family or the community. The new landscape of individual funding provides a new context, but not a new endeavour.

References

Brock, C., Australian Early Intervention Association (NSW Chapter) & Early Intervention Coordination Project (N.S.W.). (1996). *Recommended practices in family-centred early intervention.* New South Wales, Australia: Ageing & Disability Department.

Bruder, M. B., Dunst, C., Wilson, C., & Stayton, V. (2013). Predictors of confidence and competence among early childhood interventionists. *Journal of Early Childhood Teacher Education, 34*(3), 249–267.

Bruder, M. B., Mogro-Wilson, C., Stayton, V., Smith, B. J., & Dietrich, S. (2009). The national status of in-service professional development systems for early childhood intervention and early childhood special education practitioners. *Infants & Young Children, 22*(1), 13–20.

Buchanan, A. (2003). *The predictors of empowerment for parents and carers of people with intellectual disabilities within the direct consumer funding model.* Western Australia, Perth: Disability Services Commission.

Dickens, K., Matthews, L. R., & Thompson, J. (2010). Parent and service providers' perception regarding the delivery of family-centred paediatric rehabilitation services in a children's hospital. *Child: Care, Health and Development, 37*(1), 64–73.

Dunst, C. J. (1997). Conceptual and empirical foundations of family-centered practice. In R. J. Illback, C. T. Cobb, & H. M. Joseph (Eds.), *Integrated services for children and families* (pp. 75–93). Washington, DC: American Psychological Association.

Dunst, C. J. (2002). Family-centered practices: Birth through high school. *The Journal of Special Education, 36*(3), 139–147. doi:10.1177/00224669020360030401

Dunst, C. J., & Trivette, C. M. (2009). Let's be PALS: An evidence-based approach to professional development. *Infants & Young Children, 22*(3), 164–176.

Dunst, C. J., & Trivette, C. M. (2012). Moderators of the effectiveness of adult learning method practices. *Journal of Social Sciences, 8,* 143–148.

Dunst, C. J., Trivette, C. M., & Deal, A. G. (1988). *Enabling and empowering families.* Cambridge, MA: Brookline Books.

Dunst, C. J., Trivette, C. M., & Raab, M. (2013). An implementation science framework for conceptualizing and operationalizing fidelity in early childhood intervention studies. *Journal of Early Childhood Intervention, 35*(2), 85–101.

Dunst, C. J., Trivette, C. M., & Raab, M. (2015). Utility of implementation and intervention performance checklists for conducting research in early childhood education. In O. Saracho (Ed.), *Handbook of research methods in early childhood education* (pp. 247–276). Charlotte, NC: Information Age Publishing.

Dyke, P., Buttigieg, P., Blackmore, A. M., & Ghose, A. (2006). Use of the Measure of Processes of Care for families (MPOC-56) and service providers (MPOC-SP) to evaluate family-cented services in a paediatric disability setting. *Child: Care, Health and Development, 32*(2), 167–176.

Fisher, K. R., Gleeson, R., Edwards, R., Purcal, C., Sitek, T., Dinning, B., Laragy, C., D'aegher, L., & Thompson, D. (2010). *Effectiveness of individual funding approaches for disability support.* Canberra: Australian Government Department of Families, Housing, Community Services and Indigenous Affairs.

Fixsen, D., Naoom, S., Blase, K., Friedman, R., & Wallace, F. (2005). *Implementation research: A synthesis of the literature.* Retrieved from http://nirn.fpg.unc.edu/sites/nirn.fpg.unc.edu/files/resources/NIRN-MonographFull-01-2005.pdf

Fordham, L., Gibson, F., & Bowes, J. (2011). Information and professional support: Key factors in the provision of family-centred early childhood intervention services. *Child: Care, Health and Development, 38*(5), 647–653. doi:10.1111/j.1365-2214.2011.01324.x

Fordham, L., & Johnston, C. (2014). Family-centred practice for inclusive early years education. In K. Cologon (Ed.), *Inclusive education in the early years* (pp. 171–188). Melbourne: Oxford University Press.

Friedman, M., Woods, J., & Salisbury, C. L. (2012). Caregiver coaching strategies for early intervention providers: Moving towards operational definitions. *Infants & Young Children, 25*(1), 62–82.

Hollo, A. (2009). *Early childhood intervention practitioner competencies.* Retrieved from http://www.eciavic.org.au/documents/item/24

Jeglinsky, I., Autti-Rämö, I., & Brogren Carlberg, E. (2011). Two sides of the mirror: Parents' and service providers' view on the family-centredness of care for children with cerebral palsy. *Child: Health, Care and Development, 38*(1), 79–86. doi:10.1111/j.1365-2214.2011.01305.x

Johnston, C. F. (2003). Formal and informal networks: Australia. In S. L. Odom, M. J. Hanson, J. A. Blackman, & S. Kaul (Eds.), *Early intervention practices around the world* (pp. 281–299). Baltimore, MD: Paul H. Brookes.

Johnston, C. F., Tracey, D. K., Mahmic, S., & Papps, F. A. (2013). *Getting the best from Disability Care Australia: Families, information and decision making: Report of a project undertaken for the practical design fund Department of Families, Housing, Community Services and Indigenous Affairs.* Sydney, New South Wales, Australia: University of Western Sydney.

Joyce, B., & Showers, B. (2002). *Student achievement through staff development* (3rd ed.). Alexandria, VA: Association for Supervision and Curriculum Development.

Karlsson, P., Johnston, C., & Barker, K. (under review) Stakeholders' views of the introduction of assistive technology in the classroom: How family-centred is Australian practice for students with cerebral palsy?

King, G., King, S., Rosenbaum, P., & Goffin, R. (1999). Family-centred caregiving and well-being of parents of children with disabilities: Linking process with outcome. *Journal of Pediatric Psychology, 24*(1), 41–53.

King, S. M., Rosenbaum, P. L., & King, G. A. (1995). *The Measure of Processes of Care (MPOC): A means to assess family-centred behaviours of health care providers.* Hamilton, ON, Canada: CanChild Centre for Childhood Disability Research.

KPMG. (2014). *Interim report: Review of the approach to transition to the full NDIS.* Retrieved from http://www.ndis.gov.au/sites/default/files/documents/kpmg_paper.pdf

Lord, J., & Hutchison, P. (2003). Individualised support and funding: building blocks for capacity building and inclusion. *Disability & Society, 18*(1), 71–86.

Lord, J., Kemp, K., & Dingwall, C. (2006). *Moving towards citizenship: A study of individualized funding in Ontario.* Toronto: Individualized Funding Coalition for Ontario.

McWilliam, R. A. (2015). Future of early intervention with infants and toddlers for whom typical experiences are not enough. *Remedial and Special Education, 36*(1), 33–38.

Miller, P. S., & Stayton, V. (2005). DEC recommended practices: Personnel preparation. In S. Sandall, M. L. Hemmeter, B. J. Smith, & M. E. McLean (Eds.),

142 *Johnston et al.*

DEC recommended practices in early intervention/early childhood special education
(pp. 189–219). Missouri, MT: Division for Early Childhood.

National Disability Insurance Scheme. (2014, July). *Early childhood intervention.*
Retrieved from http://www.ndis.gov.au/document/869

National Disability Insurance Scheme. (n.d.). *What is the NDIS?* Retrieved from
http://www.ndis.gov.au/what-is-the-ndis

National Professional Development Center on Inclusion. (2008). *What do we mean by professional development in the early childhood field?* Retrieved from http://npdci. fpg.unc.edu

Raghavendra, P., Murchland, S., Bentley, M., Wake-Dyster, W., & Lyons, T. (2007). Parents' and service providers' perceptions of family-centred practice in a community-based paediatric disability service in Australia. *Child: Care, Health and Development, 33*(5), 586–592.

Robinson, S., Gendera, S., Fisher, K. R., Clements, N., & Eastman, C. (2011). *Evaluation of the self directed support pilot: Second report.* New South Wales, Australia: Social Policy Research Centre, University of New South Wales.

Salisbury, C. L., & Cushing, L. S. (2013). Comparison of triadic and provider-led intervention practices in early intervention home visits. *Infants & Young Children, 26*(1), 28–41.

Sandall, S., McLean, M., & Smith, B. (2000). *DEC recommended practices in early intervention/early childhood special education.* Longmont: Sopris West.

Siebes, R. C., Wijnroks, L., Ketelaar, M., van Schie, P. E. M., Vermeer, A., & Gorter, J. W. (2007). One-year stability of the Measure of Processes of Care. *Child: Care, Health and Development, 33*(5), 604–610.

Snyder, P., Hemmeter, M. L., & McLaughlin, T. (2011). Professional development in early childhood intervention: Where we stand on the silver anniversary of PL 99–457. *Journal of Early Intervention, 33*(4), 357–370.

Summers, J. A., Hoffman, L., Marquis, J., Turnbull, A., Poston, D., & Nelson, L. L. (2005). Measuring the quality of family-professional partnerships in special education services. *Exceptional Children, 72*(1), 65–81. Retrieved from http://journals. cec.sped.org/ec/

Turnbull, A. P., Turbiville, V., & Turnbull, H. R. (2000). Evolution of family-professional partnerships: Collective empowerment as the model for the early twenty-first century. In J. P. Shonkoff & S. J. Meisels (Eds.), *Handbook of early childhood intervention* (2nd ed., pp. 630–650). Cambridge, UK: Cambridge University Press.

Tyson, A., Brewis, R., Crosby, N., et al. (2010). *A report on in control's third phase: Evaluation and learning 2008–2009.* London: In Control.

Workgroup on Principles and Practices in Natural Environments, OSEP TA Community of Practice: Part C Settings. (2008, March). *Seven key principles: Looks like /doesn't look like.* Retrieved from http://www.ectacenter.org/~pdfs/topics/fami lies/Principles_LooksLike_DoesntLookLike3_11_08.pdf

9 Development of community-based services for children with disabilities and their families

John Forster

The introduction of a National Disability Insurance Scheme (NDIS) in Australia, which is currently being trialled for full implementation by 2019, will change the nature of services for all persons with a disability, including young children. In its trial phase, the NDIS is promoting a model of service delivery that involves a transdisciplinary approach with one member of the early childhood intervention team, being a primary service provider or key worker, supporting a family and child participation in natural environments. The introduction of a national approach to services for young children with disabilities represents a significant departure from a past, in which each State and territory developed its own approach to early childhood intervention (ECI). In Victoria, a model similar to that being proposed by the NDIS has been evolving over the past decade or so. One of the significant features of the Victorian approach has been the coordination of all its early childhood services, typically regarded as covering birth to six years of age. One of the dilemmas in the introduction of the NDIS is the separation of services for children with a disability from services for children without disabilities and delays.

This chapter briefly examines some of the factors that led to different approaches to services for children with a disability or delay being adopted across Australia, in both specialist early childhood intervention and general early childhood settings. It then focuses on developments in Victoria, where administrative arrangements meant that the evolution of services for children with a disability were part of significant reforms to services for young children in general. It proposes that reforms to services for children with a disability and delays in Victoria occurred in a political and policy context that was focused on improving services for all young children. As a result, specific services for children with a disability incorporated current understandings of what best promotes young children's development and services designed for the general population of children aspired to meet the needs of all children, including children with a disability. It concludes that the NDIS creates a different context for future developments.

National disability insurance scheme

The NDIS was proposed following a Productivity Commission (2011a) inquiry into disability care and support that found the existing provision of supports are "underfunded, unfair, fragmented, and inefficient" (p. 5). It is being introduced to address a range of service gaps, rationing, a "lottery" of access to supports and a lack of either a lifelong approach to support or control by persons with a disability over the services they receive. As part of this change, responsibility for the administration of services is being transferred from state and territory governments to a national government agency, the National Disability Insurance Agency (NDIA). The NDIA is charged with creating a market in which consumers have choice and control over the services they receive. Young children with a disability and their families are being included in this new market. The Productivity Commission noted the challenge the NDIS would inevitably face in choosing or targeting early interventions to be funded or purchased, including the standard of evidence to be used (p. 628).

To date the NDIA has published four documents related to recommended practices for young children with disabilities or delays. One document, on working with children in natural environments, was developed by a Workgroup on Principles and Practices in Natural Environments, Office of Special Education Programs Technical Assistance Community of Practice (2008) in the USA. It proposes that because young children learn best in the context of everyday experiences and interactions with familiar people in familiar settings, the primary role of early intervention services should be to support the family members and caregivers to promote a child's development while engaged in those settings. It assumes that "all families, with the necessary supports and resources, can enhance their children's learning and development" (p. 3) and that services need to be highly individualised in their responses to each family and develop out of that family's priorities.

Two further documents elaborate on aspects of this approach. In a fact sheet, the NDIA (2014) reports that it has expert advice that a transdisciplinary, family-centred and key worker approach is most beneficial for families. This approach involves one professional becoming the primary point of contact between the family and the early intervention team, building a trusted relationship and enabling a coordinated approach to service that includes the family in all the decision-making. A review of different types of early childhood intervention teams (NDIA, 2013) recommends the benefits of a team of professionals, made up primarily of therapists, working closely together in a highly coordinated manner. As a result, families do not have to manage multiple uncoordinated services, which can be stressful. It also reduces the potential of families receiving contradictory advice or having unrealistic demands made on them to support multiple strategies.

Services for children with disabilities across Australia

In introducing a national approach to services for children with a disability aged birth to six years (i.e., birth to school entry), the NDIS is charged with developing a consistent approach on what have been very different approaches across the six states and two territories that make up Australia. These differences have been the result of different approaches to what a service for a child with a disability should achieve, influenced by different literatures, different purposes and different administrative arrangements.

In a report for the Australian Government on the evidence for early childhood intervention, KPMG (2011) noted that there were two fields of literature informing the development of services in Australia. According to the report, while these literatures shared a common starting point, that "early intervention refers to the strategies, practices and therapies designed to help children with a disability or developmental delay to participate as fully as they are able in social, educational and economic life," one approach is focused on strategies "to support children and families with emerging needs relating to a child's disability or developmental delay," while the other approach seeks to modify "the natural environments in which children develop – that is, the environments that children inhabit and experience in their everyday lives – to improve the functioning of both children and their families" (KPMG, 2011, p.17). In the first approach, services are directed towards addressing the impact of the child's disability. The other approach takes a more holistic approach that recognises the influence of the child's environment in a child's development and the importance of services that support that environment.

These different approaches are evident in the descriptions used by different governments to describe the purposes of their programs. The websites of the Victorian Department of Education and Training (n.d., Early Childhood Intervention Services, para. 3, n.d.) and the Tasmanian Education Department (Early Childhood Intervention Service, para. 5, n.d.) are both explicit that their services support the child's environment, with services providing "parents and families with the knowledge, skills and support to meet the needs of their child and to optimise the child's development" and "to participate in family and community life." The website of the Western Australian Disability Commission (Early Childhood Development, para 3, n.d.) describes its services as using a "family-centred approach which recognises that every family is unique." The website of the New South Wales Ageing, Disability and Home Care (Early Intervention for Children, para. 1, n.d.) has a more rights-based focus, that "every child, regardless of their needs, has the right to participate fully in their community and to have the same choices, opportunities and experiences as other children." The starkest example of the difference emerged when the Australian Government became directly involved in providing services for children with a disability in 2008, through its Helping Children with Autism program and Better Start for Children with a Disability Initiative. Its website describes its programs as providing grants for the purchase of professional therapeutic and educational services for a child with a specific diagnosis of disability (Department of Social Services, n.d.(a); n.d.(b)).

One area of consistency that has been noted is that services for young children with a disability have continued to treat them as a separate population. Eligibility for services generally requires some form of formal diagnosis of disability or developmental delay. Children who are vulnerable for other reasons, for example, those at environmental risk or with health-related issues, are not eligible for these services (Kemp & Hayes, 2005; Sukkar, 2013). Each jurisdiction has adopted different approaches to screening for services and how that is used and a range of eligibility requirements (Moore, 2012; Sukkar, 2013).

One of the influences shaping the orientation of services has been the administrative context in which they have developed. A comparison of developments in Australian Capital Territory (ACT), South Australia and Victoria, three of the nine jurisdictions, illustrates both similarities and differences. It should be noted that with the introduction of the NDIS some of these services may have already ceased to exist. The three jurisdictions cover substantially different geographical areas and have significantly different population sizes. In each case, both an Education Department and a department with responsibility for health/disability and providing therapy, or allied health services, have developed service responses.

The allied health services in the three jurisdictions work with quite different populations. In the ACT, the publicly funded allied health services for young children with a disability have been provided directly by the ACT Government. ACT Therapy Services has provided services to children with delays in development, aged from birth to eight years and adults to the age of 65 years, where the disability was identified before the individual reached the age of 18 years (ACT Government, n.d.(a)). In South Australia, the Department for Communities and Social Inclusion (2013) both provides allied health services in metropolitan regions and funds non-government organisations, such as Novita Children's Services. Novita Children's Services (n.d.) works with children from birth to young adults and promotes its services as allied health therapy services, psychology services and equipment prescription. In Victoria, allied health services have been funded through an ECI program. Government and non-government teams, which also include teachers, focus exclusively on children aged birth to school entry (Victorian Department of Education and Training (n.d.). The population served by the programs in each jurisdiction has influenced the degree to which they have focused on young children.

The approach taken by departments responsible for education has also varied significantly. In the ACT, the Department of Education and Training has provided programs for approximately 300 children based on their age and the nature of the child's disability. Services have included playgroups and small classes in a mainstream preschool or specialist school settings for children aged two to three years, and small groups in a preschool setting for children aged three to school entry age. These services, which were connected closely to the school system, focused on special education, and there has been limited support for children with a disability in general community children's services (ACT Government, n.d.(b); n.d.(c); ACT Government, 2009). The South Australian Department for Education and Child Development (2012) reports a multi-tiered approach to supporting children with a disability with a strong emphasis on community inclusion. This involves a state-wide service centre for the education of preschool children with disabilities and significant developmental delay, a network of nine inclusive preschool programs for children with high support needs, with up to six children attending each program, and supports to children who attended a local preschool. Victoria's Department of Education and Training has historically operated a program which involves children aged 2.8 years to school age attending programs attached to special schools (Department of Education and Early Childhood Development, 2011). It also has separate programs that support the inclusion of children with a disability in community children's services (Department of Education and Early Childhood Development, 2013). Across these programs there are clear differences in whether the focus is on the child's disability or supporting the environment to be more responsive to a child with a disability.

Evolution of services for children with a disability in Victoria

One jurisdiction that has moved towards the type of service proposed by the NDIS is Victoria, where services for children with a disability have evolved significantly since the early 2000s. These changes included: a greater focus on the importance of parents and other significant adults in the development of children; a shift from group-based programs at a professional centre to individualised services provided in the home and the community; one professional, a key worker, taking the lead role in both the relationship with the family and the implementation of individualised services; and recognition of the potential of community-based children's services, including child care and preschool, to support the developmental needs of all children, including a child with a disability. These changes occurred in a context in which there was increased interest in the development of young children generally, leading to a political engagement in reform. Early childhood intervention had an existing evidence base that complemented the interest in early childhood development, particularly the important role played by families in children's learning and development. The implementation of new approaches to services was supported by engagement by both government policy makers and non-government organisations. The reforms to early childhood intervention services can be seen as part of much broader reforms designed to meet the needs of all children which resulted in a new approach to early childhood education and care (ECEC).

Recognition of the importance of early childhood development

In the early 2000s the Victorian Government, like other Australian and international governments, took an increasing interest in the importance of the early years of children's lives for their future development. This interest was stimulated by new research on both the development of young children and the economic benefits of early intervention. A growing body of research, such as that brought together in *From neurons to neighborhoods: The science of early childhood development* (Committee on Integrating the Science of Early Childhood Development, 2000), for example, provided a compelling description of the importance of early life experiences to a child's later development. It highlighted the critical influence that positive relationships with adults had on a child and the highly interactive interplay between a child's innate drive to develop and the environment in which he or she lives. This greater understanding of what supports children's development linked with research into the economic benefits of early intervention for children. The human capital argument proposed that as children's skill development built on earlier skill acquisition, it was more efficient to support a child's early development. There was also evidence of cost benefits in early intervention for later savings, such as in the criminal justice system, health services and special education (Heckman & Masterov, 2004; Moore, 2006). Two key policy areas that emerged were the importance of support for positive parent-child interactions (Centre for Community Child Health, 2007) and the potential of services for young children to improve the opportunities of children at risk of poor developmental outcomes (Harrison, Goldfeld, Metcalfe, & Moore, 2012).

Political engagement

Early childhood became a high priority for the then Victorian Labour Government. In August 2003, Premier Stephen Bracks established a Children's Advisory Committee "to assist the government in ensuring that development and learning are optimised for all Victorian children from pregnancy through transition to school (0–8 years of age)" (State of Victoria, 2004, p. 7). Following the Committee's report, the Government announced the establishment of an Office for Children in the Department of Human Services in March 2005. The first Minister for Children was appointed. The new Office's responsibilities, which replaced the Community Care Division, included:

- universal early childhood care, education, health and disability programs; programs to assure the safety and wellbeing of children, including child protection,
- juvenile justice services and programs to support vulnerable young people, and
- state concessions programs targeted to lower-income families and individuals.The early years services included child care regulation, early childhood intervention, kindergarten and maternal and child health.

(Department of Human Services, 2005a)

The momentum continued into 2006, when the Office for Children and Royal Children's Hospital Melbourne hosted a visit by Professor Jack Shonkoff, who spoke at a range of public events and attended private meetings with Ministers and the Premier (Flottman & Page, 2012). After Bracks's resignation, the new Premier, John Brumby, announced the formation of a new Department of Education and Early Childhood Development. This Department had two ministers, the Minister for Education and the Minister for Children and Early Childhood Development. The Department was responsible for developing and implementing a birth-to adulthood approach to learning and development (Department of Education and Early Childhood Development, 2008a).

Victoria's interest was then subsumed into national discussion which followed the election in 2007 of a new federal Labour Government, led by Kevin Rudd. In the 2008 Melbourne Declaration on Educational Goals for Young Australians (Ministerial Council on Education, Employment, Training and Youth Affairs, 2008), the national meeting of Education Ministers acknowledged the importance of the period from birth to eight years in a child's development, and in particular the first three years. The Melbourne Declaration also noted the capacity of ECEC services to influence children's development "within and beyond the home" (p. 15) and to improve transition to school, length of time at school and future participation in employment.

Policy developments

One of the features of Victoria's approach to policy development has been the linking of both its targeted and more universal policies. When the Victorian Government released its 2003 *Early Childhood Intervention Services Vision and Key Priorities* (Department of Human Services, 2003) policy, it clearly linked services for children with a disability to its overall approach to young children. The policy included a number of goals. The first was to create a comprehensive and integrated continuum of child and family services in which ECIS was to provide additional supports for children with a disability or developmental delay not usually available through the universal services. The second goal was for ECIS to develop strong collaborative relationships with universal services such as maternal and child health, playgroups, family services, child care and preschool, so these services could meet the core needs of children with a disability or developmental delay and their families (Department of Human Services, 2003, p. 5). The third goal highlighted the need to build parents' capacity to care for their child and promote the family's independence and choice in navigating services. This was a departure from an earlier approach of providing separate services for children with a disability.

In 2008, the policy Blueprint for Early Childhood Development and School Reform (Department of Education and Early Childhood Development, 2008b) described a continuum of learning and development from the years prior to and through school and beyond that was inclusive of all Victorian children. It promoted the importance of collaboration between families, schools, early childhood services and the broader community. It also identified that some children and young people would need a more individualised approach and that the government was committed to further reforms to ensure schools and children's services were able to meet the needs of all children.

When the policy debate about reform in ECEC became a national issue, its focus became narrower. A wide range of children's services such as child care and preschool were brought under one national framework, underpinned by a uniform legislative framework, a national Early Years Learning Framework (EYLF), a National Quality Standard and a rating system accessible to parents into what are collectively known as the National Quality Framework (Australian Children's

Education and Care Quality Authority, n.d.). The EYLF (Department of Education, Employment and Workplace Relations, 2009) identified five outcomes for all children attending ECEC services, including:

- children have a strong sense of identity,
- children are connected with and contribute to their world,
- children have a strong sense of wellbeing,
- children are confident and involved learners, and
- children are effective communicators.

(p. 19)

It also recognised families as children's first and most influential teachers.

Victoria continued its more integrated approach when it released its *Victorian Early Years Learning and Development Framework (VEYLDF) for all children from birth to eight years* (DEECD and VCAA, 2011), which linked the EYLF outcomes to the first two levels of the Victorian Essential Learning Standards, a set of common state-wide standards used by schools to plan student learning programs, assess student progress and report to parents. The VEYLDF was promoted as a guiding framework for all professionals working with young children. Its definition of early childhood professional embraced ECI workers, play therapists and health professionals, as well as those working in education and care (DEECD and VCAA, 2011, p. 5). The VEYLDF's eight Practice Principles for Learning and Development included: family-centred practice; partnerships with professionals; high expectations for every child; equity and diversity; respectful relationships and responsive engagement; integrated teaching and learning approaches; assessment for learning and development; reflective practice (p. 9). These practice principles incorporated elements that had already been shaping specific services for children with a disability.

Evidence base for early childhood intervention

Service development in Australia has largely drawn on international research for guidance. While there has been some interest from universities, the sector has largely relied on inviting international researchers to speak on their areas of expertise (Kemp & Hayes, 2005; Moore, 1997). Moore (1997) had characterised the evolution of services for children with a disability towards a more family-orientated approach as a change from:

- a treatment model to a promotion orientation,
- professionally directed to family-centred practice,
- a child-focused to a family-focused approach, and
- simple linear causal models to complex transactional models.

In the early 2000s, the role of families was the subject of ongoing debate about "family centred practice" (Dempsey & Keen, 2008; Kemp & Hayes, 2005; Moore & Larkin, 2005; Moore, 2008).

Two of the major influences on Victorian services were the work of Carl Dunst, Carol Trivette and colleagues, and the work of Michael Guralnick (Yooralla, 2000). This research focused on the important role that families played in their child's development and provided an approach to supporting early childhood development in the context of a family that was specific to children with a disability. The family systems approach promoted by Dunst and Trivette (2009) from the late 1980s focused on family-centred practice and included:

- viewing the family as a social unit embedded within social networks as the focus for intervention,
- reorientating the professional/family relationship away from being professionally dominated to one in which the relationship has the characteristics of capacity building and help giving,
- ensuring that what drives the interventions are the families concerns and priorities, and
- recognition that families bring their own knowledge and expertise and skills to the situation of raising a child with a disability and have an independent capacity to mobilise supports and resources to advance their situation.

(Dunst, Trivette, & Deal, 1988; Dunst & Trivette, 2009)

Guralnick's developmental systems model, in part, reframed early childhood intervention as supporting families to respond to the additional challenges, or stressors, created by having a child with a disability, in order that the family could fulfil its role of providing the necessary positive relationships, learning opportunities and a healthy and safe environment fundamental to a child's development (Guralnick 2005, 2011). These approaches were central to the development of new services.

Role of government and non-government organisations

The implementation of new service models in Victoria involved government departments initiating change through new policies and individual non-government organisations investing in their own service developments. The peak body for non-government organisations, Early Childhood Intervention Australia (ECIA), also initiated discussions across organisations, for example on identifying service outcomes (ECIA, 2005). Some of the significant developments follow.

In 2005, the State Government released *Program Framework for Early Childhood Intervention Services* (Department of Human Services, 2005b). As well as reaffirming the importance of developing family's skills to support their child's wellbeing, development and life experience, it introduced the importance of using everyday routines and activities to promote early childhood learning and development. The benefits of working with a child in his or her natural environments were described as assisting the child to:

Generalise skills

- learn to understand and accept differences,
- learn appropriate and effective social skills,
- participate in his/her community, and
- have a sense of belonging.

Natural environments were described as the settings that were typical for other children of a similar age. Naturalistic interventions were described as "strategies that identify and use opportunities for learning throughout the child's natural activities, routines, and interactions, follow the child's lead, and use natural consequences" (Department of Human Services, 2005, p. 5). This *Framework* also emphasised the importance of services working to achieve individual outcomes identified with the family/parent(s)/carer(s) through a planning process which identified opportunities for development in a variety of settings, including "the client's home, on-site or in a community setting" (p. 15).

Individual ECI organisations took a lead in implementing policy and practice. One example was the work of a small agency in northern Melbourne, Broad Insight Group, which in 2000 and 2001 had begun to change from running group programs to a more individualised approach. The new approach recognised that each family's needs were different and changed over time. It placed primary emphasis on engaging parents and other significant adults who had strong relationships with the child in creating learning opportunities for the child in the everyday settings in which the child spent time, including in the home or community. One of the influences of this change was the "Using the opportunity" approach developed by the Cerebral Palsy Association in Western Australia (Kleinitz & Symes, 2006; McLoughlin & Stonehouse, 2006).

Another contribution to changing perceptions on supports to families was made by the organisation SCOPE, through its "More than my child's disability" project (Larkin & Moore, 2005; Scope, 2004). This project evaluated how family centred the organisation's services were. As part of this process, a review of the literature on the effectiveness of family-centred practice found that:

- families reported greater satisfaction with services, lower parental stress and better parental well being,
- children benefitted most and functional performance improved when interventions were embedded in the everyday environments of families,
- the most important predictor of parental stress was related to a child's behavioural problems (or lack of) and social support networks, and
- effective services combined good clinical or technical skills, good interpersonal skills and a collaborative approach with families.

(Larkin & Moore, 2005, p. 23)

These findings reinforced the need to understand the impact of a child's disability on the family and for services to respond to the pressures placed on families. They also highlighted the complex skills staff working in this model of early intervention needed.

Sector wide discussions about the outcomes of early intervention were organised by ECIA (Victoria Chapter), the peak body for non-government ECI organisations. A process involving a series of forums, discussions and revisions over a 14-month period produced *Starting with the End in Mind Outcome Statements for Early Childhood Intervention Services* (ECIA, 2005). This report endorsed outcomes and objectives for the child, the family and community. Influenced by the work of the World Health Organisation (2002) on the International Classification of Functioning, Disability and Health, one set of outcomes focused on "functioning" and another on "participating." The development of outcomes for the community and participation consolidated the transition to services supporting families in their everyday lives.

In recognition of the broadening expectations being placed on staff working in services, ECIA, with support from the Victorian Government, developed a set of competencies staff needed. This initial process identified six areas, including:

- childhood development,
- family-centred practice,
- communication skills,
- service planning and delivery,
- structure and function of service system, and
- capacity building.

(Coulthard, 2008)

Following a review of 14 competency models (Coulthard & Hollo, 2009), these were further refined into six areas, which included:

- developing the abilities of children with disabilities,
- strengthening family participation in a child's development,
- optimising community inclusion for children with disabilities,
- delivering service,
- engaging others, and
- developing own capabilities.

(Hollo, 2009)

The work on competencies highlighted the need for staff working with children with a disability to have knowledge of general child development. This was new for the majority of the workforce as a result of their allied health background.

Turning the work on competencies into a staff orientation program was undertaken by another non-government organisation (Noah's Ark, Inc., 2010). This organisation developed a program which described the research and approaches underpinning the new directions. Initially developed for its own staff, this orientation program was opened to staff from other agencies and later adapted to be relevant to professionals who had worked in services for children with a disability for longer periods of time but who had not been exposed to newer research and the implications of that research for working with families and children.

Noah's Ark Inc. also produced a resource called the Transdisciplinary Key Worker model (Alexander & Forster, 2012). Noah's Ark had commenced transitioning its 17 centre-based programs to home visiting in Melbourne's western suburbs in 2003. Visiting families, many of which had multi-cultural or low socio-economic backgrounds, at home led to different types of relationships. Discussing family priorities and routines led to new conversations. Parents were more likely to become open about a wide range of issues, for example, family finances, housing and personal relationships. Some staff felt uncomfortable in these conversations, while others felt the child's developmental needs were getting lost.

A review was undertaken to better understand this new relationship with families and its boundaries. It identified that the key worker, or family liaison, component of the role included:

- emotional support,
- information and advice,
- identifying and addressing needs,
- service coordination, and
- advocacy.

(Success Works, 2009)

The resource included the research and practices related to each of these areas. It further established that the model involved a professional with either an allied health or education background acting as the primary point of contact for families, linking the family with a team from multiple disciplines and leading the family's practical intervention plan in relation to their child. This broader role was considered to have a number of important components:

- family liaison,
- using one's own discipline,
- using transdisciplinary skills,
- team consultations, and
- consultations to early childhood services.

It is a similar approach to the primary service provider model (Shelden & Rush, 2012) developed in the USA.

Due to the absence of tertiary courses in ECI in Australia, each organisation has had to develop its own training program. For example, Noah's Ark staff receives training in developing partnerships with families, including family-centred practice, strength-based practice (Glass & Associates, n.d.) and family partnerships (Davis & Day, 2010). They also receive training related to parent-child interactions (Psychology Foundation, n.d.) and coaching parent's interaction with their child (Rush & Sheldon, 2011). Additionally, there is a focus on supporting interventions in the everyday routines of families (McWilliam, 2010).

Reforms to early childhood education and care

The other area of service development for young children with a disability in Victoria has been through changes to services for children generally. The National

Quality Framework for ECEC clearly articulates that services are for all children in the community, and the national EYLF has identified outcomes expected for all (Australian Children's Education and Care Quality Authority, n.d.). Petriwsky (2010) describes this latest period of educational reforms as one of "participation rights" in which the purpose of inclusion extends beyond access and support to programs enhancing the learning of all children through the development of both pedagogy and curriculum (p. 347). Current barriers include overcoming a focus on disability specific services and developing a comprehensive and integrated continuum of evidence-informed practices that strengthen professional competencies (DEECD, 2009, 2011).

While both the international and national literature support the benefits of well-implemented inclusion (Centre for Education Statistics and Evaluation, 2014; National Professional Development Center on Inclusion, 2009, 2011), the limited Australian research has questioned the capacity of staff in children's services to respond to diverse needs of children with a disability (Grace, Llewellyn, Wedgwood, Fenech, & McConnell, 2008; Kishida & Kemp, 2009). These concerns were also raised by the Productivity Commission (2011b), which noted significant gaps between the opportunities available to children with additional needs and those of other children. It reported that if the developmental outcomes of children with additional needs were to improve, then they needed to be given priority in the further ECEC reforms. In particular, the Commission's report identified a need to increase the training for the generally unqualified staff who worked with children with high support needs (p 147).

Responsibility for building the capacity of staff in ECEC services remains unclear. One of the earliest attempts to build staff capacity in Victoria started in 1990 with the piloting of regional teams that included both professionals with a background of working with children with a disability and pools of aides. The professionals' role was to visit State-funded kindergartens, offer professional advice and discuss with staff how their programs might be modified. This approach proposed shifting the focus of support from the child with a disability to the whole preschool program (McLeod, 1993). This approach was not pursued by a new State Government, and by 1997, the pilot programs had lost the capacity to provide professional advice (Centre for Community Child Health, 2002). Responsibility shifted to ECI programs, although the nature of its role was never clarified with the result that staff from disability services and staff in children's services had very different expectations about what was to be achieved through the inclusion of a child with a disability (McLoughlin & Stonehouse, 2006).

Greater clarity the process of building the capacity of staff including children was achieved by the Commonwealth Inclusion and Professional Support Program for child care, which supports children from indigenous backgrounds, children whose family origins are outside Australia and children with high support needs, including children with disabilities. The design of this program included a number of capacity-building components, such as professional development and geographically based teams of Inclusion Support Facilitators. While an Inclusion Support Facilitator role includes supporting services with planning, advice and support to include a child and access to professional development and access to resources (DSS, 2015), it does not extend to advice on individual children's learning and development plans.

More recently, the first joint position statement between Early Childhood Australia (ECA), representing the ECEC field, and ECIA, representing professionals from specific services for children with a disability, calls for greater collaboration between the two fields. The "Position Statement on the inclusion of children with a disability in early childhood education and care" (ECA & ECIA, 2012) recognises that children with a disability have the same rights as other children, and additional rights as a consequence of their disability. It affirms the right of all children to "access and participate in ECEC programs" and raises the importance of services being "resourced and supported to the level required to fully include children with a disability" (ECA & ECIA, 2012, p. 2). It was developed through consultations held in State and territory capitals, a national online survey, contributions from expert reference groups and negotiations with the State and Territory Chapters of both ECA and ECIA.

The development and implementation of a comprehensive strategy to build the capacity of ECEC services remains the next step for children with a disability to benefit fully from ECEC services. This requires a number of approaches, including increasing the flexibility of the pedagogy used in programs, providing educators with professional support, making better support materials available and increasing the amount of information on working with children with disabilities available through tertiary courses. This has commenced from within ECEC services with the examination of new approaches to a pedagogy that will meet the learning and development needs of all children. One example is the focus on engaging children through "intentional teaching" (Barnes, 2012; Marbina, Church, & Tayler, 2010) in order to be responsive to different learning needs. Educators will also need access to professional support to assist them when a child's learning and developmental needs are complex. While this role has been studied internationally (for example, Buysse & Wesley, 2004; Dinnebeil & McInerney, 2011), there is still a lack of policy clarity around this role in Australia. Similarly, there has not been a coordinated development of resources to support educators in their work with children with a disability. The major local resources have been produced by non-government organisations focused on children with a disability. Yooralla has published, and subsequently updated, *A Piece of Cake? Inclusive Practices in Early Childhood Settings* (Boschetti & Stonehouse, 2007; Stonehouse & Boschetti, 2012), which encourages educators to develop more complex responses to children with diverse needs through reflective practice. Noah's Ark Inc. has recently partnered with Chisholm TAFE, a technical and further education or vocational education provider, to turn a resource it developed, *Participating and Belonging: Inclusion in Practice* (Webster & Forster, 2012), into an accredited unit for people studying for an early childhood qualification.

Implications for the future

The introduction of the NDIS represents a major change in the policy context for services for young children with a disability in Victoria. There was a significant development in these services from the early 2000s which included a greater focus on the importance of parents and other significant adults in the development of children; a shift from group-based programs at a professional centre to individualised services provided in the home and the community; one professional, a Key Worker, taking the lead role in both the relationship with the family and the implementation of services; and recognition of the potential of community-based children's services, including child care and preschool, to support the developmental needs of all children, including a child with a disability.

The fundamental premise of services for children with a disability in Victoria during this period was that they were provided *in addition* to a universal platform of services for all children and families. Central to this view was the understanding that children with disabilities and their families had needs like other families and would benefit from other community services. It also shifted the orientation of services from a focus on the child's disabilities to managing the impact of disability in the context of the broader challenges of raising children. This led to redesigning programs so they were based in family's everyday lives, routines and activities. It also encouraged a focus on how children with a disability could benefit from participation in services for all children, such as ECEC.

The introduction of the NDIS significantly changes the paradigm for future reform. The NDIS approach combines a number of elements: an insurance approach; consumer choice and control; and community engagement (Commonwealth of Australia (2013). The insurance approach includes taking a life-long approach to support, including examining the benefits of early intervention. The notion of consumer choice and control transforms the way in which services have been funded. Whereas services were previously funded by government grants, under the NDIS, consumers purchase services from a market of service providers. There is a commitment to persons with a disability being engaged in the community.

The approaches being introduced by the NDIS had previously been introduced for adults with a disability. There are a range of complexities for services for young children with a disability that will need to be addressed. The central dilemma in this new approach is that it is separating services for young children with a disability from other services from young children. For example, in Victoria it is shifting services for children with a disability into a policy context where early childhood development is not the primary focus. At an administrative level, there is potential for a significant divide between services for children with a disability, which will be administered by a federal government agency, and services for children generally, which will be administered by State and Territory Governments. This divide creates a challenge to further reform based on an approach that services for children with a disability should occur in the context of a universal platform of services for all children and families. Under the new arrangements, different levels of government are already drawing boundaries around their responsibilities. It is yet to be seen whether these new arrangements continue, or put at risk, the slow transition from the full segregation of children with a disability that occurred during the institutional era to all young children enjoying the benefits of what the Australian community has to offer.

158   *Forster*

References

Ageing, Disability and Home Care. (n.d.). *Early intervention for children.* Retrieved from http://www.adhc.nsw.gov.au/individuals/support/for_families_ and_children/early_intervention_for_children

Alexander, S., & Forster, J. (2012). *The key worker: Resources for early childhood intervention professionals.* Melbourne, Victoria: ECII, Noah's Ark Inc.

Australian Children's Education and Care Quality Authority. (n.d.) *Introducing the national quality framework, Australian children's education and care quality authority.* Retrieved from http://www.acecqa.gov.au/national-quality-framework

ACT Government. (2009). *Policy framework for children and young people with a disability and their families.* Canberra, Australian Capital Territory. Retrieved from http://www.communityservices.act.gov.au/__data/assets/pdf_file/0013/60061/Children_and_Young_People_Policy.pdf

ACT Government. (n.d. (a)). *Community services: therapy act eligibility criteria.* Retrieved from http://Www.Communityservices.Act.Gov.Au/Therapy_Act/Policies/Eligibility_Criteria

ACT Government. (n.d. (b)). *Education and training directorate: disability education.* Retrieved from http://www.det.act.gov.au/school_education/disability_education

ACT Government. (n.d. (c)). *Education and training directorate: specialist schools.* Retrieved from http://www.det.act.gov.au/school_education/disability_education/specialist-schools

Barnes, S. (2012). *Making sense of 'intentional teaching'.* PSC Alliance. Sydney, NSW: Children's Services Central. Retrieved from http://www.cscentral.org.au/Resources/intentional-teaching-web.pdf

Boschetti, C., & Stonehouse, A. (2007). *A piece of cake? Inclusive practices in early childhood settings.* Melbourne, Victoria: Yooralla Society.

Buysse, V., & Wesley, P. (2004). *Consultation in early childhood settings.* Baltimore, MD: Brookes Publishing Co.

Centre for Community Child Health (CCCH). (2002). *New frontiers in early childhood inclusion.* Melbourne, Victoria: Noah's Ark Inc. Retrieved from http://www.noahsarkinc.org.au/wp-content/uploads/2013/03/New-Frontiers-in-Early-Childhood-Inclusion-2.pdf

Centre for Community Child Health. (2007). Parenting Young children. Policy Brief No 9, Melbourne, Victoria: author. Retrieved from http://www.rch.org.au/uploadedFiles/Main/Content/ccch/PB9_Parenting.pdf

Centre for Education Statistics and Evaluation. (2014). *Children with disability in inclusive early childhood education and care: literature review.* Sydney, NSW: NSW Department of Education and Communities. Retrieved from https://www.det.nsw.edu.au/media/downloads/our-services/children-and-youth/ecec/funding/community-preschool-funding/LiteratureReview-PDSP.PDF

Commonwealth of Australia. (2013). *National Disability Insurance Scheme Act 2013.* No. 20, 2013. Canberra, ACT: Author.

Committee on Integrating the Science of Early Childhood Development. (2000). *From neurons to neighborhoods: The science of early childhood development.* In J. P. Shonkoff & D. A. Phillips (Eds.), *Board on Children, Youth, and Families, Commission on Behavioral and Social Sciences and Education.* Washington, DC: National Research Council and Institute of Medicine; National Academy Press.

Coulhard, N. (2008). *Service trends and practitioner competencies in early childhood intervention: A review of the literature.* Melbourne, Victoria: ECIA (Vic Chapter).

Coulthard, N., & Hollo, A. (2009). *Practitioner competencies and service trends in early childhood intervention: A review of the literature.* Melbourne, Victoria: ECIA (Vic Chapter).

Davis, H., & Day, C. (2010). *Working in partnership: The family partnership model.* London: Pearson.

Dempsey, I., & Keen, D. (2008). A review of processes and outcomes in family-centered services for children with a disability. *Topics in Early Childhood Special Education, 28*(1), 42–52.

Department for Communities and Social Inclusion. (2013). *Annual Report 2012–13.* Adelaide, South Australia: Government of South Australia. Retrieved from http:// www.dcsi.sa.gov.au/__data/assets/pdf_file/0017/13517/2012-13-DCSI-Annual-Report-full-colour.pdf

Department for Education and Child Development. (2012). *Annual Report 2012.* Adelaide, South Australia: Government of South Australia. Retrieved from http:// www.decd.sa.gov.au/docs/documents/1/DECDAnnualReport2012.pdf

Department of Education and Early Childhood Development. (2008a). *Annual Report 2007–2008.* Melbourne, Victoria: State of Victoria. Retrieved from http://www.education.vic.gov.au/Documents/about/department/200708deecannualreport.pdf

Department of Education and Early Childhood Development. (2008b). *Blueprint for Education and Early Childhood Development.* Melbourne, Victoria: State of Victoria.

Department of Education and Early Childhood Development. (2009). *Early childhood intervention reform project literature review.* Melbourne, Victoria: State of Victoria. Retrieved from http://www.education.vic.gov.au/Documents/childhood/providers/needs/ecislitreviewsept2009.pdf

Department of Education and Early Childhood Development. (2011). *Early childhood intervention reform project: Revised literature review.* Melbourne, Victoria: State of Victoria. Retrieved from http://www.education.vic.gov.au/Documents/childhood/providers/needs/ecislitreviewrevised.pdf

Department of Education and Early Childhood Development (DEECD) & Victorian Curriculum and Assessment Authority (VCAA). (2011). *Victorian Early Years Learning and Development Framework: For all children from birth to eight years.* Melbourne, Victoria: State of Victoria. Retrieved from http://www.education.vic.gov.au/Documents/childhood/providers/edcare/veyldframework.pdf

Department of Education and Early Childhood Development. (2011). *Victorian specialist schools.* Retrieved from http://www.education.vic.gov.au/Documents/school/teachers/teachingresources/diversity/vicspecialsists.pdf

Department of Education and Early Childhood Development. (2013). *Annual Report 2012–13.* Melbourne, Victoria: State of Victoria. Retrieved from http:// www.education.vic.gov.au/Documents/about/department/201213deecdannual-report.pdf

Department of Education and Training (n.d.). *Early childhood intervention programs.* Retrieved from http://www.education.vic.gov.au/childhood/parents/needs/pages/ecis.aspx

Department of Education, Employment and Workplace Relations. (2009). *Belonging, Being and Becoming: The Early Years Learning Framework for Australia.* Canberra, ACT: Commonwealth of Australia. Retrieved from https://www.coag.gov.au/sites/default/files/early_years_learning_framework.pdf

Department of Human Services. (2003). *Early childhood intervention services vision and key priorities.* Melbourne, Victoria: State of Victoria. Retrieved from http://www.education.vic.gov.au/Documents/childhood/providers/needs/ecisvision.pdf

Department of Human Services. (2005a). *Annual Report 2004–05.* Melbourne, Victoria: State of Victoria. Retrieved from http://www.dhs.vic.gov.au/__data/assets/pdf_file/0007/527128/19-DHS-Annual-Report-04-05.pdf

Department of Human Services. (2005b). *Early childhood intervention services (ECIS) program framework.* Melbourne, Victoria: State of Victoria. Retrieved from https://www.eduweb.vic.gov.au/edulibrary/public/earlychildhood/intervention/framework2005.pdf

Department of Social Services. (n.d. (a)). *Better start program.* Retrieved from https://www.dss.gov.au/our-responsibilities/disability-and-carers/program-services/for-people-with-disability/better-start-for-children-with-disability-initiative

Department of Social Services. (n.d. (b)). *Helping children with autism.* Retrieved from https://www.dss.gov.au/our-responsibilities/disability-and-carers/program-services/for-people-with-disability/helping-children-with-autism

Department of Social Service. (2015). *Inclusion and professional support program guidelines for 2013–2016.* Canberra, ACT: Australian Government. Retrieved from https://www.dss.gov.au/sites/default/files/documents/06_2015/dss_ipsp_programme_guidelines_2013_-_2016_final_may_2015.pdf

Dinnebeil, L., & McInerney, W. (2011). *A guide to itinerant early childhood special education services.* Baltimore, MD: Brookes Publishing Co.

Disability Commission. (n.d.). *Early childhood development.* Retrieved from http://www.disability.wa.gov.au/services-support-and-eligiblity/services-supports-and-eligibility-new/services/services-provided-by-the-commission/therapy-services/early-childhood-development-/

Dunst, C., Trivette, C., & Deal, A. (1988). *Enabling and empowering families: Principles and guidelines for practice.* Cambridge, MA: Brookline Books.

Dunst, C. J., & Trivette, C. M. (2009). Capacity-building family-systems intervention practices. *Journal of Family Social Work, 12*(2), 119–143.

Early Childhood Australia and Early Childhood Intervention Australia. (2012). *Position statement on the inclusion of children with a disability in early childhood education and care.* Retrieved from http://www.ecia.org.au/documents/item/31

Early Childhood Intervention Australia (Victoria). (2005). *Starting with the end in mind: Outcome statements for warly childhood intervention services.* Melbourne, Victoria: ECIA (Victorian Chapter).

Education Department. (2015). *Early childhood intervention services.* Retrieved from http://www.education.tas.gov.au/parents_carers/schools-colleges/Programs-Initiatives/Pages/Early-Childhood-Intervention-Services.aspx

Flottman, R., & Page J. (2012). Getting early childhood onto the reform agenda: An Australian case study. *International Journal of Child Care and Education Policy, 6*(1), 17–33. Retrieved from http://www.icep.re.kr/archive/archive/index.jsp

Glass, B., & Associates. (2015). *The strengths approach – what is it?* Bernadette Glass & Associates. Retrieved from http://www.bernadetteglass.com.au/

Grace, R., Llewellyn, G., Wedgwood, N., Fenech, M., McConnell, D. (2008). Far from Ideal: Everyday experiences of mothers and early childhood professionals negotiating an inclusive early childhood experience in the Australian context. *Topics in Early Childhood Special Education, 28*(1), 18–30.

Guralnick, M. (2005). An overview of the developmental a systems model for early intervention. In M. Guralnick (Ed.), *The developmental systems approach to early intervention.* Baltimore, MD: Paul H. Brookes Publishing.

Guralnick, M. (2011). Why early intervention works: A systems perspective. *Infants & Young Children, 24*(1), 6–28.

Harrison, L. J., Goldfeld, S., Metcalfe, E., & Moore, T. (2012). *Early learning programs that promote children's developmental and educational outcomes.* Resource sheet no. 15. Produced for the Closing the Gap Clearinghouse. Australian Institute of Health and Welfare and Australian Institute of Family Studies, Canberra. Retrieved from http://www.aihw.gov.au/uploadedFiles/ClosingTheGap/Content/Publications/2012/ctgc-rs15.pdf

Heckman, J. J., & Masterov, D. V. (2004). *The Productivity Argument for investing in Young Children.* Invest in Kids Working Group. Working Paper No. 5, September, 2004. Washington, DC: Committee on Economic Development.

Hollo, A. (2009). *Early childhood intervention practitioner competencies.* Melbourne, Victoria: ECIA (Victorian Chapter). Retrieved from http://www.eciavic.org.au/documents/item/24

Kishida, Y., & Kemp, C. (2009). The engagement and interaction of children with Autism Spectrum Disorder in segregated and inclusive early childhood center-based settings. *Topics in Early Childhood Education, 29*(2), 105–118.

Kemp, C., & Hayes, A. (2005). Early intervention in Australia: The challenge of systems implementation. In M. J. Guralnick (Ed.), *The developmental systems approach to early intervention* (pp. 401–423). Baltimore, MD: Paul H. Brooks Publishing Co.

Kleinitz, P., & Symes, L. (2006). *What are the challenges and the choices for early childhood intervention services in implementing change?* Paper delivered at the Early Childhood Intervention Australia (Victorian Chapter) Annual Conference, Melbourne. Retrieved from http://www.eciavic.org.au/documents/item/34

KPMG. (2011). *Reviewing the evidence on the effectiveness of early childhood intervention.* Report to the Department of Families, Housing, Community Services and Indigenous Affairs. Retrieved from https://www.dss.gov.au/sites/default/files/documents/05_2012/childhood_int_effectiveness_report_0.pdf

Marbina, L., Church, A., & Tayler, C. (2010). *Practice principle 6: Integrated teaching and learning approaches.* Victorian Early Years Learning and Development Framework evidence paper. Melbourne, Victoria: University of Melbourne. Retrieved from https://www.eduweb.vic.gov.au/edulibrary/public/earlylearning/evi-integteachlearn.pdf

Ministerial Council on Education, Employment, Training and Youth Affairs. (2008). *Melbourne declaration on educational goals for young Australians.* Melbourne, Victoria: Author. Retrieved from http://www.curriculum.edu.au/verve/_resources/national_declaration_on_the_educational_goals_for_young_australians.pdf

McLeod, J. (1993). *A different way: An evaluation of the pilot projects in integration support.* Victoria: Victorian Coordinating Committee for the Commonwealth Special Education Program.

McLoughlin, J., & Stonehouse A. (2006). *Inclusion in children's services: Next steps.* Melbourne, Victoria: Noah's Ark Incorporated. Retrieved from http://www.noahs arkinc.org.au/wp-content/uploads/2013/03/Inclusion-in-Childrens-Services-Next-Steps2006.pdf

McWilliam, R. A. (2010). *Routines-based early intervention: supporting young children and their families.* Baltimore, MD: Paul H. Brookes.

Moore, T. (1997). Promoting the healthy functioning of young children with developmental disabilities, and their families, the evolution of theory and research. *Family Matters, 44.* Melbourne, Victoria: Australian Institute of Family Studies.

Moore, T. (2006). *Early childhood and long term development: The importance of the early years.* Evidence into Action Topical Paper, for the Australian Research Alliance for Children & Youth. Parkville, Victoria: Centre for Community Child Health. Retrieved from https://www.aracy.org.au/publications-resources/command/download_ file/id/97/filename/Early_childhood_and_long_term_development_-_ The_importance_of_the_early_years.pdf

Moore, T. G. (2008*). Early childhood intervention: Core knowledge and skills.* CCCH Working Paper 3. Parkville, Victoria: Centre for Community Child Health.

Moore, T. (2012). *Rethinking early childhood intervention services: Implications for policy and practice,* Pauline McGregor Memorial Address presented at the 10th Biennial National Conference of Early Childhood Intervention Australia, and the 1st Asia-Pacific Early Childhood Intervention Conference. Retrieved from http:// www.rch.org.au/uploadedFiles/Main/Content/ccch/profdev/ECIA_National_ Conference_2012.pdf

Moore, T., & Larkin, H. (2005). *"More than my child's disability. . ." : A comprehensive literature review about family-centred practice and family experiences of early childhood intervention services.* Melbourne, Victoria: SCOPE.

National Disability Insurance Agency (NDIA). (2013). *Early Childhood Intervention – Transdisciplinary Approach to Service Provision.* Retrieved from http://www. ndis.gov.au/sites/default/files/media/teamwork_in_early_child_intervention_ services.pdf

National Disability Insurance Agency (NDIA). (2014). *Teamwork in early childhood intervention services: recommended practices.* Retrieved from http://www.ndis. gov.au/sites/default/files/media/transdiciplinary_approach_to_service_provision may2014.pdf

National Professional Development Center on Inclusion. (2009). *Research synthesis points on early childhood inclusion.* Chapel Hill: The University of North Carolina, FPG Child Development Institute, Author. Retrieved from http://npdci.fpg.unc.edu

National Professional Development Center on Inclusion. (2011). *Research synthesis points on practices that support inclusion.* Chapel Hill: The University of North Carolina, FPG Child Development Institute, Author. Retrieved from http://npdci. fpg.unc.edu

Noah's Ark. (2010). *Orientation framework for new early childhood intervention practitioners.* Melbourne, Victoria: Author, unpublished.

Novita Children's Services. (n.d.). *Services: How Novita Can Help Develop Your Child's Potential.* Retrieved from http://www.novita.org.au/Content.aspx?p=9

Petriwskyj, A. (2010). Who has rights to what? Inclusion in Australian early childhood programs. *Contemporary Issues in Early Childhood, 11*(4), 342–352.

Productivity Commission. (2011a). *Disability care and support.* Report no. 54. Canberra, ACT: Australian Government. Retrieved from http://www.pc.gov.au/ inquiries/completed/disability-support/report

Productivity Commission. (2011b). *Early childhood development workforce*. Research report. Canberra: Australian Government. Retrieved from http://www.pc.gov.au/inquiries/completed/education-workforce-early-childhood/report

Psychology Foundation. (n.d.). *First three years – make the connection website*. Retrieved from http://firstthreeyears.org/index.html

Rush, D. D., & Shelden, M. L. (2011). *The early intervention coaching handbook*. Baltimore, MD: Paul H. Brookes.

SCOPE. (2004). *"More than my child's disability . . .": A study of the experiences and family centred practices of scope early childhood intervention services and supports*. Melbourne, Victoria: Scope (Vic) Ltd.

Shelden, M. L., & Rush, D. D. (2012). *The early intervention teaming handbook: The primary service provider approach*. Baltimore, MD: Paul H. Brookes.

State of Victoria. (2004). *Joining the dots: report of the victorian children's advisory committee*. Melbourne, Victoria: Author. Retrieved from http://www.cyf.vic.gov.au/__data/assets/pdf_file/0016/17008/min_pcac_report_joining_the_dots.pdf

Stonehouse, A., & Boschetti, C. (2012). *A piece of cake – Linking inclusive practice to the EYLF and VEYLDF*. Melbourne, Victoria: Yooralla.

Success Works. (2009). *Working with families: The key worker role at Noah's ark*. Melbourne, Victoria: Noah's Ark Inc. Unpublished.

Sukkar, H. (2013). Early childhood intervention: An Australian perspective. *Infant & Young Children: An Interdisciplinary Journal of Early Childhood Intervention*, 26(2), 94–110.

Webster, A., & Forster, J. (2012). *Participating and belonging: Inclusion in practice*. Melbourne, Victoria: ECII, Noah's Ark Inc.

Workgroup on Principles and Practices in Natural Environments, OSEP TA Community of Practice: Part C Settings. (2008, February). *Seven Key Principles: Looks Like/ Doesn't Look Like*. Retrieved from http://www.ndis.gov.au/sites/default/files/documents/seven_key_principles.pdf

World Health Organization. (2002). *Towards a common language for functioning, disability and health: ICF, the international classification of functioning, disability and health*. Geneva: Author. Retrieved from http://www.who.int/classifications/icf/icfbeginnersguide.pdf?ua=1

Yooralla. (2000). *The turning point: Rethinking the early childhood intervention service delivery model*. Melbourne, Victoria: Yooralla.

10 Working with families in schools

Wendy Goff and June McLoughlin

In this chapter, we describe a place-based, family-centred approach to supporting the health, development, wellbeing and learning of vulnerable children and their families. We provide insight into the processes, challenges, opportunities and possibilities embedded in a place-based, family-centred community school established in Australia. Throughout the case study discussed, different approaches to guide and support professionals in their work with vulnerable children, families and communities are presented, and various examples of some of these "approaches in action" are provided. Practical strategies and take-away messages for coming together and working with key service delivery partners to better support children and families are also offered.

Over the past few decades, there has been an unprecedented social change, both in Australia and beyond. The rapid explosion of digital technology, the globalisation of ideas, changing economic conditions, extended work hours and a greater social mobility has resulted in significant social change across the globe (Moore & Fry, 2011). Such change has not only altered the conditions in which families are now raising young children, but it has also changed the communities and circumstances in which young children are now growing and living (Moore & Fry, 2011). Through this change, communities across the globe have become both complex and multidimensional (Moore & Fry, 2011), and the challenges posed to families on a daily basis are now multifaceted.

A variety of researchers have demonstrated that the health and wellbeing of individuals and families is intricately linked to the social connections and relationships within their communities (Bryderup & Trentel, 2013; Herz, 2015; Hunt, 2013). Such links have included improved community participation (Simplican, Leader, Kosciulek, & Leahy, 2015), benefits to mental health (Petersen, Baillie, & Bhana, 2012) and greater family support systems (Angley, Divney, Magriples, & Kershaw, 2015). Despite the identification of such benefits, the social changes that have occurred over the past few decades have posed some new challenges for families in their ability to forge such connections and relationships. As a result, some families are now experiencing high levels of vulnerability that are characterised by complex needs and low levels of social support.

Family-centred service provision

Families have long been considered as a primary context for a child's development (Grace & Bowes, 2011). Families shape children's experiences in different ways and provide opportunities for children to "form relationships with others outside the family through the family's links to the community" (Bowes & Warburton, 2014, p. 100). When the family does not have or cannot make such community links, opportunities for wider support and input into a child's experiences and development are either restricted or not afforded.

In recent years, research into the efficacy of family-centred service provision to enhance the lives of young children has presented some promising findings. In fact, Australian reviews into the effectiveness of the practice have demonstrated that both the theoretical evidence and practical benefits that emerge as a result of family-centred work are significant (Dempsey, Keen, Pennell, O'Reilly, & Neilands, 2009; Moore & Larkin, 2005). Likewise, a synthesis of 52 studies conducted across seven different countries highlighted a number of direct and indirect benefits to families, parents and children (Dunst, Trivette, & Hamby, 2008). Such benefits included positive changes in child behaviour, improved self-efficacy for both families and children and changes in family and child functioning (Dunst et al., 2008).

Dunst (2002) defines family-centredness as exemplified by "beliefs and practices that treat families with dignity and respect" and that are also "individualised, flexible and responsive" (p.139). Such practices are described as having both "relational and participatory components" (Dunst, 2002, p. 139) that are drawn upon concurrently to achieve desired outcomes. Within a family-centred approach, families are recognised as experts of their own lived experiences and are therefore "actively involved in decisions and choices" (Dunst, 2002, p. 139). This involvement includes the voice of the family in the formulation of the goals and outcomes that are being worked towards. It is also embedded in the notion that families are "worked with," not "worked on."

In relation to policy, the family system is integral to economic operation and functioning (Peers, 2015). However, in Australia, government services have been challenged to support families in ways that are family-centred and ways that address multiple needs and varying levels of complexity. Current reforms and initiatives are driven by the notion that multiple needs demand multiple solutions, and that these solutions should involve "tackling social problems at multiple levels simultaneously" (Moore & Fry, 2011, p. 16). However, such reforms and initiatives often position families at the periphery rather than at the centre of intervention.

In the following section of this chapter, we introduce a place-based, family-centred approach to supporting the health, development and wellbeing of vulnerable children and families in Victoria, Australia. In doing so, we highlight what is possible when government put families at the centre of service provision, including what can be achieved through such action. By examining the place-based, family-centred approach and then presenting and explicating the challenges and opportunities afforded through this model, we hope to provide insight into how similar practices and outcomes might be achieved by those working with vulnerable families in other contexts.

Doveton College

Doveton is a suburb of Victoria, Australia, that is situated approximately 31kms southeast of the Melbourne central business district. In the 2013 Australian Census, 11,127 people resided in the Doveton community, 45.5% of families were identified as speaking a language other than English at home and the median household income was $AUD822 per week (Australian Bureau of Statistics, 2013). Since 2006 the community has been identified through the Socio-Economic Index for Areas of Relative Socio-economic Disadvantage as in the lowest quintile of disadvantage compared to all other Australian communities.

In 2009, a philanthropic organisation, The Colman Foundation, approached the Victorian State Government with their desire to become directly involved in the education and support of young children and families who are experiencing social and economic disadvantage. During this time, the State Government was amidst statewide school reform, and an agreement was reached for the Colman Foundation and the government to come together to better support the families and children in the Doveton community. The agreement met by both parties involved the construction of a purpose-built, prenatal to year nine, community-focused school.

The partnership was the first government social partnership to establish a learning facility in Australia. It involved an initial $1.8-million-dollar investment by the Colman Foundation, a $27 million dollar investment by the government and an annual funding commitment from the Colman Foundation for the next eight years. In 2012, Doveton College opened its doors to the Doveton community.

The Doveton model of service delivery

Doveton College works on a place-based, family-centred, integrated community service delivery model. A place-based approach is focused on community strengthening and "seeks to address the collective problems of families and communities at a local level" (Moore & Fry, 2011, p. 29). There are three components of service incorporated within the model: *services that are embedded within the College* (early learning, schooling, playgroup, maternal and child health care, family support services); *services that are provided to, and located at the College* (allied health, general practitioner, paediatrician, refugee services, adult education and training); and *services that are provided through referral from the College but that are offered off site* (housing, counseling, financial support services). Figure 10.1 provides a visual representation of the delivery model.

The model has been designed as a comprehensive, integrated approach to supporting families. It has numerous goals that are both multi-dimensional

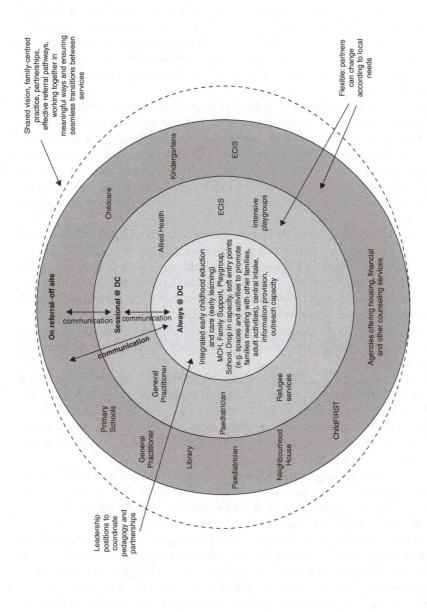

Shared vision, family-centred practice, partnerships, effective referral pathways, working together in meaningful ways and ensuring seamless transitions between services

Flexible: partners can change according to local needs

On referral–off site

Sessional @ DC

Always @ DC

communication

communication

communication

Childcare

Kindergartens

ECIS

Allied Health

ECIS

Intensive playgroups

Integrated early childhood eduction and care (early learning) MCH, Family Support, Playgroup, School. Drop in capacity, soft entry points (e.g. spaces and activities to promote families meeting with other families, adult activities), central intake, information provision, outreach capacity

Primary Schools

General Practitioner

General Practitioner

Library

Paediatrician

Paediatrician

Neighbourhood House

Refugee services

ChildFIRST

Agencies offering housing, financial and other counseling services

Leadership positions to coordinate pedagogy and partnerships

Figure 10.1 The Doveton College service delivery model

Source: Created by the author

and collaborative in nature. Integration of service delivery is at the core of the model, but this delivery is also considered within a dynamic living system. Family needs drive the model, and support starts with, and through, the identification and formation of service connections that might support an identified need of the family (both identification and formation are achieved in conjunction with the family). Focus within the model then moves toward coordination of these service connections. This involves bringing several services together to formulate a support plan (once again, this is achieved through active family involvement). The final stage of the model involves integration of services to action the plan.

The model ensures that service delivery is not only comprehensive in scope, but that it can also serve multiple purposes and address individual complexity and difference. It is dynamic in nature and provides a way for service delivery to be driven *by families for families*. It is also tailored to accommodate changing needs and provides a means for service to enter and exit at different times according to need. In relation to children, it provides a way to recognise young children as part of their family, their school and their community systems.

Doveton College is home to approximately 660 school-aged children, with a further 145 children enrolled in the early learning centre. The college also accommodates a variety of professionals, including a general practitioner, mental health care providers, child and allied health professionals, a pediatrician, social welfare workers, youth workers and educators. The partnerships developed with these various professionals have resulted in a variety of services on site, providing immediate access to families and children. This has eliminated many of the usual barriers to service provision such as transport difficulties and long waiting times.

The college can be described as a community-learning centre whereby school and community resource is woven together to support the needs of families and children. There are a variety of child and family services functioning within the college, such as parenting support, playgroups and adult education programs. Such groups are driven by community and family needs and are integrated within and alongside the learning environment.

Whilst we acknowledge that Doveton College is a unique example, what we aim to highlight in the remainder of this chapter are the various strategies and processes that are embedded within the Doveton model. We believe that these strategies and processes are transferrable to different circumstances and contexts, and can be effectively employed by those working in similar communities. In order to do this, we draw on the implementation of the place-based, integrated, family-centred, community service delivery model to highlight a variety of practical examples that demonstrate the challenges and opportunities that have been encountered at Doveton College. Our aim is to highlight a number of strategies and processes that can be employed by others working with vulnerable children and families in different contexts.

Challenges, opportunities and possibilities

Implementing the model at Doveton College has not been without challenges. However, as with any challenge, it has also provided an opportunity to work through and develop solutions, and in some cases, a variety of solutions. This has been the strength of the model as it has unfolded in action. It has provided a way to recognise and tackle complexity, but also a way to move forward and overcome obstacles.

One of the initial challenges faced during the implementation of the Doveton model centred on the people who were recruited to work at the college. The model demanded a shift in thinking and, in some instances, an unlearning of how systems operate and work together. It necessitated all staff employed at the college to re-think their work with families and children and to reconceptualise and develop new ways of working.

According to Dunst (2002), a family-centred approach requires "a particular set of beliefs, principles, values, and practices for supporting and strengthening family capacity to enhance and promote child development and learning" (p. 139). What was discovered during the implementation of the model at Doveton was that developing such beliefs, principles, values and practices takes both time and support.

Time provision was a strategy that was incorporated into the implementation plan. It provided an opportunity for staff at the college to develop and engage in relational practices, but it also provided the opportunity to embed participatory practices into everyday work (Dunst et al., 2008). Time was provided for collaboration with both families and colleagues, but time was also provided to think about how what was being learned (through such collaboration) could be embedded into day-to-day practice. This was an integral component of the process of implementation, and we believe a component that (although is easily transferrable to other contexts) is often overlooked during the development of similar models.

Another challenge that emerged during the early stages of implementation centred round inter-agency collaboration. At the systems level, different organisations have different structures, different networks, diverse leadership and varied policy imperative. All of these factors emerged as a significant challenge at Doveton, particularly when one of the aims of the college was to provide an integrated wrap-around service for families. Whilst the individuals working within the college demonstrated a willingness to consider new possibilities and seek out new opportunities to work together, it was the systems in which they were employed that posed some genuine obstacles for inter-agency collaboration to take place. This included the limitations placed on the differing organisations by their governance and funding models; resource for collaboration was not necessarily allocated by all organisations.

According to Horwath and Morrison (2011), "little is known about the organisational conditions . . . that can promote or inhibit collaborative practices" (p. 369). At Doveton it was evident that the individuals within the different organisations wanted to work together, but as the work unfolded, it was also evident that the organisational conditions that were initially in place were prohibiting this work from happening. A coordinated approach was imperative to the model, so this posed a significant problem during the early stages of implementation. In order to overcome this challenge, the development of a shared service philosophy was seen as a way forward.

A shared service philosophy provided a way to embed some common practices into the different systems and draw on these shared initiatives to move forward in ways that were conducive to collaboration and service innovation. It also provided a way to speak back to differing systems through the development and use of a common and shared language. This work during the early stage of the project provided valuable insight into inter-agency collaboration, including what might be necessary to move forward to break down systemic barriers. Those preparing to collaborate with different organisations might draw on what was learned at Doveton, and develop a shared service philosophy prior to coming together. Such an approach would ensure that organisational challenges, such as those experienced at Doveton, would be eliminated.

As the implementation of the model continued, there were also a variety of affordances that were not necessarily linked to overcoming challenge, but instead naturally emerged. For example, the provision of a variety of services in one physical location immediately removed some of the barriers to access that many vulnerable families might experience. According to Grace, Bowes, Trudgett, McFarlane and Honig (2010), typical barriers include costs of services, transport expenses and availability/opening hours. The Doveton model eliminated many of these barriers through the coordination of service to the one physical space.

The physical environment also provided the opportunity for the wider Doveton community to make use of the space that was not being used and to develop an increased community presence within the college. Groups that have emerged since the implementation of the model include sewing groups, men's support groups, refugee support groups, work and learn programs and a fruit and vegetable co-op. Whilst the physical space at Doveton has been purpose-built and has included the support of significant financial investment, the same affordances could be facilitated in other contexts through an assessment of current existing physical space. This might include something as simple as identifying space that is not often utilised, or offering the service to community after operating hours. Such initiatives can promote community engagement and provide those most isolated in the community with community connections.

Affordances to children

In relation to children's learning, an integrated learning model that is focused on stage (rather than age) has been embedded within the Doveton model. This shift in focus has ensured that a personalised learning approach is naturally afforded, where level of personal progression determines a learner's individual achievement rather than aged-based outcomes. Such an approach not only recognises the complexity of some children's lives, but it also harnesses the gains made in working through and overcoming challenges. It has also provided an opportunity to draw on family as a resource to support and celebrate the individual achievements of children, recognising and extending children's learning beyond the classroom.

The shift away from more traditional ways of working with children and families has been challenging for some of the educators at the college, as it has demanded a different way of thinking about teaching and learning and a different way of viewing an educator's work with families. In order to support personnel through this change, strong leadership has been imperative. The college leadership team is comprised of an Executive Principal, Director of Family and Children's Services, two Assistant Principals and the Business Manager. A Parent Advisory Group and a Family and Community Services Reference Group support the leadership team in all facets of planning and implementation and provide direction from the family and community perspectives.

This team has been actively involved in mentoring the educators at the college through both change and challenge. This mentoring has involved engaging staff in new processes, providing support for innovation and experimentation and the provision of targeted professional development. It has also been driven by the notion of developing people. According to Leithwood et al. (2010), "developing people" is embedded in a distributed leadership style whereby leadership is shared amongst different people who can contribute to an individuals development in different ways. Within a framework of family-centredness, this is a worthwhile consideration for leadership teams.

The bi-directional processes that take place within and between the systems in which children live and learn have also been important components of supporting children's learning and development (Bronfenbrenner, 1977; Bronfenbrenner & Morris, 1998). Whilst the early learning centre at Doveton is play-based and driven by the interests of children, support provided to individual children is afforded through the relationships that are forged between educators, families and partner services. By recognising relationships as resources to be drawn upon to support the learning and wellbeing of children, each individual child is recognised as part of a wider system, and in turn, this wider system is recognised as a vital component of children's learning and wellbeing.

Community strengthening is at the heart of place-based models (Moore & Fry, 2011), and in this case, strengthening the Doveton community was the vision. What has been learned through the Doveton model is that "empowering" people and community is not something that can necessarily be achieved; empowerment comes from within person and within the community itself. Educators and service providers can work together to support individuals and their communities, but empowerment is not something that can be gifted from one to another.

Malone (1997) suggests that "when most people talk about [notions of] empowerment, they mean relatively timid shifts of power within a fairly conventional, hierarchical structure" (p. 23). Such shifts might be suited to the priorities of some contexts, but this was not what was being sort in the Doveton model. Empowerment in the Doveton model was a reciprocal process whereby educators, service providers and families were all empowered through their successes together. At times this involved supporting a family to overcome challenge and realise potential, and at other times it involved the family supporting educators to better understand the needs of children. Empowerment in the Doveton model was a bi-directional process and therefore achieved in many different ways by different individuals.

Key messages

Whilst there are a variety of lessons that can be learned through the implementation of the Doveton model, we believe that there are three key messages for those about to embark on similar work. We list these messages below.

1) *There will be challenges.* Some of these challenges will be predictable, whilst others will emerge throughout the journey. The key to overcoming such challenges is to recognise the opportunities that challenges afford.
2) *Do not underestimate the potential of people.* People are the most significant resource that can be drawn upon when embarking on such work. However, what people can offer can only be drawn upon if the strengths of people are recognised.
3) *Be patient and persistent.* This work involves learning and it will take time before these new learnings are put into practice. Remember, change takes time.

A concluding comment

Whilst we appreciate that the Doveton model is unique and well resourced, we also believe that the lessons learned through the Doveton journey can provide some valuable insight to others embarking on similar endeavours. In this chapter we have attempted to highlight this insight through the different examples presented.

References

Angley, M., Divney, A., Magriples, U., & Kershaw, T. (2015). Social support, family functioning and parenting competence in adolescent parents. *Maternal and Child Health Journal, 19*(1), 67–73.

Australian Bureau of Statistics. (2013). *Doveton SA2.* Retrieved from http://stat.abs.gov.au/itt/r.jsp?RegionSummary&region=212021295&dataset=ABS_REGIONAL_ASGS&geoconcept=REGION&datasetASGS=ABS_REGIONAL_ASGS&datasetLGA=ABS_REGIONAL_LGA&regionLGA=REGION&regionASGS=REGION

Bowes, J., & Warburton, W. (2014). Family as the primary context of children's development. In J. Bowes, R. Grace, & G. Hodge (Eds.), *Children, families and communities* (4th ed.). South Melbourne, Victoria: Oxford University Press.

Bronfenbrenner, U. (1977). Toward an experimental ecology of human development. *American Psychologist, 32*(7), 513–531.

Bronfenbrenner, U., & Morris, P. (1998). The ecology of developmental processes. In W. Damon & R. M. Lerner (Eds.), *Handbook of child psychology: Theoretical models of human development* (5th ed., Vol. 1, pp. 993–1029). New York: Wiley.

Bryderup, M., & Trentel, M. (2013). The importance of social relationships for young people from a public care background. *European Journal of Social Work, 16*(1), 37–54. doi:10.1080/13691457.2012.749219

Dempsey, I., Keen, D., Pennell, D., O'Reilly, J., & Neilands, J. (2009). Parent stress, parenting competence and family-centred support to young children with an intellectual or developmental disability. *Research in Developmental Disabilities, 30*(3), 588–566.

Dunst, C. (2002). Family-centred practices: Birth through high school. *Journal of Special Education, 36*(3), 139–147.

Dunst, C., Trivette, C., & Hamby, D. (2008). *Research synthesis and meta-analysis of studies of family-centred practices*. Asheville, NC: Winterberry Press.

Grace, R., & Bowes, J. (2011). Using an ecocultural approach to explore young children's experiences of prior-to-school care settings. *Early Child Development and Care, 181*(1), 13–25.

Grace, R., Bowes, J., Trudgett, M., McFarlane, A., & Honig, T. (2010). *Barriers to participation: The experience of disadvantaged young children, their families and professionals in engaging with early childhood services*. NSW Australia: NSW Department of Human Services.

Herz, A. (2015). Relational constitution of social supports in migrants' transnational personal communities. *Social Networks, 40*, 64–74.

Horwath, J., & Morrison, T. (2011). Effective inter-agency collaboration to safeguard children: Rising to the challenge through collective development. *Children and Youth Services Review, 33*, 368–375.

Hunt, J. (2013). Engaging with Indigenous Australia – exploring the conditions for effective relationships with Aboriginal and Torres Strait Islander communities. *Issue paper no.5 — Closing the gap clearing house*. Canberra: Australian Institute of Health and Welfare.

Leithwood, K., Louis, K., Wahlstrom, K., Anderson, S., Mascall, B., & Gordon, M. (2010). How successful leadership influences student learning: The second installment of a longer story. In A. Hargreaves, A. Lieberman, M. Fullan, & D. Hopkins (Eds.), *Second international handbook of educational change* (Vol. 23, pp. 611–630). Dordrecht Heidelberg London New York: Springer.

Malone, T. (1997). Is empowerment just a fad? Conrol, decision making and IT. *Sloan Management Review, 38*(2), 23–35.

Moore, T., & Fry, R. (2011). *Place-based approaches to child and family services: A literature review*. Parkville, Victoria: Murdoch Childrens Research Institute and The Royal Children's Hospital Centre for Community Child Health.

Moore, T., & Larkin, H. (2005). *"More than my child's disability": A comprehensive literature review about family-centred practice and family experiences of early childhood intervention services* (pp. 1–69). Glenroy, Victoria: Scope (Vic) Ltd.

Peers, C. (2015). What is 'human' in human capital theory? Marking a transition from industrial to postindustrial education. *Open Review of Educational Research, 2*(1), 55–77.

Petersen, I., Baillie, K., & Bhana, A. (2012). Understanding the benefits and challenges of community engagement in the development of community mental health services for common mental disorders: Lessons from a case study in a rural South African subdistrict site. *Transcultural Psychiatry, 49*(3–4), 418–437.

Simplican, S., Leader, G., Kosciulek, J., & Leahy, M. (2015). Defining social inclusion of people with intellectual and developmental disabilities: An ecological model of social networks and community participation. *Research in Developmental Disabilities, 38*, 18–29.

Part V
Working with families and young children in other countries

The tugs and pulls and trials and tribulations which are almost always found within and between the different ecological systems in which early childhood intervention is a subsystem are described in the chapters in this section of the book. These influences include, but are not limited to, governmental legislation (or lack thereof), funding streams, interagency agreements and disagreements, agency policies and practices, differences in the beliefs and practices of professionals from different disciplines, and administrative and organisational supports (or lack thereof) for supporting or discouraging the use of family-centred early childhood intervention practices. Each of the chapters includes rich descriptions of the challenges and opportunities offered by family systems and family-centred approaches to early childhood intervention.

One of the most important messages communicated in several chapters is that becoming a family-centred program or organisation is difficult enough, but that remaining a family-centred program or organisation is even more difficult (Serrano et al., Chapter 11; Hiebert-Murphy et al., Chapter 12). Knowing and acting on those conditions is therefore absolutely necessary if family-centred practices are ever to become a routine way of implementing early childhood intervention (Dempsey & Carruthers, 1997; Dunst & Espe-Sherwindt, 2016). The authors of all three chapters share "real life" experiences in their respective countries that readers will find helpful for understanding the broader-based contexts of attempts to implement family-centred early childhood intervention. These experiences include the complexities of engaging parents and other carers in interventions in ways that not only promote child learning and development, but also support and strengthen family member confidence and competence.

Serrano et al. (Chapter 11) describe the evolution of family-centred early childhood intervention in Portugal, and the challenges and opportunities afforded by national early childhood intervention legislation. The authors also describe how lessons learned in Portugal have informed adoption of family-centred practices in Spain. Hiebert-Murphy et al. (Chapter 12) describe their efforts to develop and implement family-centred and family-strengthening practices in Manitoba, Canada, and share key issues and findings in terms of their ability to promote the adoption and use of these approaches to early childhood intervention (see Trute & Hiebert-Murphy, 2013). Blackman (Chapter 13) describes how family experiences in early childhood intervention in England have been directly and indirectly influenced by broader-based macrosystem influences, and how those systems factors shaped the provision of early childhood intervention. All three chapters include information for understanding and informing the adoption and use of family systems and family-centred early childhood intervention practices.

References

Dempsey, I., & Carruthers, A. (1997). How family-centered are early intervention services: Staff and parent perceptions? *Journal of Australian Research in Early Childhood Education, 1*, 105–114.

Dunst, C. J., & Espe-Sherwindt, M. (2016). Family-centered practices in early childhood intervention. In B. Reichow, B. A. Boyd, E. E. Barton, & S. L. Odom (Eds.), *Handbook of early childhood special education* (pp. 37–55). Cham, Switzerland: Springer International.

Trute, B., & Hiebert-Murphy, D. (Eds.). (2013). *Partnering with parents: Family-centred practice in children's services*. Toronto, Canada: University of Toronto.

11 Family systems and family-centred intervention practices in Portugal and Spain
Iberian reflections on early childhood intervention

Ana M. Serrano, Joana M. Mas, Margarita Cañadas and Climent Giné

"Searching the dream is searching for truth"- Fernando Pessoa

This chapter includes descriptions of the current status of early childhood intervention (ECI) in Portugal and Spain, the long path that Portugal has taken in adopting and implementing capacity-building family-centred services and how the Portugal model and lessons learned have influenced the adoption of this model in Spain. Despite recent changes in ECI in Spain, the conceptual model and professional practices prevailing in ECI in these two countries differ. The ECI system in Portugal has a legislative framework that places the family system at the centre of attention and ensures the use of capacity-building, family-system intervention practices. In contrast, Spain has only recently begun to experience major changes toward understanding the family as pivotal in the ECI process and the changes that are needed in order to have capacity-building characteristics and consequences for children and families. This is currently the focus of transformation (reflection and change) towards adoption of a family-centred model (FCM) in Spain.

In order to understand the current state of ECI in each country, we briefly describe the historical, conceptual and legislative bases of ECI in both Portugal and Spain. Then we will proceed to an analysis of the current reality of practices in Portugal and the process of transformation in Spain. We conclude the chapter by describing some future directions and by discussing events that have been key to making a paradigm shift in how ECI is practised, and the national and international support network that has been created during this process.

Conceptual and legislative foundations of early childhood intervention in Portugal and Spain

Early childhood intervention in Portugal

In Portugal, 25 April 1974 represents a crucial turning point in how ECI has evolved, and how changes that occurred on this date have had a tremendous impact on the ways in which services are provided to children and their families. Considerable changes were made in the area of child care and protection; several initiatives emerged for children with special needs (SN), and preschool education was recognised as being part of the official educational system (Serrano & Boavida, 2011). The country, aided by investment and support from the European Community, increased its rates of preschool attendance from 33% in 1996 to 67% in 1997–98 (Clements, 1999), and from 67% in 1997–1998 to 80% in 2008 (OECD, 2011). In the health services arena, a number of follow-up programs were started for high-risk newborns in maternity and paediatric clinics in many of the major public hospitals in the country. Through a network of primary care health centres and local, secondary and tertiary hospitals, Portugal's National Health Service provided free health care to most of the population. In the last 30 years, there has been a significant increase in the quality of maternal and child health services, resulting in a dramatic decrease in the infant mortality rate from 24.2 in 1,000 live births in 1980 to 3.3 in 1,000 live births in 2008 (OECD, 2011).

Origins of early childhood intervention in Portugal

All these changes led to the development of the first ECI services in Portugal. These included the development of a centre-based ECI program for children with cerebral palsy at the Cerebral Palsy Center in Lisbon in the 1970s. During the 1980s, with the support provided by the Directorate of Guiding and Psychology Intervention Services in Lisbon, a Portage ECI Program was begun by translating and using the Portage materials in their work with young children with SN and their families as part of a home-based ECI program (Coutinho, 1999; Pereira, 2009; Pimentel & Almeida, 1999; Pereira, 2009; Serrano, 2003; Serrano & Boavida, 2011; Veiga, 1995). Despite the fact that these programs had much to offer, they were child-centred and acted independently from other services. This lack of articulation with other services led to fragmented service delivery.

The Coimbra early intervention project

From late 1980s to end of the 1990s ECI in Portugal has progressed from an emerging service, provided in the context of a child-centred perspective, to a rapidly changing service expansion with a totally different conceptual framework. Part of this evolution was triggered by the implementation of a community-based program of ECI in Coimbra – The Coimbra Early Intervention Project (PIIP), located in the central region of the country (Boavida & Carvalho, 2003; Boavida, Espe-Sherwindt, & Borges, 2000). The project aimed to provide individualised district-wide services to children under three years of age who were at risk for or were SN and their families by using both formal and informal resources already available in the community and by creating a collaborative effort involving health, education and social services (Serrano & Boavida, 2011). The Coimbra Project was the first coordinated interdisciplinary, interagency ECI program in Portugal, involving health care, education and social work, and other existing resources in the community (Boavida & Borges, 1994). The PIIP provided training to all professionals involved in the program and promoted a strong collaboration among researchers and experts in the field, both in Portugal and abroad for personnel preparation.

As a result of its successes, the Coimbra project greatly influenced the development of the Portuguese legislation regarding ECI services, and is considered a precursor of the national model which was created later by the legislation and enacted in 2009. As Serrano and Boavida (2011) noted, "the implementation of the Coimbra Project constituted the starting point of a *no return* process for the development of ECI in Portugal" (p.128). The project's success contributed to and influenced both professionals' and policy-makers' awareness of the need to integrate and coordinate the service delivery of multiple community agencies and develop regulations on the provisions of services to ensure that children with SN and their families received needed supports, resources, and services.

Early childhood intervention legislation

As a result of the Coimbra ECI experience, a task force was established to formulate polices for ECI in Portugal in 1994. This was in response to the need to create an organisational and integrated model of shared interservice responsibilities for ECI. This task force was comprised of representatives from the Ministry of Education, Ministry of Social Affairs and Ministry of Health, and had the mission of developing the first ECI legislation (Joint Executive Regulation (JER), nr. 891/99) (Despacho conjunto n.° 891/99) aimed at establishing and organising services for young children with SN and their families. According to the law, ECI services require the inclusion of three basic elements: (1) the family as the focus for planning and delivering community-based early intervention supports and services in addition to the education and treatment of the child; (2) the provision of ECI that is multidisciplinary and interagency, which includes professionals from education, health and social services in order to provide comprehensive developmental services to children from birth to six and their families; and (3) the development and implementation of an Individualised Early Intervention Plan (IEIP) according to a family-focused philosophy.

The legislation, unfortunately, was not widely adopted, and ECI was successfully implemented only in specific areas in Portugal, especially in the central region of the country and in Alentejo (Almeida, 2009; Pinto et al., 2012). In other regions, it was not implemented because of a lack of involvement from regional political authorities. Part of this failure resulted from the fact that JER, issued by the government, was not empowered to promote widescale adoption of ECI, as is the case for Parliament-approved Public Laws. Consequently, an intense advocacy and awareness campaign was initiated that involved parents, professionals and faculty members within the civil society in the country followed. The campaign's goal was to guarantee the rights of these children and families and culminated in the enactment of Public Law (PL) 281 on October 6, 2009 (Decreto-Lei n.º 281/2009 de 6 de Outubro).

The parliament approved a new legislation for the provision of ECI services (PL 281/09) that had many similarities with the JER. It created a National System for Early Childhood Intervention (SNIPI). However, an examination of both pieces of legislation reveals that they are poorly conceptualised, resulting in less than ideal family involvement. Fortunately, since the beginning of the new millennium, ECI has gained a growing audience, and professionals, agencies and families have become more aware of the significant paradigm shift that occurred in Portugal that was described earlier. We hope this shift will result in more beneficial provision of best practice ECI than was facilitated by the legislation itself (Serrano & Boavida, 2011).

These numerous societal and legislative changes pose new challenges to families, ECI practitioners, trainers and planners. It is also important to remark that the implementation of ECI services in Portugal was a *bottom-up* process, which helped maintain the changes needed to ensure that a paradigmatic shift (Healy, Keesee, & Smith, 1989) towards a capacity-building, family-centred model of intervention occured.

Early childhood intervention in Spain

The political and territorial organisation of Spain into 17 Autonomous Communities, with their own parliaments and governments, makes it difficult to provide a general conceptual and legislative vision, as there are different realities in different places concerning regulations, funding, composition of professional teams, conceptual models, etc. Nevertheless, we intend to describe the most important features that characterise the evolution of ECI in Spain on the basis of three main stages: origins, development and present state-of-affairs. At the outset, we should note that presently ECI in Spain is a consolidated service, which has been integrated into a network of public social services.

Origins of early childhood intervention in Spain

The origins of ECI in Spain can be traced to the 1970s. The interest of a few eager professionals who were working with children with development disorders had the idea that if "treatment" could be started sooner, better child outcomes would be realised. These types of ECI programs or services were first called "early stimulation" services (Guinea, Lleonhart, Ssilvestre, Martinez, Zaurín, & Giné, 1983) and now are described as early childhood intervention.

The earliest approaches to ECI in Spain conceptualised professional practice from a clinical perspective where delays or deviations in functioning were thought to reside in the child, and where intervention or "treatment" focused on alleviating the consequences of either real or perceived deficits (Giné, Vilaseca, Gràcia, & García-Díe, 2004). This pathological view of intervention was also applied to the family. As noted by Cunningham (2000), it was automatically assumed that the families with a child with disability necessarily suffered as a result of the child's condition or developmental delay and so they should also be focus of treatment. Summarising, the beginning of the "early stimulation" is characterised by a concept of intervention focused on the child, aimed at correcting deficits, where interventions were carried out by professionals who acted as experts in altering changes in child and family functioning.

Development of early childhood intervention

The decades of the 1980s and 1990s represent important changes in the development and implementation of ECI services in Spain. At least three aspects of those changes need to be considered. Firstly, the administration of ECI in the different Autonomous Communities in Spain became more centralised, and the centralised administration took on responsibility for regulating and funding ECI services. These initiatives occurred within already existing programmes, by recognising and often funding them, and by creating new public services.

Secondly, it is important to note the role that professional organisations had – and continue to have – throughout the entire process of reshaping the landscape of ECI in Spain. Professional organisations interested in ECI have had a huge influence on their members, the administration, and the broader-based society. In every Autonomous Community, professionals organised themselves into local associations, which became the foundations of a national ECI body that included all of the separate associations of early intervention professionals in Spain. These associations have been very active, mainly in terms of training and the development of professionals entering ECI and in their explicit recognition of the importance of ECI. They publish journal articles, organise congresses and conferences and offer training activities (courses, workshops, seminars etc.) both at a local and a national level.

Thirdly, during the 1980s and 1990s, the model that dominated ECI both from a conceptual perspective and in terms of professional practice focused on (a) child (and family) deficits; (b) treatment with a goal to correct or rehabilitate poor functioning; (c) an expert or professionally centred model; and (d) professionals as the decision-makers in terms of most or all aspects of the ECI process (including identification of the needs of the child and family, treatment, transition to school and how parents should do at home). These characteristics, taken together, are what Dunst and Trivette (2009) describe as a traditional ECI paradigm.

Contemporary early childhood intervention

In the second half of the 1990s, there were a number of important changes in how ECI was implemented in Spain. Initially, there was a change in the children who were served in ECI which included children with emotional-relational difficulties, children who were at risk for developmental delays and disabilities and children with problems associated with disadvantaged socio-cultural environments. As a result, the focus of early intervention for children with a disability was expanded and included chidren with a number of different kinds of identified conditions.

Professionals increasingly become aware of the need to give the family greater prominence in two important ways. Starting with a growing recognition by the professionals of the need to involve the family in early intervention, this new awareness led to the publication of the *Libro Blanco de la Atención Temprana* [White Paper of Early Intervention] (GAT, 2000). The definition of ECI in this White Paper includes a description of the family as the focus of intervention. Also, the publication of the *Manual of Best Practices in Early Intervention: Guidelines for Quality* (FEAPS, 1999) includes a description of how professionals could make the transition from a rehabilitation model to an educational model of ECI. This manual includes tenets that are highly consistent with an ecological approach to ECI that places the family at the centre of ECI practices.

Despite the fact that the traditional paradigm continues to be widely used by Spanish professionals, some important steps have been taken that indicate advances have been made towards adoption of a family-centred model. Firstly, reference should be made to the training of professionals. During the 1990s and the following years, well-known ECI professionals (Bjorck, Dunst, Espe-Sherwindt, Guralnick, McWilliam, Peterander and Turnbull, among others) have made presentations at congresses and conferences and have had opportunities to participate in other ECI activities. These professionals have been able to discuss alternatives to the traditional ECI paradigm and increase awareness of the need and benefits for a change towards an ecological, family-centred approach of ECI.

Secondly, research on family quality of life carried out by researchers at the Ramon Llull University (Barcelona, Spain) included the participation of ECI professionals, which contributed to an increased recognition of the importance of ecological and systems approaches to ECI and the pivotal role of the family in the development of their children. The international collaboration of Robin McWilliam (USA) and Ana Serrano (Portugal), particularly in the last few years, has provided Spanish professionals the opportunity to become familiar with the importance of working with children and their families in natural environments; engaging children meaningfully in daily routines and everyday learning activities; and identifying family resources and supports as the basis for family systems interventions (Correia & Serrano, 1998; McWilliam, 2010, 2011, 2012; McWilliam et al., 2011; Pereira & Serrano, 2014; Rapport, McWilliam, & Smith, 2004; Serrano, 2007; Serrano & Boavida, 2011; Serrano & Pereira, 2014).

Finally, the implementation of these principles started with the experience of an ECI program in Valencia, L'Alqueria, and how FEAPS had an important role to play in terms of developing a new programme and approach to transform ECI services in Spain. The program in La Alquería began to implement family-centred practices in 2010. The first steps towards this goal consisted of team meetings that included discussions and reflections on the need for new knowledge and intervention skills. This was followed by training in the routines-based ECI model by Robin McWilliam. Several team members visited the USA and Portugal to learn more about other types of ECI approaches and practices. Families were also asked to evaluate practices to help professionals reflect on their current practices and improve their relationships with families. Throughout the process of learning to use family-centred practices, the support provided by experienced experts such as Robin McWilliam, Climent Giné, Ana Serrano and Marylin Espe-Sherwindt proved essential. The FEAPS programme includes training conferences and workshops and the participation of more than 38 ECI centres and their staff at these training opportunities. The programme had adopted four guiding principles: (a) promote adoption and use of a family-centred ECI model; (b) promote and optimise the competencies of parents and children in family educational practices; (c) base ECI practices on child and family strengths; and (d) aim to improve family empowerment (Dunst & Trivette, 2009). Besides the centres that are run by FEAPS, 25 other ECI centres have requested training on the family-centred ECI model.

Analysis of early childhood intervention practices in Portugal and Spain

Using the conceptual and legislative situation of ECI in each country as a backdrop, we will now present some reflections on how the capacity-building, family-centred practices are being implemented. We first analyse the state of current practices in ECI in Portugal and then describe the ongoing transformation of ECI practices and services in Spain.

Early childhood intervention practices in Portugal

We analyse ECI practices in Portugal in context of the PL 281 (2009) described earlier, and some of the premises that are foundational to that legislation. The principles that are included in the legislation are based on the belief that ECI practices ought to be evidence based, and include four key practice components for the provision of services in the Portuguese ECI system (Decreto-Lei n.º 281/2009 de 6 de Outubro):

1 a family-centred, capacity-building model for guiding the provision of ECI services,
2 natural contexts for learning and development assuring inclusive supports,
3 integration and coordination of ECI services across various agencies and services, and
4 use a transdisciplinary approach to service provision.

Although the legislation itself, as mentioned before, does not explicitly include these particular premises, the foundations of professional practices in Portugal and various documents that have been used to develop regulatations and operationalise language in the legislation as part of everyday practice to include these premises (e.g., Manual for Local Early Intervention Teams[1]).

The law defines ECI as encompassing a range of community services and supports (formal and informal) provided by Local Early Intervention (LEI) teams consisting of professionals from health, education and social services. By using a community resources-based model, the system assures proximity of services and inclusive solutions to meeting and attaining family identified concerns and expectations (Trivette, Dunst, & Deal, 1997). Ideally, local teams are based in local health centres, as health is considered the primary access to the ECI system and as a way to involve community health centres in the ECI system (Serrano & Boavida, 2011). Moreover, services are focused not only on the child but also include the family as part of planning and delivering community-based ECI supports and services (Dunst & Trivette, 2009).

The organisational structure for providing services is located within five regions in Portugal: North, Central, Lisbon, Alentejo and Algarve, each with a coordinating commission composed of one representative from the three departments (health, education and social security). Nationally, the Ministries of the three departments have a central coordination responsible for the development of regulations involving ECI (see Figure 11.1). There are two representatives from each of the three departments National Commission. As such, the law defines a national action structure that is responsible for services coordination between the three government departments.

The LEI teams in each region have professionals from different disciplines, such as early childhood special educators, physicians, psychologists, social security professionals, occupational therapists, physical therapists, speech therapists, nurses and other professionals with specific training in the area of child development.

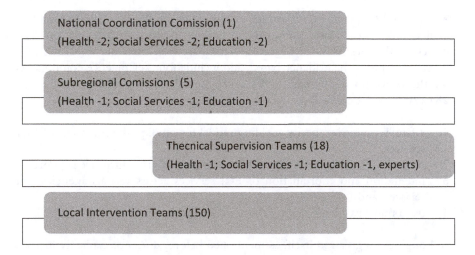

Figure 11.1 Organisation chart of Portuguese early intervention system

Source: Briggs (1989), adapted by Rosseti, L.M. (1990). *Infant-Toddler Assessment: An Interdisciplinary Approach.* Boston, MA: Little, Brown. The authors adopted the model into their local context.

There are currently 150 LEI teams in the five regions in Portugal. These professionals are assigned to the education, health and social services systems by local NGOs, taking into consideration the specific concerns of the families and the existing community resources (Pereira & Serrano, 2014). Within each LEI team there is a case coordinator (called a mediator) who works closely with the family and mediates the relationships between the family and the LEI team (see Figure 11.2). Team members are expected to engage in role release while working on the ECI teams. Research and experience has found that role release is an important aspect of professional development that needs to be addressed in order to impact positively the quality of ECI practices (Foley, 1990; Sheldon & Rush, 2001).

All children from zero to six years of age who are at risk for or have an SN and their families are eligible for ECI services. The LEI is also responsible for ongoing monitoring of children not found eligible for ECI services. This includes periodic assessment of the children and their families as the result of risk factors associated with developmental delays.

The development of an Individualised Early Intervention Plan is also a central feature of the Portuguese legislation. This plan is developed and implemented according to a family-centred philosophy and from the collective results involving a collaboration process between the family and the LEI team members. The law also requires the development of a *transition plan* whenever there are transitions

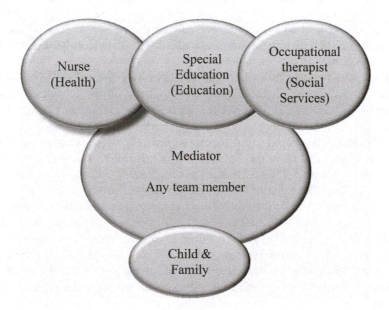

Figure 11.2 A transdisciplinary model with a mediator between the team and the family

Source: Created by the author

of the child to different programs and service delivery systems, including pre-school and primary school.

The full implementation of the PL 281 (2009) has not yet occurred, but the latest reports from SNIPI (2013) clearly demonstrate the importance of services coordination. In particular, this coordination has helped ensure ECI is provided to children and families despite the economic crisis Portugal has experienced in the past eight years. Another positive aspect of the implementation of the law is the increase in the number of children and families receiving services in all regions of the country, and especially the increased equity in the distributions of numbers of children and families being served in those regions. A recent data report from a National SNIPI Report notes that between 2011 and 2012, there was a 55% increase in the number of children being served, and between 2012 and 2013, there was a 22 % increase of children being served. In 2011, 7,545 children and their familes were served in ECI, and in 2013, the number of children and families that were served almost doubled (n = 14,273). These increases can be attributed to an emphasis on both child identification and referral, which has contributed to the ever-increasing number of children and families being served since the enactment of the law.

In terms of adherence to family-centred principles and practices, national studies in Portugal have yielded encouraging findings (Maia, 2012; Pereira, 2003; Pereira, 2009; Tegethof, 2007). Studies conducted before the enactment of the law showed that professionals had an understanding and knowledge of basic theoretical concepts related to family-centred principles. The results from these studies indicated that professionals and organisations were making efforts toward increased adoption and use of family-centred practices, and that families were generally satisfied with these services (Maia, 2012; Pereira, 2003; Pereira, 2009; Tegethof, 2007).

These early studies also found that practices were generally aligned with the main characteristics of the relational component of family-centred practices described by Dunst (2000), but the participatory component revealed some weakness (i.e., the results indicated a greater adherence by professionals to relational practices compared to participatory practices), which is not unique to Portugal (Dunst, Boyd, Trivette, & Hamby, 2002; Dunst & Trivette, 2005; Dunst, Trivette, & Hamby, 2008). Findings highlighted an awareness on the part of professionals of the value of help being provided to parents and families within natural settings, as well as the use of service coordination (mediation) to improve the supports provided by ECI programs and professionals (Maia, 2012). Other findings from these studies showed a need to involve families more actively in the different phases of the intervention process. Further, results indicated the need to develop IEIP in order to increase an emphasis on mobilisation and strengthening families' informal social support networks and their use of existing community-based resources and services for addressing family concerns and priorities.

The need to invest in personnel preparation has become increasingly apparent as the rapid changes in the ECI system have posed a major challenge in terms of the number of new professionals entering ECI. As a result, the National

Association of Early Intervention recently proposed a project in collaboration with the SNIPI to provide in-service training to ECI professionals involved in LEI teams. This project involves the development of an orientation guide to practices titled 'Recommended Practices in Early Intervention: A Guide for Professionals'. Along with this initiative, supervision of professional practice is seen as a crucial feature for promoting adherence to family-centred practices, and involves professionals constantly reflecting on their day-to-day practices with children and their families to help them deconstruct misconceptions from more traditional ways of working with families. This type of supervision is being provided by the Universities of Oporto and Minho to the LEI teams in the northern region of the country but has not yet been extended to other regions in Portugal.

According to Boavida (2014), the state of affairs of the ECI system in Portugal can be understood in terms of the following points:

- lack of parents' participation in the different levels of ECI throughout the ECI system,
- need to improve the adoption and adherence to family-centred, capacity-building principles and practices through personnel preparation of ECI professionals,
- high staff turnover within LEI teams due to administrative procedures of personnel distribution in the different departments, and
- lack of adequate financial support to fund ECI due to the economic crisis experienced by Portugal.

Overall, and despite the many difficulties faced in implementing its ECI legislation, Portugal has made considerable progress in improving the quality of ECI practices. However, as the Chinese proverb reminds us, we still have the rest of "a thousand kilometres to walk on our journey." We are aware of the gains achieved throughout the past 20 years and we believe that the foundations of a high-quality ECI system are being put into place to ensure that children and families receive the supports, resources and services they require in way that has empowering consequences.

Early childhood intervention practices in Spain

As described earlier, some ECI services in Spain are currently undergoing a deep and intense process of change towards the adoption and use of a family-centred approach to working with children and their families. We now describe different aspects of this transformation process – both challenges and opportunities – for ECI professionals and families. Our discussion is placed in the context of the four elements of a capacity-building, family system intervention model (Dunst & Trivette, 2009; Trivette, Dunst, & Hamby, 2010) which we use as a framework to describe the state of affairs of ECI in Spain.

Our comments come from three diferent sources: (1) two studies on family-centred practices in ECI recently conducted in our country (Ferreira, 2014;

Giné, Gràcia, & Vilaseca, 2014; Mas et al., 2014; Simon et al., 2014), (2) congresses and meetings that focused on the transformation of ECI in Spain (II International Congress on Family and Disability, 2014; Meeting on Progress in the Transformation Processes of EI services, FEAPS, 2014), and (3) results from the ongoing assessment of training provided to professionals to facilitate the implementation of family-centred practices.

Ongoing challenges in Portugal and Spain

Family concerns and priorities

It has been a challenge for both families and professionals to shift their focus from basing ECI on professionally identified needs to ECI based on family-identified concerns and priorities. There are two reasons why it has been challenging for families to recognise the importance of considering both the needs of their children and the family's needs. The first has to do with recognising the fact that families have needs, and that those needs can and should be the focus of attention of ECI professionals. The second reason arises from the recognition that family-identified needs for their child are important, and that those needs can and likely will be different from the child needs that professionals identify (Mas et al., 2014). It has also been difficult for professionals to: (a) shift the focus of attention solely from the child with SN to both the child and the family; (b) base interventions on family identified rather than only professional identified needs; (c) respect family's decisions, particularly when they differ from those of professionals, and to refrain from imposing their beliefs on families; (d) actively engage the family in ECI to meet both child and famly needs; and (e) set aside their priorities for child-level interventions and focus on the priorities identified by families (Ferreira, 2004; Mas et al., 2014).

One paticular type of intervention has provided both parents and professionals the opportunity to make the shift to ECI based on family-identified needs. Conceptualising and implementing ECI in terms of family routines has permitted families to identify everyday settings that are challenging to them and to focus on functional child outcomes in those settings that improve family life (Mas et al., 2014). Besides offering families the opportunity to express their concerns and needs in terms of everyday routines, this approach to ECI has facilitated professionals' abilities to see everyday family life from the perspective of the family rather than the professional (Ferreira, 2014). For example, professionals have found that intervention methods and procedures such as the routine-based interview (McWilliam, 2010) helpful in terms of developing a better understanding of families' everyday life situations. As a result, intervention in natural settings and everyday routines has provided an opportunity for professionals to recognise family concerns within the contexts of the everyday activities of the child and family (Ferreira, 2014).

Family member abilities and interests

The shift from a deficit-based to strengths-based approach to ECI with families has been a novel, complex, gratifying and a competency-enhancing experience.

Novel because families had rarely been asked about what they do well, their strengths, and what they like doing and what is important to them. Complex because it is hard for some families to think about themselves in terms of their strengths. Usually the first response is "I don't know" or "You tell me." As a result, it is a difficult process for them to recognise their strengths and interests and to think about how they can use strengths to achieve goals they have set both for their child and their family. It has been particularly gratifying and competency enhancing because it offers families the possibility to see that they have strengths and that they were doing better than they thought (Mas et al., 2014). It also helps them recognise their parenting confidence and competence. For example, Ferreira (2014) found that it is very motivating for families to see that they have important roles to play in helping their children learn and develop.

The shift from a deficit-based to strengths-based perspective has helped professionals view families from an alternative perspective, to recognise that many families are doing well with their children. Professionals now are more likely to acknowledge that families have many things to contribute to their children's learning and development, and that children can and do learn a lot from the interactions they have with their families. However, one aspect of this approach to ECI that has been challenging for professionals has been knowing how to work with families starting from their strengths, because they have typically been taught to use interventions to correct or remediate deficits. Moreover, a strengths-based approach necessitates that professionals be respectful of each family's lifestyle and cultural values, beliefs and practices. This approach has required a radical change in professional practices that continues to be a challenge for using other than deficit-based practices.

Supports and resources

Extending ECI to include informal resources and supports in addition to professional services for meeting child and family needs has been challenging, but not as much as other changes inherent in a family-centred approach. This expansion has facilitated professionals' recognition, identification and understanding of the range of resources and supports available in both their communities and in the family. For example, the mapping of family and community supports has proved to be a very powerful tool for families to become aware of their informal and formal social networks, and which supports are most helpful and which supports are available but not used. This was noted by professionals at the meeting on Progress in the Transformation Processes of EI services, organized by FEAPS in December 2014.

It has been encouraging to find that many ECI professionals utilise the great potential of informal supports for meeting child and family needs. For example, many professionals and families see that developing an intervention plan starting from the learning opportunities (resources) available as part of daily routines and using these opportunites as informal sources of support to promote child learning and development not only makes sense but is also more effective/efficient.

Moreover, both parents and professionals consider the discussions held about learning opportunities in the context of everyday activities and routines as being a more positive (strengths-based) approach to ECI. As a result, home visits are viewed as "meetings that help to understand much better the possibilities that [everyday] routines offer as sources of learning" (Ferreira, 2014, p. 8).

Capacity-building help-giving practices

According to Dunst (2000), capacity-building, family-centred practices include two types of help giving: participatory help giving and relational help giving. As Dunst and Trivette (2009) describe:

> *Relational helpgiving includes practices typically associated with good clinical practice (e.g., active listening, compassion, empathy, respect) and help-giver positive beliefs about family member strengths and capabilities. . . . Participatory help-giving includes practices that are individualized, flexible, and responsive to family concerns and priorities, and which involve informed family choices and involvement in achieving desired goals and outcomes.*
>
> (p. 131)

Of the two types of help giving, participatory practices have not only been a challenge for professionals but also for families. As previously noted, professionals have had difficulites involving families in informed decision-making and basing ECI practices on family priorities. This has required ECI professionals to examine their practices to determine how they can improve their use of family-centred approaches to intervention.

Professionals have also voiced concerns about the way in which they work with families, since a capacity-building approach is so different from the expert model that they have traditionally used for intervention purposes. This is the case, to a large degree, because they more often than not decide about most aspects of child-level interventions (e.g., assessment and intervention practices), which limits the role family have in terms of decision-making and involvement in their children's early intervention. This often results in professionals acknowledging the fact that one of their greatest weaknesses is not knowing how to involve families in decisions regarding the role that they want to play in intervention and which aspects of intervention they consider most important to improve child and family functioning (Cañadas, 2013).

Professionals also recognise that it is very difficult for them abandon their perceived obligation as professionals to solve child and family problems or to put into place the resources and supports to meet family-identified needs. As a result, ECI professionals have increasingly requested training on how to work effectively with families to improve child and family functioning in ways that enhance parental capacity.

As indicated earlier in this section of the chapter, the paradigm shift that is necessitated by adoption of capacity-building, help-giving practices has been a challenge for families, but at the same time, has been a great opportunity for improving family involvement in ECI. It has allowed families to recognise and accept the fact that their needs, concerns, abilities, resources etc. can and should play a pivitol role in how ECI services are delivered. This has allowed families to have an active role during all aspects of the ECI process. This has permitted a shift from being mere recipients of services to being able to collaborate with professionals in the identification and decision-making process involving their children and family. We end this section with the comment of a father[2] that illustrates how this change has influenced both families and professionals: "Now we take part of it and discuss the problems that we encounter at home. Before, during the sessions we observed what the therapist did. Now we share it and each one makes their contribution."

Future directions

We conclude the chapter by highlighting those aspects of ECI that need to be considered to facilitate further adherence to family-centred, capacity-building practices in Portugal, and how experiences and lessons learned in Portugal can be extended and used to further develop family-centred ECI in Spain. In terms of strengthening the Portuguese ECI system, the major priorities for the future will be the development of methods, procedures and strategies to increase family active participation in ECI, improving child identification practices to locate more children eligible for ECI, professional preparation and in-service training that address the skills and competencies necessary to the development of capacity-building, family systems interventions practices and providing transdisciplinary services and improving interagency collaboration for promoting and ensuring high-quality ECI services. In Spain, the priorities include planning to continue the transformational process (training and reflexion) described in the FEAPS (2014) report and responding to professionals' requests for ways to become more family centred. ECI professionals in Spain have expressed the need for specific training on how to adopt and use capacity-building, family-centred practices based on recommendations from different proponents of family-centred practices from research and practice on family-centred intervention (e.g., Bruder, 2000; Dunst, Bruder, & Espe-Sherwind, 2014; Espe-Sherwindt, 2008), and especially training that promotes practitioners' use of strengths-based, capacity-building practices (Dunst, Trivette, & Hamby, 2008). The focus of this professional preparation will be the use of evidence-based, family-centred practices (Dempsey & Keen, 2008; Odom & Wolery, 2003; Trivette et al., 2010).

The achievement of these outcomes will be facilitated by the development of instruments or checklists for promoting: (a) professionals' understanding and use of family centred practices; (b) the assessment of professional use of these practices; (c) measuring the adoption, application and adherence to the key characteristics of this model (Dunst, 2004); and (e) evaluating the extent to which use of the practices and model are related to child and family outcomes (Boston, Zimmerman, Trivette, & Dunst, 2013; Dempsey & Keen, 2008; Trivette et al.,

2010).Therefore, we think that researchers interested in family-centred practices can play an important role in providing support to ECI professionals during this process. We also believe that this work can inform how government can develop policies consistent with a family-centred model and allocate funding by describing criteria for the provision of ECI services in terms of a family-centred approach.

The experiences in our two countries has resulted in Portugal and Spain initating a collaborative relationship among different stakeholders at both the national and international level. At a national level, different initiatives (such as conferences, congresses, research etc.) have occured which have served as support networks that enabled progress toward adoption and use of capacity-building, family-centred practices. Besides the collaborative work between our two countries, other international researchers such as Carl Dunst (Orelana Hawks Puckett Institute, NC, USA), Robin McWilliam (National Early Childhood Inclusion Institute, Chapel Hill, NC, USA) and Marylin Espe-Sherwindt (Family Child Learning Centre, OH, USA) have made important contributions in helping rethink ECI in both Spain and Portugal. This increased knowledge and understanding can be used to enhance the quality of life of the families and children who receive ECI services. Therefore, we see a strong collaborative network of knowledge and support among families, professionals and researchers as important to further improvements in ECI as a result of *global* thinking.

Notes

1 Manual that was developed by the EI system and operatioanlizes the legislation for EI professionals.
2 This father's comment was collected at the meeting on Progress in the Transformation Processes of EI services, FEAPS, 2014.

References

Almeida, I. C. (2009). *Estudos sobre a intervenção precoce em Portugal: ideias dos especialistas, dos profissionais e das famílias* [Studies of early intervention in Portugal: Ideas of specialists, professionals and families]. Lisboa: Instituto Nacional de Reabilitação.

Boavida, J., & Borges, L. (1994). Community involvement in early intervention: A Portuguese perspective. *Infants & Young Children, 7*(1), 42–50.

Boavida, J. (2014, December). *La propuesta de atención temprana centrada en la familia en Portugal: Avances en el proceso político legislativo* [Family centered Early Intervention in Portugal: Advances in the political and legal process]. Paper presented at Jornadas Avances en la transformación de servicios de atención temprana Hacia servicios centrados en la familia y en sus contextos cotidianos, FEAPS, Madrid, Spain.

Boavida, J., & Carvalho, L. (2003). A comprehensive early intervention training approach: Portugal. In S. L. Odom, M. J. Hanson, J. A. Blackamn, & S. Kaul (Eds.), *Early intervention practices around the world* (pp. 213–252). Baltimore, MD: Paul H. Brooks Publishing.

Boavida, J., Espe-Sherwindt, M., & Borges, L. (2000). Community-based early intervention: The Coimbra Project (Portugal). *Child: Care, Health and Development,* 26(5), 343–354.

Boavida, J. (2014, December). *La propuesta de atención temprana centrada en la familia en Portugal: Avances en el proceso político legislativo [Family centered Early Intervention in Portugal: Advances in the political and legal process].* Paper presented at Jornadas Avances en la transformación de servicios de atención temprana Hacia servicios centrados en la familia y en sus contextos cotidianos, FEAPS, Madrid, Spain.

Boston, S., Zimmerman, G., Trivette, C., & Dunst, C. J. (2013). Algoma client-centred care tool: An evaluation scale for assessing staff use of client-centred practices. *Practical Evaluation Reports,* 5(2), 1–12.

Bruder, M. B. (2000). Family-centered early intervention: Clarifying our values for the new millennium. *Topics in Early Childhood Special Education,* 20, 105–116.

Cañadas, M. (2013). *La participación de las familias en los servicios de atención temprana en la Comunidad Valenciana* [Families participation in EI services of Valencia Region] (Unpublished doctoral dissertation). Universidad Católica de Valencia – San Vicente Mártir, Valencia, España.

Clements, B. (1999). The efficiency of Education Expenditure in Portugal. Working paper of the International Monetary Fund.

Correia, L. M., & Serrano, A.M. (Orgs.). (1998). *Envolvimento Parental, em Intervenção Precoce: Das práticas centradas na criança às práticas centradas na família* [Parent involvement on Early Intervention: From child centered to family centered practices]. Porto: Porto Editora

Coutinho, M.T. B. (1999). *Intervenção Precoce: Estudo dos efeitos de um programa de formação parental destinado a pais de crianças com Síndroma de Down* [Early Intervention: Studiesy of the effects of a parent education program for parents of children with Down Syndrome]. (Unpublished doctoral dissertation), Faculdade de Motricidade Humana de Universidade Técnica de Lisboa.

Cunningham, C. C. (2000). Familias con niños con Síndrome de Down. In M. A. Verdugo (Ed.), *Familias y Discapacidad Intelectual* (pp. 41–71). Madrid: Colección Feaps.

Decreto-Lei n.º 281/2009 de 6 de Outubro [Decree-Law No. 281/2009 of October 6]. Diário da República, 1. série, N.º 193.

Despacho conjunto n.º 891/99 [Joint Executive Regulation No. 891/99]. Diário da República, 2. série, N.º 244 de 19 de Outubro de 1999. Ministérios da Educação, da Saúde e do Trabalho e da Solidariedade.

Dempsey, I., & Keen, D. (2008). A review of processes and outcomes in family-centered services for children with a disability. *Topics in Early Childhood Special Education,* 28(1), 42–52.

Dunst, C. J. (2000). Revisiting "rethinking early intervention." *Topics in Early Childhood Special Education,* 20, 95–104.

Dunst, C. J. (2004). Traveling the transCanada highway: Mapping the adoption, application and adherence to family support principles. *Spring Printemps,* 1(1), 41–48.

Dunst, C. J., Boyd, K., Trivette, C. M., & Hamby, D. W. (2002). Family-oriented program models and professional helpgiving practices. *Family Relations,* 51, 221–229.

Dunst, C. J., Bruder, M. B., & Espe-Sherwindt, M. (2014). Family capacity-building in early childhood intervention: Do context and setting matter? *School Community Journal, 24*(1), 37–48.

Dunst, C. J., & Trivette, C. M. (2005). *Measuring and evaluating family support program quality* (Winterberry Press Monograph Series). Asheville, NC: Winterberry Press.

Dunst, C. J., & Trivette, C. M. (2009). Capacity-building family systems intervention practices. *Journal of Family Social Work, 12*, 119–143.

Dunst, C. J., Trivette, C. M., & Hamby, D. W. (2008). *Research synthesis and meta-analysis of studies of family-centered practices* (Winterberry Monograph Series). Asheville, NC: Winterberry Press.

Espe-Sherwindt, M. (2008). Family-centred practice: Collaboration, competency, and evidence. *Support for Learning, 23*, 136–143. doi:10.1111/j.1467-9604.2008.00384.x

FEAPS. (2014). *Memoria 2014 [Report 2014]*. Unpublish document

Ferreira, D. (2014). *Prácticas Centradas na Família: Um estudo de caso do Centro de Educación Infantil y de Atención Temprana da Universidade Católica de València* [Family centered practices: A case study of the Early Childhood Intervention Centre of the Catholic University of València] (Unpublished master dissertation). Instituto de Educação, Universidade do Minho, Portugal.

Foley, G. M. (1990). Portrait of the arena evaluation: Assessment in the transdisciplinary approach. In E. Biggs & D. Teti (Eds.), *Interdisciplinary assessment of infants: A guide for early intervention professionals* (pp. 271–286). Baltimore, MD: Paul H. Brookes.

GAT.(2000). *Libro blanco de la atención temprana* [White Paper of Early Intervention] Madrid, Espanya: Ministerio de Trabajo y Asuntos Sociales.

Giné, C., Vilaseca, R., Gràcia, M., & García-Dié, M. T. (2004). Early intervention in Spain : Some directions for future development. *Infants & Young Children, 17*, 247–257.

Guinea, C., Lleonhart, M., Silvestre, N., Martínez, I., Zaurín, L., & Giné, C. (1983). L'estimulació primerenca: definició i algunes experiències actuals. [Early stimulation: Definition and some current experiences]. *Educar, 4*, 75–89.

Healy, A., Keesee, P. D., & Smith, B. S. (1989). *Early services for children with special needs: Transactions for family support*. Baltimore, MD: Brookes Publishing Co.

Maia, M. F. (2012). *A intervenção precoce nas Associações Portuguesas de Paralisia Cerebral: perceções das famílias, dos profissionais e dos diretores de serviço. [Early Intervention in Portuguese Associations of Cerebral Palsy: Perceptions of families, professionals and administrators]*. University of Minho, Portugal (Unpublished doctoral dissertation).

Mas, J. M., Balcells, A., Giné, C., Gracia, M., González, A., Galván, M. J., & Simó, D (2014, July). *Work with families in Early Intervention Centers in Spain: Opportunities and challenges*. Paper presented at the 4th International Association for the Scientific Study of Intellectual and Developmental Disabilities (IASSIDD) Europe Congress, Viena (Austria).

McWilliam, R. A. (2012). Implementing and preparing for home visits. *Topics in Early Childhood Special Education, 31*, 224–231. doi:10.1177/0271121411426488

McWilliam, R. A. (2011). The top 10 mistakes in early intervention – and the solutions. *Zero to Three, 31*, 11.

McWilliam, R. A. (2010). *Routines-based early intervention. Supporting young children and their families.* Baltimore, MD: Brookes.

McWilliam, R. A., Casey, A.M., Ashley, D., Fielder, J., Rowley, P., DeJong, K., Mickel, J., Stricklin, S. B., & Votava, K. (2011). Assessment of family-identified needs through the routines-based interview. In M. E. McLean & P. Snyder (Eds.), *Young exceptional children monograph series No. 13: Gathering information to make informed decisions* (pp. 64–78). Missoula, MT: The Division for Early Childhood of the Council for Exceptional Children.

Odom, S. L., & Wolery, M. (2003). A unified theory of practice in early intervention/early childhood special education evidence-based practices. *The Journal of Special Education, 37*, 164–173.

Origins of Early Childhood Health Data. (2011). Retrieved from www.oecd.org/social/family/database

Pereira, A. P. (2003). *Práticas centradas na família: Identificação de comportamentos para uma prática de qualidade no Distrito de Braga.* [Family centered: Identification of behaviors towards a quality practice in the District of Braga]. University of Minho, Portugal (Unpublished Master dissertation).

Pereira, A. P. (2009). *Práticas centradas na Família em Intervenção Precoce: Um estudo nacional sobre as práticas dos profissionais* [Family centered early intervention practices: A national study about professional practices]. University of Minho, Portugal (Unpublished doctoral dissertation).

Pereira, A. P., & Serrano, A. M. (2014). Early intervention in Portugal: Study of professionals' perceptions. *Journal of Family Social Work, 17*, 263–282.

Pimentel, J. S., & Almeida, I. C. (1999) *Formação Básica em Intervenção Precoce [Basic training in Early Intervention].* Curso Básico Portage. Lisboa: Associação Portage

Pinto, A. I., Grande, C., Aguiar, C., De Almeida, I. C., Felgueiras, I., Pimentel, J. S., Serrano, Ana Maria, Carvalho, Leonor, Brandão, Maria Teresa, Boavida, Tânia, Santos, Paula, Lopes-Dos-Santos, P. (2012). Early childhood intervention in Portugal: An overview based on the developmental systems model. *Infants & Young Children, 25*, 310–322.

Rapport, M. J. K., McWilliam, R. A., & Smith, B. J. (2004). Practices across disciplines in early intervention. *Infants & Young Children, 17*, 32–44.

Serrano, A. M. (2003). *Formal and informal resources among families with young children with special needs in the District of Braga, Portugal.* (Unpublished doctoral dissertation). Instituto de Estudos da Criança, Universidade do Minho, Portugal.

Serrano, A. M. (2007). *Redes sociais de apoio e sua relevância para a Intervenção Precoce* [Social support networks and its relevance to early intervention]. Porto: Porto Editora.

Serrano, A. M., & Boavida, J. F. (2011). Early childhood intervention: The Portuguese pathway towards inclusion. *Revista Educación Inclusiva, 4*(1), 123–138.

Serrano, A. M., & Pereira A. P. (2014). Modelo centrado en la família en contextos de vulnerabilidad de salud mental [Family centered model in contexts of mental vunerability]. In P. G. Cuevas, C. S. Romero (Coord.), *Primera Infancia y vulnerabilidad proyecto kids strengths* (pp. 141–168). Madrid: Editorial: SANZ Y TORRES

Sheldon, M. L., & Rush, D. D. (2001). The ten myths about providing early intervention services in natural environments. *Infants & Young Children, 14*, 1–13.

Simón, C., Pró, M. T., Dalmau, M., Vilaseca, R., Salvador, F., Izuzquiza, D. . . . Baqués, N. (2014, July). *Promoting family-centered practices in Early Intervention Centers for children with intellectual or developmental disabilities.* Potser presented at 4th International Association for the Scientific Study of Intellectual and Developmental Disabilities (IASSIDD) Europe Congress, Vienna (Austria).

SNIPI. (2013). *National committee annual report.* Lisbon: SNIPI.

Tegethof, M. I. (2007). *Estudos sobre a intervenção precoce em Portugal: ideias dos especialistas, dos profissionais e das famílias* [Studies about early intervention in Portugal: Ideas of experts, professionals and families]. Universidade do Porto, Portugal (Unpublished doctoral dissertation).

Trivette, C. M., Dunst, C. J., & Deal, A. G. (1997). Resource-based approach to early intervention. In S. K. Thurman, J. R. Cornwell, & S. R. Gottwald (Eds.), *Contexts of early intervention: Systems and settings* (pp. 73–92). Baltimore, MD: Paul Brookes.

Trivette, C. M., Dunst, C. J., & Hamby, D. W. (2010). Influences of family-systems intervention practices on parent-child interactions and child development. *Topics in Early Childhood Special Education, 30*(1), 3–19.

Veiga, M. E. (1995). *Intervenção precoce e avaliação – Estudo introdutório [Early Intervention and assessment- An introductory study*]. Porto: O Fio de Ariana.

12 Implementing family-centred practice in childhood disability services in Manitoba, Canada

Diane Hiebert-Murphy, Barry Trute, and Alexandra Wright

Family-centred practice (FCP) has been internationally recognised as highly relevant to the delivery of children's disability services. Despite being widely endorsed in children's services, it appears that shifts in professional practice and service delivery policy have been minimal (Craft-Rosenberg, Kelley, & Schnoll, 2006; Patterson & Hovey, 2000). According to Dempsey and Keen (2008), the integration of FCP in childhood disability services is still in an "adolescent phase of development" (p. 43).

Although the term "family-centred" has often been used interchangeably with other terms such as family-focused and family-based, it has over time become more carefully defined and consistently applied across various service sectors (Allen & Petr, 1996; Johnson, 1990; Trute, 2007; Walton, Sandau-Beckler, & Mannes, 2001). At the most fundamental level, family-centred practice involves a partnership between service recipients and service providers (Dunst, 2002; Roberts, Rule, & Innocenti, 1998; Trute & Hiebert-Murphy, 2013). Allen and Petr (1996) suggest that family-centred service delivery recognises the centrality of the family in the lives of individuals, promotes fully informed choices by families, and focuses on family strengths and capabilities. A primary aim of FCP in the context of services for young children is to strengthen and empower parental functioning and to assist in the enhancement of the family as a vital resource for the positive development of children.

Dunst, Trivette and Hamby (2007) describe how family-centred service delivery includes both relational elements (i.e., the ability to establish a collaborative working relationship with families) and participatory elements (i.e., strategies that empower families and increase their capacity to meet their needs). Such an approach focuses on family-identified needs and priorities and engages in professional-family collaborations that result in service/support plans that are individualised for the family and congruent with the family's style, preferences, and cultural norms (Dunst, Trivette, & Deal, 1988). The relational component has been further explicated as the development of a "working alliance" between family members and professionals (Trute & Hiebert-Murphy, 2013), while the participatory component can be seen as anchored in empowerment practice (Levine, 2013).

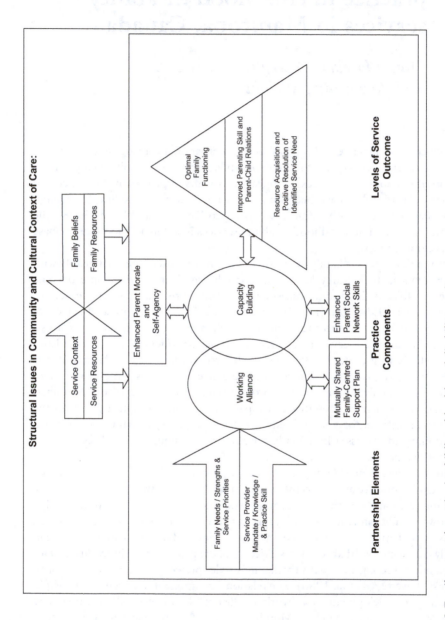

Figure 12.1 Family-centred practice in childhood health and disability services

Source: Trute, B. (2013). Basic family-centred practice concepts and principles. In B. Trute & D. Hiebert-Murphy (Eds.), *Partnering with parents: Family-centred practice in children's services* (p. 38). Toronto: University of Toronto Press. Used with permission.

Figure 12.1 illustrates our understanding of FCP in the context of childhood health and disability services. As described by Trute (2013), FCP considers the broad social context in which families are situated. Attention is given to the ways in which structural factors (such as class and racial/cultural background) frame families' experiences. Context also includes elements of the service system that determine how service is delivered and accessed and the external support resources that are available to families. Families' beliefs about disability and attitudes towards seeking help from outsiders as well as resources that families have to address their perceived needs constitute other elements of the context. Aided by the development of a working alliance, families' needs, strengths, beliefs, and service priorities interact with service providers' mandate, knowledge, and practice skills. Through the identification of priority needs and a collaborative planning process, a support plan is developed that addresses identified needs and builds families' capacity (by increasing parent morale and sense of agency and by enhancing families' skills in utilising social network support). These components of FCP are not necessarily sequential, nor are they mutually exclusive; they are iterative resulting in a dynamic exchange between families and professionals. The goals of FCP include improved child, parent-child, and family functioning; enhanced parenting skills and sense of mastery; and resolution of identified service needs.

There is evidence that FCP results in increased parental satisfaction with services (Law et al., 2003) and a reduction in family need (Trute, Hiebert-Murphy, & Wright, 2008). Despite the appeal and evidence supporting the benefits of this approach to practice, the process of changing service delivery systems and professional practice to fully realise these principles is complex. Some research has attempted to illuminate the process of implementing FCP in service delivery. A number of factors have been identified as barriers to implementing FCP principles such as adherence to the medical model or professional-centred approach to service delivery (Dunst, Johanson, Trivette, & Hamby, 1991), lack of interprofessional collaboration (Bruce, Letourneau, Ritchie, Larocque, Dennis, & Elliott, 2002), high caseloads and paperwork demands (Campbell & Halbert, 2002; Dinnebeil, Hale, & Rule, 1996), limited resources (Dinnebeil et al., 1996), and inadequate practitioner training (Bruder, 2000).

In this chapter, we examine the delivery of services to families of children with disabilities in Manitoba, Canada, and describe efforts made to strengthen the family-centredness of these services. Our research on the process of implementation of FCP is discussed. Our observations of implementation challenges to delivering family-centred services in the Province of Manitoba are also considered.

Context of child disability services in Manitoba

Manitoba is a province in Canada that is home to approximately 1.3 million people spread over a large geographic area (Statistics Canada, 2014a). The population is diverse, with approximately 15% of the population self-identifying as Aboriginal (Statistics Canada, 2008a). Further, immigrants comprise 13% of the population

(Statistics Canada, 2008b). The majority of the population (about 61%; Statistics Canada, 2014b) reside in the province's capital city with the reminder of the population living in smaller urban centres and rural (in some cases, relatively isolated) areas. Manitoba's child population (ages zero to 19 years) comprises 26% of the total population (Healthy Child Manitoba, n.d.). The rate of Manitoba children six to 17 years of age who received educational funding for disabilities in 2001–2006 was 4.3% (Brownell et al., 2008).

According to Canada's constitution, responsibility for health and social services rests with provincial governments, who are highly dependent on funds from the federal government to support the programs and services they provide. In Manitoba, services for children with disabilities and their families are non-mandated and discretionary. No specific legislation exists that dictates the province's responsibility to support families with children with disabilities, although there is legislation to protect the rights of children with disabilities (e.g., human rights legislation and the Healthy Child Manitoba Act) and child welfare legislation that addresses the need to support families in meeting the basic needs of children. A provincial government-run program (Children's DisABILITY Services [CDS]) has existed since the 1980s to provide community-based supports to families who may need assistance meeting the demands of caring for children with disabilities. In 2013–2014, provincial funding for CDS equaled $CAD27,870.00, which included funding and support for the delivery of individualised services to 5,040 children and their families, funding support for regional child therapy services (e.g., occupational therapy, speech therapy, physiotherapy) which served an estimated 46,000 children across the province, and funding for applied behavior analysis programming for 227 children (Government of Manitoba, 2014).

Accessing services

Upon meeting eligibility criteria, CDS assigns a family service worker (in Australia, the UK, and the USA, similar positions have been termed "key worker" or "primary service coordinator") to each family. Family service workers are service coordinators who provide ongoing and long-term support to families. They are expected to develop support plans with each family. A range of services is offered by CDS including, for example, respite care, special supplies and equipment, child development services, therapy, and behavioural services (see Government of Manitoba, 2015). In addition to direct services, family service workers assist families in identifying other sources of support available through non-governmental organisations, as well as the health and education systems. Family service workers remain involved with the family over the long term as the child transitions from early intervention to school-based support to, when applicable, services for adults with disabilities.

Development of FCP in Manitoba provincial services

It is difficult to identify a particular point in time when family support programs "become" family-centred because there are elements of FCP that exist within

Table 12.1 Core features of family-centred services

Family-centred services:

- are individualised to meet each family's needs and priorities
- are responsive to community and cultural norms
- are based on a partnership between professionals and families
- recognise strengths in all families
- engage families in an explicit planning process
- increase families' sense of competence and capacity to meet their needs
- increase families' ability to advocate for resources
- work with families to mobilise the resources of both the formal service delivery system and their informal networks

other approaches to service delivery. The relational component of FCP includes practices that would be identified as core skills for all helping professionals including, for example, the ability to engage with families, develop collaborative working relationships, and respect the individuality of families. The ability to establish a strong working relationship is paramount in FCP (Trute & Hiebert-Murphy, 2007). In addition, there are distinct practice elements in a family-centred model. For example, FCP represents a shift in power where professionals relinquish the role of expert whenever possible in favour of partnerships with families, with shared responsibilities and acknowledgement of differing bases of expertise (Trute & Hiebert-Murphy, 2013). Further, FCP emphasises the participatory elements of practice which seek to enhance families' capacity to define their needs and preferences and identify and engage resources to meet those needs (through the use of formal and informal supports). It is the participatory component, or empowerment practice, in particular that represents a significant shift from traditional models of service delivery (see Table 12.1 for a summary of key elements of family-centred services).

Creating momentum for change: Research on resilient families

The provision of services to families with children with disabilities has a long history in Manitoba and has involved service coordination and family support functions. There are a number of noteworthy activities that can be identified as significant in the evolution of service delivery in CDS in a way which charted the course towards FCP. The first involved research that focused on family strengths in the context of childhood disability (Trute & Hauch, 1988a). This was one of the first research projects to focus on resilient families raising children with disabilities. Key factors related to positive outcomes for families were identified and included strong relationships between the parents/couple and effective use of social network resources including support from extended family and friends. In-depth research was conducted with a cross-sectional sample of families to further assess the impacts of social support resources on family functioning (Trute &

Hauch, 1988b). This research challenged a deficit-focused view of families, which assumes that families with children with disabilities will be overwhelmed and experience difficulties coping with the demands they face. In addition, the research highlighted the importance of informal sources of support in family well-being. These early studies were presented to administration and staff of CDS to facilitate better understanding of, and bolster commitment to, the principles of a family-centred model of service delivery.

Transitioning to family-centred services: The role of training

In response to ongoing discussion of how best to deliver services to Manitoba families with children with disabilities, a decision was made by key government leaders in 1999 to formally adopt a province-wide staff training program to advance FCP within the province's child disability program. As part of this initiative, a training strategy was developed by consultants at the University of Manitoba that provided training in FCP to all managers, supervisors, and family service workers employed in the program. Training materials were developed to fit with the perceived needs of staff and included didactic teaching about FCP as well as opportunities to explore the application of the principles in case studies. The four-day training occurred initially with program leaders and supervisors. This was followed by a second four-day block of training for all family service workers in the province that was conducted jointly by CDS supervisors and university consultants. Follow up occurred between a family-centred practice consultant and service delivery teams, which largely involved case consultation regarding the application of FCP principles in complex family situations.

Studying the implementation process: The family strengths in childhood disability project

The decision to formally adopt FCP presented an opportunity to conduct research on the implementation process. In 2000, the Family Strengths in Childhood Disability Project was collaboratively developed by researchers and CDS administrators to both study the functioning of families with young children with disabilities and track the experiences of families and staff with FCP. The research engaged families as they entered the service delivery system and followed up with them one year later. Data on family functioning and the perceived family-centredness of services were collected from parents. Data were also collected from service providers.

The research examined factors related to family adjustment and needs, and identified potential targets for family-centred intervention. Results indicated that family functioning could be predicted by parent identified need for family counselling, parenting morale (Trute & Hiebert-Murphy, 2005), and parental appraisal of the family impact of the child's disability (Trute, Hiebert-Murphy, &

Levine, 2007). The research also suggested that attention be given to parental self-esteem as an important predictor of parenting stress (Trute, Worthington, & Hiebert-Murphy, 2008). Maternal self-esteem, in particular, was found to mediate the relationship between parenting stress and family adjustment (Thompson, Hiebert-Murphy, & Trute, 2013). The level of emotional support received from maternal and paternal grandmothers was also identified as important in moderating mothers' parenting stress (Trute, Worthington et al., 2008). Three factors were found to be important to how families enter the service delivery systems: how problems in child development are recognised, the process of obtaining a formal diagnosis of disability, and how linkage between diagnostic services and community-based support services occurs (Hiebert-Murphy, Trute, & Wright, 2008). These factors resulted in differing patterns of entry associated with different needs for service suggesting that attention must be given to these processes when working with families.

The research also provided evidence of the value of a family-centred approach to service delivery. Findings confirmed that a positive working alliance between parents and professionals is important in parents' satisfaction with services. Further, the perceived family-centredness of services was strongly related to satisfaction with services after controlling for the quality of the working alliance (Trute & Hiebert-Murphy, 2007) demonstrating that a FCP model contributes to parent satisfaction with service delivery beyond what is achieved by a positive working relationship. Family-centred practice was also found to be related to a reduction in family need for psychosocial support resources (Trute, Hiebert-Murphy et al., 2008).

There are a number of findings that speak directly to the issue of implementation of FCP. Research with front-line staff and supervisors identified organisational culture and climate (e.g., caseload, training, supervision), policy issues, and the practices of other service providers with whom they collaborate as key factors affecting the implementation of FCP (Wright, Hiebert-Murphy, & Trute, 2010). Parents reported that effective services require skilled practitioners, an adequately resourced service delivery system, and program policies and procedures that are responsive to family needs (Hiebert-Murphy, Trute, & Wright, 2011).

Key issues and challenges in implementing FCP

In the remainder of the chapter, we discuss parents' and staff members' perceptions as well as additional issues that we have observed as particularly relevant to the implementation of FCP (see Table 12.2). In their assessment of child disability services, parents identified factors at the level of the individual worker, the organisation, and the broader service delivery context that they perceive as necessary for services to be effective. It is the interaction of factors at each of these levels that results in a service delivery system that adequately addresses the needs and concerns of families. Any one factor will be limited in the extent to which it moves the system towards being truly family-centred.

Table 12.2 Factors that facilitate the implementation of family-centred practice

Organisational level:

- Commitment of key stakeholders (i.e., senior policymakers, program managers, and staff supervisors) to FCP
- Policy that supports the implementation of FCP and identifies key indicators that FCP is being implemented (e.g., individualised support plans are developed with families)
- Program policies that are flexible to accommodate differing family needs
- Mechanisms for parent/family feedback and input in policymaking
- Commitment of resources for training and supervision intra- and inter-organisationally to ensure that front-line staff have support in developing skills needed for FCP
- Supervisors with the skills and time to provide practice supervision that is focused on ensuring that family service workers incorporate family-centred principles into their practice
- A plan for ongoing training in FCP for new staff as they enter the service delivery system
- Education/training opportunities for parents/family members which provide information about the service delivery system and orient them to the principles of FCP
- Collaborations among providers of services to families that promote seamless delivery of services
- Caseloads that allow family service workers to establish relationships with families and maintain ongoing contact
- A network of adequately resourced support services to assist families

Worker level:

- Strong interpersonal skills (e.g., workers who are friendly, warm, and supportive)
- Skills for establishing a positive working relationship with parents
- Ability to be responsive to parents (i.e., listen, respond to parent-initiated requests)
- Skills for working in partnership with families
- Knowledge and skills to provide families with information that allows them to participate in decisions regarding the services provided to their child and/or family
- Skills for interaction with families that increase each family's ability to cope more effectively in the future
- Recognition that all families have strengths and the skills to identify and build on these strengths in intervention
- Skills for engaging families in decision-making to the extent that families are able and willing
- Education in the core elements of FCP and opportunities for ongoing practice supervision

Worker skills

Parents in our study clearly articulated qualities and behaviours of workers that they found helpful. They described both interpersonal characteristics and clinical skills important for effective practice (Hiebert-Murphy et al., 2011). It was seen as essential that family service workers have the ability to engage families and build relationships with them. Parents identified personal qualities of workers that facilitate this process (e.g., friendly, warm, supportive), as well as specific behaviours important in establishing relationships with parents (e.g., listening, having face-to-face meetings, responding promptly to phone calls). The ability to establish a solid working alliance with families is regarded as a core skill (Mitchell & Sloper, 2003) and is congruent with what Dunst and Trivette (1996) describe as the relational component of FCP. As Pretis (2006) emphasises, although there may be more technical aspects of FCP, the personal competencies of the practitioner are a main source of impact in work with families.

Relational skills are commonly considered essential for helping relationships. As such, it is expected that parents would identify these skills as important. What is surprising is the variability in relational competence that parents perceived among workers. It is possible that not all family service workers had professional training in a helping discipline (where presumably they would learn core helping skills). It is also likely that even with similar training there will be differences in the skill level of workers. This parent feedback suggests that it should not be assumed that family service workers have relationship building skills. Attention may need to be given to building competence in this area beginning in the orientation of new workers and following up with ongoing practice supervision and continuing professional training. Without these core helping skills that facilitate the development of a strong working alliance, advanced training in specific FCP techniques is not likely to result in positive outcomes.

Beyond qualities and skills generic to the helping relationship, parents also identified specific worker behaviours that closely align with FCP principles. For example, parents identified a number of behaviours consistent with developing partnerships with parents. They appreciated being treated as equals, having control over the final decisions affecting the services that were provided to their child and/or family, and receiving information that allowed them to participate in the service delivery process. The ability to engage with families and invite them to participate and share in decision-making to the extent that they are able or willing is a hallmark of FCP. Intervention that contributes to a family's capacity to identify its needs and seek supports and resources to address those needs is central to the participatory element of FCP. This requires the ability to identify strengths in all families, even those with high levels of need who are struggling to meet the basic needs of their members, and intervene in a way that builds on those strengths. FCP requires workers to show sensitivity to each family's needs and resources and adapt the intervention to engage families in partnerships to the greatest extent possible. Regardless of the ability, resources, and functioning of a particular family, in order for practice to be family-centred, the intervention should increase the family's sense of competence and skill in addressing its needs. An emphasis on family empowerment is key to FCP and is one of the features that distinguishes FCP from other practice approaches. From an FCP perspective, positive outcomes include both a reduction in unmet needs and increased capacity to meet needs that arise in the future.

While most workers value practice approaches that result in client empowerment, FCP is explicit that family empowerment should be a goal of intervention.

Therefore, the meeting of immediate needs should occur in a way which strengthens the family and increases its capacity to identify future needs and secure the resources that are needed to meet those needs. The "how" or process of intervention is a central focus in FCP. While FCP attends to what is needed in the present, the way in which the FCP worker engages with the family to enhance the family's resiliency and ability to cope more effectively with life challenges in the future is important. That is, the identification of present family needs, and the implementation of possible solutions or responses to those needs, should reflect a process that focuses on family priorities, engages families in an explicit planning process, explores resources available in the formal service system as well as the informal network of family and friends, and shares responsibility for decision-making, implementation, and evaluation of plans with family members. These features of FCP are distinct and extend the role of the family service worker beyond case manager or service coordinator.

Despite having received formal training in FCP, not all Manitoba workers were perceived by parents as possessing the skills needed to empower families. Parents reported that these practice elements were not uniformly present across workers. Workers were not consistently engaging in an explicit planning process that resulted in individualised family support plans. Parents perceived considerable differences among workers in the extent to which they were engaged as partners. This raises questions about how best to prepare workers to practice in a family-centred way.

Most family service workers in Manitoba were professional social workers and believed that their specific education provided them with a knowledge and value base consistent with FCP (Wright et al., 2010). It has been observed, however, that although social workers are well suited for FCP because of their familiarity with systems theory and ecological assessment (Hartman & Laird, 1983), they are often not well trained in the skills that are required for practice in early intervention (Malone, McKinsey, Thyer, & Straka, 2000). Furthermore, it should not be assumed that social workers will necessarily hold views that are congruent with a family-centred approach to practice. In a national survey in the United States, for example, while the majority of social workers reported attitudes that were "parent-friendly" and consistent with family-centred beliefs (e.g., that parents are experts on their children, that information should be shared openly with parents), there was a substantial minority of social workers who espoused attitudes that were assessed to be "antithetical to parent empowerment" (e.g., disagree with sharing information with parents, believe that parents' views are important mostly to inform workers about family dynamics; Johnson et al., 2003, p. 95).

Programs that educate professionals from different disciplines to work in childhood disability services (e.g., social work, psychology, occupational therapy, physical therapy, speech pathology, nursing) should include instruction in FCP and offer opportunities for supervised practice experience in child disability programs. Such education would help students develop foundational knowledge and skills in how to work with families and how to practice in a family-centred way. This beginning knowledge and skill could then be nurtured through more advanced professional development opportunities. Exposure to a family-centred conceptualisation of intervention at an early stage in professionals' training would orient them towards strength-based, empowerment practice and prepare them for work in systems which espouse FCP principles. Knowledge of FCP could be included in university curriculum as well as ongoing professional development opportunities and organisational knowledge transfer initiatives.

Shifting to a family-centred approach may be especially challenging for professionals who have been trained in traditional helping models. Being facilitators and partners may not be professional roles comfortable to those who have been trained to be experts who take charge of the helping process and "do for" families rather than "work with" families. Being attuned to the process of intervention with a focus on how all helping activities can build on the strengths of families and enhance the capacity of families to meet their needs is a dramatic shift from traditional helping roles. Such a shift is unlikely to occur easily or quickly. Workers will have to be convinced that this practice method is effective and efficient and will need opportunities to learn and practice the skills required. Initial education in FCP must be further developed through ongoing training, combined with supervision that integrates FCP elements.

If professionals are to shift the way that they provide services, there must be organisational support and planning for ongoing staff development. Regular training, supervision, and peer support will influence the extent to which professionals are able to fulfill all aspects of their role (e.g., service coordinator, counsellor, broker, advocate; Sloper, Greco, Beecham, & Webb, 2006). Many resources (e.g., books, web-based resources, videos) exist to support training activities and offer tools such as individualised family support plans (Klassen, Trute, & Hiebert-Murphy, 2013) and Collaborative Helping maps (Madsen, 2014) to facilitate practitioners' implementation of the principles in practice. Feedback on FCP training has suggested the need for case examples, discussion of complex families, and hands-on experience (Craft-Rosenberg et al., 2006). Involving parents as co-instructors in training has also been suggested as a way of enhancing the training experience (McBride, Sharp, Hains, & Whitehead, 1995). Workers may need opportunities to observe more experienced professionals practice from a family-centred perspective, attempt the practice skills in their work, and receive feedback on their practice. Although there was a carefully designed training strategy that included follow up support in Manitoba, there have been ongoing challenges to training and staff development: (a) new staff have been hired who do not have background training in FCP; (b) the shift from program specific to generic supervision within provincial programs for children has meant that supervisors are not necessarily trained in, or committed to, family-centred principles and practice; and (c) there has been a lack of resources for building a strong internal, sustainable staff development program. Each of these factors has made it difficult to maintain momentum in the implementation process.

It should be noted that preparation for FCP is also indicated for the family side of the family-professional partnership (Hiebert-Murphy, 2013). That is, training for parents (and youth) is needed so that they understand their role as partners.

Informed family members can best make decisions regarding the extent to which they want to engage in service planning and intervention strategies. For many families, participation as service partners will evolve over time as they feel more confident and capable. Although some pilot work on preparing parents for FCP occurred in Manitoba, an ongoing strategy for offering such training has not been developed.

Organisational context

Regardless of the skills of practitioners, FCP will not be fully realised without an organisational context that supports the integration of family-centred principles. Within Manitoba, the decision to formally adopt FCP came as a result of collaborations between senior policymakers, researchers, and key stakeholders in the practice community. While this group of strong advocates for adopting FCP across childhood disability services was relatively small, efforts were made to expand this group to include managers and supervisors, who would be responsible for overseeing the implementation in various regions of the province. The planning group decided on an initial four-day training for all supervisors in the province. This training provided an opportunity to discuss FCP and ensure that all managers had a common understanding of the approach and goals for changes in the service delivery system. The training also gave supervisors an opportunity to consider challenges to moving forward with the initiative.

Following the training of supervisors, staff members and key collaborators were brought together for training. This required a considerable investment of resources in travel, accommodation, staff time, and training costs. Bringing together staff from various regions across the province strengthened the message that this was a system-wide change and provided the opportunity to discuss specific challenges that staff face in their locales. The training strategy was essential for communicating the commitment to the shift and for equipping staff with the knowledge that they needed. Further resources were allocated to providing supervision in FCP to all service delivery regions in the province. In addition, policymakers encouraged the use of individualised family support plans to document the extent to which collaborative planning between workers and families was occurring.

Our research found that as the implementation process unfolded, a number of organisational factors were identified as barriers to effective service delivery. Parents identified a number of program policies that did not meet their needs and were perceived as inflexible and unfriendly to families (Hiebert-Murphy et al., 2011). Working within the constraints of such policies can create tensions between families and workers. Further, policies that do not reflect family realities create conditions which are in conflict with FCP principles. For example, the way in which respite services were allocated left some families fearful that a failure to utilise all of their approved respite hours within a specified time period could threaten the availability of those resources or result in the services being reduced. This constrained the ability of families to use respite services in a way which best addressed their needs.

Staff also perceived challenges with program policies. They identified a lack of policy or conflicting policies, inconsistent policies across jurisdictions, and policies that were based on criteria such as the child's age or diagnosis that were restrictive and constrained their ability to be responsive to families' needs (Wright et al., 2010). Family service workers also commented that their organisation's mandate sometimes created difficulties implementing a family-centred model. If the needs that family members identified were outside the mandate of the organisation, the family service worker was unable to adequately respond to those needs. The extent to which collateral agencies and professionals also worked from a family-centred perspective either mitigated or compounded the problem. Staff reported that it was difficult to work in a family-centred way without the buy-in of collateral agencies or professionals. If other service providers had narrow mandates or worked from an "expert" stance, family service workers found that the delivery of services to the family did not meet the ideals of FCP. Parents were also aware of the challenges of negotiating between complex service delivery systems including child disability, health, education, and child welfare sectors and identified a lack of communication between service providers as well as jurisdictional issues as problematic. Other researchers have identified the need for clarity and consistency in policies on cross-jurisdictional, interdisciplinary, and intra-organisational levels in order to deliver services that are family-centred (e.g., Harbin et al., 2004). Implementing FCP requires applying a family-centred lens to the policies that govern programs and the allocation of resources. The organisation's internal context, including its culture and climate, should reflect family-centred policies, procedures, and organisational practices. On a program level, FCP requires that services be flexible and comprehensive (Dunst, Trivette, & Deal, 1994; Shelton & Stepanek, 1995), as well as accessible (Dunst et al., 1994; Stroul, 1995).

The issue of program and system resources was also raised by parents and staff. It is difficult to be family-centred in a system with inadequate resources where service delivery is driven more by what is available than by what families need. On one level, inadequate staff resources impact the interaction between families and family service workers. For example, both parents and staff commented on how large caseloads create conditions under which it is difficult for family service workers to be responsive to the individual needs and priorities of families. Families perceived difficulty accessing their family service workers and, in some instances, reported an inability of family service workers to respond in a timely manner. Some parents recognised that the problem was situated in the system and not the individual family service worker. They perceived the need to hire more staff to meet the demands. Family service workers described how large caseloads limited their availability to have ongoing contact with families. Not only does the number of families for which a family service worker has responsibility have an effect, but the needs of the families and the resulting activity impact practice. Responding to a high number of families frequently in crisis can make finding time to engage with other families in a more proactive, preventative manner challenging. The issue of staff resources and its impact on FCP has been raised by others (e.g., Coyne, O'Neill, Murphy, Costello, & O'Shea, 2011). Without a commitment to reasonable caseloads that acknowledge the level of need of the families, the extent to which FCP will be implemented will be limited.

Families were also well aware of the scarcity of resources within the service system. This was realised when experiencing lengthy waitlists for services for their child and/or family. This was especially distressing for families who experienced barriers to entry into the service system and perceived urgency to the acquisition of early intervention services for their children (Hiebert-Murphy et al., 2008). In some cases, program policies were seen as a way to ration limited resources rather than facilitate the delivery of needed supports. As a result, family service workers can be placed in a difficult position of helping families identify needs, only to then have to communicate the realities of a system in which there are inadequate resources to meet families' needs. This is especially challenging when the scarce resources involve highly specialised services (e.g., speech therapy) and there are limited options for meeting those needs. Further, scarce resources can put family service workers in a position of making difficult decisions about where to place resources. Some families feared that if their children demonstrated modest positive outcomes as a result of specific interventions, they were at risk of losing those services or having the services cut back. This created tension in parents' relationships with family service workers and the perception that the service system was not equipped to support families in the long term.

Broader policy context

The issue of resources is complex and reflects a number of challenges within the broader policy context. As noted earlier, in Canada, health and social services are a provincial responsibility under the constitution. However, funding for these services stems largely from the federal government's health transfer and social transfer of tax revenue to provinces based on the rate of economic growth and per capita numbers (Fierlbeck, 2013). While there is federal and provincial legislation that provides policy direction for services for childhood disability, child disability services are non-mandated. As a result, funding for these services is capped; the provision of disability services is treated as a privilege rather than a basic right of citizens. Child disability support programs must work within the limits of their budgets. Increased demands for service must be managed and result in waitlists for services and reductions in types and/or levels of service. Family service workers within the provincially funded service system must work creatively with families to try to establish support plans within this environment. While there are options to how some needs can be met (using services offered in the non-profit sector or utilising informal sources of support), there are certain services for which alternate service providers do not exist or which are only available through the private sector, limiting accessibility for families.

Within the child disability field, resource allocation must also address the demands of particular groups who lobby for increased resources for interventions that address their specific needs. An example is the demand for specialised intervention for young children diagnosed with autism spectrum disorder (ASD). The prevalence of ASD (based on the number of children identified in hospital/physician records and education records) for Manitoba children aged five to nine years increased from 0.49% in 1996–2001 to 0.88% in 2001–2006 (Brownell et al., 2008). Advocacy regarding access to intensive applied behaviour analysis intervention for children diagnosed with ASD has placed pressure on the Manitoba government to increase funding for these services. Even when such demands result in new funding, it impacts the budgeting process and the extent to which additional resources are likely to be available to address the needs of children with other disabilities.

The accessibility of services is further complicated by differences between urban and rural areas. Rural and remote communities have few options with regards to services. While provincially funded programs are available across the province, there is more limited access in rural areas to the services offered by the network of non-profit organisations that provide support to families with children with disabilities. Specialised health services are also much more limited outside of the major urban area; families must often commute to this urban centre to receive such care. This reality challenges the implementation of FCP, which purports the need for comprehensive, accessible services (Dunst et al., 1994; Shelton & Stepanek, 1995; Stroul, 1995).

As noted earlier, Manitoba has a sizeable Aboriginal population (approximately 175,000 people in 2006), with about 57,000 people living on one of 62 reserves throughout the province (Government of Manitoba, n.d,). Although health and social services are a provincial responsibility, services for Aboriginal people living on reserves are a federal responsibility. Constitutional issues create jurisdictional issues including ineligibility of Aboriginal children living on reserve for provincial services (Minister of Health, 2000). Disputes between which level of government is responsible for the costs of services can be seriously detrimental to meeting the needs of Aboriginal children and families. For example, a high-profile case of an Aboriginal child named Jordan from a reserve in Northern Manitoba, who eventually died in hospital care because of disagreements about which level of government should provide the services needed to support the child in his home community, illustrates how jurisdictional issues can work to the detriment of service provision (First Nations Child and Family Caring Society, 2015). The outcome of this case was the adoption of "Jordan's Principle" which has been initiated to ensure that service costs be paid initially by the government of first contact with reimbursement pursued later. Such jurisdictional matters in Canada create challenges to the implementation of family-centred principles in services for Aboriginal families.

Conclusion

The potential outcomes of family-centred services are highly appealing: greater satisfaction with services, reduced family need, and increased capacity of families. Developing service delivery systems that are family-centred, however, is challenging. Our experience with FCP in childhood disability services in Manitoba suggests that a number of issues must be addressed for implementation to be successful.

First of all, there must be a commitment to family-centred principles by senior policymakers and managers responsible for decision-making regarding program policies and resources. Implementation of family-centred principles requires a willingness to shift program policies and practices so that they align with the philosophy of FCP. Further, the assessment of the family-centredness of the service system may identify the need for increased staff or expanded support services in order to facilitate increased partnership with families. While individual family service workers can make shifts in how they interact with families, for a service delivery system to be truly family-centred the entire organisation must shift so that policies and practice are congruent with family-centred principles. The policy infrastructure must support the basic tenets of FCP (e.g., individualised, culturally responsive, seamless service delivery), and the organisational culture must value professional-parent partnerships and family empowerment to produce a positive climate for those providing/implementing services. Implementing FCP at the organisational level involves assessment and redrafting of organisational policies and practice standards to ensure that they align with family-centred principles. In addition, the service system needs to be adequately resourced so that the principles of FCP can be enacted. Family service workers' caseloads must allow them to maintain ongoing relationships with families and be proactive in working with families to identify and address needs rather than reactive to family crises. As well, there must be sufficient support services available to assist families when the need for such services is identified. Implementing FCP may well require advocacy for resources in order to better support families. Shifting organisational policies and advocacy for resources will be ongoing processes that should be done in partnership with families. An important element of implementation is developing mechanisms within organisations that encourage family involvement in these processes and ensure that families have a voice in decision-making regarding organisational policies and resource allocation. It should be noted that the implementation of FCP within specific organisations or programs does not occur in isolation; the extent to which a family-centred lens is adopted across all professional disciplines, service delivery sectors, and organisations/collateral services that work with families impacts the degree to which families will experience the service system as family centred.

Once a commitment to FCP is made, well-planned professional training in family-centred service principles, and the components of FCP intervention skills, is vital to moving implementation forward. While training is essential, it is important to understand training as an ongoing, developmental process. A one-time training, regardless of its comprehensiveness, is unlikely to result in sustained change. An intensive introduction to FCP principles and their application to a specific service delivery context may be a good first step in a broader plan that addresses ongoing support for the development of skills. However, the impact of the training will diminish over time if there is no follow up to support the change. Ongoing supervision is needed that provides family service workers with feedback on how to integrate the principles of FCP into their work. Family service workers may need assistance in developing the skills needed for working in partnership with families. They will also likely need support in enhancing the ways in which their practice encourages family empowerment. Developing the capacity of family service workers to work in family-centred ways is key to sustaining a shift in practice.

Our involvement in the efforts to increase the family-centredness of services in Manitoba has highlighted issues that emerge in implementation. These issues are complex and not likely to be easily addressed in any jurisdiction. Implementation of FCP is best seen as a lengthy process requiring the strong commitment of, and partnership between, policymakers, program staff, families, and researchers.

References

Allen, R. I., & Petr, C. G. (1996). Toward developing standards and measurements for family-centered practice in family support programs. In G. Singer, L. Powers, & A. Olson (Eds.), *Family support policy and America's caregiving families: Innovations in public-private partnerships* (pp. 57–86). Baltimore, MD: Brookes.

Brownell, M., De Coster, C., Penfold, R., Derksen, S., Au, W., Schultz, J., & Dahl, M. (2008). *Manitoba child health atlas update*. Winnipeg, MB: Manitoba Centre for Health Policy.

Bruder, M. B. (2000). Family-centered early intervention: Clarifying our values for the new millennium. *Topics in Early Childhood Special Education, 20*, 105–115. doi:10.1177/027112140002000206

Bruce, B., Letourneau, N., Ritchie, J., Larocque, S., Dennis, C., & Elliott, M. R. (2002). A multisite study of health professionals' perceptions and practices of family-centered care. *Journal of Family Nursing, 8*, 408–429. doi:10.1177/10748 4002237515

Campbell, P. H., & Halbert, J. (2002). Between research and practice: Provider perspectives on early intervention. *Topics in Early Childhood Special Education, 22*, 213–226. doi:10.1177/027112140202200403

Coyne, I., O'Neill, C., Murphy, M., Costello, T., & O'Shea, R. (2011). What does family-centred care mean to nurses and how do they think it could be enhanced in practice. *Journal of Advanced Nursing, 67*, 2561–2573. doi:10.1111/j.1365-2648.2011.05768.x

Craft-Rosenberg, M., Kelley, P., & Schnoll, L. (2006). Family-centered care: Practice and preparation. *Families in Society, 87*, 17–25. doi:10.1606/1044-3894.3480

Dempsey, I., & Keen, D. (2008). A review of processes and outcomes in family-centered services for children with a disability. *Topics in Early Childhood Special Education, 28*, 42–52. doi:10.1177/0271121408316699

Dinnebeil, L. A., Hale, L. M., & Rule, S. (1996). A qualitative analysis of parents' and service coordinators' descriptions of variables that influence collaborative relationships. *Topics in Early Childhood Special Education, 19*, 322–347. doi:10.1177/027112149601600305

Dunst, C. J. (2002). Family-centered practices: Birth through high school. *Journal of Special Education, 36*, 141–149. doi:10.1177/00224669020360030401

Dunst, C. J., Johanson, C., Trivette, C. M., & Hamby, D. (1991). Family-oriented early intervention policies and practices: Family-centered or not? *Exceptional Children, 58*, 115–126.

Dunst, C. J., & Trivette, C. M. (1996). Empowerment, effective helpgiving practices and family-centered care. *Pediatric Nursing, 22*, 334–337, 343.

Dunst, C. J., Trivette, C. M., & Deal, A. G. (1988). *Enabling and empowering families: Principles and guidelines for practice.* Cambridge, MA: Brookline Books.

Dunst, C. J., Trivette, C. M., & Deal, A. G. (Eds.). (1994). *Supporting and strengthening families.* Cambridge, MA: Brookline Books.

Dunst, C. J., Trivette, C. M., & Hamby, D. W. (2007). Meta-analysis of family-centered helpgiving practices research. *Mental Retardation and Developmental Disabilities Research Reviews, 13,* 370–378. doi:10.1002/mrdd.20176

First Nations Child and Family Caring Society. (2015). *Jordan's principle.* Retrieved from http://www.fncfwc.ca/advocacy-activities/jordans-principle/

Fierlbeck, K. (2013). Introduction: Renewing federalism, improving health care: Can this marriage be saved? In K. Fierlbeck & W. Lahey (Eds.), *Health care federalism in Canada: Critical junctures and critical perspectives* (pp. 3–23). Montreal, Quebec: McGill-Queen's University Press.

Government of Manitoba. (n.d.). *Aboriginal People in Manitoba.* Retrieved from http://www.gov.mb.ca/ana/pdf/pubs/abpeoplembweb.pdf

Government of Manitoba. (2014). *Manitoba Family Services Annual Report 2013–2014.* Retrieved from http://www.gov.mb.ca/fs/about/annual_reports.html

Government of Manitoba. (2015). *Children's disability services.* Retrieved from http://gov.mb.ca/fs/pwd/css.html#content

Harbin, G. L., Bruder, M. B., Adams, C., Mazzarella, C., Whitbread, K., Gabbard, G., & Staff, I. (2004). Early intervention service coordination policies: National policy infrastructure. *Topics in Early Childhood Special Education, 24,* 89–97. doi:10.1177/02711214040240020401

Hartman, A., & Laird, J. (1983). *Family-centered social work practice.* New York: Free Press.

Healthy Child Manitoba. (n.d.). *2012 report on manitoba's children and youth.* Retrieved from http://www.gov.mb.ca/healthychild/publications/hcm_2012report.pdf

Hiebert-Murphy, D. (2013). Parent preparation for family-centred services. In B. Trute & D. Hiebert-Murphy (Eds.), *Partnering with parents: Family-centred practice in children's services* (pp. 157–175). Toronto: University of Toronto Press.

Hiebert-Murphy, D., Trute, B., & Wright, A. (2008). Patterns of entry to community-based services for families with children with developmental disabilities: Implications for social work practice. *Child & Family Social Work, 13,* 423–432. doi:10.1111/j.1365-2206.2008.00572.x

Hiebert-Murphy, D., Trute, B., & Wright, A. (2011). Parents' definition of effective child disability support services: Implications for implementing family-centered practice. *Journal of Family Social Work, 14,* 144–158. doi:10.1080/10522158.2011.552404

Johnson, B. H. (1990). The changing role of families in health care. *Children's Health Care, 19,* 234–241. doi:10.1207/s15326888chc1904_7

Johnson, H. C., Cournoyer, D. E., Fliri, J., Flynn, M., Grant, A. M., Lant, M. A., Parasco, S., & Stanek, E. J. (2003). Are we parent-friendly? Views of parents of children with emotional and behavioral disabilities. *Families in Society, 84,* 95–108. doi:10.1606/1044-3894.80

Klassen, T., Trute, B., & Hiebert-Murphy, D. (2013). The family-centred support plan: An action strategy for parent and professional partners. In B. Trute & D. Hiebert-Murphy (Eds.), *Partnering with parents: Family-centred practice in children's services* (pp. 176–197). Toronto: University of Toronto Press.

Law, M., Hanna, S., King, G., Hurley, P., King, S., Kertoy, M., & Rosenbaum, P. (2003). Factors affecting family-centred service delivery for children with disabilities. *Child: Care, Health and Development, 29*, 357–366. doi:10.1046/j.1365-2214.2003.00351.x

Levine, K. (2013). Capacity building and empowerment practice. In B. Trute & D. Hiebert-Murphy (Eds.), *Partnering with parents: Family-centred practice in children's services* (pp. 107–129). Toronto: University of Toronto Press.

Madsen, W. C. (2014). Applications of collaborative helping maps: Supporting professional development, supervision and work teams in family-centered practice. *Family Process, 53*, 3–21. doi:10.1111/famp.12048

Malone, D. M., McKinsey, P. D., Thyer, B. A., & Straka, E. (2000). Social work early intervention for young children with developmental disabilities. *Health & Social Work, 25*, 169–180. doi:10.1093/hsw/25.3.169

McBride, S. L., Sharp, L., Hains, A. H., & Whitehead, A. (1995). Parents as co-instructors in preservice training: A pathway to family-centered practice. *Journal of Early Intervention, 19*, 343–55. doi:10.1177/105381519501900408

Minister of Health. (2000). *FAS/FAE initiative information and feedback sessions. National synthesis report, June 2000.* Retrieved from http://research4children. com/data/documents/FASDHealthCanadaFASFAEInitiativeInformationand FeedbackSessionsNationalSynthesisReportpdf.pdf

Mitchell, W., & Sloper, P. (2003). Quality indicators: Disabled children's and parents' prioritizations and experiences of quality criteria when using different types of support services. *British Journal of Social Work, 33*, 1063–1080. doi:10.1093/bjsw/33.8.1063

Patterson, J. M., & Hovey, D. L. (2000). Family-centred care for children with special health needs: Rhetoric or reality. *Families, Systems & Health, 18*, 237–251. doi:10.1037/h0091849

Pretis, M. (2006). Professional training in early intervention: A European perspective. *Journal of Policy and Practice in Intellectual Disabilities, 3*, 42–48. doi:10.1111/j.1741-1130.2006.00051.x

Roberts, R. N., Rule, S., & Innocenti, M. S. (1998). *Strengthening the family-professional partnership in services for young children.* Baltimore, MD: Brookes.

Shelton, T. L., & Stepanek, J. S. (1995). Excerpts from family-centered care for children needing specialized health and developmental services. *Pediatric Nursing, 21*, 362–364.

Sloper, P., Greco, V., Beecham, J., & Webb, R. (2006). Key worker services for disabled children: What characteristics of services lead to better outcomes for children and families? *Child: Care, Health and Development, 32*, 147–157. doi:10.1111/j.1365-2214.2006.00592.x

Statistics Canada. (2008a). *Population reporting an aboriginal identity, by age group, by province and territory (2006 census) (Manitoba, Saskatchewan, Alberta, British Columbia).* Retrieved from http://www.statcan.gc.ca/tables-tableaux/sum-som/l01/cst01/demo40c-eng.htm

Statistics Canada. (2008b). *Immigrant population by place of birth, by province and territory (2006 census) (Manitoba, Saskatchewan, Alberta, British Columbia).* Retrieved from http://www.statcan.gc.ca/tables-tableaux/sum-som/l01/cst01/demo34c-eng.htm

Statistics Canada. (2014a). *Statistics Canada, CANSIM, Table 051–0001.* Retrieved from http://www.statcan.gc.ca/tables-tableaux/sum-som/l01/cst01/demo 02a-eng.htm

Statistics Canada. (2014b). *Statistics Canada, CANSIM, Table 051–0056.* Retrieved from http://www.statcan.gc.ca/tables-tableaux/sum-som/l01/cst01/demo05a-eng.htm

Stroul, B. A. (1995). Case management in a system of care. In B. J. Friesen & J. Poertner (Eds.), *From case management to service coordination for children with emotional, behavioral, or mental disorders: Building on family strengths* (pp. 3–25). Baltimore, MD: Paul H. Brookes.

Thompson, S., Hiebert-Murphy, D., & Trute, B. (2013). Parental perceptions of family adjustment in childhood developmental disabilities. *Journal of Intellectual Disabilities, 17*, 23–37. doi:10.1177/1744629512472618

Trute, B. (2007). Service coordination in family-centered childhood disability services: Quality assessment from the family perspective. *Families in Society, 88*, 283–291. doi:10.1606/1044-3894.3626

Trute, B. (2013). Basic family-centred practice concepts and principles. In B. Trute & D. Hiebert-Murphy (Eds.), *Partnering with parents: Family-centred practice in children's services* (pp. 19–44). Toronto: University of Toronto Press.

Trute, B., & Hauch, C. (1988a). Building on family strength: A study of families with positive adjustment to the birth of a developmentally disabled child. *Journal of Marital and Family Therapy, 14*, 185–193. doi:10.1111/j.1752-0606.1988.tb00734.x

Trute, B., & Hauch, C. (1988b). Social network attributes of families with positive adaptation to the birth of a developmentally disabled child. *Canadian Journal of Community Mental Health, 7*(1), 5–16.

Trute, B., & Hiebert-Murphy, D. (2005). Predicting family adjustment and parenting stress in childhood disability services using brief assessment tools. *Journal of Intellectual & Developmental Disability, 30*, 217–225. doi:10.1080/13668250500349441

Trute, B., & Hiebert-Murphy, D. (2007). The implications of 'working alliance' for the measurement and evaluation of family-centered practice in childhood disability services. *Infants & Young Children, 20*, 109–119. doi:10.1097/01.IYC.0000264479.50817.4b

Trute, B., & Hiebert-Murphy, D. (2013). *Partnering with parents: Family-centred practice in children's services.* Toronto: University of Toronto Press.

Trute, B., Hiebert-Murphy, D., & Levine, K. (2007). Parental appraisal of the family impact of childhood developmental disability: Times of sadness and times of joy. *Journal of Intellectual and Developmental Disability, 32*, 1–9. doi:10.1080/13668250601146753

Trute, B., Hiebert-Murphy, D., & Wright, A. (2008). Family-centred service coordination in childhood health and disability services: The search for meaningful service outcome measures. *Child: Care, Health and Development, 34*, 367–372. doi:10.1111/j.1365-2214.2008.00819.x

Trute, B., Worthington, C., & Hiebert-Murphy, D. (2008). Grandmother support for parents of children with disabilities: Gender differences in parenting stress. *Families, Systems & Health, 26*, 135–146. doi:10.1037/1091-7527.26.2.135

Walton, E., Sandau-Beckler, P., & Mannes, M. (Eds.). (2001). *Balancing family-centered services and child well-being.* New York: Columbia University Press.

Wright, A., Hiebert-Murphy, D., & Trute, B. (2010). Professionals' perspectives on organizational factors that support or hinder the successful implementation of family-centered practice. *Journal of Family Social Work, 13*, 114–130. doi:10.1080/10522150903503036

13 Family experiences of early childhood intervention services for young children with speech, language and communication needs in England

Carolyn Blackburn

It is now well established that speech language and communication (SLC) skills are crucial for children's social, educational and long-term outcomes (Gowsami, 2008; Roulstone et al., 2010; Whitebread & Bingham, 2011). In England, children's early language and cognitive development has been the subject of successive Government policy initiatives placing emphasis on the role of early childhood practitioners (ECPs) to identify, assess and support any problems with children's development as early as possible with appropriate intervention so that children's developmental trajectory can be optimised. This chapter includes descriptions of parents' experiences with early childhood intervention (ECI) services for young children with speech, language and communication needs (SLCN) in one Local Authority (LA) in England. It highlights the difficult and subjective nature of early identification of problems with SLC and illustrates this with a vignette of a child diagnosed with autism. The author argues that identification of young children's progress requires ongoing monitoring and assessment and ECI can be very effective for young children with SLCN. However, ECI services are currently more responsive and accessible to parents whose children who have severe and complex SLCN than those who have mild to moderate SLCN. This raises questions about how young children at risk from special educational needs and disabilities (SEND) are supported and how children's trajectories can be optimised in line with policy intentions.

Background to the chapter

Children's early SLC skills are acquired in the micro social and cultural context of relations with caregivers who ideally provide a degree of sensitive mind-minded interpretation to children's early vocalisations and gestures beginning in infancy. Meins and Fernyhough (2006) defined mind-mindedness as an individual's "tendency to adopt the intentional stance in their interactions with and representations of others" (p. 2). Mind-mindedness characterises social interaction involved in early caregiver-child interactions, and in particular, the proclivity of a mother to treat her child as an individual with a mind from an early age. Sensitive caregivers attribute intent to an infant's early vocalizations by interpreting the possible meaning of infant behaviour and vocalisations. In order to understand what an infant is trying to communicate in their early babbling and coos, it is thought necessary to recognise that the infant is actually *intending* to convey some message. Therefore, when caregivers listen and respond to their infant's early behaviours and vocalisations, they demonstrate mind-mindedness. They perceive these vocalisations as intentional communication rather than inconsequential utterances without agenda or meaning, and interpret them using past knowledge of the child and concurrent gestures.

The basic components of language (phonology, semantics, syntax and pragmatics) are mastered over time starting with the pre-speech stage, which lasts from birth to about the end of the first year or early part of the second and ends with the appearance of single words at approximately twelve months old (Smith, Cowie, & Blades, 2008). Achievements in the pre-linguistic stage include the appearance of intentions to communicate, evident in signals and gestures that have meaning for both the infant and caregiver and the discovery of symbols. In other words, children develop the understanding that objects and artefacts have names. The ability to use and understand words develops from a complex series of interactions between infants and caregivers, including eye contact, episodes of intersubjective joint attention using eye movements and gestures and turn-taking between infants and their caregivers. As children mature and their SLC skills become increasingly more complex, adults mediate the interactions between children and the activities, resources and objects in their environments. Scaffolding children's communication and thinking through guided participation is also an important adult role (Bruner, 1983; Rogoff, 2003). For the majority of typically developing children, the acquisition of SLC occurs naturally in this manner. However, in a review of provision for children with SLCN (Bercow, 2008) a national prevalence for SLCN of 6–8% was found and this is discussed in more detail later on. Overall, the prevalence of SLCN has been noted to have increased by 58% between 2005 and 2011 (Dockrell et al., 2012). As a result, there has been an increasing English policy emphasis on the early years (birth to five), recognition of the centrality of language in children's learning and development, the effectiveness of early intervention and the role of early ECPs in the early identification, assessment and support of children's early language difficulties and delays, as discussed and demonstrated below.

For example, an independent report on the English Early Years Foundation Stage (EYFS) (Tickell, 2011) included the argument that early identification followed by appropriate intervention was most effective to help children overcome specific obstacles to learning. A progress check for children between the ages of two and three was recommended by Tickell (2011) in order to provide a summary of children's development for parents in prime areas of social and emotional development, communication and language development and physical development that were regarded as essential foundations for children's life, learning and success.

A new EYFS statutory framework setting out standards for learning, development and care from birth to five and focusing on the three prime areas of learning was introduced in September 2012 and updated in 2014 (DfE, 2012, 2014). This placed stronger emphasis on the role of ECPs in the important function of ECI.

The nature and effectiveness of particular types of early ECI services for SLCN is too broad for the focus of this chapter. However, the literature located in the scientific field of ECI notes that interventions based on developmental systems, family-centred approaches are particularly effective. As Guralnick (2011) points out, regardless of the aetiology of a child's difficulties or the "label" provided for them,

> *Systems features such as adopting a family-centered approach, requiring individualised interventions, and ensuring coordination of services supported by a research base, in addition to generally agreed-upon values and principles, have now achieved international consensus.*

(p. 7)

For example, in their meta-analysis of 70 ECI studies, Dunst, Trivette and Hamby (2008) found that family-centred practices benefitted families by strengthening parents' relationships with professionals and improving engagement in their children's learning and education in meaningful ways. In order to achieve this, professionals working in ECI services needed to promote self-efficacy and be responsive to parents' information and resource needs, that is, be responsive and helpful in a participatory and relational manner. In other words, a capacity-building paradigm is called for (Dunst & Trivette, 2009).

This discussion has highlighted the significance of relationships in children's learning and development. This includes relationships at the proximal level that occur between people (caregivers and infants), as well as more distant relationships such as those between policy intentions and delivery of ECI services to families consistent with bio-ecological models such as that proposed by Bronfenbrenner (1979). Relationships between professionals that work in ECI services and families can also serve to promote children's development if they operate in a manner that is perceived by families to be helpful. This chapter includes a discussion of family perspectives on ECI services for early SLCN and an example of one child's ECI experience through the theoretical lens of bio-ecology to provide an explanatory framework.

Bio-ecology and potential for change

Contemporary scientific study of children's development is characterised by a commitment to the understanding of the dynamic relationships between the developing individual and the integrated multilevel ecology of human development (Lerner, 2005). Characterised by a temporally or historically embedded person-context relational process, the developmental systems approach to understanding child development embraces models of dynamic change across the ecological system and by relational change-sensitive methods. This assumes that children influence the people and institutions in their ecology as much as they are influenced by them, suggesting that children's development is both a product and outcome of the variables within the environments they inhabit. The plasticity or potential for systematic change associated with the engagement of an active child with his or her active context presents the possibility that intervention provides the opportunity to improve the course and context of child development from "what is" human development to "what could be" human development (Bronfenbrenner, 2005). These contexts range from the *microsystems* that refer to the developing child and the immediate environment of home and preschool; their linkages in the *mesosystems*, or indirect influences in the immediate setting (for example, the LA), intermediate *exosystems*, through to the *macrosystem* of society, comprising patterns of value, culture, political, economic and legal organisation. The chrono-system acknowledges changes over time (for example, policy changes, macro-time or children's maturation over time). Relationships between different contexts or systems that children inhabit are therefore influential in their development.

Bronfenbrenner (1979, 2005) conceptualised these relationships between children and the environments they inhabited in his bio-ecological model, in which he explained the importance for human development of interrelated ecological levels, conceived of as nested systems. This suggests that ideally policy must operate in harmony with practice and take into account the diverse range of family rhythms, patterns, and processes that occur within communities as well as the resources and stressors that serve to promote or compromise relationships within the multiple contexts identified within Bronfenbrenner's model. An overview of child and family policy is therefore provided below.

English child and family policy

In light of the significant influence that policy is perceived to exert on children's development, an overview of recent English policy provides the background to this chapter. Since the late 1990s, child and family policy has exemplified the major tenants of English Government policy, which underpin a drive to ensure a socially cohesive and economically productive and stable society. Concerned that society had become fragmented and families dysfunctional, and in line with Europe-wide political moves towards social liberalism, broader policy aims have highlighted matters such as gender equality and the accommodation of different family structures and cultures. Because of this, the early years have become a central focus for government policy, planning and development for the first. The provision of child care and nursery education for under-fives and strengthening parental responsibility have been prioritised, in part so that more women could join the workforce, but also to ensure that all children have equal opportunities to succeed in life. Early childhood has been perceived as the period during which the foundations for future success and happiness are laid:

> *The early years of a child's life are critical to their future success and happiness. We are determined to invest in better opportunities for our youngest children. . . we*

need to do more to provide help to parents with the difficult job of raising children successfully throughout their childhood and adolescence.

(Home Office, 1998, pp. 15–16)

Unfolding child and family policy developments have also reflected the wider social policy goals of tackling established problems with poverty and raising standards of educational outcomes for all children (Baldock, Fitzgerald, & Kaye, 2013). With one in three children living in poverty in 1988, the Government has been concerned about the risk that poverty poses to children and families (Baldock et al., p. 46). Research evidence suggests that this risk includes the link between economic disadvantage to parental stress, low responsiveness in parent-child interactions and a range of poor cognitive and social-emotional outcomes in young children. This includes children's inadequate language acquisition, self-regulation and confidence to interact or express their needs (Whitebread & Bingham, 2011). Consequently, the Government made an ambitious, and arguably naive, claim that the cycle of deprivation could be broken within two decades:

(O)ur historic aim that ours is the first generation to end child poverty forever, and it will take a generation. It is a 20-year mission, but I believe it can be done.

(Blair, p. 7)

In order to achieve this aim, the Government has driven initiatives for both expansion and consolidation of early childhood and family services, including welfare reforms, in order to provide good quality child care and education for all children and a range of targeted services for vulnerable groups.

Focussing on SLCN, a landmark government-commissioned review of services for children and young people with SLCN further signalled the centrality of SLC in early development, learning and later academic and lifelong success (Bercow, 2008). The author reported a national prevalence of SLCN of 7% of all children in England, with 1% of children having severe or complex SLCN needing long-term specialist provision, and a further 50% of five-year-olds living in the most disadvantaged areas having SLC significantly below those of their peers. Bercow (2008) defined the term SLCN as:

Encompassing a wide range of difficulties related to all aspects of communication in children, including difficulties with fluency, forming sounds and words, formulating sentences, understanding what others say and using language socially (p. 13).

Bercow argued that the majority of difficulties and delays could be identified as early as the second year of life and that the benefits of ECI were so significant that they could reduce the possible risk of later academic and behavioural problems, emotional and psychological difficulties, poorer employment prospects, challenges to mental health and, in some cases, a descent into criminality (Bercow, 2008, p. 7).

However, Bercow (2008) was concerned that professionals involved in early identification, such as health visitors (HVs), teaching assistants (TAs), teachers and practitioners working in early childhood settings were not sufficiently well trained. In addition, parents had reported that speech and language therapists (SLTs) and HVs did not always take their concerns seriously. Therefore, he suggested that improved early identification may result from improved knowledge in the children's workforce and joined-up multi-agency working. This would mean that there was improved communication and information sharing between agencies and common working practices that would promote a more responsive service for families, noted earlier to be important. The problems with training and knowledge to implement ECI have also been noted by others, most notably Locke et al. (2002) and Mroz and Hall (2003), who both called for greater clarity for ECPs so that fewer children 'slipped through the net' and missed out on the reported benefits of ECI.

Consecutive ECI policy reports following the Bercow (2008) review emphasised the centrality of language in children's development and the requirement for early childhood practitioners to identify, assess and support children's difficulties and delays in the acquisition of language early in liaison with multi-agency HVs and SLTs. For example, the significant economic returns of intervening early to improve children's SLC skills was noted by Allen (2011, 13) whose recommendation to form an Early Intervention Foundation was recently taken forward by Government with a view to

> *Breaking the inter-generational cycles of dysfunction . . . resulting from social disruption, broken families and unmet human potential.*
>
> (Allen, 2013, p. 2)

Nutbrown (2012) noted that for ECPs, a "key part of understanding how and when children typically develop was being able to notice signs of slower, or different development and whether an apparent delay in development was an indication of other special educational needs or disabilities [SEND]" (pp. 19–20). She was particularly concerned that ECPs should be equipped with the knowledge about what to look for in this regard, how to respond to it and how to interact with parents and the multi-agency professionals that play a part in supporting a child with SEND. It was against this backcloth of intense focus on young children's development in the microcontext of family relationships and early childhood settings that the study to be reported in this chapter was set. The requirement for ECPs to identify problems with children's early language development has already been noted. However, the difficult and subjective nature of early identification were highlighted in the empirical literature, as shown below.

Background literature

The professional difficulties inherent in early identification were summarised by Law et al. (1998) who noted that the common use of the term "delay" by professionals in describing children's SLCN suggested that it was possible to characterise children with delays along a single axis. Law et al. (1998) argue that this is problematic as speech and language represents a complex interaction of functions. This is because children may present with different levels of delay and with qualitative differences in the difficulties they experience. For example, in some children, expressive speech alone can be affected; for others, problems may occur in expressive language and/or verbal comprehension. Furthermore, whilst there is a strong correlation between comprehension and production of language, approximately 10% of children show significantly higher levels of comprehension than production, particularly those children who are described as "late talkers" (Hulme & Snowling, 2009). Moreover, although many children described as late talkers at the age of two catch up with their peers by the age of five, they may experience later problems with reading and writing tasks in formal learning that could sometimes take years to become manifest (Hulme & Snowling, 2009).

This has important implications for early years practice in light of the role already discussed for early childhood practitioners in identifying delays and difficulties in young children's SLC and referring to specialist professionals for ECI. It may not be easy for practitioners to assess whether aspects of SLC are delayed or a sign of SEND without specialist knowledge. The consequences of this were illustrated by Law et al. (1998, vii), who reported that a substantial proportion of children identified by specialists on the basis of expressive language delay alone were likely to have difficulties which resolved spontaneously in the preschool period. Although it was impossible to predict at the time of identification which of the children with expressive delay were likely to have persistent problems, it was certainly the case that children with expressive and receptive delays were less likely to experience a spontaneous recovery. Therefore, the issue of which children were likely to need intervention from specialist services would, therefore, seem to require detailed professional knowledge of the technicalities of SLC development. As Dale, Price, Bishop and Plomin (2003) noted:

> *Nearly two thirds of late talkers move into the normal range before preschool and distinguishing transient from persistent delays is notoriously difficult for clinicians and researchers.*
>
> Cited in Fernald and Marchman (2012, p. 203)

When late talking does not resolve itself, a diagnosis of specific language impairment (SLI) may be the result, particularly when a child's language has failed to develop typically for no obvious reason. Therefore, hearing loss, physical disability, emotional disturbance, parental neglect and brain injury should all be ruled out before the diagnosis is made (Bishop, 2008). Children with SLI do not usually produce their first words until up to six months later than their typically developing peers, with word combinations appearing significantly later (Hulme & Snowling, 2009). It is more common for children with SLI to have difficulties with expressive language or production of words than receptive language or comprehension of words. Most commonly, there are problems with slow lexical development and a delay in learning to combine words together (Hulme & Snowling, 2009).

Hulme and Snowling (2009) noted that if patterns of development resemble those seen in typically developing younger children, then any difference in a child's SLC development is most accurately described as a delay. Deviant or disordered SLC development, in contrast, represents development in which a delay in the rate at which *particular* skills in certain key areas could be observed such as thought processing, social communication skills or forming particular sounds. So for children with SLI, their oral language skills would be weaker than expected compared with their reasoning or conceptualising. Some children with SLI may have had speech difficulties, others may have had difficulties using language socially and some may well be able to communicate effectively despite expressive language problems (Hulne & Snowling, 2009).

Added to this, Dockrell et al. (2012) noted that expressive language disorders rarely occurred alone, distinguishing between specific difficulties with vocabulary and grammar particularly in the early stages of development was challenging and children have been reported to move from one diagnostic group to another. These changes have been difficult to explain in theoretically meaningful ways leading to questions about whether children with SLI formed a qualitatively distinct group or were best understood as the lower end of the normal distribution. This exemplified the difficulty for generalist ECP practitioners in being equipped with sufficient specialist knowledge in order to determine the difference between delay and disorder and refer children to other professionals such as SLTs.

Parents' experiences of early childhood intervention services

In a study concerned with the policy-to-practice context to delays and difficulties in acquisition of SLC in the first five years (Blackburn, 2014; Blackburn &

Table 13.1 Prevalence of speech, language and communication needs reported by practitioners

Children by age	Number of children	Number of children with SLCN	Number with children with SLCN as a percentage of total
Children aged 0–12 months	103	0	0
Children aged 12–24 months	239	7	2.9%
Children aged 24–48 months	1,406	188	13.4%
Children aged 48–60 months	551	92	16.7%
Total for all age groups	**2,299**	**287**	**12.5%**

Source: Author's study

Aubrey, 2016), the author surveyed and interviewed ECPs and parents and conducted structured observations of adult-adult and adult-child interactions in early childhood settings within one LA in England. Analysis of the survey and practitioner interviews showed that practitioners were using a wide range of tools to monitor children's progress and that the prevalence of SLCN reported by practitioners was overall higher than suggested by Bercow, as shown in Table 13.1.

This could indicate an over-identification of problems with children's language and serve to reinforce the highly subjective nature of identification of problems. The focus of this chapter, however, is family experiences of ECI services in the microcontexts of home and early childhood settings, as well as the professionals who provide specialist-targeted intervention, such as HVs and SLTs, at the exosystem level.

Family experiences of early childhood intervention

The author interviewed nine parents of children with SLCN in order to understand young children's SLCN from parents' perspectives, taking into account the wider family relationships with parents, grandparents and close friends. The children came from varied home backgrounds, as shown in Table 13.2.

Interviews with parents were intended to provide insight into children's earliest social and communication development and factors that may affect it, such as genetic factors, maternal health, childbirth and early environmental factors. It was also intended to describe and analyse parents' understanding of children's early communication development and their perceptions about early childhood care and education and health professionals involved, thereby illuminating the context of practice. Interviews with parents showed that children included in the study had a range of SLCN that fell within the Bercow definition, as shown in Table 13.3. The children all attended early childhood settings.

Interestingly, out of nine parents, the first person to notice a problem with the child's SLC had been the parents for seven of the children (child-2, 3, 4, 5, 6, 7 and 9), a senior health practitioner for one (child-8, identification occurred in a hospital setting following cardiac arrest at the age of four months) and the early childhood setting for the remaining child (child-1). On noticing that their child was developing differently than their peers, these seven parents contacted their HV or practitioners in early childhood settings, depending on the age of their child, in order to seek help for their child.

For one parent (child-1), the early childhood setting had identified problems with the child's SLC development, and the parent reported tension between her views and those of the ECPs at the nursery that her son was attending. She commented on her frustration about the perceived pressure within society to encourage and mould her son's development at an unreasonably rapid rate to ensure that all children reached similar stages of development at a particular age. She was confident that upon entering formal education at the age of five, all children would reach a particular stage of development that would enable them to access the curriculum, and resented the competitive nature of parenting that she had experienced within her son's early years setting.

Table 13.2 Background of children involved in the study

Child's age and gender	Child's family background	Language(s)	Child's health experiences
Male 2 years 3 months	Lives at home with mum (aged 28 and a PA) and dad (aged 32 and a tyre fitter/mechanic). Mum is now pregnant with second baby.	English	Born a week early following a long labour but a normal delivery. He was small in size and ill as a baby. Did not drink milk due to gastroenteritis. Weaned at 14 weeks due to weight loss which was thought to be a result of lactose intolerance. He also had a hernia at one year and there was an episode at the same time of excessive thirst and needing constant nappy changes. There was concern over diabetes, which was disproved.
Male 3 years	Lives at home with mum (aged 39 and a full-time housewife) and dad (aged 43 and a machine maintenance engineer). Mum has Bechets Syndrome (auto immune disorder) and has to take medication and steroids for this which continued through pregnancy. She is also partially sighted. Dad has diabetes.	English	Normal pregnancy and labour. Born with an extra finger on each hand and has very slow growing toenails. Walks with feet turned out and has been referred to a podiatrist.
Male 3 years 5 months	Lives at home with mum (aged 39 and a nurse), dad (aged 39 and a technician), brother aged seven, sister aged 18 months and a student lodger.	English, Ilocano Tagalog	Normal pregnancy and labour. In infancy, he was rushed to hospital, choking with milk and vomiting. Milk brand was changed and difficulties ceased.
Female 4 years 1 month	Lives at home with mum (aged 39 and a supermarket assistant, dad (aged 41 and an auditor) and brother aged seven. Brother also had SLCN, as did dad and his sister.	English	Normal pregnancy and labour. No health issues.
Male 4 years, 2 months	Lives at home with mum (aged 40 and a full-time housewife), dad (aged 45 and a trainer/assessor) and brother aged five months. Oldest brother	English	Normal pregnancy and labour. Gets a lot of colds and mum was not certain that his hearing had been checked since he was a baby.

Male 4 years, 4 months	has SLCN, physical and social and emotional difficulties and was born seven weeks premature. Lives with mum (aged 40 and an optician); dad (aged 41 and a development consultant) and sister aged seven. Sister has social and emotional difficulties and has extra support at school to support this.	English	Normal pregnancy, long labour. Suffered from frequent and persistent ear infections from birth. Grommets were fitted at two. Mum visited a sleep clinic as sleep was disrupted until 18 months old. He was sick from birth, placed in a neonatal due to a heart murmur. Diagnosed with autism at four years four months. Fragile X has also been suggested
Female 4 years 4 months	Lives with mum (aged 34 and a cleaner, mum's partner (aged 52 and a health care assistant), twin sister and older sister aged eleven (older sister has a different biological father to the twins.) Partner also has twins who live with their own mother. Sees her natural father at weekends with her twin sister and elder sister.	English	Normal pregnancy, emergency caesarean section delivery due to foetal distress and umbilical cord being wrapped around baby's neck.
Male 5 years 1 month	Lives with his dad (aged 40 and a full-time carer for his son), brother, aged nineteen, and sister, aged thirteen, but has another natural sibling aged three who lives with his natural mother (aged 24 and a full-time housewife). Has two step siblings who live with his dad's current partner aged one and two. Another step sibling aged 21 lives on his own. Natural mother has Job Syndrome and mental health issues.	English	Normal pregnancy and labour. Childhood bronchiolitis at age four months with cardiac arrest. Diagnosed with Cerebral Palsy, Microcephaly and Global Developmental Delay
Male 5 years 2 months	Lives with mum (aged 29 and full-time housewife) and dad (aged 31 and graphic designer). Dad's cousin had cerebral palsy and his brother had Duchene muscular dystrophy. Mum has had eight miscarriages.	English Polish	Normal pregnancy and labour. Diagnosis of autism, severe language impairment and global developmental delay.

Source: Author's study

Table 13.3 Speech, language and communication needs of children involved in the study

Child	Gender	Age	Home Language(s)	Description of child's SLC
1	Male	2 years, 3 months	English	Delayed speech and difficulty with control of emotions and behaviour. Screams in a shrill voice when he wants something. Exhibits tantrums, immature behaviour, hurts peers by biting or hitting them. Can make some things clear using gesture. Passes out in temper if he cannot have his own way or express his emotions verbally.
2	Male	3 years, 5 months	English	Some speech, lots of muttering, will come and take adults to objects he wants. Plays alone most of the time but will sometimes interact with peers. Understands most of what is said to him. Attention and listening skills are limited and can be over-excited when hugging and cuddling other children. Has hurt other children in disputes over toys in the past, does not like eye contact and will only eat facing away from others.
3	Male	3 years, 5 months	Ilocano Tagalog English	Delayed language development (uses single words and babble, pointing and gesture). Is beginning to follow some simple instructions within nursery routine which have been learned over time, but struggles with new concepts. Will play alongside peers but does not interact with them.
4	Female	4 years, 1 month	English	Speech and language difficulties. Word findings problems and difficulties discriminating between the letter "S" and "P". Difficulty forming sentences. Has recently started to stammer. Good understanding and interaction with adults and peers.
5	Male	4 years, 2 months	English	Delayed speech, babbles a lot and speech is difficult to understand. Has good listening skills, is attentive and joins in with adult-led activities. Interacts well with other children. Has forked tongue.
6	Male	4 years, 4 months	English	Had no verbal communication skills on joining the nursery at the age of three. Now he uses mainly verbal communication, but also gestures sometimes, for example, will take adult by hand to what he wants. Uses photographs occasionally. Will interact with familiar adults and is content to play alongside peers.
7	Female	4 years, 4 months	English	Delayed language development (probably specific language difficulty). Speech is supported with visual cues. Sometimes substitutes semantically related words or uses gesture and pointing. Sociable, spontaneously communicates through actions, facial expressions and speech. Listening skills are gradually improving. Sometimes needs adult attention to refocus on a task.

8	Male	5 years, 1 month	English	Communicates using pointing, gesture, facial expression, beginning to sign "more" and will say "no" in context. Demonstrates a good understanding of what is being asked of him. Has a short attention span but will maintain interest if the activity is highly motivating, for example painting. Very sociable, enjoys being with the other children but tends to engage in "rough" play.
9	Male	5 years, 2 months	Polish English	Communicates mainly through picture exchange using photographs. Has some speech but it is non-functional. Understanding is at a one key word level. Prefers to play alone. Will listen in a 1:1 situation but is inattentive in group situations.

Source: Author's study

Disappointingly, five parents (child-2, 6, 7, 8 and 9) reported that their concerns about their child's development had not been taken seriously by health professionals when their child was very young (under the age of three). Two of these stated that they had been passed from one professional to another resulting in additional and undue stress for the parents and increased concern about their child's future progress. As noted by one parent:

> *It's difficult to remember exactly how old he was [when he was referred for assessment] because we were sent from pillar to post and I think someone just thought, "oh, they are over reacting." But obviously being a parent, there is something called "gut feeling."*

(child-9, parent interview)

In addition, there were negative reports from parents about HVs, such as them not being sufficiently well trained about children with complex needs, being dismissive of parents concerns and not referring a child to SLTs, despite children's scores on developmental checks being recorded as low (child-2 and child-8). There seemed to be a "wait and see" attitude, a suggestion from HVs that as all children developed differently, children at the age of two or three were too young for professionals to intervene (child-6). Two of these children were subsequently diagnosed with autism (child-6 and child-9), two with speech sound problems (child-4 and child-7) and the other child already had a diagnosis of cerebral palsy (child-8). Another parent reported that she had not attended any HV clinics, as the timing and availability of them did not coordinate with her working patterns, suggesting that health services were not operating in harmony with parents' needs (child-1). One parent, whose child was exposed to three home languages and who was learning English as an additional language (EAL), was recommended by an SLT to focus on communicating in English to her child in order to reduce any possibility of confusion for the child and to aid his English language development (child-3). This confused her, as she had read that bilingualism was an asset in education.

Although parents reported that they were interested in addressing problems with their child's SLC development and seeking professional help with this, questions were raised about the training for health professionals in relation to timely EI and children with complex needs, as well as their methods for ensuring family-centred participatory and relational approaches. Most interestingly for children who were attending combined early childhood placements (a mainstream EC setting combined with a specialist EC setting, child-4 and child-6) there was a procedural difference according to whether children had mild to moderate SLCN or severe and complex SLCN. For children with mild to moderate SLCN, communication between the two early years settings was informal and parents were not involved in this communication process. Parents communicated with practitioners in each setting and the SLT separately. However, for children with complex and severe SLCN, communication between different early childhood settings and with parents was more formal; there were multi-agency Team around the Child

(TAC) meetings where the child's progress and successes were discussed and shared, and parents attended these. Overall, it was easier for parents to gain access to ECI services such SLT if their child had complex and severe SLCN than mild to moderate. However, once identified and in receipt of support, children made adequate progress in their early years setting, as demonstrated by the following vignette.

Case study: Vignette

Child-6 had English as his home language and attended a mainstream private day nursery for three mornings per week and a specialist outreach nursery assessment centre for two mornings per week. Practitioners in the settings communicated with each other and pedagogical strategies were coordinated through TAC meetings and shared SLT targets. The statement of SEN for Child-6 indicated that he had significant and complex SLC difficulties. The statement reported that he could understand and follow basic instructions and would occasionally engage with incidental conversation. Although he used some full sentences, they were learned by rote rather than constructed by him, and he was extremely difficult to understand unless a familiar adult was available to interpret his meaning. He was reported to use single words to converse, although he was beginning to construct two-word sentences such as "want puzzle." His play was reported to be mostly solitary, with some interactive play occurring with one particular child in his specialist setting.

In the interview, the mother of child-6 acknowledged that although she knew his SLC was "not where it's supposed to be," it had improved considerably over the previous 18 months since he had joined nursery. She reported that, although he still could be easily upset or frustrated when he could not express himself, she could have a conversation with him and he could verbalise his needs. For example, that morning he had actually said "I want an apple" followed by "Thank you," then "Mummy, can I have toast," whereas prior to starting nursery, he had more limited verbal skills. Overall, the parents of child-6 were satisfied that their child had made progress, and it was now their hope that he would attend a mainstream primary school, although his mother had concerns that the delayed insertion of grommets to rectify hearing problems and late referral to ECI services had contributed to his delayed SLC skills. Child-6 was three years old by the time he was referred by a health professional to ECI services. In addition to the combined early years placement, he was also referred to other specialist home-based ECI services, such as *Portage* and play services.

The manager of the mainstream setting explained that the child's SLC difficulties had been identified "quite late" and she felt he had "slipped through the net." The manager of his mainstream setting also stated that although he had no verbal communication skills on joining the nursery at the age of three and would mainly cry to indicate a response, his main communication strategy now was verbal communication, with the occasional use of gestures. For example, he would sometimes lead an adult by the hand to an object that he wanted. He was also reported to use photographs occasionally to show adults something that he wanted. He would interact with familiar adults and was content to play alongside peers. Practitioners in the setting had received training to use signing; however, the manager explained that they needed time to embed the training into practice. Activities provided for child-6 in this setting were planned for all children aged three to five and designed to promote a broad range of socio-emotional, communication, cognition and physical development skills in line with the goals of the EYFS.

In contrast, the practitioner in his specialist setting reported that child-6 used a number of strategies to communicate, including signing, symbols and photographs (Picture Exchange Communication System) and gesture, as well as speech as the setting used a "total communication" approach. The practitioner noted that he was quite "chatty" and talkative when he was happy and mentioned his friendship with another child who was diagnosed with autism, which she reported as rare as "children with autism tended to be rather solitary." Activities provided for child-6 in this setting were closely matched to his own developmental needs and focused on communication and cognition.

Communication between the two early years settings was coordinated with regular Team around the Child meetings attended by health and education professionals and parents. Pedagogical strategies were shared between the two early years settings, and jointly agreed targets were set reinforcing the ideology of joined-up working. However, as noted above, the use of augmentative and assistive communication systems such as signs as symbols was more embedded within the specialist setting than the mainstream, which had an influence on the child's communicative interactions and friendships in the two settings. Nevertheless, the effective communication at the mesosystem level between the two microsystem contexts of early childhood settings and home served to reinforce the influence of the integrative nested contexts on children's learning and development as suggested by Bronfenbrenner, especially for children with complex and severe SLCN.

This vignette seemed to exemplify the benefits of ECI and suggest that even though identification of language problems had not occurred within the second year of life, as suggested by Bercow (2008), children can make satisfactory progress and succeed. Therefore, identification of difficulties is a process of ongoing monitoring and assessment rather than a single event and ECI can be extremely effective even when administered later than policy intentions suggested. Furthermore, there appeared to be benefits for child-6 in attending a combined specialist and mainstream early childhood placement alongside specialist home-based ECI services.

Discussion and conclusion

This chapter has provided a policy-to-practice discussion of young children's SLCN suggesting that Bronfenbrenner's bioecological model can be used as a framework to understand the relationship between the nested social contexts that children grow and develop. The harmony between the broader political macrosystem and practices within the microsystems of home and early childhood settings as well as communication between them at the mesosystem level has the potential to influence and be influenced by children's characteristics and development.

At the macrosystems level, policy documents are produced by government on the basis of production, contestation and compromise in manifestos, political ideologies and expert reports. Successful implementation relies on the skills and qualifications of the early years workforce to work with children, families and other professionals, as the quality of early years provision is integrated with the qualifications of practitioners at the microsystem context of practice. This includes health professionals such as HVs and SLTs as well was practitioners in EC settings and effective communication and collaboration between them and with families at the mesosystem context. There has been an intense policy focus in England on young children's SLC with an overall aim of reducing the number of children living in poverty and improving children's cognitive and language outcomes.

However, at the practice or microsystem level, the case examples reported here suggest that children with severe and complex SLCN were able to access considerable support from SLTs, even if some parents felt dissatisfied with services they received from health professionals. In addition, at the mesosystem level, communication between early childhood settings and health practitioners was coordinated through regular meetings and could be described as joined-up in harmony with policy intentions at the macrosystem level. However, this was not the case for children with mild to moderate and therefore less easily recognisable SLCN or children with EAL. Although children with mild to moderate SLCN and EAL had some access to specialist services, it was not comparable to that offered to children with severe and complex SLCN and was less coordinated or joined up. This raised the question of how those children at risk from developing SEND might have their developmental trajectory optimised.

Implications for policy are that as suggested earlier by Bercow (2008). Communication between agencies such as health and education would benefit from improvements, and perhaps joint training would serve to promote improved relations between agencies at the mesosystem level. Most importantly, questions are raised about the relational processes that inhere in ECI services for children with SLCN and their families and the lack of family-centred practices given the importance of this stressed by Dunst and Trivette (2009), and this is an area for further research. At the practice level, initiatives from policy for joint professional training and improved professional communication would help in this regard. Also at the practice level, whilst the professionals working in the mainstream early childhood setting for child-6 had received training for augmentative communication approaches, this needed to be better embedded within the setting and activities provided for children with complex SLCN could be more closely matched to their developmental needs.

Abbreviations

ECI – Early Childhood Intervention
HVs – Health Visitors
LA – Local Authority
SEND – Special Educational Needs and Disabilities
SLC – Speech, language and communication
SLCN – Speech, language and communication needs
SLTs – Speech and Language Therapists

References

Allen, G. (2011). *Early intervention: Smart investment, massive savings. The second independent report to her majesty's government.* London: HM Government.

Baldock, P., Fitzgerald, D., & Kay, J. (2013). *Understanding early years policy* (3rd ed.). London: Sage Publications.

Bercow, J. (2008). *The Bercow report. A review of services for children and young people (0–19) with speech, language and communication needs.* Nottingham: Department of Children, Schools and Families.

Bishop, D. (2008). Mental capital wellbeing: Making the most of ourselves in the 21st century State-of-Science Review: SR-D1 Specific Language Impairment. Government Office for Science.

Bishop, D., Price, T., Dale, P., & Blomin, R. (2003) Outcomes of early language delay. *Journal of Speech, Language, and Hearing Research, 46,* 561–575.

Blackburn, C. (2014). *The policy-to practice context to the delays and difficulties in the acquisition of speech, language and communication in the first five years.* Unpublished doctoral thesis University of Birmingham.

Blackburn, C., & Aubrey, C. (2016 in press). Policy-to-practice context to delays and difficulties in the acquisition of speech, language and communication in early years. *International Journal of Early Years Education.*

Blair, T. (1999). Beveridge revisited: A welfare state for the 21st century. In R. Walker (Ed.), *Ending child poverty* (pp. 7–18). Bristol: The Poverty Press.

Bronfenbrenner, U. (Ed.). (2005). *Making human beings human: Bioecological perspectives on human development.* California: Sage Publications.

Bronfenbrenner, U. (1979). *The ecology of human development.* Cambridge: Harvard University Press.

Bruner, J. (1983). *Child's talk learning to use language.* Oxford: Oxford University Press.

Department for Education (DfE). (2012, 2014). *Statutory framework for the early years foundation stage.* [Online]. Retrieved from https://www.gov.uk/government/policies/improving-the-quality-and-range-of-education-and-childcare-from-birth-to-5-years/supporting-pages/early-years-foundation-stage

Dockrell, J., Ricketts, J., & Lindsay, G. (2012). *Understanding speech, language and communication needs: Profiles of need and provision*. London: Department for Education.

Dunst, C. J., & Trivette, C. M. (2009). Capacity-building family systems practices. *Journal of Family Social Work, 12,* 119–143.

Dunst, C. J., Trivette, C. M., & Hamby, D. W. (2008). *Research synthesis and meta-analysis of studies of family centered practices*. Asheville, NC: Winterberry Press.

Fernald, A., & Marchman, V. A. (2012). Individual differences in lexical processing at 18 months predict vocabulary growth in typically developing and late-talking toddlers. *Child Development, 83*(1), 203–222.

Goswami, U. (2008), *Learning difficulties: Future challenges*, Mental Capital and Wellbeing Project. London: HMSO: Government Office for Science.

Guralnick, M. J. (2011). Why early intervention works: A systems perspective. *Infants & Young Children, 24,* 6–28. doi:10.1097/IYC.0b013e3182002cfe

Home Office. (1998). *Supporting families: A consultation document*. London: The Stationery Office.

Hulme, C., & Snowling, M. J. (2009). *Developmental disorders of language learning and cognition*. West Sussex: Wiley-Blackwell.

Law, J., Boyle, J., Harris, F., Harkness, A., Nye, C. (1998). Screening for speech and language delay: A systematic review of the literature. *Health Technology Assessment, 2*(9), 1–184.

Lerner, R. M. (2005). Foreword: Urie Bronfenbrenner: Career contributions of the consumate developmental scientist. In U. Bronfenbrenner (Ed.), *Making human beings human: Bioecological perspectives on human development* (pp. ix–xxvi). Thousand Oaks, CA: Sage Publications.

Locke, A., Ginsborg, J., & Peers, I. (2002). Development and disadvantage: Implications for the early years and beyond. *International Journal of Language and Communication Disorders, 37*(41), 3–15.

Meins, E., & Fernyhough, C. (2006). *Mind-mindedness coding manual*. Unpublished manuscript. Durham, UK: Durham University.

Mroz, M., & Hall, E. (2003, September). Not yet identified: The knowledge, skills, and training needs of early years professionals in relation to children's speech and language development. *Early Years: An International Journal of Research and Development, 23*(2), 117–130.

Nutbrown, C. (2012). *Review of early education and childcare qualifications: Final report*. London: Department for Education.

Rogoff, B. (2003). *The cultural nature of human development*. Oxford: Oxford University Press.

Roulstone, S, Law, J., Robert Rush, R., Clegg, J., & Peters, T. (2010). *Investigating the role of language in children's early educational outcomes*. DfE Research Report DFE-RR134.

Smith, P, Cowie, H., & Blades, M. (2008). *Understanding children's development*. Oxford: Blackwell Publishing.

Tickell, C. (2011). *The early years foundations for life, health and learning: An independent report on the early years foundation stage to Her Majesty's Government*. Retrieved from https://www.gov.uk/government/collections/tickell-review-reports

Whitebread, D., & Bingham, S. (2011). *School readiness: a critical review of perspectives and evidence*. Occasional Paper No: 2 Association for the Professional Development of Early Years Educators (TACTYC)/ University of Cambridge

Part VI

Conclusions and future directions

The contributors to this volume describe theory, research, and practice that informed the development and implementation of different approaches to family systems and family-centred approaches to early childhood intervention. The content of individual chapters reflects the authors' extensive knowledge and experience working with young children with special needs and their families, and how that knowledge and experience informed different approaches to early childhood intervention in different types of programs and settings, and in different countries under different opportunities and constraints.

A content analysis of each chapter identified both major and minor themes that inform further developments in early childhood intervention, as well as areas in which additional research and practice are indicated. The major themes include the utility of social and family systems theories for conceptualising the focus of early childhood intervention, the implications of family-centred practices for strengthening family-early childhood practitioner relationships, the conditions under which early childhood intervention is most likely to have family capacity-building and empowering characteristics and consequences, the need for a shift in focus from deficit-based to strengths-based early childhood intervention practices, and the delineation of the outcomes and benefits that can be expected to be either directly or indirectly realised from systems and family-centred approaches to early childhood intervention. The minor (but no less important) themes include an explicit focus on university and in-service professional development to build workforce capacity to use family systems and family-centred early childhood intervention practices, the need to build interagency collaboration around shared family-centred beliefs and practices, and the challenges and opportunities afforded by government legislation, policy, programs, etc. that can have macro-system influences on how early childhood intervention is conceptualised and practised.

Readers should find the experiences and lessons learned from the contributors invaluable for informing their own work with young children with special needs and their families. The experiences and lessons learned hopefully will stimulate thoughtful discussions about ways to improve early childhood intervention.

Part VI

Conclusions and Future Directions

14 Contributions of family systems and family-centred practices for informing improvements in early childhood intervention

*Carl J. Dunst, Hanan Sukkar
and Jane Kirkby*

Contemporary interest in early childhood intervention for young children with developmental disabilities or developmental delays can be traced to the 1960s (see Caldwell, 1970; Shonkoff & Meisels, 1990). This interest was, in part, the result of findings from studies of young children and their families experiencing multiple risk factors (poverty, low parent educational achievement, single-parent household, poor housing, etc.) where early childhood intervention (at the time called infant stimulation, early education, or early enrichment) was found to promote and enhance child learning and development compromised by the risk factors (e.g., Karnes, Teska, & Hodgins, 1970; Tjossem, 1976). It was shortly thereafter that the potential value of early childhood intervention for promoting and enhancing the learning and development of young children with identified disabilities, significant developmental delays, and children at risk for poor developmental outcomes due to medical conditions or biological risk factors began to appear (e.g., Barrera et al., 1976; Cooper, Moodley, & Reynell, 1974; Denhoff, 1981; Scarr-Salapatek & Williams, 1972).

Two types of early childhood intervention evolved from early attempts to alter the developmental outcomes of young children with or at risk for disabilities or developmental delays. One type of early childhood intervention involved professionals intervening directly with young children to treat aberrations associated with a disability or to prevent delays associated with disabilities (e.g., Hensley & Patterson, 1970). Another type of early childhood intervention involved professionals working with children's parents or other primary care providers to help them learn to provide their children different types of experiences to promote and enhance learning and development (e.g., Jew, 1974).

The second approach, which is the focus of this volume, first appeared in the late 1960s and early 1970s where parents were typically taught to use professionally identified or prescribed early education or therapeutic practices to facilitate early childhood learning and development (e.g., Bricker & Casuso, 1979; Sandow, Clarke, Cox, & Stewart, 1981). There has been considerable debate about the ways in which parents and other family members ought to be involved in early childhood intervention and the relationships early childhood practitioners ought to have with children's primary caregivers (e.g., Foster, Berger, & McLean, 1981; Mahoney et al., 1999; Turnbull & Summers, 1985; West & Rheingold, 1978; Winton, Sloop, & Rodriguez, 1999). These debates, in part, were the consequence of different assumptions about parenting capabilities and the approaches professionals use to engage parents in their children's early childhood intervention (Lee, 2015).

Despite early calls for the adoption of family-centred and family and social systems intervention models and practices (Bronfenbrenner, 1975; Dokecki & Strain, 1973; Schaefer, 1970), it was not until the 1980s that these types of models and practices started to receive serious attention (e.g., Dunst, 1985; Seligman & Darling, 1989; Zigler & Weiss, 1985). Since that time, significant and important advances have been made which contributed to rethinking and reframing how early childhood intervention with young children and their families ought to be conceptualised and implemented (Broderick, 1993; Cowan, Powell, & Cowan, 1998; Guralnick, 2008). These efforts have led to a better understanding of the importance of systems theories for conceptualising early childhood intervention, the role and importance of family-centred practices for engaging parents in early childhood intervention, and the influences of systems and family-centred approaches to early childhood intervention for building and strengthening child, parent, and family capacity.

The contributors to this volume describe and address different aspects of systems theories and/or family-centred practices that can inform changes and improvements in the ways to intervene more effectively with young children and their families. The contents of the chapters include a rich tapestry of information on theory, research, and practice for conceptualising and implementing early childhood intervention with young children with special needs and their families. Contributors have provided readers a wealth of information relevant for understanding the many factors that contribute to not only a better understanding of early childhood intervention, but also innovative thinking about how to move from theory and research to practice in ways that are likely to have intended outcomes and benefits. Close inspection of the chapters in this volume finds a number of recurring themes and associated considerations that contributors identified as important for ensuring that early childhood intervention will have optimal child, parent, and family benefits and outcomes. We describe those themes and considerations to both highlight the current state of knowledge and practice and to point out future directions.

Major themes and considerations

Major themes that unify the majority of chapters in this volume are social and family systems theories, family-centred practices, family capacity-building and parent empowerment practices, strengths-based practices, and the parent and family outcomes, in addition to child outcomes, that are the desired outcomes and benefits of early childhood intervention. These themes and associated considerations are what stand out as having major implications for changing and improving how practitioners conceptualise and work with young children and their families.

Systems theories and approaches

Descriptions of different aspects of systems theories and their implications for practice are included in nearly every chapter in this volume. These include ecological systems theory (Bronfenbrenner, 1992), social systems theory (Friedman & Allen, 2010), family systems theory (Combrinck-Graham, 1990; Dunst & Trivette, 2009a), and the developmental systems model (Guralnick, 2005). The common theme found in the chapters is that young children and their parents and other family members are best understood as a social unit where the behaviour of any one family member is likely to influence the behaviour of other family members, and that the family social unit is embedded in other social systems where events reverberate and can directly or indirectly influence individual family member behaviour and the family as a unit.

Guralnick (Chapter 2) describes how different patterns of family interaction influence and contribute to child social and cognitive competence, and how different family resources contribute to both patterns of family interactions and child development. Guralnick's (2001) developmental systems model was used by Forster (Chapter 9), for example, to describe how the model has "reframed early childhood intervention as [focusing] on supporting families . . . in order that the family could fulfil its role of providing the necessary positive relationships, learning opportunities, and a healthy and safe environment fundamental to a child's development." Both Serrano et al. (Chapter 11) and Hiebert-Murphy et al. (Chapter 12) described how the developmental systems model broadens the focus and scope of early childhood intervention based on theory and research in both the developmental and interventions sciences. Guralnick's model has been employed widely to conceptualise and reframe early childhood intervention practices (see especially Guralnick, 2005). Guralnick's development systems model has also been used by a number of researchers and practitioners to capture the relations between family systems influences and child development (Hauser-Cram & Howell, 2005) as part of conceptualising early childhood intervention (e.g., Hu & Yang, 2013; Pinto et al., 2012; Shulman, Meadan, & Sandhaus, 2012; Sukkar, 2013).

The family systems early childhood intervention model described by Dunst (Chapter 3) is based on a number of tenets from Bronfenbrenner's (1979, 1986, 1992) ecological systems theory, which was used to identify the types of supports and resources that are needed for parents to carry out parenting responsibilities (Bronfenbrenner, 1979) and for parents to provide their children development-enhancing child learning opportunities (Bronfenbrenner, 1986). Bronfenbrenner's ecological system theory was used by Holman (Chapter 5), Kennedy (Chapter 6), and Blackburn (Chapter 13) to describe different ways of conceptualising early childhood intervention. Holman (Chapter 5), for example, describes how Bronfenbrenner's ecological systems theory was used in one Australian State to frame the informal, formal, and broader-based systems influences that became the focus of early childhood intervention (Department of Education and Early Childhood Development, 2009).

Family-centred practices

The call for use of family-centred practices and a family-centred approach to early childhood intervention is a major focus of most chapters. Despite the fact that different contributors employ different sources of information and evidence for defining the key characteristics of family-centred practices, there are remarkable similarities for how these practices are operationalised. The key characteristics include different types of relationship-building practices and practices for meaningfully involving family members in informed decision-making and acting on those choices (Dunst & Espe-Sherwindt, 2016; Espe-Sherwindt, 2008). Johnston et al. (Chapter 8) list 10 core family-centred relational and participatory practices, including, but not limited to, treating families with respect, sharing information with families in a complete and unbiased manner, promoting family choice and decision-making, employing competency-enhancing help-giving practices, and enhancing family strengths and capabilities (Fordham & Johnston, 2014). Dempsey and Keen (Chapter 3) and Hiebert-Murphy et al. (Chapter 12) describe similar types of relational and participatory family-centred practices as the defining characteristics of this approach to early childhood intervention (see also Allen & Petr, 1998; Dempsey & Keen, 2008; Dunst & Espe-Sherwindt, 2016; M. Law et al., 2005; Moore & Larkin, 2005; Shelton & Stepanek, 1994; Trute, 2013).

The importance of building and strengthening family member-practitioner partnerships and collaboration is mentioned by a number of contributors as a key characteristic of family-centred practices. For example, Dempsey and Keen (Chapter 4) stated that "family-centred practice fosters family engagement, *collaboration*, and decision making, [and] sees families *as partners*, and focuses on family strengths in the process of facilitating child development" (emphasis added). Kennedy (Chapter 6), Sukkar (Chapter 7), Johnston et al. (Chapter 8), Forster (Chapter 9), Goff and McLoughlin (Chapter 10), and Serrano et al. (Chapter 11) all discuss different aspects of family-professional partnerships and collaboration as crucial for family-centred early childhood intervention to be optimally effective (Ashton et al., 2008; Turnbull, Turbiville, & Turnbull, 2000).

Another theme relates to the fact that becoming a family-centred practitioner is not easily accomplished, and evidence from a number of sources indicates that the use of family-centred practices is not as widespread as is generally believed (Dempsey & Carruthers, 1997; Dempsey & Keen, 2008; Dunst & Trivette, 2005; Wright, Hiebert-Murphy, & Trute, 2010). The struggles in promoting the use of family-centred practices in different countries are made explicitly clear by Johnston et al. (Chapter 8), Hiebert-Murphy et al. (Chapter 12), and Serrano et al. (Chapter 11) in terms of early childhood practitioners having the knowledge and skills necessary to establish family-professional partnerships and collaboration, and a belief that family members are equals in the early childhood intervention enterprise (Dinnebeil, Hale, & Rule, 1996; Oster, 1985).

A number of contributors either implicitly or explicitly note that family-centred practices are a way of engaging parents and other primary caregivers in the use of other kinds of early childhood intervention practices (e.g., Dempsey and Keen, Chapter 4; Serrano et al. Chapter 11; Blackman, Chapter 13). Whereas family-centred practices have often been misunderstood as an alternative to other kinds of early childhood intervention practices, family-centred practices are now recognised as a particular approach to how other child, parent-child, parent, and family interventions are implemented (Coogle, 2012; Dunst & Espe-Sherwindt, 2016).

Family capacity-building and parent empowerment practices

The importance of family capacity-building and empowering practices to support and strengthen child, parent, and family functioning is echoed by many contributors to this volume. Contributors both explicitly and implicitly note that early childhood intervention is not likely to be optimally effective if intervention practices do not strengthen existing family member functioning and promote acquisition of additional family member functional and adaptive capabilities.

The contributors who emphasise family capacity-building and empowering practices as a focus of early childhood intervention note that this requires a major shift in how practitioners interact with, treat, and involve family members meaningfully in different types of interventions. Dempsey and Keen (Chapter 4) and Johnston et al. (Chapter 8), for example, contend that family capacity building will more likely be realised when family members have sufficient opportunity to exercise existing knowledge and skills and acquire new competencies. This type of practice is described in other chapters as either participatory opportunities or parent engagement strategies that encourage informed choices and family member actions based on those choices (e.g., Dunst, Chapter 3; Sukkar, Chapter 7; Hiebert-Murphy et al., Chapter 12).

There continues to be misunderstanding and confusion as to whether early childhood practitioners routinely employ family capacity-building and parent empowerment practices. For example, despite claims that parents are involved in early childhood intervention in a capacity-building manner, evidence indicates that this is not generally the case (see e.g., Dunst, Bruder, & Espe-Sherwindt, 2014; Korfmacher et al., 2008). This is the result, in part, of a failure to fully understand the key characteristics of capacity-building and empowering practices, and how those practices are used to involve parents and other family members in early childhood intervention in ways supporting and strengthening parent and other primary caregivers' confidence and competence (Levine, 2013; Rouse, 2012).

Family capacity building and parent empowerment in early childhood intervention can be, and often is, difficult to accomplish. A number of contributors note different reasons for this difficulty and offer suggestions for promoting early childhood practitioners' understanding and use of family-centred, capacity-building and empowering practices. Dempsey and Keen (Chapter 4), for example, point to implementation science (Kelly & Perkins, 2012) as a way of conceptualising which implementation practices (e.g., professional development) are used to promote practitioners' use of desired intervention practices (e.g., family-centred and capacity-building practices). An implementation science framework has increasingly been used in early childhood intervention (e.g., Dunst, Trivette, & Raab, 2013) for employing different kinds of professional development practices to support and promote early childhood practitioners' use of capacity-building intervention practices with parents and other family members with considerable success (e.g., Dunst, Trivette, & Raab, 2014; Swanson, Raab, & Dunst, 2011).

Strengths-based practices

Each of the chapters in this volume includes descriptions of some aspect of strengths-based practices as an important feature of family-centred intervention and why those practices are more likely to contribute to optimal positive benefits. Two aspects of these descriptions stand out as especially relevant for conceptualising and implementing early childhood intervention: (1) operationally differentiating between strengths-based and deficit-based practices (Eloff & Ebersöhn, 2001) and (2) conceptualising and operationalising family member strengths as particular types of behavioural capabilities, abilities, and interests (Swanson et al., 2011).

Holman (Chapter 5), Kennedy (Chapter 6), and Serrano et al. (Chapter 11) note the differences between strengths-based and deficit-based practices and the need to employ strengths-based practices in order for early childhood intervention to have capacity-building characteristics and consequences. Dunst (Chapter 3) contends that strengths-based practices constitute one of five intervention approaches that, taken together, operationally define a capacity-building paradigm for conceptualising and implementing early childhood intervention.

One of the most important contributions authors make to family-centred early childhood intervention is the description and operationalisation of family member strengths as skills, abilities, and interests that are the building blocks for improving child, parent, and family functioning. Guralnick (Chapter 2), for example, notes that research on children with disabilities had identified "strengths exhibited by children that could be capitalised upon when designing early [childhood] intervention." Dunst (Chapter 3) and Holman (Chapter 4) also describe how parents' skills, abilities, and interests constitute strengths that engage them in positive parent-child interactions and which are used to obtain needed child and family supports and resources.

Kennedy (Chapter 6), Sukkar (Chapter 7), and Hiebert-Murphy et al. (Chapter 12) describe how strengths-based intervention practices contribute to improved child, parent, and family functioning. In addition, Serrano et al. (Chapter 11) and Hiebert-Murphy et al. (Chapter 12) describe how the use of strengths-based practices contributes to early childhood practitioners' improved sense of competence and confidence as a result of seeing changes and improvements in child and family capacity building.

As noted by Rappaport (1981), all people have existing strengths and the capacity to become more competent, and by focusing on strengths rather than deficits or weaknesses, we are more likely to make a real difference in the lives of the people with whom professionals work. There is a considerable amount of evidence that strengths-based practices have value-added benefits to the people who experience those practices (e.g., Caspe & Lopez, 2006; Schlesinger, 2007). Yet, strengths-based practices are not widely used in early childhood intervention or other types of intervention programs (e.g., Lietz, 2011; Sousa, Ribeiro, & Rodrigues, 2007). Chapters in this volume as well as descriptions elsewhere (e.g., Wartel, 2003; Ylvén & Granlund, 2009) provide excellent guidance about how to infuse strengths-based practices into early childhood intervention.

Desired outcomes

Contributors to this volume emphasise a broad range of child, parent, and family outcomes as the desired benefits of early childhood intervention. As noted by Guralnick (Chapter 2), "the overarching goal of early [childhood] intervention is to maximise children's social and cognitive competence." The child outcomes described as the desired benefits of early childhood intervention by Forster (Chapter 9) include a sense of identity, sense of wellbeing, confident and involved learners, effective communicators, and a connectedness to and contributor to their world. This, as well as other child outcomes, has been described as the kinds of child behaviour and competencies necessary for young children to be able to interact with their social and non-social environment in functional and meaningful ways (Mannan, Summers, Turnbull, & Poston, 2006; Parrish & Phillips, 2003).

Several contributors describe a number of different parent and family outcomes that are the desired benefits of early childhood intervention. Dempsey and Keen (Chapter 4) identify parental belief appraisals, parenting capabilities, a sense of empowerment, decreased stress and enhanced wellbeing, and parenting confidence and satisfaction as desired parent and family outcomes of early childhood intervention. Hiebert-Murphy et al. (Chapter 12) added to this list reduced family needs and the increased capacity of families as desired outcomes of family-centred early childhood intervention. Elsewhere, other researchers and practitioners described improved family functioning, strong social relationships and connections, building strong social support systems networks, and family quality of life as desired outcomes of early childhood intervention (e.g., Epley, Summers, & Turnbull, 2001; Raspa et al., 2010; Turnbull, Summers, Lee, & Kyzar, 2007). Holman (Chapter 5) and Johnston et al. (Chapter 8), however, note a need to identify which child, parent, and family behaviour and skills are most important for measuring individual family member and overall family functioning for evaluating whether early childhood intervention is optimally effective (see e.g., Dempsey & Keen, 2008).

Inasmuch as different family and social systems theorists posit indirect effects of systems factors on child, parent, and family functioning, it is likely to be the case that family-centred practices would be indirectly related to some parent and family outcomes and will almost certainly be indirectly related to most child outcomes. Dempsey and Keen (Chapter 4) review research on the use of explanatory models of the family-centred processes associated with desired outcomes and note the contributions the results from these studies have made toward a better understanding of system influences on child, parent, and family outcomes. Explanatory models have been used by a number of researchers for mapping pathways of the influence of family-centred practices on desired family, parent, and child outcomes (e.g., Bailey, Nelson, Hebbler, & Spiker, 2007; Dunst & Trivette, 2009b; King, King, Rosenbaum, & Goffin, 1999; M. Law et al., 2003; Thompson et al., 1997; Trivette, Dunst, & Hamby, 2010) and serve as frameworks for how to conceptualise and test the indirect effects of systems and family-centred practices on child, parent, and family outcomes.

Minor themes and considerations

In addition to the major themes described above, a number of minor but no less important themes can be found in the descriptions of many of the contributors to this volume. These include the need for both pre-service and in-service professional development to enhance early childhood practitioner capacity to understand and use systems and family-centred approaches to early childhood intervention, the importance of interagency collaboration for the broad-based institutionalisation of family-centred practices, and the roles and influences of governmental legislation, policy, and funding have on how early childhood intervention is practised.

Workforce capacity

The ability of early childhood practitioners to understand and use family and social systems and family-centred approaches is certainly dependent on the quality of both pre-service and in-service professional development and the ongoing supports of the practitioners' organisations. Sukkar (Chapter 7) and Hiebert-Murphy et al. (Chapter 12) note the need to include family-centred knowledge and practices as part of pre-service professional preparation if university graduates are likely to be prepared to work with young children and their families in a family-centred manner. As noted by Sukkar (Chapter 7), Johnston et al. (Chapter 8), and Hiebert-Murphy et al. (Chapter 12), as well as Kennedy (Chapter 6), Forster (Chapter 9), and Goff and McLaughlin (Chapter 10), ongoing in-service staff training and supports are needed for practitioners to be able to employ systems and family-centred approaches to early childhood intervention. For example, Johnston et al. (Chapter 8) noted that "[a]t the centre of building staff capacity is effective professional development and the mentoring or coaching of staff by [early childhood] practitioner experts."

Pre-service professional development and ongoing supports may be a necessary but are not a sufficient condition for ensuring that early childhood practitioners use systems and family-centred approaches and practices. As noted by Hiebert-Murphy et al. (Chapter 12), "Regardless of the skills of practitioners, [family-centred] practices will not be fully realised without an organisational context that supports the integration of family-centred principles" into day-to-day practice. Dempsey and Keen (Chapter 4) and Johnston et al. (Chapter 8) also noted the need for organisational supports if early childhood practitioners are able to use systems and family-centred approaches to early childhood intervention.

There is no guarantee, however, that organisational supports together with effective professional development will result in the use of systems and family-centred approaches to early childhood intervention. This is illustrated with data from an early childhood intervention program that adopted the use of family systems and family-centred practices and provided early childhood practitioners considerable amounts of training and supports to be able to work with young children and their families in a family-centred manner (e.g., Dunst & Trivette, 1988a; Dunst & Trivette, 1988b; Dunst, Watson, Roper, & Batman, 2011). As part of the evaluation of staff use of family-centred practices, Dunst and Trivette (2005) monitored the family-centredness of practitioners' practices in the early childhood intervention programme over a 14-year period and concluded, among other things, that "high levels of [practitioner] adherence to family support principles [and family-centred practices] are difficult to attain and even more difficult to maintain " (p. 39). They went on to say that anything and everything within and outside a program or organisation that can negatively affect practitioner adherence to family-centred practices can and will likely do so and that ongoing "vigilance and more vigilance" (p. 41) is needed by program directors and administrators if the use of family systems and family-centred practices are to be attained and maintained.

Interagency collaboration

The need for interagency collaboration, understanding, and a commitment to family and social systems and family-centred approaches to early childhood intervention was noted by a number of contributors as conditions necessary to broadly institutionalise the use of these types of practices. Goff and McLaughlin (Chapter 10) describe both the challenges and opportunities in establishing interagency collaborations and the concerted effort it takes to bring diverse partners together around a shared vision for how to work with young children and their families in a family-centred manner. These contributors noted that because "different organisations have different structures, different networks, [and] diverse leadership . . . and policy imperatives," the establishment of interagency collaboration can be a daunting but not an insurmountable task.

Serrano et al. (Chapter 11) both extend and elaborate on the challenges and opportunities in establishing interagency collaboration by noting that professionals from different disciplines within the same program or organisation and between different agencies working with young children and their families often have quite different perspectives of what constitutes appropriate kinds of early childhood intervention practices. For example, these contributors noted that for some professionals from certain disciplines, it is difficult for practitioners to shift focus from deficit-based to strengths-based practices, which makes the transition from professionally centred to family-centred practices difficult at best.

We believe it is safe to say that the more agencies that are involved in early childhood intervention, the more divergent the policies for how to work with young children and their families. We also contend that the more diverse the professional backgrounds of the practitioners in those agencies, the more difficult it is to "get everyone on the same page" in terms of adoption and use of systems and family-centred practices.

Governmental influences

Governmental influences including, but not limited to, early childhood intervention and other child and family legislation, policies guiding the provision of early childhood intervention, and the manner in which services, supports, and resources are funded will likely shape and influence all aspects of early childhood intervention. These different considerations are what Bronfenbrenner (1979) describes as macrosystem factors indirectly influencing parenting and child development. Each of the chapters in the *Working with Families of Young Children in Australia* and *Working with Families of Young Children in Other Countries* sections of the book include descriptions of both the opportunities and tensions afforded by governmental involvement.

There is little doubt that the *National Disability Insurance Scheme* (NDIS) (Commonwealth of Australia, 2013, 2014) is in the forefront of changes in early childhood intervention in Australia. Although it is at the beginning phases of widespread implementation, both Johnston et al. (Chapter 8) and Forster (Chapter 9) point out potential benefits of funding-driven early childhood intervention, although, as Forster notes, the NDIS "represents a significant departure from [the] past [where] each state and territory developed its own approach to early childhood intervention." This is the case because the primary responsibility for administering early childhood intervention funding has shifted from States and Territories to a National Government Agency. If not carefully monitored, this can result in less rather than more flexibility in the services, supports, and resources available to young children and their families and how they are provided as suggested by preliminary analyses of the *National Disability Insurance Scheme* (e.g., Biddle et al., 2014; Soldatic, van Toorn, Dowse, & Muir, 2014).

An important component of the *National Disability Insurance Scheme* is the assignment of a primary service provider (Kennedy, Chapter 6) or key worker (Alexander & Forster, 2012) to each child and family, whose responsibilities include assisting the family in making informed choices and the coordination of family-identified services. There are, however, indications that this may not be working as intended at least in some States and Territories. One editor of this volume has been told on a number of occasions by early childhood intervention experts that the primary service provider assigned to work with young children and their families often has neither training nor experience in child or family development, and that this has resulted in less than fruitful relationships between the providers and parents, and in some cases, the use of professionally centred rather than family-centred practices contrary to consumer-driven and capacity-building foundations of the Act (Commonwealth of Australia, 2013, 2014).

Hiebert-Murphy et al. (Chapter 12) describe the challenges that are posed by non-mandated and discretionary services for young children with disabilities and their families in one Canadian province. As these contributors note, the lack of early childhood legislation and policy has sometimes resulted in disagreements about which agency or organisation is responsible for which type of services and this, in turn, is often detrimental to which services, resources, and supports are made available to young children and their families.

The chapter by Serrano et al. (Chapter 11) includes a rich source of information on the evolution of early childhood intervention in Portugal and how the passage of legislation establishing a *National System for Early Childhood Intervention* has resulted in both opportunities and challenges for families, early childhood practitioners, and both pre-service and in-service professional development specialists. The chapter also includes a description of the challenges faced by proponents of family-centred early childhood intervention in Spain, where they are applying lessons learned in Portugal to facilitate understanding and use of family-centred intervention practices in Spain. The Serrano et al. chapter is an excellent case study of the factors and conditions both facilitating and inhibiting progress in adoption of social and family systems, family-centred, and family capacity-building practices in two different countries.

There is little doubt that legislation or some type of formal authoritative mandate can lead to increased provision of much needed early childhood intervention supports, resources, and supports to young children and their families. However, legislation and mandates can have unintended adverse consequences. Dunst (2012), for example, noted that prior to the passage of early intervention legislation in the United States, early childhood intervention was conceptualised and operationalised in terms of the experiences, activities, and learning opportunities used to influence child development, but that following the passage of Federal legislation, early childhood intervention was immediately changed and defined entirely in terms of professional services. One cannot but sense a concern and tension in how early childhood intervention is described by a number of contributors in light of legislative changes in Australia and Portugal potentially influencing who, how, and in what manner young children with disabilities and their families are involved in early childhood intervention.

Conclusions

The purposes of this volume were to (1) provide different perspectives on systems theories and family-centred practices and (2) provide descriptions of the use of the theories and practices in early childhood intervention for supporting and strengthening child, parent, and family functioning. The goal was to provide readers information useful for conceptualising and implementing early childhood intervention with young children with disabilities and developmental delays and their families. Nearly all the contributors to this volume include information on the real-life opportunities and challenges experienced in using different systems models and frameworks for conceptualising and implementing early childhood intervention and for using family-centred principles and practices to improve child, parent, and family outcomes. Readers should benefit immensely from exchanges of ideas shared by contributors.

The use of systems theories for conceptualising early childhood intervention and the use of family-centred principles and practices for implementing early childhood intervention will no doubt continue to evolve. The contributors to this volume provide useful directions for future developments by noting both successful applications and difficulties encountered in using systems and family-centred concepts and ideas for improving the provision of early childhood intervention.

Lessons learned by contributors not only inform future directions in terms of theory, research, and practice, but also provide readers a wide range of methods and strategies to consider as part of efforts to implement changes and improvements in early childhood intervention. As noted in the first chapter of this volume, young children with developmental disabilities and delays are most likely to benefit from early childhood intervention when parents and other family members receive the supports and resources they need to be able to engage their children in adult-child interactions and learning opportunities promoting child development. As noted by many contributors, this is more likely to be realised if early childhood practitioners work with families in ways that are empowering and capacity-building. A lot is known about how to do this, yet much more needs to be learned about how to do this in optimally effective ways. We are confident that readers' own thinking and work will be informed by the contents of this volume.

References

Alexander, S., & Forster, J. (2012). *The key worker: Resources for early childhood intervention professionals.* Malvern, Victoria, Australia: Noah's Ark.

Allen, R. I., & Petr, C. G. (1998). Rethinking family-centered practice. *American Journal of Orthopsychiatry, 68*, 4–15. doi:10.1037/h0080265

Ashton, J., Woodrow, C., Johnston, C. F., Wangmann, J., Singh, L., & James, T. (2008). Partnerships in learning: Linking early childhood services, families and schools for optimal development. *Australian Journal of Early Childhood, 33*(2), 10–17.

Bailey, D. B., Jr., Nelson, L., Hebbler, K., & Spiker, D. (2007). Modeling the impact of formal and informal supports for young children with disabilities and their families. *Pediatrics, 120*, 992–1001. doi:10.1542/peds.2006-2775

Barrera, M. E. C., Routh, D. K., Parr, C. A., Johnson, N. M., Arendshorst, D. S., Goolsby, E. L., & Schroeder, S. R. (1976). Early intervention with biologically handicapped infants and young children: A preliminary study with each child as his own control. In T. J. Tjossem (Ed.), *Intervention strategies for high risk infants and young children* (pp. 609–628). Baltimore, MD: University Park Press.

Biddle, N., Al-Yaman, F., Gourley, M., Gray, M., Bray, J. R., Brady, B., . . . Montaigne, M. (2014). *Indigenous Australians and the National Disability Insurance Scheme.* Canberra, Australia: Australian National University.

Bricker, D., & Casuso, V. (1979). Family involvement: A critical component of early intervention. *Exceptional Children, 46,* 108–116. doi:10.1177/001440297904600204

Broderick, C. B. (1993). *Understanding family process: Basics of family systems theory.* Newbury Park, CA: Sage.

Bronfenbrenner, U. (1975). Is early intervention effective? In B. Z. Friedlander, G. M. Sterritt, & G. E. Kirk (Eds.), *Exceptional infant: Vol. 3. Assessment and intervention* (pp. 449–475). New York: Brunner/Mazel.

Bronfenbrenner, U. (1979). *The ecology of human development: Experiments by nature and design.* Cambridge, MA: Harvard University Press.

Bronfenbrenner, U. (1986). Ecology of the family as a context for human development: Research perspectives. *Developmental Psychology, 22,* 723–742.

Bronfenbrenner, U. (1992). Ecological systems theory. In R. Vasta (Ed.), *Six theories of child development: Revised formulations and current issues* (pp. 187–248). Philadelphia, PA: Jessica Kingsley.

Caldwell, B. M. (1970). The rationale for early intervention. *Exceptional Children, 36,* 717–726.

Caspe, M., & Lopez, M. E. (2006). *Lessons from family-strengthening interventions: learning from evidence-based practice.* Retrieved from http://www.hfrp.org/

Combrinck-Graham, L. (1990). Developments in family systems theory and research. *Journal of the American Academy of Child and Adolescent Psychiatry, 29,* 501–512. doi:10.1097/00004583-199007000-00001

Commonwealth of Australia. (2013). *National Disability Insurance Scheme Act 2013 (No. 20, 2013).* Canberra, Australia: Author.

Commonwealth of Australia. (2014). *National Disability Insurance Scheme Act 2013: Operational guideline – planning and assessment – supports in the plan – supports for early childhood.* Canberra, Australia: Author. Retrieved from http://www.ndis.gov.au/sites/default/files/documents/og_plan_assess_supports_early_childhood.pdf

Coogle, C. G. (2012). A study of family centered help giving practices in early intervention. *Electronic Theses, Treatises and Dissertations.* Retrieved from http://diginole.lib.fsu.edu/etd/4778

Cooper, J., Moodley, M., & Reynell, J. (1974). Intervention programmes for preschool children with delayed language development: A preliminary report. *British Journal of Disorders of Communication, 9,* 81–91. doi:10.3109/13682827409011613

Cowan, P. A., Powell, D., & Cowan, C. P. (1998). Parenting interventions: A family systems perspective. In W. Damon, I. E. Sigel, & K. A. Renninger (Eds.), *Handbook of child psychology: Vol. 4. Child psychology in practice* (5th ed., pp. 3–72). New York: Wiley.

Dempsey, I., & Carruthers, A. (1997). How family-centered are early intervention services: Staff and parent perceptions? *Journal of Australian Research in Early Childhood Education, 1,* 105–114.

Dempsey, I., & Keen, D. (2008). A review of processes and outcomes in family-centered services for children with a disability. *Topics in Early Childhood Special Education, 28,* 42–52. doi:10.1177/0271121408316699

Denhoff, E. (1981). Current status of infant stimulation or enrichment programs for children with developmental disabilities. *Pediatrics, 67*, 32–37.

Department of Education and Early Childhood Development. (2009). *Victorian Early Years Learning and Development Framework: For all children from birth to eight years.* Melbourne, Australia: Victorian Department of Education and Early Childhood Development and Victorian Curriculum and Statement Authority.

Dinnebeil, L. A., Hale, L. M., & Rule, S. (1996). A qualitative analysis of parents' and service coordinators' descriptions of variables that influence collaborative relationships. *Topics in Early Childhood Special Education, 16*, 322–347. doi:10.1177/027112149601600305

Dokecki, P. R., & Strain, B. A. (1973). Early childhood intervention 2001: Transactional and developmental perspectives. *Peabody Journal of Education, 50*(3), 175–183. doi:10.1080/01619567309537907

Dunst, C. J. (1985). Rethinking early intervention. *Analysis and Intervention in Developmental Disabilities, 5*, 165–201. doi:10.1016/S0270-4684(85)80012-4

Dunst, C. J. (2012). Parapatric speciation in the evolution of early intervention for infants and toddlers with disabilities and their families. *Topics in Early Childhood Special Education, 31*, 208–215. doi:10.1177/0271121411426904

Dunst, C. J., Bruder, M. B., & Espe-Sherwindt, M. (2014). Family capacity-building in early childhood intervention: Do context and setting matter? *School Community Journal, 24*(1), 37–48.

Dunst, C. J., & Espe-Sherwindt, M. (2016). Family-centered practices in early childhood intervention. In B. Reichow, B. Boyd, E. Barton, & S. L. Odom (Eds.), *Handbook of early childhood special education* (pp. 37–55). Cham, Switzerland: Springer International.

Dunst, C. J., & Trivette, C. M. (1988a). A family systems model of early intervention with handicapped and developmentally at-risk children. In D. R. Powell (Ed.), *Parent education as early childhood intervention: Emerging directions in theory, research, and practice* (pp. 131–179). Norwood, NJ: Ablex.

Dunst, C. J., & Trivette, C. M. (1988b). Toward experimental evaluation of the family, infant and preschool program. In H. B. Weiss & F. H. Jacobs (Eds.), *Evaluating family programs* (pp. 315–346). New York, NY: de Gruyter.

Dunst, C. J., & Trivette, C. M. (2005). *Measuring and evaluating family support program quality.* Asheville, NC: Winterberry Press.

Dunst, C. J., & Trivette, C. M. (2009a). Capacity-building family systems intervention practices. *Journal of Family Social Work, 12*(2), 119–143. doi:10.1080/10522150802713322

Dunst, C. J., & Trivette, C. M. (2009b). Meta-analytic structural equation modeling of the influences of family-centered care on parent and child psychological health. *International Journal of Pediatrics, 2009*, 1–9. doi:10.1155/2009/596840

Dunst, C. J., Trivette, C. M., & Raab, M. (2013). An implementation science framework for conceptualizing and operationalizing fidelity in early childhood intervention studies. *Journal of Early Intervention, 35*(2), 85–101. doi:10.1177/1053815113502235

Dunst, C. J., Trivette, C. M., & Raab, M. (2014). Everyday child language learning early intervention practices. *Infants & Young Children, 27*(3), 207–219. doi:10.1097/IYC.0000000000000015

Dunst, C. J., Watson, A., Roper, N., & Batman, D. (2011). Factors associated with employee appraisals of adherence to learning organization principles and practices.

E-Journal of Organizational Learning and Leadership, 9(2), 81–93. Retrieved from http://www.leadingtoday.org/weleadinlearning/Winter2011/Article%205%20-%20Jones.pdf

Eloff, I., & Ebersöhn, L. (2001). The implications of an asset-based approach to early intervention. *Perspectives in Education*, 19(3), 147–157. Retrieved from http://reference.sabinet.co.za/sa_epublication_article/persed_v19_n3_a11

Epley, P. H., Summers, J. A., & Turnbull, A. P. (2001). Family outcomes of early intervention: Families' perceptions of need, services, and outcomes. *Journal of Early Intervention*, 33, 201–219. doi:10.1177/1053815111425929

Espe-Sherwindt, M. (2008). Family-centred practice: Collaboration, competency and evidence. *Support for Learning*, 23, 136–143. doi:10.1111/j.1467-9604.2008.00384.x

Fordham, L., & Johnston, C. F. (2014). Family-centred practice for inclusive early years education. In K. Cologon (Ed.), *Inclusive education in the early years* (pp. 171–188). Melbourne, Australia: Oxford University Press.

Foster, M., Berger, M., & McLean, M. (1981). Rethinking a good idea: A reassessment of parent involvement. *Topics in Early Childhood Special Education*, 1(3), 55–65. doi:10.1177/027112148100100311

Friedman, B. D., & Allen, K. N. (2010). Systems theory. In J. R. Brandell (Ed.), *Theory and practice in clinical social work* (2nd ed., pp. 3–20). Thousand Oaks, CA: Sage.

Guralnick, M. J. (2001). A developmental systems model for early intervention. *Infants & Young Children*, 14(2), 1–18.

Guralnick, M. J. (2008). Family influences on early development: Integrating the science of normative development, risk and disability, and intervention. In K. McCartney & D. Phillips (Eds.), *Blackwell handbook of early childhood development* (pp. 44–61). Oxford, England: Blackwell.

Guralnick, M. J. (Ed.). (2005). *The developmental systems approach to early intervention*. Baltimore, MD: Brookes.

Hauser-Cram, P., & Howell, A. (2005). The development of young children with disabilities and their families. In R. M. Lerner, F. Jacobs, & D. Wertlieb (Eds.), *Applied developmental science: An advanced textbook* (pp. 377–397). Thousand Oaks, CA: Sage.

Hensley, G., & Patterson, V. W. (Eds.). (1970). *Interdisciplinary programming for infants with known or suspected cerebral dysfunction*. Boulder, CO: Western Interstate Commission for Higher Education.

Hu, X. Y., & Yang, X. J. (2013). Early intervention practices in China: Present situation and future directions. *Infants & Young Children*, 26(1), 4–16. doi:10.1097/IYC.0b013e3182736cd3

Jew, W. (1974). Helping handicapped infants and their families: The delayed development project. *Children Today*, 3, 7–10.

Karnes, M. B., Teska, J. A., & Hodgins, A. S. (1970). The effects of four programs of classroom intervention on the intellectual and language development of 4-year-old disadvantaged children. *American Journal of Orthopsychiatry*, 40, 58–76. doi:10.1111/j.1939-0025.1970.tb00679.x

Kelly, B., & Perkins, D. F. (Eds.). (2012). *Handbook of implementation science for psychology in education*. New York: Cambridge University Press.

King, G., King, S., Rosenbaum, P., & Goffin, R. (1999). Family-centered caregiving and well-being of parents of children with disabilities: Linking process with outcome. *Journal of Pediatric Psychology*, 24, 41–53.

Korfmacher, J., Green, B., Staerkel, F., Peterson, C., Cook, G., Roggman, L., . . . Schiffman, R. (2008). Parent involvement in early childhood home visiting. *Child and Youth Care Forum, 37,* 171–196. doi:10.1007/s10566-008-9057-3

Law, M., Hanna, S., King, G., Hurley, P., King, S., Kertoy, M., & Rosebaum, P. (2003). Factors affecting family-centred service delivery for children with disabilities. *Child: Care, Health and Development, 29,* 357–366.

Law, M., Teplicky, R., King, S., King, G., Kertoy, M., Moning, T., . . . Burke-Gaffney, J. (2005). Family-centred service: Moving ideas into practice. *Child: Care, Health and Development, 31*(6), 633–642. doi:10.1111/j.1365-2214.2005.00568.x

Lee, Y. H. (2015). The paradox of early intervention: Families' participation driven by professionals throughout service process. *International Journal of Child Care and Education Policy, 9*(1), 1–19. doi:10.1186/s40723-015-0007-x

Levine, K. (2013). Capacity building and empowerment practice. In B. Trute & D. Hiebert-Murphy (Eds.), *Partnering with parents: Family-centred practice in children's services* (pp. 107–129). Toronto, Canada: University of Toronto.

Lietz, C. A. (2011). Theoretical adherence to family centered practice: Are strengths-based principles illustrated in families' descriptions of child welfare services? *Children and Youth Services Review, 33*(6), 888–893. doi:10.1016/j.childyouth.2010

Mahoney, G., Kaiser, A. P., Girolametto, L., MacDonald, J., Robinson, C., Safford, P., & Spiker, D. (1999). Parent education in early intervention: A call for a renewed focus. *Topics in Early Childhood Special Education, 19,* 131–140. doi:10.1177/027112149901900301

Mannan, H., Summers, J. A., Turnbull, A. P., & Poston, D. J. (2006). A review of outcome measures in early childhood programs. *Journal of Policy and Practice in Intellectual Disabilities, 3,* 219–228. doi:10.1111/j.1741-1130.2006.00083.x

Moore, T., & Larkin, H. (2005). *"More than my child's disability": A comprehensive literature review about family-centred practice and family experiences of early childhood intervention services.* Glenroy, Victoria, Australia: SCOPE.

Oster, A. (1985). *Equals in this partnership: Parents of disabled and at-risk infants and toddlers speak to professionals.* Washington, DC: National Center for Clinical Infant Programs.

Parrish, D. M., & Phillips, G. (2003). *Developing an early childhood outcomes system for OSEP: Key considerations.* Retrieved from http://www.researchgate.net/profile/Deborah_Parrish/publication/254344325_Developing_an_Early_Childhood_Outcomes_System_for_OSEP_Key_Considerations/links/54ca8cef0cf2c70ce5225f63.pdf

Pinto, A. I., Grande, C., Aguiar, C., de Almeida, I. C., Felgueiras, I., Pimentel, J. S., . . . Lopes-dos-Santos, P. (2012). Early childhood intervention in Portugal: An overview based on the developmental systems model. *Infants & Young Children, 25*(4), 310–322. doi:10.1097/IYC.0b013e3182673e2b

Rappaport, J. (1981). In praise of paradox: A social policy of empowerment over prevention. *American Journal of Community Psychology, 9,* 1–25. doi:10.1007/BF00896357

Raspa, M. J., Bailey, D. B., Jr., Olmsted, M. G., Nelson, R., Robinson, N., Simpson, M. E., . . . Houts, R. (2010). Measuring family outcomes in early intervention: Findings from a large-scale assessment. *Exceptional Children, 76,* 496–510. doi:10.1177/001440291007600407

Rouse, L. (2012). Partnerships in early childhood education and care: Empowering parents or empowering practitioners. *Global Studies of Childhood, 2*(1), 14–25. doi:10.2304/gsch.2012.2.1.14

Sandow, S. A., Clarke, A.D. B., Cox, M. V., & Stewart, F. L. (1981). Home intervention with parents of severely subnormal pre-school children: A final report. *Child: Care, Health and Development, 7*, 135–144. doi:10.1111/j.1365-2214.1981.tb00831.x

Scarr-Salapatek, S., & Williams, M. L. (1972). A stimulation program for low birth weight infants. *American Journal of Public Health, 62*, 662–667. doi:10.2105/AJPH.62.5.662

Schaefer, E. S. (1970). Need for early and continuing education. In V. H. Denenberg (Ed.), *Education of the infant and young child* (pp. 61–82). New York: Academic Press.

Schlesinger, B. (2007). *Strengths in families: Accentuating the positive.* Retrieved from http://www.vifamily.ca/library/cft/strengths.html

Seligman, M., & Darling, R. B. (1989). *Ordinary families, special children: A systems approach to childhood disability.* New York: Guilford Press.

Shelton, T. L., & Stepanek, J. S. (1994). *Family-centered care for children needing specialized health and developmental services* (3rd ed.). Bethesda, MD: Association for the Care of Children's Health.

Shonkoff, J. P., & Meisels, S. J. (1990). Early childhood intervention: The evolution of a concept. In S. J. Meisels & J. P. Shonkoff (Eds.), *Handbook of early childhood intervention* (pp. 3–31). Cambridge, UK: Cambridge University Press.

Shulman, C., Meadan, H., & Sandhaus, Y. (2012). Young children with disabilities in Israel: System of early intervention service delivery. *Infants & Young Children, 25*(4), 297–309. doi:10.1097/IYC.0b013e318267770a

Soldatic, K., van Toorn, G., Dowse, L., & Muir, K. (2014). Intellectual disability and complex intersections: Marginalisation under the National Disability Insurance Scheme. *Research and Practice in Intellectual and Developmental Disabilities, 1*(1), 6–16. doi:10.1080/23297018.2014.906050

Sousa, L., Ribeiro, C., & Rodrigues, S. (2007). Are practitioners incorporating a strengths-focused approach when working with multi-problem poor families? *Journal of Community and Applied Social Psychology, 17*, 53–66. doi:10.1002/casp.875

Sukkar, H. (2013). Early childhood intervention: An Australian perspective. *Infants & Young Children, 26*(2), 94–110. doi:10.1097/IYC.0b013e31828452a8

Swanson, J., Raab, M., & Dunst, C. J. (2011). Strengthening family capacity to provide young children everyday natural learning opportunities. *Journal of Early Childhood Research, 9*, 66–80. doi:10.1177/1476718X10368588

Thompson, L., Lobb, C., Elling, R., Herman, S., Jurkiewicz, T., & Hulleza, C. (1997). Pathways to family empowerment: Effects of family-centered delivery of early intervention services. *Exceptional Children, 64*, 99–113. doi:10.1177/001440299706400107

Tjossem, T. D. (Ed.). (1976). *Intervention strategies for high risk infants and young children.* Baltimore, MD: University Park Press.

Trivette, C. M., Dunst, C. J., & Hamby, D. W. (2010). Influences of family-systems intervention practices on parent-child interactions and child development. *Topics in Early Childhood Special Education, 30*, 3–19. doi:10.1177/0271121410364250

Trute, B. (2013). Basic family-centred practice concepts and principles. In B. Trute & D. Hiebert-Murphy (Eds.), *Parenting with parents: Family-centred practice in children's services* (pp. 19–44). Toronto, Canada: University of Toronto Press.

Turnbull, A. P., Summers, J. A., Lee, S.-H., & Kyzar, K. (2007). Conceptualization and measurement of family outcomes associated with families of individuals with intellectual disabilities. *Mental Retardation and Developmental Disabilities, 13*, 346–356. doi:10.1002/mrdd.20174

Turnbull, A. P., & Summers, J. A. (1985, April). *From parent involvement to family support: Evolution to revolution.* Paper presented at the Down Syndrome State-of-the-Art Conference, Boston, MA.

Turnbull, A. P., Turbiville, V., & Turnbull, H. R. (2000). Evolution of family-professional partnerships: Collective empowerment as the model for the early twenty-first century. In J. P. Shonkoff & S. J. Meisels (Eds.), *Handbook of early childhood intervention* (2nd ed., pp. 630–650). Cambridge: Cambridge University Press.

Wartel, S. C. (2003). A strengths-based practice model: Psychology of mind and health realization. *Families in Society, 84,* 185–191. doi:10.1606/1044-3894.104

West, M. J., & Rheingold, H. L. (1978). Infant stimulation of maternal instruction. *Infant Behavior and Development, 1,* 205–215. doi:10.1016/S0163-6383(78)80031-9

Winton, P. J., Sloop, S., & Rodriguez, P. (1999). Parent education: A term whose time is past. *Topics in Early Childhood Special Education, 19,* 157–161. doi:10.1177/027112149901900306

Wright, A., Hiebert-Murphy, D., & Trute, B. (2010). Professionals' perspectives on organizational factors that support or hinder the succcessful implementation of family-centered practice. *Journal of Family Social Work, 13,* 114–130. doi:10.1080/10522150903503036

Ylvén, R., & Granlund, M. (2009). Identifying and building on family strengths: A thematic analysis. *Infants & Young Children, 22*(4), 253–263. doi:10.1097/IYC.0b013e3181bc4d87

Zigler, E., & Weiss, H. (1985). Family support systems: An ecological approach to child development. In R. Rappaport (Ed.), *Children, youth, and families* (pp. 166–205). New York: Cambridge University Press.

Index